Freud
as Philosopher

Freud
as Philosopher

METAPSYCHOLOGY AFTER LACAN

RICHARD BOOTHBY

ROUTLEDGE NEW YORK AND LONDON

Published in 2001 by
Routledge
29 West 35th Street
New York, NY 10001

Published in Great Britain by
Routledge
11 New Fetter Lane
London EC4P 4EE

Routledge is an imprint of the Taylor & Francis Group.

Library of Congress Cataloging-in-Publishing Data

Boothby, Richard, 1954–
    Freud as philosopher : metapsychology after Lacan / Richard Boothby.
        p. cm.
    Includes bibliographical references and index.
    ISBN 0–415–92589–4—ISBN 0–415–92590–8 (pbk.)
        1. Psychoanalysis and philosophy. 2. Freud, Sigmund, 1856–1939. 3. Lacan, Jacques,
    1901– I. Title.

    BF175.4.P45 B66 2001
    150.19'5—dc21   00–068964

Where is my metapsychology? In the first place, it remains unwritten. Working-over material systematically is not possible for me; the fragmentary nature of my observations and the sporadic character of my ideas will not permit it. If, however, I should live another ten years, remain capable of work during that time . . . then I promise to make further contributions to it.

—Sigmund Freud, letter to Lou Andreas-Salomé

ACKNOWLEDGMENTS

We are grateful for permission to reprint selected excerpts from the following: *Crises in Continental Philosophy: Selected Studies in Phenomenology and Existentialism*, edited by Arleen B. Dallery, Charles E. Scott and P. Holley Roberts. Copyright 1990. Reprinted by permission of State University of New York Press. *The Origins of Psychoanalysis: Letters to Wilhelm Fliess* by Sigmund Freud, edited by Marie Bonaparte, Anna Freud, and Ernst Kris, authorized translation by Eric Mosbacher and James Strachey. Copyright 1954 by Basic Books, Inc. Reprinted by permission of Basic Books, a member of Perseus Books, L.L.C. *The Psychopathology of Everyday Life* by Sigmund Freud, edited and translated by James Strachey. Copyright © 1965, 1960 by James Strachey. translated copyright © by Alan Tyson. Used by permission of W. W. Norton & Company, Inc. *The Standard Edition of the Complete Psychological Works of Sigmund Freud*, translated and edited by James Strachey. Sigmund Freud © Copyrights. Reprinted by permission of The Institute of Psychoanalysis and the Hogarth Press. *Six Lectures on Sound and Meaning* by Roman Jakobson, translated by James Mepham. Reprinted by permission of MIT Press. *Principles of Psychology*

Volume 1 by William James. Reprinted by permission of Dover Books. *Ecrits: A Selection* by Jacques Lacan, translated by Alan Sheridan. Copyright © 1966 by Les Editions du Seuil. English translation copyright © 1977 by Travistock Publications. Used by permission of W. W. Norton & Company, Inc. *The Four Fundamental Concepts of Psycho-Analysis* by Jacques Lacan, translated by Alan Sheridan. Copyright © 1975 by Les Editions du Seuil. English translation copyright © 1977 by Alan Sheridan. Used by permission of W. W. Norton & Company, Inc. *The Seminar of Jacques Lacan: Book I: Freud's Papers on Technique 1953–1954* by Jacques Lacan, translated by John Forrester. Copyright © 1975 by Les Editions du Seuil. English translation copyright © 1988 by Cambridge University Press. Used by permission of W. W. Norton & Company, Inc. *The Seminar of Jacques Lacan: Book II: The Ego in Freud's Theory and in the Technique of Psychoanalysis* by Jacques Lacan, translated by Sylvia Tomaselli. Copyright © 1978 by Les Editions du Seuil. English translation copyright © 1988 by Cambridge University Press. Used by permission of W. W. Norton & Company, Inc. *The Seminar of Jacques Lacan Book VII—The Ethics of Psychoanalysis* by Jacques Lacan, edited by Jacques-Alain Miller, translated by Dennis Porter. Copyright © 1986 by Les Editions du Seuil. English translation copyright © 1992 by W. W. Norton & Company, Inc. Used by permission of W. W. Norton & Company, Inc, and from Routledge. *Phenomenology of Perception* by Maurice Merleau-Ponty, translated by Colin Smith. Reprinted by permission of Northwestern University Press.

The author gratefully acknowledges the support of the Loyola College Center for the Humanities in the writing and publication of this book.

CONTENTS

PREFACE

This book could be described in a number of ways. First and foremost, it is a study of Sigmund Freud's theory of the unconscious and, in particular, what Freud called his "metapsychology." At the same time, it is a treatment of Jacques Lacan's radical reinterpretation of psychoanalysis, a treatment that seeks both to clarify key aspects of Lacan's thought and to map its relation to Freud. Then again, it is a work of philosophy that draws new implications from the psychoanalytic theory of the unconscious and does so by means of introducing a number of original concepts.

It both is and is not the book I wanted to write. It succeeds in laying out the rudiments of an idea, though not always with the ease and elegance I might have wished for. The idea occurred to me in 1985 in one of those exceptional flashes of insight, vividly intense and absolutely compelling, that seem suddenly to penetrate to the heart of a problem. Yet for all its appearance of instantaneous clarity, it was an idea that required a great deal of time and labor to articulate. The lightness and transparency of the original inspiration now seem somewhat compromised by the workman-like style with which I have had to unfold it.

But I remark upon the distance between the conception and execution of my idea less to make apology for my insufficiencies as a writer than to introduce a larger point that is central to this book. For the book is ultimately concerned with the profound tension between simultaneity and succession. It is the tension between the instant flash of insight and the extended time required for its discursive elaboration, the tension between the image and the word. In one sense, everything is present with the first crystallization of the image. As Coleridge recognized, the image is the product of a seemingly magic fusional power. The image is the pregnant source of a virtually inexhaustible stream of realizations. At the same time, however, it is only through the labor of thought mediated by language that an idea, nascent in the body of the image, ripens and truly comes to birth. Only by traversing the pathways of discourse is the mute cargo of the image made available for deliberation.

Upon further reflection, this first sense of the relation of image and word, according to which the inchoate potency of the image is unfolded by the word, gives way to a deeper mystery. If the germ of the image is brought to fulfillment only by being trellised along the frame of language, it must also be said that language and its formative influence are always already there from the start. Human perception is always preinformed by the categories of speech and language. The seed of the image is sown by the word. Thus this paradox: the universe of language by means of which the human subject struggles to speak itself is at the same time the originary condition without which there could be no subject at all. The house of language is at once the destination of the human journey and also its point of departure.

Freud touched upon this paradox in his concept of *Nachträglichkeit*, the term rendered in English as "deferred action" and somewhat more aptly in French as "*après coup*." By *Nachträglichkeit* Freud referred to the wrinkled temporality of human destiny, the circumstance that the human subject is never fully coincident with itself but is always at once behind and ahead of itself. *Nachträglichkeit* describes the elemental enigma discovered by psychoanalysis: that every seeking of an object of love is an attempt to refind an object *that was in fact never possessed*. As our discussion unfolds, this paradoxical temporality of retroaction will increasingly emerge at the very center of Freud's theoretical construction, and we will see it related to the master problem of all his work: the complex and dynamic relation of the image and the word.

A prime objective of the book, then, is to develop a new understanding of the meaning of *Nachträglichkeit* and of its place and function in the psychoanalytic theory of the unconscious. But the trajectory of the argument is itself *nachträglich*: the real import of the opening three chapters is achieved only in the fourth and fifth chapters. This is not to diminish the value of the first chapters. They develop the guiding perspective for the book as a whole and offer interpretations of some of Freud's most important concepts and case studies. Without the material they develop the final chapters would be unintelligible. Nevertheless, the concluding chapters significantly augment and restructure the conceptual framework developed to that point. Unfortunately for those who would like to sample a section here and there, this book is understandable only as a whole. I can only beg the reader's patience to consider it as such.

LIST OF BIBLIOGRAPHICAL
ABBREVIATIONS USED IN THE TEXT

BT   Heidegger, Martin. *Being and Time.* Translated by John MacQuarrie and Edward Robinson. New York: Harper and Row, 1962.

CL   Masson, Jeffrey, ed. *The Complete Letters of Sigmund Freud to Wilhelm Fliess.* Edited and translated by Jeffrey Masson. Cambridge: Harvard University Press, Belknap Press, 1985.

E   Lacan, Jacques. *Écrits.* Paris: Editions du Seuil, 1966.

E:S ———. *Écrits: A Selection.* Translated Alan Sheridan. New York: W. W. Norton & Co., 1977.

FFC ———. *The Four Fundamental Concepts of Psychoanalysis.* Edited by Jacques-Alain Miller. Translated by Alan Sheridan. New York: W. W. Norton & Co., 1981.

I   Husserl, Edmund. *Ideas Pertaining to a Pure Phenomenology and to a Phenomenological Philosophy: First Book, General Introduction to a Pure Phenomenology.* Translated by F. Kersten. Dordrecht: Kluwer, 1982.

L   G. W. F. Hegel. *Logic, Being Part One of the Encyclopedia of the Philosophical Sciences.* Translated by William Wallace. Oxford: Clarendon Press, 1975.

MM   Bergson, Henri. *Matter and Memory.* Translated by Nancy Paul and W. Scott Palmer. New York: Zone Books, 1991.

OT   Foucault, Michel. *The Order of Things.* New York: Vintage Books, 1970.

P   James, William. *Principles of Psychology.* 2 vol. New York: Dover Books, 1950.

PP   Merleau-Ponty, Maurice. *Phenomenology of Perception.* Translated by Colin Smith. London: Routledge and Kegan Paul, 1962.

S.I   Lacan, Jacques. *The Seminar of Jacques Lacan, Book I, Freud's Papers on Technique, 1953–1954.* Edited by Jacques-Alain Miller. Translated by John Forrester. New York: W. W. Norton & Co., 1988.

S.II   ———. *The Seminar of Jacques Lacan, Book II, The Ego in Freud's Theory and in the Technique of Psychoanalysis, 1954–1955.* Edited by Jacques-Alain Miller. Translated by Sylvana Tomaselli. New York: W. W. Norton & Co., 1988.

S.III   ———. *The Seminar of Jacques Lacan, Book III, The Psychoses.* Edited by Jacques-Alain Miller. Translated by Russell Grigg. New York: W. W. Norton & Co., 1993.

S.VII   ———. *The Seminar of Jacques Lacan, Book VII, The Ethics of Psychoanalysis.* Edited by Jacques-Alain Miller. Translated by Dennis Porter. New York: W. W. Norton & Co., 1992.

S. X   ———. "Le Séminaire, Livre X, Angoisse," Transcription based on students' notes. Unpublished translation by Cormac Gallagher.

SE   Freud, Sigmund. *The Standard Edition of the Complete Psychological Works of Sigmund Freud.* 24 vol. Edited and Translated by J. Strachey, A. Freud et .al. London: Hogarth Press & the Institute of Psycho-analysis, 1955.

SM   Jakobson, Roman. *Six Lectures on Sound and Meaning.* Translated by James Mepham. Cambridge: MIT Press, 1981.

WP   Nietzsche, Friedrich. *The Will to Power.* by Walter Kaufmann. Translated by Walter Kaufmann and R. J. Hollingdale. New York: Vintage Books, 1967.

VI   Merleau-Ponty, Maurice. *The Visible and the Invisible.* Edited by Claude Lefort. Translated by Alphonso Lingis. Evanston: Northwestern University Press, 1968.

Returning to Metapsychology

This book seeks to regrasp the meaning of Freud's psychoanalytic theory and to chart its relation to some of the main currents of contemporary philosophy. But another book about Freud? Attacks on Freud's ideas seem only to have intensified in recent years, swelling a tide of criticism that nearly scuttled a major exhibition of his papers at the Library of Congress. After five years of controversy the exhibition finally opened, in altered form, in 1998. Psychoanalytic therapy is struggling to survive under pressure from behavioral and cognitive techniques and from a burgeoning industry of psychopharmacology. Already in 1993, a *Time* magazine cover pointedly asked "Is Freud Dead?" To revisit Freud's theories in the chilly atmosphere that now surrounds his legacy might well appear to be a quixotic enterprise. Why bother?

Amid the sound and fury of his critics it is easy to forget that Freud is the most influential thinker of the twentieth century, having left his impress on a host of fields well beyond the borders of psychology, including anthropology and sociology, film and media studies, literature and poetics, aesthetics and art history, history and biography, philosophy and theology. Equally remarkable, Freud's enduring presence in the academy is matched or even exceeded by the diffusion of his ideas in the popular domain, where the jargon of psychoanalysis has permeated the most everyday kinds of discourse. The very immensity of the shadow cast by Freud, in and out of the university, amply justifies continuing efforts to better understand his work.

But that is not all. Precisely to the extent that we appreciate the enormity of Freud's influence, we are bound to be struck by a remarkable paradox: the most criticized and most forcefully repudiated part of the psychoanalytic theory was precisely the part most prized by the master himself—what Freud called his "metapsychology." In its premises and conclusions alike, the Freudian metapsychology has generally been rejected by posterity, both inside and outside of the psychoanalytic community. If we accept Freud's own estimate of the importance of metapsychology, then we must reckon with the possibility that we may not yet have fully grasped what Freud himself was after. If we have failed to understand the basic terms of Freud's metapsychology, can we be said to have understood Freud at all?

What justifies another book on Freud is above all the unanswered question of metapsychology. In what follows, I will argue that the rejection of metapsychology is based on misunderstandings of its basic concepts. The result is a profound misconstrual of the real meaning of Freud's work and a failure to grasp its true radicality. Describing his hopes for metapsychology, Freud remarked that "when I was young, the only thing I longed for was philosophical knowledge, and now that I am going over from medicine to psychology I am in the process of attaining it."[1] Metapsychology was Freud's answer to metaphysics. The most unfortunate consequence of rejecting Freud's metapsychology consists in losing the philosophical richness of his thought, of truncating the conceptual horizon that the metapsychology opens up. Without the wide sweep of the metapsychological perspective, psychoanalysis becomes merely one of a legion of talking therapies, distinctive merely for its thematics of the Oedipus and castration complexes.

To Recall Freud's Witch

Freud coined the term "metapsychology" very early—indeed, it falls from his pen in February 1896, only a week after the first published appearance of the word "psycho-analysis."[2] In a letter to Wilhelm Fliess, Freud defined metapsychology very generally as "my psychology that leads behind consciousness" (SE, 1:274). Metapsychology thus refers to the assumption of the unconscious itself, as well as to the structures that condition its relations with consciousness. It comprises the distinction of primary and secondary processes, the tripartite division of ego, id, and superego, and the activities of defense, repression, resistance, and symptom formation. Metapsychology is therefore the most comprehensive and all-encompassing viewpoint, one that seeks to coordinate the battery of psychoanalytic concepts into an integrated theoretical architecture. If the term "psychoanalysis" refers first of all to a therapeutic technique, a method of engaging the speaking subject in the interpersonal field of the transference, it was by means of metapsychology that Freud sought to place psychoanalytic experience within a comprehensive account of the working of the mind. It is this virtual identity of metapsychology and psychoanalytic theory that makes the repudiation of metapsychology so provocative. The question of metapsychology is nothing less than the question of psychoanalytic theory itself.

To say that metapsychology formed for Freud himself the most valued portion of his theory is not to deny Freud's own ambivalence toward it. Of the twelve papers written by Freud and originally intended for a collection to be entitled *Zur Vorbereitung einer Metapsychologie* (Preliminaries to a metapsychology), only five have survived: "Instincts and Their Vicissitudes," "Repression," "The Unconscious," "A Metapsychological Supplement to the Theory of Dreams," and "Mourning and Melancholia." The other seven papers, the existence of which became known only in the course of Ernest Jones's review of Freud's letters, were apparently destroyed by Freud himself. Jones's research has shown that five of the seven missing papers dealt with the topics of consciousness, anxiety, conversion hysteria, obsessional neurosis, and the transference neuroses in general. More indirect evidence suggests that the other two papers were concerned with sublimation and projection (or paranoia). We can only conclude that Freud's dissatisfaction with the seven papers was sufficiently intense to wish them not only withheld from publication but disposed of altogether. We may readily suppose that a similar dissatisfaction with his efforts at metapyschology was responsible for Freud's attempt to suppress the *Project for a Scientific Psychology* of 1895—which was posthumously published—a work that deserves more than any other, with the possible exception of *Beyond the Pleasure Principle*, to be considered Freud's most sustained attempt at metapsychology. The text of the *Project* survived thanks only to the happy circumstance that Fliess did not destroy his copy and that Marie Bonaparte, after finding the manuscript among Freud's letters to Fliess, ignored Freud's explicit instructions to burn it.

Freud's restless dissatisfaction with his metapsychology is also discernible in texts that successfully found their way into print. In one of his very last papers, "Analysis Terminable and Interminable," Freud once again attempts to orient his compass with the help of a metapsychological perspective. Summoning his "Witch Metapsychology," Freud maintains that "without metapsychological speculation and theorizing—I had almost said 'phantasying'—we shall not get another step forward. . . . Unfortunately," he goes on to say, "here as elsewhere, what our Witch reveals is neither very clear nor very detailed" (SE, 23:225). Similar self-critical reminders of the limits to Freud's powers of theoretical construction are frequent throughout his oeuvre and betoken his enduring sense of conceptual inadequacy. Indeed, Freud's complaints of his limited success at theoretical exposition constitute a veritable leitmotif of his text. They provide a measure of his intellectual honesty yet also underscore the magnitude of his theoretical ambitions. The question remains whether we, the inheritors of Freud's theories, bring a comparable breadth of vision to the task of interpreting them.

What, then, did Freud mean by metapsychology? The key concept that underlies the whole system of metapsychological ideas is that of psychical energy. The notion of a mobile energy, capable of variable investments or "cathexes" and susceptible of transfer along a chain of associated representations, remained throughout Freud's career his single most important theoretical construction. The concept of psychical energy clearly points back toward Freud's theoretical precursors in the nineteenth century, especially to the psychophysics of Gustav Theodor Fechner, yet it is essential to grasp the distinctive uses to which Freud put it. It was in terms of the buildup and release of energetic tensions that Freud conceived the nature of pleasure and pain. Moreover, the notion of psychical energy was virtually consubstantial with Freud's concept of libido. It was thus the energetic metaphor that enabled Freud to posit the psychical equivalence of apparently disparate psychical contents and as such provided the basis for his understanding of the processes of displacement and condensation that guide the dream-work and the formation of symptoms. Energetics was likewise the theoretical taproot for Freud's concepts of repression and resistance, inasmuch as Freud came to think of the process of defense as a play of cathexis and anticathexis of energies. It was in terms of a distribution of energy that Freud distinguished between object love and the narcissistic investment that is constitutive of the ego, the distinction that led him to envisage "a libidinal cathexis of the ego, from which some is later given off to the object-cathexes much as the body of an amoeba is related to the pseudopodia which it puts out" (SE, 14:75). So, too, it was the energetic assumption that opened the way to distinguishing between primary and secondary processes in terms of free and bound energies. In his 1915 paper "The Unconscious," Freud reaffirmed the indispensability of energetics, claiming that the distinction between bound and unbound energies "represents the deepest insight we have gained up to the present into the nature of nervous energy, and I do not see how we can do without it" (SE, 14:88). Finally, the concept of psychical energy underlay Freud's notion of the instincts or drives and thus formed the foundation of his most daring theoretical construction: the supposition of the two primordial drives of life and death.[3] In the theory of the dual drives, the energetic metaphor, far from being left behind as an artifact of an early, exploratory period, comes to occupy the very center of Freud's most mature and far-reaching synthesis, according to which the entirety of the psychical process down to its minutest increment is to be reckoned in terms of the two great destinies of energy: the gathering together into ever greater unities under the influence of Eros and the splitting apart and disintegration effected by the death drive.

If the energetic metaphor can thus be seen to undergird virtually the whole of Freud's theory, much of its value for psychoanalytic practice consists in the way in which it forms a bridge between theoretical abstraction and immediate lived experience. The metaphor of energy readily renders the phenomenology of bodily experience by situating the body in a field of interacting quantities of force. It resonates with the daily cycle of morning freshness and evening fatigue, for example, and corresponds to our immediately convincing sense of being at times infused with a feeling of power and readiness for activity while at other times we are overwhelmed by a sluggish inertia, at a loss for the resources to take up even the most trivial tasks. On the level of the most immediately given sense of embodiment, the body is unreflectively experienced in terms of the ease and difficulty of its movements, while the surrounding world of things is encountered first of all as allowing and facilitating movement or of resisting and frustrating it.

If the concept of psychic energy readily lends itself to accounts of bodily experience, even more striking is its aptness to describe the affective states with which psychoanalysis is typically confronted. In anxiety, for example, the psychoanalytic affect par excellence, we seem to perceive the effects of a pent-up quantity of force vainly in search of release. So, too, mania and dementia suggest the presence of an intense and chaotic overcharge of energy. In like fashion, it is tempting to characterize the behavior of the hysteric in terms of an excessive charge spread over the entire surface of the personality, as if to compensate for an internal lack or vacuity. The compulsive repetitions of the obsessive, on the other hand, are readily conceived as an excessively intense focus of energy, comparable in some way to a tightly coiled eddy in the flow of experience. Precisely the opposite impression is invited by depression, in which the listless and apathetic subject seems empty and, as the word itself suggests, deflated or depressurized.

Despite its theoretical centrality and its clinical relevance, however, the concept of energetics has remained a highly problematic one.[4] Indeed, in one way or another the rejection of Freud's metapsychology can be traced to a rejection of energetics. With respect to the concept of psychic energy itself, it has been repeatedly charged, especially by critics of the scientific pretensions of psychoanalysis, that Freud's concept corresponds to no scientifically recognized form of energy. Faced on the one hand with the excesses of Wilhelm Reich's quest to capture "orgone" energy and confronted on the other hand with the existentialist critique of Freud as over-mechanical and deterministic, many otherwise enthusiastic supporters of psychoanalysis have felt inclined to dispense altogether with Freud's references to psychical energy. Thus Roy Grinker has remarked that "the series of words—instinct, drive, action, force, force, and energy—are misconceptions. There is no relation of 'psychic energy' to any known form of energy, and it is not remotely related to the physical concept of force."[5] Other analysts insist on the enduring relevance of Freudian energetics for clinical description yet despair of finding an adequate conceptual grounding for it. As L. Breger puts it,

> psychoanalytic theory deals with many aspects of human thought and action, but above all it is a theory of motivation. Its empha-

sis on the basic urges and forces that underlie human psychology—on man's unconscious impulses, on sexuality and aggression—have made it the most influential theory of human
motivation. Yet the conceptual underpinning of the motivational
theory—the concepts of psychic energy, of libido, of conserva-
tion or economy, of the life and death instincts—has long been
its weakest aspect.[6]

Even more striking than the attacks on Freud's concept of psychic
energy itself have been the successive waves of criticism aimed at the most
far-reaching and highly speculative extrapolation of the energetic perspective: the theory of the life and death drives.[7] Here, too, criticism among
Freud's followers aims at a portion of the theory considered indispensable
by Freud himself. Despite continuing hesitations over the details of his
construction, he was increasingly convinced of its fundamental value and
importance. Freud reaffirmed the theory of the dual drives in his later and
most famous works, including *The Ego and the Id, Civilization and Its
Discontents, The New Introductory Lectures,* and *An Outline of Psycho-analysis.* More than a decade after introducing the two great drives, Freud
remarked that "to begin with, it was only tentatively that I put forward the
views I have developed here, but in the course of time they have gained
such a hold on me that I can no longer think in any other way" (SE,
21:119). In his last major article, "Analysis Terminable and Interminable,"
Freud insisted more strenuously than ever on the necessity of the dual
drive hypothesis, claiming that "only by the concurrent or mutually opposing action of the two primal instincts—Eros and the death instinct—never
by one or the other alone, can we explain the rich multiplicity of the phenomena of life" (SE, 23:243).

Yet for all the importance placed upon it by Freud himself, the theory
of the death drive was from the beginning viewed with suspicion, if not
downright hostility, even among many of Freud's closest followers. As
Ernest Jones observed, *Beyond the Pleasure Principle* "is noteworthy in
being the only one of Freud's which has received little acceptance on the
part of his followers. Thus of the fifty or so papers that have been directed
to the topic one observes that in the first decade only half supported
Freud's theory, in the second decade only a third, and in the last decade,
none at all."[8] For many, perhaps even the majority in the psychoanalytic

community, Freud's hypothesis that "the aim of all life is death" (SE, 18:38) signaled an unwarranted excess of theorizing. David Rapaport called the theory of the death drive "a speculative excursion which does not seem to be an integral part of the [psychoanalytic] theory."[9] Other commentators, seeking to explain how Freud could have spun such an obviously fantastic and implausible hypothesis, reckoned the death drive to be an expression of Freud's horror at the murderous spectacle of World War I or a precipitate of the generally morbid intellectual milieu of the time. Henri Ellenberger has suggested, for example, that "Freud's concept of the death instinct can be best understood against the background of the preoccupation with death shared by a number of his eminent comtemporaries: biologists, psychologists, and existential philosophers."[10] Still others suspected a more personal motivation, rooted in Freud's sadness at the deaths of his son and daughter or in worries over his own mortality. Paul Roazen notes that "an unusual number of elderly analysts . . . thought Freud's cancer preceded his theory of the death instinct."[11] Whatever the reasons adduced for its rejection, the majority judgment of Freud's followers has been clear: the final theory of the dual drives as Freud formulated it is unacceptable. Kenneth Colby thus speaks for many others in roundly concluding that "the postulation of a death instinct we now know was based on a misapplication of physical principles to living organisms. Today it is only an interesting part of psychoanalytic history."[12]

The troubled legacy of Freud's metapsychology unsettles our understanding of Freud at the most elemental level. The challenge before us is to regrasp the meaning of Freud's metapsychological speculations, relimning his basic distinctions and striving to make new sense of them. Our efforts must center first upon the notion of psychical energy itself, along with its companion concepts of *Besetzung*, or cathexis, and of binding and unbinding. We must then retrace the meaning of Freud's mature theory of the dual drives. Indeed, our capacity to arrive at a satisfactory reconception of the life and death drives may be taken as a key measure of the success or failure of our approach. We can also state in advance the general aim of such a reconception. Our investigation must fulfill Freud's intention to conceive of the entirety of psychical processes in terms of the grand opposition between Eros and death. The capacity to account for the most palpable manifestations of the conflict between the two "eternal adversaries," the epochal struggle between love and destructiveness described at the end of *Civilization and Its Discontents,* was only part of Freud's hope for his dual drive hypothesis. He also longed to show how, beneath the level of their most spectacular effects, the two great pulsional forces are at work with one another in every microincrement of the mind's operation. It was precisely this dream of reconceiving the hidden working of the psychical process that led Freud to liken his theory of the two elemental drives to the Empedoclean dialectic of *Philia* and *Neikos.*

The Lacanian Return to Freud

In setting ourselves the task of regrasping Freud's conceptual apparatus, we will take the work of Jacques Lacan as a privileged clue. Arguably the most theoretically ambitious and sophisticated of all Freud's interpreters, Lacan enriches psychoanalysis by bringing it into dialogue with other theoretical traditions, prominent among them phenomenology and existential philosophy, structuralist linguistics and anthropology. This theoretical refounding of psychoanalysis recalibrates the tools of analytic practice but also extends the implications of psychoanalysis beyond the consulting room, demonstrating the extent to which Freud's theories are deeply resonant with other important intellectual movements of the twentieth century.

The basic concepts of psychoanalysis, Lacan maintains, "can only become clear if one establishes their equivalence to the language of contemporary anthropology, or even to the latest problems in philosophy, fields in which psychoanalysis could well regain its health."[13] Rightly interpreted, however, Freud's text becomes itself an unparalleled resource for the enrichment of other disciplines. From a Lacanian vantage point, Freud is seen to augment and extend intellectual traditions in which he never directly participated. Through Lacan's rereading, Freud emerges as a philosophical thinker of the first order, whose contribution is to be ranked with that of Heidegger or Hegel. "Of all the undertakings that have been proposed in this century," Lacan claims, "that of the psychoanalyst is perhaps the loftiest, because the undertaking of the psychoanalyst acts in our time as a mediator between the man of care and the subject of absolute knowledge" (E:S, 105). And elsewhere: "They say Freud isn't a philosopher. I don't mind, but I don't know of any text concerning the working up of scientific theory which is philosophically more profound" (S.II, 93–94).

If Lacan offers an especially promising path of "return to Freud," it is by no means an easy path to follow. In the first place there is the notorious difficulty of Lacan's style, which Jeffrey Mehlman has fairly described as "Mallarmean in hermetic density, Swiftian in aggressive virulence, Freudian in analytic acumen."[14] Still more apt might be Joseph Conrad's description of the enigmatic Kurtz:

> The man presented himself as a voice. . . . [O]f all his gifts the one that stood out preeminently, that carried with it a sense of real presence, was his ability to talk, his words—the gift of expression, the bewildering, the illuminating, the most exalted and the most contemptible, the pulsating stream of light, or the deceitful flow from the heart of an impenetrable darkness.[15]

For many people otherwise interested in knowing what Lacan is up to, the torture of ploughing through his prose is too high a price to be paid. And indeed, Lacan often gives the maddening impression that he intentionally resists being understood. "I like to leave the reader no other way out than the way in," he says, "which I prefer to be difficult" (E:S, 146). One advantage of this choice is to prevent *too easy a reading*. As Lacan sees it, the masterfully lucid prose form by which Freud sought to make himself understandable, even to a lay audience, paradoxically contributed to widespread misunderstandings of his thought. The possibilities for distortion are multiplied to the extent that many of Freud's concepts appear assimilable to commonsense notions. The activity of repression, for example, is all too easily imagined as a mechanical process analogous to hiding something away in a box or cupboard—an image that, however wildly inadequate to the complexity of the psychical process Freud has in mind, is at times called up by Freud's own manner of speaking. Or again, the relation of the ego to the id and superego is too readily reduced to a conflict between the claims of base animality and duty to a higher nature. Pressed into this mold, Freud's discovery is trimmed to fit the Sunday school banality of a weak but well-intentioned self torn between its devil and its angel. The attractiveness of such notions derives precisely from their immense crudity, a circumstance that would concern us less were it not for the frequency with which they can be discerned not only in the vulgar reception of Freud's theories but also in discussions by people who ought to know better. Lacan's punishing style ups the ante for achieving a more sophisticated understanding by first denying us such comfortable oversimplifications. As he puts it himself, Lacan "provides an obstacle to the experience of analysis being served up to you in a completely cretinous way."[16] The difficulty of Lacan's prose frustrates the flat-headed certainties of commonsense and helps restore the note of utter strangeness and even violence to common sense that is an essential feature of the Freudian perspective.

But there is more to it than that. The insistent obscurity of Lacan's style is intended not only to break old habits of thought but also to establish new ones. In the opacity of his own discourse, Lacan aims to produce in the reader an experience that bears some likeness to the analytic encounter with the unconscious. His style is an appropriate reflection of the fact, as he says, that "obscurity is characteristic of our field" (FFC, 187). Alternately intriguing and frustrating, Lacan excites a hunger for insight yet denies facile understanding. The result is that the reader is held in a concentrated suspense akin to the attitude of the psychoanalyst who must listen attentively for what is significant yet refuse the temptation to round off what is heard to fit within the contour of a pat understanding. Lacan's discourse trains us to listen less for what is known than for what is unknown. He thus succeeds in reopening the mysteriousness of the unconscious. Reading Lacan, we are repeatedly brought up against the most elemental considerations as if for the first time.

The difficulties posed by Lacan's style are compounded by the fact that he rereads Freud's theory by reference to a battery of highly original concepts that are unfamiliar to traditional students of psychoanalysis. Prime among these new Lacanian concepts are the three cardinal categories of imaginary, symbolic, and real. To provide a brief sketch of the three categories:

Lacan defines the Freudian ego as a precipitate of the *imaginary*. During the "mirror phase," the psychically formative period between the ages of six months and two years, the contours of the infantile ego are laid down in identification with the perceptual unity of the body image. In this conception, Lacan rediscovers the profound appropriateness of Freud's term "narcissism" and opens up a whole series of new problematics around the function of perception and the meaning of the object relation in psychoanalysis.

Beyond the identifications staged by the imaginary, Lacan locates the linguistically mediated cognitions of the *symbolic*. In his concept of the symbolic, Lacan draws upon the structuralist conception of language as a diacritical system in an effort to provide a new understanding of the nature and destiny of unconscious desire, that of "the unconscious structured like a language." The claim is a provocative one, yet it becomes increasingly plausible when we reread Freud's great case studies with an eye to the way in which the workings of the unconscious are revealed over and again to turn around plays on words and phonemic linkages. As a grand system of differences, the structure of language comprises an immense and precisely articulated web, impossible of perceptual representation, in which the desire of the subject unknown to the ego finds its circuit toward expression.

The first two registers of imaginary and symbolic are triangulated by a third, that of the *real*, by which Lacan points enigmatically toward an unencompassable horizon that remains unthinkable and unknowable. The real forever outstrips everything figured by the imaginary or signified by the symbolic. As much an expression of the ineffable ground of the subject's own being as that of the world beyond it, the real escapes all representation, even as its indeterminate force may be encountered in the experience of the uncanny or evidenced in the effects of the trauma.

Lacan's innovative categories, particularly his conception of the imaginary ego, serve to mark a sharp departure from the prevailing interpretation of Freud's theory, especially in the United States, informed by "ego psychology." Given its initial impetus by Anna Freud and developed by Heinz Hartmann, Ernst Kris, Rudolph Lowenstein, and others, ego psychology conceives the primary task of psychic life to be *adaptation* to reality. The accomplishment of this task falls upon the executive ego, whose powers of synthesis and defense enable it to mediate the three-way conflict between the pressures of instinctual drives emanating from within the organism, the constraints of external reality, and the demands of conscience levied by the superego. For these theorists, the strengthening of the ego and the enlargement of the "conflict-free sphere" over which it holds sway become the primary goals of psychoanalysis.

For Lacan, nothing could be further from the essential aims of analysis. Far from being the key to health and happiness, the ego from a Lacanian viewpoint is the heart of the problem. "The ego," Lacan argues, "is structured exactly like a symptom. At the heart of the subject, it is only a privileged symptom, the human symptom *par excellence,* the mental illness of man" (E:S, 16). In Lacan's view, it is the imaginary character of the ego that is decisive. Although the elaboration of psychic structure must necessarily pass through the formation of an ego, the imaginary institution of the ego is stabilized only at the price of a profound alienation of the subject from its own desire. The effect of this alienation is a profound misrecognition, or *méconnaissance,* with the result "that the ego hasn't a clue about the subject's desire."[17] Thus Lacan claims that "the ego, whose strength our theorists now define by its capacity to bear frustration, is frustration in its essence" (E:S, 42). Whatever its powers of unity and integration, the ego remains a kind of internal object whose effects on the rest of the psychic system are generally stultifying. "Literally," Lacan insists, "the ego is an object."[18] The ego is never capable of achieving more than a partial synthesis. It inevitably excludes the heterogeneity of the subject's desire. Lacan therefore distinguishes emphatically between the imaginary ego and the subject beyond the ego. It is the subject, not the ego, that is addressed by the action of psychoanalysis. Indeed, the aim of analysis is less a strengthening of the ego than a kind of controlled deconstruction of it. "What is at issue, at the end of analysis," Lacan insists, "[is] a twilight, an imaginary decline of the world, and even an experience at the limit of depersonalization" (S.I, 232).

Lacan's distinction between the ego (*moi*) and the subject (*je*) marks a radical point of contrast with the perspective of the ego psychologists, but it is not as different from that of Freud as it may at first appear. Indeed, the alienating disjunction posed by Lacan between the ego and the subject of the unconscious is homologous with the Freudian distinction between the ego and the id. Underlining precisely this homology, Lacan notes that the German "*Es*" is audible as the initial letter of the French "*sujet.*" What is less recognizably Freudian is Lacan's contention that the desire of this *Es-sujet* is sustained and circuited by means of the structures of language. The Lacanian subject is "strung along" by the unfolding of the chain of signifiers; its very being is conditioned by the organization of a linguisitic code. Lacan's innovation here is to introduce the influence of linguistic structure on the level of primary process, to insist that even the most ostensibly primitive functions of the drives are subject to the formative effects of a symbolic order. As he puts it, with every intention to provoke:

> If what Freud discovered with a perpetually increasing sense of shock has a meaning, it is that the displacement of the signifier

determines the subjects in their acts, in their destiny, in their refusals, in their blindnesses, in their end and in their fate, their innate gifts and social acquisitions notwithstanding, without regard for character or sex, and that, willingly or not, everything that might be considered the stuff of psychology, kit and caboodle, will follow the path of the signifier.[19]

If the first great lodestar of Lacanian psychoanalysis is a distinctive conception of the signifier, the second, equally unfamiliar to orthodox Freudians, is the concept of the Other. For Lacan, the unconscious is "the discourse of the Other." Human desire is "the desire of the Other." It is difficult to overestimate the importance for Lacan of this reference to the Other. Directly or indirectly, everything in Lacanian theory is bound up with it. Lacan's entire effort is aimed at raising it as a question: "Who, then, is this other to whom I am more attached than to myself, since, at the heart of my assent to my own identity it is still he who agitates me?" (E:S, 172).

One of the primary objectives of the following discussions is to clarify the meaning of these Lacanian innovations and to assess their value in close readings of Freud's own text. But we cannot fail to be struck at the outset by the magnitude of the challenge. Indeed, in reading Lacan, one can often feel that Lacan's claim of fidelity to Freud rings somewhat hollow. The Lacanian turn to language seems closer to Ferdinand de Saussure or Claude Lévi-Strauss than to Freud. Lacan's evocation of the Other appears less Freudian than Hegelian. Does Lacan really return to Freud's theory or does he reinvent it altogether? The question seems especially pressing for our aim of reevaluating Freud's metapsychology and its pivotal concept of energetics. For what could be more foreign to Lacan than Freud's appeal to energetics? Isn't the hallmark of a Lacanian psychoanalysis the emphasis on form over force? Does the Lacanian algebra of the signifier not render Freud's energetic metaphor more obsolete than ever? As Lacan puts the question to analysts: *"[H]ave you ever, for a single moment, the feeling that you are handling the clay of instinct?"* (FFC, 126). Yet the concept of psychical energy and the drive theory that springs from it form the conceptual spine of Freud's metapsychology. No effort to reconsider the meaning of the metapsychology can ignore it. What, then, is the place of energetics in the context of Lacan's claim that the unconscious is structured like a language?

Along the course of our inquiry, we will have to provide an answer to this question. Yet to do so, we must be prepared to traverse a broad terrain of theory. In what follows, I will argue that what makes Lacan's "return" possible is Freud's complex relation to himself, the way in which Freud's invention of psychoanalysis allowed him to glimpse something that Freud himself could not fully articulate. And nowhere is this inchoate dimension of Freud's thought more palpable than in his metapsychology. Like the dreams he analyzed, the manifest terms of Freud's metapsychology conceal a latent content that can be brought to light only by transposition into concepts Freud didn't possess. The primary task of this book is to trace some of the main lines of that transposition. All the more appropriate, then, to begin by taking our bearings with respect to a point that lies outside the psychoanalytic field altogether.

CHAPTER ONE

Toward the Unthought Ground of Thought

Most philosophical evaluations of psychoanalysis accept the basic meaning of the Freudian doctrine as given from the outset and immediately pass on to its philosophical implications (its scientificity, its bearing on problems of truth, subjectivity, ethical responsibility, etc.). By contrast, we propose to reread Freud's text with an eye to a theory the meaning of which has yet to be determined. Such a reading requires a conceptual frame within which the fundamentals of Freud's thought can be rediscovered. To establish such a frame is the business of the present chapter—a labor that will require us to traverse the work of a large number of figures, from William James, Henri Bergson, and Friedrich Nietzsche, through Christian von Ehrenfels and Edmund Husserl, to Martin Heidegger and Maurice Merleau-Ponty. We begin, however, with a topic apparently even more remote from Freud's metapsychological speculations: the paintings of Claude Monet.

Monet's Pursuit of the *"Enveloppe"*

During the fall of 1890, while Freud was in Vienna completing the drafts of his first book, the monograph on aphasia, Claude Monet bought the plot of land in Giverny that became his base of operations for the final period of his work. Over the course of the following four decades, Monet would conduct a novel experiment in painting, the so-called Series paintings. Beginning with the fifteen Grainstacks, exhibited in 1891, Monet went on to produce similar serial treatments of Poplars, the Rouen Cathedral, Mornings on the Seine, the views of London Bridge, and, finally, the Water Lilies of his Giverny garden. As many writers have observed, the paintings of this great cycle somehow belong together. What, then, was their subject? What was it that Monet sought to realize in them? In answering these questions, we will find ourselves unexpectedly drawn into some of the decisive currents of twentieth-century thought—currents that will eventually lead us back, equipped with new resources, to our central concern with the theory of the unconscious.

Let us begin with the earliest of the Series, the Grainstack paintings. What is most immediately remarkable about these paintings is their barrenness of subject matter. With few exceptions, their composition is limited to one or two mounds of hay in an open field. The effect is therefore completely different from that of Jean-François Millet's "Autumn, Grainstacks," in which the stacks are surrounded by gleaners, animals, and farm buildings. Millet's haystacks are placed firmly within the context of human activity and emerge as symbols of pastoral tranquility, of the seasonal cycle, and of rural community. Nothing of the kind is present in Monet's paintings. Yet it is precisely the stark and arresting isolation of Monet's haystacks that points us toward the real subject matter of the paintings. For Monet's interest lies not so much in the stacks themselves as in the light that animates them. It is not the focal subject matter of the paintings that most concerns him, but rather the way in which the ostensible subject presents an occasion to register infinitely less tangible aspects of the total environment in which it is situated. "For me the subject is insignificant," claimed Monet, "what I wish to reproduce is what is between the subject and myself."[1] To that end, as Thadée Natanson remarked, Monet might just as well have decided to paint a "cube of stone."[2] The haystacks themselves function, as Gustave Geffroy pointed out, as *objets passagers,* merely transitory objects, that serve to reflect the subtle effects of light and air that surround them. The comparison of the stacks to reflective screens is evoked by Monet's own commentary. "These haystacks, in an empty field," he remarked, "are mirror-like objects in a kind of open thoroughfare where environmental influences, atmospheric effects, puffs of breeze, and short-lived light effects manifest themselves."[3] In a letter to Geffroy, Monet described his aim in the Grainstacks as the attempt "to render what I'd call 'instantaneity,' the '*enveloppe*' above all, the same light spread over everything."[4]

Monet's Grainstacks remind us that the objects of vision are always situated in a total environment of light. However, the light-sphere in which objects come to visibility is not in itself visible. Monet's project in the Grainstacks is therefore a paradoxical one, intimately bound up with the paradoxes of vision itself. Monet attempts to render the invisible conditions of visibility. It is this sharpened interest in the medium of illumination itself that distinguishes the Series paintings from Monet's earlier work and prompts us to amend Jules Castagnary's definition of the Impressionist painter as rendering "not the landscape but the sensation produced by the landscape."[5] The Grainstack paintings do not merely reproduce the sensation of the scene, they bathe us in the unique diffusion of light that makes sensation possible in the first place. Monet's purpose is not merely to reproduce color but to evoke the encompassing field of illumination that conditions all appearance of color. It was precisely such a total experience of the scene that Monet later referred to as the "moment of landscape."[6]

To further develop these points, let us turn to the paintings of Rouen Cathedral. Completed between 1892 and 1895, the views of the Rouen facade constitute a series of some thirty paintings. Compositionally, this group shows even more extreme reduction and uniformity than do the Grainstacks. Unlike the earlier series, in which Monet varied the number of stacks, the distance from them, and the angle of view from which they were painted, twenty of the thirty Cathedrals are framed identically from a single vantage point. This uniformity of composition further accentuates Monet's explicit intention to produce a fully integrated series. Indeed, the point on which Monet had already insisted for his Grainstacks is even more valid for the Cathedrals: the paintings "only acquire their full value by comparison and succession of the whole series."[7] Recognizing this essential unity, Camille Pissaro complained that Monet's Cathedrals "are going to be scattered here and there, and yet it is as a whole that it must be seen."[8] Alert to the same issue, George Hamilton defended his choice of the entire series for his Charlton Lectures of 1959, lectures traditionally devoted to a single work of art.

Like the Grainstacks that preceded them, the paintings of Rouen Cathedral are attempts to capture the illuminative *enveloppe*. "It could be said," writes Joachim Pissaro, "that Monet did not, in fact, paint the cathedral. He painted this invisible mass of air between himself and the cathedral, composed of innumerable waves of sunlight, intertwined with mist and cold, that make the cathedral visible."[9] And with the Cathedrals we realize again how the *enveloppe* is less an image than a kind of sublime idea. By its very nature it cannot be conveyed in a single canvas but dawns on the viewer slowly, through comparison of a succession. Absolutely momentary, a function of what Monet called "instantaneity," the environing *enveloppe* becomes perceptible only by means of the contrasting of different times. We become aware of the utter particularity of the *enveloppe* of the cathedral depicted in "Early Morning" only when we have seen it together with "Late Afternoon," or with "Midday."

The necessity of serial treatment for the rendering of the *enveloppe* reveals an essential relativity that binds together the paintings in each of Monet's Series. Different situations of lighting are distinguishable only in relation to one another. Yet this necessary relativity, intrinsic to the depiction of the *enveloppe*, is ultimately based upon another, more fundamental relativity: that between the visible object and the conditions of illumination that bring it to presence. This second aspect of relativity deserves to be called metaphysical inasmuch as it raises questions about the identity of the objects in our experience, questions about both the discreteness and stability of objects as independent things as well as their perdurance over the passage of time. To the end of investigating this ontological relativity, Monet's choice of the Rouen Cathedral is a fitting one. Unlike the haystacks, themselves highly transitory objects that come and go with the changing of the seasons, the cathedral provides an image of massive substance and solidity. The views of the cathedral thus serve to further dramatize Monet's conviction that "a landscape does not exist in its own right. . . . [I]t is only the surrounding atmosphere that gives objects their real value."[10] It is as if Monet chose the cathedral as the ultimate challenge for his intention. His renderings of the Rouen facade succeed in communicating a sense for the ever-changing character of even the most convincing instance of stability. As a monumental testimony to permanence through time, the cathedral furnishes the perfect occasion to demonstrate the inescapable temporality of all being. "Everything changes," wrote Monet to Pissaro, "even stone."[11]

The World of the Water Lilies

When we turn to the last great period of Monet's work and to his Water Lilies, we cannot fail to note their differences from the earlier Series, concerned with evoking the luminal ambient. Is it not clear that this concern has receded in the Water Lilies? The Water Lilies are not bound to particular times of day, but appear to float in eternity. How, then, are the Water Lilies related to the earlier works?

To prepare an answer, we need only to extend the implications of our previous discussion. Monet's exploration of the *enveloppe* touches upon an ontological concern, a question about the very being of things. Monet's Series paintings explore the way in which perception of any object always occurs within what might be called a "dispositional field." The Series remind us of the fact that the "data" of sensation cannot be abstracted from an encompassing field of influences that lend specific quality and character to objects. Monet's interest is thus located precisely at the ever-shifting plane of interaction between the object and its surrounding, conditioning environment. In the paintings devoted to the depiction of the *enveloppe*, Monet is concerned specifically with the disposition of visibility. The appearance of objects, characterized by particular textures and tonalities, is a function of the dispositional field of a specific illumination. The basic point at stake can easily be generalized to include other modalities of sensory experience. The specific quality of sounds, tastes, or smells are also conditioned by an environing context of background conditions. The same notes of the oboe that round out the coloring of a light and joyful symphonic passage may sound plaintive and whining when played alone. A wine that seems oversweet and cloying with one dish reveals new subtleties and balance when served with something else.

The Water Lilies continue to explore the dispositional field, but in a new way. For an object is affected not only by a changing sensory ambient but also by the effects of the other objects that surround it. Where hay and stone meet varying conditions of lighting in the Grainstacks and Cathedrals, the Water Lilies trace the meeting of the pond flowers with clouds drifting in the sky above, the confluence of the tree trunks with the pond bank, and the barely intuitable presence of the dark earth, slumbering in the fluid depths, yet maintaining a secret intercourse with the shimmer of the water's surface. The main concern of the Water Lilies is less illumination than reflection. Indeed, for a time Monet considered "Reflections" as a title for them. Yet even "reflection" is inadequate, both because is retains too close a visual association and because the relation it suggests is too external to name the intimate correspondences at play between blossoming flower and billowing cloud. The restricted lens of these paintings reveals a cosmos in miniature, within whose compass the elemental substances—the fire of the blossoms, the overarching air, the swirl of water, and the somber earth that undergirds it—all embrace one another in an ongoing dance.

Appropriate to the cosmic vision they seek to evoke, the paintings in the series of Water Lilies are organized in various ways around the figure of the circle. The lilies themselves are basically circular, as is the pond on which they float. Five of the paintings, unique in all Monet's *oeuvre*, are actually presented on circular canvases. The fluid movement of our gaze over their surface, encouraged by the absence of sharp lines or crisply defined forms, is facilitated by their circular shape. Even more striking is the encompassing circularity of the great panels installed at the Orangerie. Intended to completely surround us, these paintings cannot be taken in at a single glance. By their very size and sweep, they overwhelm any notion of discrete and delineated objects. Standing in the midst of these enormous canvases, we feel ever more profoundly gripped by the force of Monet's essential conviction that every particular existence must ultimately be understood in its participation within the sweep of an infinite horizon.

The Water Lilies present an epiphany of the garden-world as a great skein of ceaselessly interpenetrating reflections, not only of light but of being. Against critics like Gillet who found Monet to be a sumptuous colorist, but little more than that, Georges Clemenceau contended that Monet "held for *true* what his vision revealed" and was continually willing to "sacrifice all to the expression of *that which is,* as far as he could reach that point."[12] From the viewpoint we have adopted, we can agree with

Clemenceau's defense. Monet's Series echo the founding gesture of philo-sophical thought that seeks to overcome the apparent separateness of things in order to evoke an overarching unity. They overturn our habitual mode of perceiving that construes the tissue of the real in terms of discrete and independent entities.

This intention is already clear in the earlier Series. The Cathedral paintings thus derive much of their power from the way in which they violate the implicit assumption of common sense that objects in the world are stable and unchanging points of reference. The stone of the cathedral, at first slumbering in the blue-gray morning mists, later shines forth in the yellows of midday, then bursts into the flaming red and orange of late afternoon before lapsing again into the cool and muted shadows of evening. What we took to be dead and immobile matter forces itself upon us as a living play of forces that breathes in the entirety of the world it inhabits and shines back to us an ever-changing dance of aspects. In the Water Lilies, we are similarly challenged to reexamine the commonsense assumption of ontological discreteness. What is revealed in the Water Lilies is a vision of the secret, inner communication of things, a sense for the way flower and cloud, earth and sky, are bound together by sublime affinities. Precisely because our ordinary apprehension of things is driven by a penchant for the distinctness of things, because the world of our experience usually appears to us always already cut up into independent objects, the revelation of their interconnectedness, of their participation in some embracing medium of transendence, is generally speaking a hard-won fruit of philosophical reflection, poetic transposi-tion, or religious ascesis. The Water Lilies, by contrast, confront us with the unfamiliar task of reintroducing discreteness into a vision of ecstatic fusion. Only slowly and tentatively can we disentangle the different dimensions of reality that these paintings have stirred together, reparti-tioning the elements of the world that Monet has melded together in the play of reflections and transparencies. These paintings call attention to the discreteness of things that we ordinarily take for granted by forcing us to re-create it deliberately.

If the underlying theme of Monet's art touches upon the concerns of metaphysics, it is certainly not metaphysical in the traditional sense. This is so in the first place because he communicates a sense of transcendence in and through the immanent. He evokes the invisible in the very heart of the visible. Monet's Series reach toward the realization of an idea, not by leaving the domain of the image but by entering ever more profoundly into it. Unlike the Platonic program that guides the philosopher away from the body of the visible toward the rarefied element of abstract ideality, Monet's art undertakes a reeducation of perception in its own terms.

But there is another sense in which Monet has less in common with classical metaphysics than with a modern spirit of antimetaphysical critique. Monet's art is unthinkable outside the context of a post-Kantian understanding that refuses to approach the nature of the reality except by way of the activity of a perceiving subject that apprehends it. Thus Geffroy remarks that "the sense of light could not be in a work of art as long as it was not in knowledge. . . . Painting, like the rest of human expression, had to reflect the slow discovery of things and of self which is at the kernel of human destiny."[13] In the Cathedrals, writes Hamilton, Monet investigates a "subject which must be known and explored as much within oneself as in the outer world of nature."[14] If Monet aims at the reality of being, he remains no less aware that it is only the sensitivity of our perceptual faculties that give any access to it. A concern for the activity of perception is central to Monet's effort in all the Series paintings but might be said to reach a high point in the Water Lilies, inasmuch as the surface of the lily pond readily offers itself as a metaphor of the knowing and perceiving subject. The water's surface at once reflects what is above it, supports what floats upon it, and also betrays something of what lies beneath it. So, too, the perceiving mind simultaneously turns toward the world a reflective plane, maintains forms and structures of its own, and reveals in each moment of its activity the influence of motive forces seated deeply within it. The motif of the pond surface is a thus a highly complex metaphor, one that well expresses Monet's exquisite awareness of the way in which every act of perception is the product of a multiplicity of conditions arrayed along various dimensions.

The example of Monet's Series paintings suggests a number of theoretical implications that will ultimately return us to the concerns of psychoanalysis. Let us summarize those implications under four points:

1. The objects of awareness always occur within a dispositional field. The existence of such a field is an absolutely fundamental feature of the way in which the human being is oriented in awareness. The basic tendency of mentation is configurative. It seeks to establish a series of coordinates within the sweep of an encompassing field. The parameters of the field may be established in various dimensions (spatial, temporal, even affective), and objects within it may be very differently conjugated. Monet's attempts in the early Series paintings to render the luminal *enveloppe* explore this field in terms of the specific qualities of lighting and atmosphere that lend to the entire landscape a particular quality or mood. Objects within the field are themselves saturated with this mood quality, as if they themselves possessed and emanated its peculiar energy. In the Water Lilies, the nature of the field and its effects are extended beyond the qualities of illumination to include the constant intercourse of things with one another. There is always an intimate comingling and interpenetration of things with one another. Insight into the functioning of the dispositional field is therefore insight into the inescapably complex character of all presentations. There exist no simple presentations, no monadic and independent objects, unconnected to a surrounding environment of determinative conditions.

2. The dispositional field out of which objects of perception arise always extends beyond the horizon of explicit awareness. Like the luminal *enveloppe* of the Grainstacks, the greater part of what constitutes the dispositional field remains unconscious, yet nevertheless remains active and exerts formative influences upon what does emerge into awareness. What lies outside the focus of awareness constitutes the conditioning ground for what emerges into the focus. As such, the dispositional field exerts an active and determinative force upon everything within its sphere of influence. It is from out of such a constitutive ground and in accordance with its peculiar qualities that things appear to the perceiver in a particular way.

3. Between the object of awareness and the dispositional field that surrounds it there exists a dialectical relation. Objects only become perceptible by virtue of their situation within a dispositional field and its range of effects, yet the existence and specific character of the field itself become palpable only in being registered upon definite objects. The Series paintings simultaneously accentuate both sides of this dialectical relationship. The Series evoke the luminate ambient but only by repeating a particular figure on which varying field influences are registered. Without the object on whose surface the influence of the ambient field is engaged, we would know nothing at all of its existence. The exploration of the dialectical interface of object and ambient is the very heart of Monet's intention in the series works.

4. This dialectical relation involves two correlative movements. In the first of these movements, some specific and delimited content is offered to awareness. The positing of objects is made possible by the dispositional field, just as the grainstacks in the meadow are offered to vision by the conditions of lighting that prevail at a given moment. Such object positing corresponds to an absolutely fundamental activity, a kind of elemental tropism of perception that seeks discrete entities or "things." At the same time, however, and precisely as a function of this primordial positing tropism, the dispositional field withdraws from attention. Like the luminous ambient of the *enveloppe*, the greater part of the dispositional field tends to disappear from explicit awareness. Although the influence of the dispositional field enables the perception of objects, it cannot in itself be perceived as an object. What is seen are not the conditions of lighting but the objects illuminated by them. The very awareness of objects obscures the environing and constitutive field in which they are situated. The dispositional field is always in some measure *de*-posed or *dis*-posed.

The Class of 1890: James, Bergson, and Nietzsche

"If there really is a modern art," proposed Léon Bazalgette in 1898, "an art linked to today's thought, the painter of the Cathedrals, from every point of view, is one of its representatives."[15] Especially when Monet's work is viewed from the angle we have adopted, Bazalgette's claim is a fair one. The implicit themes of Monet's Series were echoed in the intense intellectual ferment of the *fin de siècle*. It was in 1890 that William James finished his monumental two-volume *Principles of Psychology*. Meanwhile in Paris, Bergson's *Essay on the Immediate Givens of Consciousness* had been published only a year earlier, to be followed in 1896 by *Matter and Memory*. In 1886, Nietzsche published *Beyond Good and Evil*, and in 1892 the first complete public edition of *Thus Spake Zarathustra* appeared, while throughout the intervening years he wrote the notes that would be collected after his death under the title of *The Will to Power*. In all three thinkers we find an echo of the concepts we have developed in a discussion of Monet as well as a series of pointers to indicate how those concepts might be further developed.

JAMES

The lessons to be drawn from Monet's art bear very significant resemblance to the ideas set out by William James in his *Principles of Psychology*. This is so especially in the sensitivity James shows for the *context* of thought, the way in which every increment of mental life is placed within a broad and subtle network of intimate connections to other elements and other moments of the psychical process. James refuses to allow that anything in the life of the mind is simple or monadic. Of course, this is not to deny that the mind always works upon a selection and delimitation of the material before it. As James puts it, "the mind is at every stage a theatre of simultaneous possibilities. Consciousness consists in the comparison of these with each other, the selection of some, and the suppression of the rest by the reinforcing and inhibiting agency of attention."[16] James stresses that each act of thought addresses itself to a unity, that each moment of mental life is oriented toward some unitary aim or object. "Each thought," he says, "is a fresh organic unity, *sui generis*" (P, 1:279). Yet this emphasis on the unity of thought serves only to recall the manner in which the objects of attention are always situated within a diffuse horizon that lacks object-like unity. It is this elusive horizon that occupies James's greatest interest. Misunderstood or completely overlooked by most of the traditions of psychology among which he found himself, James's notion of a complex and subtle context of thought, the interlacing play of influences with which each object of thought is bound up, is closely parallel to the concept of a dispositional field.

The primary concept through which James attempts to think this broader context of thought is that of the psychical "fringe," a broad penumbra of associations that accompanies every element of thought. He thus proposes to "use the words *psychic overtone, suffusion,* or *fringe,* to designate the influence of a faint brain-process upon our thought, as it makes it aware of relations and objects but dimly perceived" (P, 1:258). James's main concern is to show the sensible continuity and unity of our thought as contrasted with the apparent discreteness of words, images, and other means by which it seems to be carried on. Between all their substantive elements there is 'transitive' consciousness, and the words and images are 'fringed' and not as discrete as to a careless view they seem. (P, 1:271)

The breadth and richness of the psychical fringe that attaches to ideas vary under different conditions. The fringe may expand, for example, under the influence of relaxation or excitement and shrink during periods of fatigue, fear, pain, etc. Indeed, one of the primary functions of our accommodation to "everyday reality" is to control the extent and intensity of fringe associations, allowing neither too great nor too restricted a latitude of communication with the broader network of thoughts and feelings.

When very fresh, our minds carry an immense horizon with them. The present image shoots its perspective far before it, irradiating in advance the regions in which lie the thoughts as yet unborn. Under ordinary conditions the halo of felt relations is much more circumscribed. And in states of extreme brain-fag the horizon is narrowed almost to the passing word. (P, 1:256)

One of the primary objectives of James's concept of the psychical fringe of ideas is to clarify the temporality of consciousness, the flowing quality of mental life by which it forms a stream of thought. By means of the notion of fringe he distinguishes between the substantive and transitive aspects of the thought stream.

As we take, in fact, a general view of the wonderful stream of our consciousness, what strikes us first is this different pace of its parts. Like a bird's life, it seems to be made of an alternation of flights and perchings. The rhythm of language expresses this, where every thought is expressed in a sentence, and every sentence closed by a period. The resting-places are usually occupied by sensorial imaginations of some sort, whose peculiarity is that they can be held before the mind for an indefinite time, and contemplated without changing; the places of flight are filled with thoughts of relations, static or dynamic, that for the most part obtain between the matters contemplated in the periods of comparative rest.

Let us call the resting-places the 'substantive parts,' and the places of flight the 'transitive parts,' of the stream of thought. It then appears that the main end of our thinking is at all times the attainment of some other substantive part than the one from which we have just been dislodged. And we may say that the main use of the transitive parts is to lead us from one substantive conclusion to another. (P, 1:243)

As this passage already makes clear, speech and language provide privileged examples for James's elucidation of the stream of thought and his concept of the psychical fringe. All of the units of language—word, sentence, paragraph, etc.—carry with them a fringe of meaning, including both retentions from what has immediately preceded in the speech chain as well as anticipations of what will follow. James will therefore claim the following:

In all cases where the words are *understood*, the total idea may be and usually is present not only before and after the phrase has been spoken, but also whilst each separate word is uttered. It is the overtone, halo, or fringe of the word, *as spoken in that sentence.* It is never absent; no word in an understood sentence comes to consciousness as a mere noise. We feel its meaning as it passes; and although our object differs from one moment to another as to its verbal kernel or nucleus, yet it is *similar* throughout the entire segment of the stream. . . . [I]n our feeling of each word there chimes an echo or foretaste of every other. (P 1:281)

The fringe of meaning guides the unfolding of the stream of thought in time, and its capacity to do so is grounded in the fact that each word stimulates an entire web of associations. Yet James applies the fringe concept not only to the semantic dimension of language but also to its more purely auditory aspect. It is in this way that James explains the peculiarities of pronunciation that characterize a particular language or dialect. The movement of the speech stream displays fringe effects that are common to all the words that enter into it. A certain fringe quality is shared by all the words uttered by a speaker in a given language and lends a distinctive color and feel to everything she or he speaks. This sort of dominant tonality of pronunciation prepares the speaker to continue in the same language making it possible, for example, for a reader to move smoothly even through an unknown text.

> How comes it about that a man reading something aloud for the
> first time is able immediately to emphasize all his words aright,
> unless from the very first he have a sense of at least the form of
> the sentence yet to come, which sense is fused with his con-
> sciousness of the present word, and modifies its emphasis in his
> mind so as to make him give it the proper accent as he utters it?
> (P, 1:253–54)

The fringe carried by a language, akin to the accent of a particular dialect, amounts to what we might call an "enunciatory disposition," a kind of total attitude, borne by the posture and bearing of the organs of speech themselves, which, once adopted, prepares the speaker to continue more fluidly in that language. Drawn into the "fringe" of a language, the speaker possesses and is possessed by a kind of phonological template, cut to the shape of that language and its sound peculiarities, such that the next words that the speaker utters tend to follow in the same pattern. Like Monet's *enveloppe* that predisposes the appearance of objects within its field in particular ways, the fringe character of a language tends to favor continuing in that language and poses an obstacle to shifting into another language. Thus James observes:

> If we know English and French and begin a sentence in French,
> all the later words that come are French; we hardly ever drop
> into English. And this affinity of the French words for one
> another is not something merely operating mechanically as a
> brain-law, it is something we feel at the time. Our understand-
> ing of a French sentence heard never falls to so low an ebb that
> we are not aware that the words linguistically belong together. . . .
> Such a vague sense as this of the words belonging together is
> the very minimum of fringe that can accompany them, if
> 'thought' at all. (P, 1:262)

Though many of James's examples of the meaning fringe attached to ideas are particularly relevant to language, he clearly intends the fringe concept to be applicable to any psychical content whatsoever. The cumulative effect of extensive experience with some object, or of repeated and varied acquaintance with a particular image or idea, enriches its associative fringe. The result is a special "sense of familiarity" or of "sentimental value."

> What is the difference between an experience tasted for the first time and the same experience recognized as familiar, as having been enjoyed before, though we cannot name it or say where or when? A tune, an odor, a flavor sometimes carry this inarticulate feeling of their familiarity so deep into our consciousness that we are fairly shaken by its mysterious emotional power. But strong and characterisic as this psychosis is—it probably is due to the submaximal excitement of wide-spreading associational brain-tracts—the only name we have for all its shadings is 'sense of familiarity.' (P 1:252)

BERGSON

Concurrent with the appearance of William James' *Principles of Psychology*, yet a good deal closer to Monet's Giverny, Henri Bergson was working on ideas that have close affinities to James's psychology. Bergson, too, was concerned to overturn the atomistic prejudice of empiricism and to appreciate of the way perception is always situated in a broad and nuanced field or horizon. He thus asserts that

> the immediate horizon given to our perception appears to us to be necessarily surrounded by a wider circle, existing though unperceived, this circle itself implying yet another outside it and so on, ad infinitum. It is, then, of the essence of our actual perception, inasmuch as it is extended, to be always only a *content* in relation to a vaster, even an unlimited, experience which contains it; this experience, absent from our consciousness, since it spreads beyond the perceived horizon, nevertheless, appears to be actually given.[17]

Like James, Bergson conceives the brain as a system of interconnecting neural pathways, in effect "a kind of central telephonic exchange: its office is to allow communication or to delay it" (MM, 30). As such, the brain always processes material in myriad connections with other material.

Although psychical states are typically oriented by focused and selective images or structured by dominant themes or concerns, each psychical element is integrated into a larger network of relations to other elements. Memories, therefore, "are not formed of recollections laid side by side like so many atoms. There are always some dominant memories, shining points round which the others form a vague nebulosity. These shining points are multiplied in the degree to which our memory expands" (MM, 171). Bergson thus makes explicit a philosophical account that could well have been taken by Monet as a credo for his work:

> That there are, in a sense, multiple objects, that one man is distinct from another man, tree from tree, stone from stone, is an indisputable fact; for each of these beings, each of these things, has characteristic properties and obeys a determined law of evolution. But the separation between a thing and its environment cannot be absolutely definite and clear-cut; there is a passage by insensible gradations from the one to the other: the close solidarity which binds all the objects of the material universe, the perpetuality of their reciprocal actions and reactions, is sufficient to prove that they have not the precise limits which we attribute to them. (MM, 209)

If Bergson's outlook is reminiscent of Monet and the concept of the dispositional field, Bergson also adds a new dimension by emphasizing the role of the practical engagment of the body in action.[18] According to Bergson, the selective function of perception that offers a series of specific images to consciousness is a response to the requirements of action. The perceiving mind is no merely passive spectator in a theater of images. Rather,

> our perception outlines, so to speak, the form of their nucleus; it terminates them at a point where our possible action upon them ceases, where, consequently, they cease to interest our needs. Such is the primary and the most apparent operation of the perceiving mind: it marks our divisions in the continuity of the extended, simply following the suggestions of our requirement and the needs of practical life. (MM, 209–10)

The problem is how and according to what principle a selection is made from among the multitude of images available to the perceiver. "The question is, then, to know how and why this image *is chosen* to form part of my perception, while an infinite number of other images remain excluded from it" (MM, 42). No answer to this question is possible on the assumption that the knowing subject is a disinterested spectator. The solution is rather to assert that the forms carved out by perception correspond to the practical purposes of the human being, engaged with the world in the maintenance of its life activity. The world is a reflection of my own projects, cut to the pattern of my own powers of action. The images I have of external objects "send back to my body, as would a mirror, its eventual influence; they take rank in an order corresponding to the growing or decreasing powers of my body. *The objects which surround my body reflect its possible action upon them*" (MM, 21).

This conclusion bears directly on the problem of the dispositional field that we have been unfolding, as it implies that a key dimension of the field within which perception of the world is shaped and oriented is informed by the vectors of embodied activity. The register of images is organized, and particular images are, in Bergson's term, "discerned," under the influence of the subject's practical engagement in the world. The image of the cup before me is constituted in part by my incipient act of grasping for it. The cup gives itself as separable from its surroundings on the tabletop because I am actively and intentionally inclined toward it. My incipient act of grasping, as well as the thirst that motivates that act, therefore constitute essential dimensions of the dispositional field in which the perception of the cup is formed. Moreover, the active posture behaves exactly as our description of the dispositional field leads us to expect: it tends itself to disappear in favor of the object it outlines. It is the cup, not my reaching hand, nor even the thirst that moves the hand, that occupies my attention. Only later and in retrospect might I reconstitute the other dimensions of the perceptual situation, including the background surroundings of the cup image, other possible image apprehensions of the cup, awareness of my own bodily comportment toward it, etc. In the press of action, everything extraneous and peripheral is edited out or disposited. In sum:

> Perception appears, then, as only a choice. It creates nothing; its
> office, on the contrary, is to eliminate from the totality of images
> all those on which I can have no hold, and then, from each of

those which I retain, all that does not concern the needs of the image which I call my body. . . . [I]f we could assemble all the states of consciousness, past, present, and possible, of all conscious beings, we should still only have gathered a very small part of material reality because images outrun perception on every side. It is just these images that science and metaphysic seek to reconstitute, thus restoring the whole of a chain of which our perception grasps only a few links. (MM, 229)

NIETZSCHE

Nietzsche develops many of the ideas present in James and Bergson in a general critique of consciousness. For Nietzsche, consciousness is a surface play, a by-product of the operation of more basic functions, a stir of dust kicked up by the dance of the instincts and affects. In thus tracing the appearances of consciousness back to a dark ground of unconscious conditions, Nietzsche, too, is a thinker of the dispositional field.

Nietzsche begins with an insight into the phenomenology of mentation, reminding us that it is not we who call up thoughts, but thoughts that call upon us. Thoughts "occur" to us. Like the famous apple that prompted Newton, a thought comes to consciousness with a force and timing of its own. Neither do I create thoughts out of nothing, nor do thoughts always obediently appear when I bid them. Rather, thoughts "befall" the thinking mind. Thinking has less the character of an *act* that is solely mine than of an *event*, something that happens to me. "I shall never tire of emphasizing a small, terse fact," Nietzsche remarks,

> namely, that a thought comes when "it" wishes, and not when "I" wish, so that it is a falsification of the facts of the case to say that the subject "I" is the condition of the predicate "think." *It* thinks, but that the "it" is precisely the famous old "ego" is, to put it mildly, only a supposition, an assertion, and assuredly not an "immediate certainty." After all, one has gone too far with this "it think"—even the "it" contains an interpretation of the process and does not belong to the process itself. One infers here according to the grammatical habit: "Thinking is an activity; every activity requires an agent, consequently——.[19]

Nietzsche makes a similar claim against the ordinary view of memory. In our actual experience of memory, bits and pieces of the past bubble into consciousness in a spontaneous chain of association. The spring out of which the stream of remembrance flows is located beyond the boundaries of conscious intention. Why are some memories retained while others are lost? For what purpose does one remnant of the past come to be wed with another, more or less unlikely and dissimilar content, so that they make their appearance together on the stage of consciousness? From the viewpoint of the ego as the master executor of memory, these questions receive no answer.

> One must revise one's ideas about *memory*: here lies the chief temptation to assume a "soul," which, outside time, reproduces, recognizes, etc. But that which is experienced lives on "in the memory," I cannot help it if it "comes back," the will is inactive in this case, as in the coming of any thought. Something happens of which I become conscious: now something similar comes—who called it? roused it?[20]

Nietzsche's treatment of consciousness thus aims first and foremost at making the hidden motivations of thought come to light as a question. "The entire conscious life," he poses, "the spirit along with the soul, the heart, goodness and virtue—in whose service do they labor?" (WP, # 674. 355). He rejects the notion of a master operator: the ego. "Ultimately," he says, "we understand the conscious ego itself only as a tool in the service of a higher, comprehensive intellect; and then we are able to ask whether all conscious willing, all conscious purposes, all evaluations are not perhaps only means through which something different from what appears in consciousness is to be achieved" (WP, #676, 357). The puppetry of mental life is controlled by forces that remain hidden from awareness.

> *In summa:* That which becomes conscious is involved in causal relations which are entirely withheld from us—the sequence of thoughts, feelings, ideas in consciousness does not signify that this sequence is a causal sequence, but apparently it is so, to the highest degree. Upon this *appearance* we have founded our whole idea of spirit, reason, logic, etc. . . .[Consciousness] is not the directing agent, but an organ of the directing agent. (WP, #524, 284)

Nietzsche's critique of the sovereignty of consciousness parallels Monet's exploration of the background ambient that brings objects to visibility yet remains itself invisible. Things come to appearance only by virtue of the activity of an encompassing dispositional frame that does not itself appear. And like Monet, Nietzsche rejects the unity of conscious contents in favor of a more global complexity. "Everything that enters consciousness as a 'unity'" he insists, "is already tremendously complex; we always have only a semblance of unity" (WP, #489, 270).

> Everything of which we become conscious is arranged, simplified, schematized, interpreted through and through—the actual process of inner "perception," the causal connections between thoughts, feelings, desires, between subject and object, are absolutely hidden from us—and are perhaps purely imaginary. (WP, #477, 264)

Complexity is the watchword for Nietzsche's conception of the mind. The apparently unitary elements of consciousness arise from a substratum of innumerable interactive forces. Nietzsche therefore takes it as a general principle that "all unity is unity only as organization and cooperation—just as a human community is a unity—as opposed to an atomistic anarchy, as a pattern of domination that *signifies* a unity, but *is* not a unity" (WP, #561, 303). The thinking mind is therefore analogous to a body politic in which a reigning power oversees a deployment of the mind's contents. "Interpretations of the world," Nietzsche suggests, "are symptoms of a ruling drive" (WP, #677, 358).

> We gain the correct idea of the nature of our subject unity, namely as regents at the head of a communality (not as "souls" or "life-forces"), also of the dependence of these regents upon the ruled and of the order of rank and division of labor as the conditions that make possible the whole and its parts. (WP, #492, 271)

A conscious thought or value is the sign of a reigning form of domination among the seething melée of forces at play in the mind. Consciousness is a weapon by means of which an ascending force seeks to secure its dominion over competing forces. The most powerful, most original forces never become conscious, but manipulate awareness by means of props or delegates. The origin of such forces, unknowable in themselves, is the body, and it is in this sense that Nietzsche maintains that "the body is a more astonishing idea than the soul" (WP, #659, 347–48). In the body, "the most distant and most recent past of all organic development again becomes living and corporeal" (WP, #659, 347). The body is therefore the ever-pregnant birth canal of becoming, a conduit of infinite complexity and mysteriousness "through which and over and beyond which a tremendous inaudible stream seems to flow" (WP, #659, 347). Nietzsche observes that "we set up a word at the point at which our ignorance begins, at which we can see no further."[21] *Body* is such a word. It is a signpost at the outermost horizon of our understanding. It marks the boundary of a region that lies outside our grasp, yet out of which flow the motive forces that inform even our most familiar thoughts and evaluations.

Gestalt Psychology and Phenomenology

Our discussions of Monet's Series paintings yielded the concept of a dispositional field. The foregoing excursus on James, Bergson, and Nietzsche illustrates how kindred ideas percolated more generally in the intellectual climate of the 1890s. Drawing upon the work of these three thinkers, the concept of a dispositional field is opened out upon dimensions of temporality, language, action, the unconscious, and the body. The path toward a more far-reaching development of these concepts is to be found in the work of two more of Monet's contemporaries, Christian von Ehrenfels and Edmund Husserl.

VON EHRENFELS

The inauguration of Monet's Series paintings in 1890 coincided not only with the publication of William James's *Principles of Psychology* but also with the appearance of Christian von Ehrenfels's enormously influential article *"Über Gestaltqualitäten"*—a significant conjunction, for if the basic principles we have discerned in Monet's art were to be made explicit in terms of a systematic psychology, those of Gestalt psychology would offer an excellent model. At first glance, Ehrenfels's work on gestalt qualities appears quite distinct from Monet's quest for the *enveloppe* of visibility. Ehrenfels takes his point of departure from the example, not of vision, but of sound, specifically the phenomenon of melody. Like Monet, however,

Ehrenfels's inquiries lead him to renounce all atomistic understandings of perception. A melody cannot be comprehended merely as a sum of individual notes but forms an intrinsic totality in which each tone is given its value by its relationship to the whole. Such a priority of wholeness over the sum of the parts makes possible the transposability of a melody from one pitch to another. Whether played in a higher or a lower register, the identity of the melody remains perfectly recognizable.

The gestalt qualities of holism and transposability discovered by Ehrenfels in the example of the melody are applicable to other dimensions of perception, including vision. The registration of color brightness, for example, clearly exhibits a similar character of transposability. Contrary to what atomistic empiricism would lead us to expect, it is not the absolute intensity of a given area of color but rather its relation to its immediate surrounding that is of primary importance in the perception of visual identity. Experiments with animals reveal this point in an especially striking way. In an experiment by Wolfgang Köhler, for example, chickens were trained to peck grain placed on a gray field and to ignore grain on a darker, adjacent field. When the chickens were then presented with grain strewn on the original gray field, now paired with a lighter field, they abandoned the original gray and fed upon the new, lighter area. The fact that the chickens transferred their response to the relatively brighter area suggests that the determining factor was not a response to a particular stimulus of a given magnitude but rather the animal's more global orientation within a field of relative magnitudes. Perception operates within an overall situation in which it is less elements in themselves than relationships between elements that are of decisive importance.

The single most important concept by which Gestalt psychology deals with the problem of unity in perception is that of the relation of figure and ground. In every perception of a unitary form, a more central, more explicitly registered figure is separated from an environing background. This figure-ground relation is of special interest for our purposes in making explicit the principles drawn from our discussion of Monet. First, the figure-ground relation is obviously unintelligible without the assumption that the mind operates in a total field. As coconstitutive moments of a total situation, figure and ground are embraced by a function of perception that operates in an organized way over a configuration of elements in a given field. Second, the figure-ground relation is obviously a dialectical one, in which two essential moments are to be distinguished. A more prominent, figural unity is separated from its environing ground by a kind of double movement in which the figure is promoted to heightened attention while the perception of the ground is dimmed down and reduced.

For the Gestalt psychologists, the figural tendency, the essential tropism of the mind toward discrete forms, is thought to operate at various levels of complexity. It comprises an automatism of perception but may also be considered a basic tendency of higher psychical functions of thought and judgment. Just as perception obeys a fundamental tropism toward *Prägnanz*, the "good" contour of a closed form, thinking seeks to resolve open questions by eliminating ambiguity and equivocation, thereby grasping the "truth" of the matter. From Kurt Koffka's point of view, it is no accident that truth has been likened for centuries to a kind of seeing and that the process of thought has been described so pervasively by visual metaphors. Gestalt perception displays what might be called the "univocal tendency" as it seeks a determinate interpretation of sensory data.

The most famous examples put forward by Gestalt psychology illustrate this tendency. It is the primary lesson of Edgar Rubin's well-known figure, for example, in which the observer can readily perceive either a vase or two faces in profile (Fig. 1). The key point concerns the difficulty of perceiving both interpretations at the same time. Perception decides for one of the two possible interpretations and is able to entertain the other only by a deliberate shift of attitude. In another famous example, that of the Necker cube (Fig. 2), we can easily adjust our point of view so as to see the cube as presenting surface "a-b-c-d" foremost, or the other way round, with surface "e-f-g-h" closest to us, but it is impossible to see the cube both ways simultaneously.

It is immediately tempting to draw from such examples, and from the primitive preference for perceptual univocity that they illustrate, a lesson applicable to more complex functions of mentation. Indeed, we might readily locate in this drive toward univocity of recognition the most primitive basis for all judgment, the function which, as Hegel noted, involves a primordial partitioning or *Urteilen*.

HUSSERL

In his phenomenology, Edmund Husserl evolved a series of concepts that directly parallel the figure-ground distinction of Gestalt psychology.

Figure 1

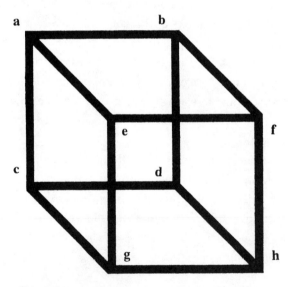

Figure 2

Indeed, from early on Gestalt psychology maintained a corroborative if not quite collaborative relationship with phenomenology. The point of departure for both schools was consideration of the foreground and background structures of the perceptual field. Husserl thus relied on a variety of conceptual pairs—focal vs. marginal, thematic vs. unthematic, actualized vs. merely potential—to explore the logical and metaphysical implications of the figure-ground structure empirically demonstrated by Koffka, Köhler, Wertheimer, and others. Husserl describes this structure in terms of an opposition between the focus of attention and a "halo of background intuitions."

> In perceiving proper, as an attentive perceiving, I am turned toward the object, for instance, the sheet of paper; I seize upon it as the existent here and now. The seizing-upon is a singling out and seizing; anything perceived has an experiential background. Around the sheet of paper lie books, pencils, an inkstand, etc., also 'perceived' in a certain manner, perceptually there, in the 'field of intuition;' but, during the advertence to the sheet of paper, they were without even a secondary advertence and seizing-upon. They were appearing and yet were not seized upon and picked out, not posited singly for themselves. Every perception of a physical thing has, in this manner, a halo of background intuitions (of background-seeings, in case one already includes in intuiting the advertedness to the really seen), and that is also a '*mental process of consciousness*' or, more briefly, 'consciousness,' and more particularly, *of* all that which in fact lies in the objective 'background' seen along with it.[22]

The fact that all attentive perceiving is girt about by a penumbra of such "background intuitions" means that the object of consciousness is always situated within a horizon of indeterminacy, which, though not in the explicit focus of attention, may at some other moment become available to further exploration. Moreover, though the intuitive background is not in itself an object of explicit attention, it always exerts a positive, constitutive force on the explicit subject matter of awareness. It is precisely such a constitutive background that we intended to designate by the term *dispositional field*. Afloat in a sea of indeterminate intuitions, the focus of consciousness is surrounded by an infinite expanse that bears upon and supports the central concern of consciousness but that remains largely unavailable to it.

> What is now perceived and what is more or less clearly co-present and determinate (or at least somewhat determinate), are penetrated and surrounded by an *obscurely intended to horizon of indeterminate actuality.* I can send rays of the illuminative regard of attention into this horizon with varying results. Determining presentations, obscure at first and then becoming alive, haul something out for me; a chain of such quasi-memories is linked together; the sphere of determinateness becomes wider and wider, perhaps so wide that connection is made with the field of actual perception as my *central* surroundings. But generally the result is different: an empty mist of obscure indeterminateness is populated with intuited possibilities or likelihoods; and only the 'form' of the world, precisely as 'the world,' is predelineated. Moreover, my indeterminate surroundings are infinite, the misty and never fully determinable horizon is necessarily there. (I, 52)

If phenomenological reflection thus discovers in the perceptual field a necessary and essential structure of focus and margin, Husserl also asserts the relevance of this structure for the field of thought in general. "*Every consciousness is either an actual or potential 'positing' consciousness*" (I, 280). The structures drawn from examination of the perceptual sphere are thus discernible in the most general way in the constitution of all conscious experience. The focal positing that underlies perception of physical objects is merely the sensory specification of what Husserl more generally calls "intentionality."

> To the essence of every intentive mental process, whatever may otherwise be found in its concrete composition, there belongs the having of at least one, but as a rule many, "positing-characteristics," "positings," interconnected by way of the relationship of founding; there is, in this plurality, then, necessarily a positing which is *archontic*, so to speak, which unifies and governs all the others. (I, 279)

The phenomenogical doctrine of intentionality implies that the essential tendency of consciousness is toward the articulation of focal actualities. Although a state of consciousness might be conceived in which a gathered focus of this sort is absent, such a state would be the exception rather than the rule. At the same time, however, Husserl concludes definitively that under no circumstances can consciousness consist solely of such focal awarenesses. The focus is always and necessarily accompanied by a relatively indeterminate margin in which explicit awareness trails off into indistinction.

> At the one time the mental process is, so to speak, *"explicit"* consciousness of its objective something, at the other time it is implicit, merely *potential*. . . . It is likewise obviously true of all such mental processes that the actional ones are surrounded by a "halo" of non-actional mental processes; *the stream of mental processes can never consist of just actionalities.*[23]

> It is the case also of a mental process that it is never perceived completely, that it cannot be adequately seized upon in its full unity. . . . [M]y whole stream of mental process is, finally, a unity of mental processes which, of essential necessity, cannot be seized upon completely in a perceiving which 'swims along with it.' (I, 97)

Even a cursory review of Husserl's conception of phenomenology reveals a deep homology between the Gestaltist figure-ground structure and the key categories by which Husserl thinks the relation between the focal concern of conscious attention, the point around which intentionality is mobilized, and the environing horizon of indeterminate intuition that surrounds it. Yet Husserl increases the scope and generality of the problems with which Gestalt psychology concerns itself, placing them within the sort of broader and more profound horizon that we have sought to mark out with the concept of the dispositional field. An even more valuable expansion and elaboration of related ideas is afforded by the work of Husserl's most illustrious student, Martin Heidegger.

Heidegger: The Disposition of Being

Although Heidegger does not explicitly rely on gestalt categories, it is not difficult to discern a broad and suggestive parallel between his most basic formulations and the concepts we have been exploring. To see it, we need only note how the Husserlian problem of the background, the constitutive horizon of consciousness that remains indistinctly or indeterminately registered in awareness, is taken up by Heidegger in a new way. Indeed, nothing could be more crucial for Heidegger's sense of the phenomenological project. It is precisely this constitutive horizon that Heidegger attempts to think in his concept of Dasein as a lighted clearing in which being comes to presence. Heidegger's appropriation of phenomenology reminds us ever more radically that the basic issues at stake in the figure-ground structure pass well beyond the sphere of sensuous perception in which they are most immediately manifest. Heidegger thinks these issues in terms of the exposure of the human being to the presencing of being in a way that enables him to reformulate the history of metaphysics in terms, not of ontology, but of *fundamental* ontology.

In *Being and Time,* Heidegger characterizes Dasein in terms of its being-in-the-world, a concept that echoes Gestalt psychology's commitment to holism. "The compound expression 'Being-in-the-world,'" says Heidegger, "indicates in the very way we have coined it, that it stands for a *unitary* phenomenon. This primary datum must be seen as a whole."[24] That Dasein's being-in-the-world is essentially whole means that entities encountered by Dasein are always implicitly conditioned by their situation within an encompassing horizon. In the first half of *Being and Time,* this unthematized horizon is analyzed in terms of Dasein's "average everydayness," the way Dasein always finds itself unreflectively bound up with its ordinary and familiar activities and involvements. Everydayness designates that state of highly routinized business-as-usual in which Dasein knows its way around. Although this characterization of Dasein's everyday way of being will finally be qualified as "inauthentic" (*uneigentlich*), it provides the guiding clue for the presentation of worldhood and thus serves to establish a basic feature of Dasein's being.

The concept of "world" functions for Heidegger, as it did for Husserl, to name something analogous to what we have called a dispositional field. Entities dealt with by Dasein in its accustomed activities are disclosed to it unreflectively as "ready to hand," that is, as already familiar and easily manipulable by virtue of being bound up with aims and activities of ordinary life. Thus I do not encounter the pen, the paper, or the ashtray on my desktop as strange and alien objects. Rather, they immediately offer themselves for my use in accordance with well-worn routines of activity. When I reach for them, they exert no claim on my attention as independent objects. In fact, they only come to my awareness obtrusively as discrete *objects* in the event of a disturbance or breakdown of their function— when, for example, I suddenly perceive that the remnant of a coffee spill has caused the paper to become stuck to the desktop or when I discover that my pen is out of ink. Entities ready-to-hand are lit up by the structure of the world and can be said to bear that structure implicitly within themselves.

At this level of his analysis, Heidegger's existential analytic is comparable to Bergson's insistence that image recognition is rooted in the incipience of actions. Like Bergson, Heidegger relates the very appearance of things in the world—this particular image or set of images rather than some other—to the active engagment of the human subject with its habituated behaviors and projects. Heidegger's example of the hammer displays this pragmatist bent. The carpenter does not regard the hammer as an object, in the sense of a discrete and separate thing that demands attention in and for itself. It is taken up as completely familiar and immediately manipulable, that is, as ready-to-hand, because it is caught up in a larger undertaking, some work that needs to be done. It is not explicitly registered upon awareness as an object in its own right because "that with which our everyday dealings proximally dwell is not the tools themselves. On the contrary, that with which we concern ourselves primarily is the work" (BT, 99). The hammer is swept along with the current of the "in-order-to" that belongs to a construction project. Like everything else in the environment of this project, the very being of the hammer is drawn into the goal of the project's accomplishment, the "toward-which" of the work being done.

The relation between individual items of equipment and the structured world of involvements in which they occur emerges with special clarity in Heidegger's treatment of reference and signs. In a sense, all items of equipment bear implicit reference: they refer to the projects with which Dasein is concernfully bound up. Yet there also exists equipment—in the form of *signs*—the explicit function of which is reference. What such equipment refers to is not simply some other item of equipment but rather the totality of relations within which equipment will be employed. The sign is thus "*an item of equipment which explicitly raises a totality of equip-*

ment into our circumspection so that together with it the worldly character of the ready-to-hand announces itself' (BT, 110). When the hammer becomes a sign (as it might, for example, hung over the door of the carpenter's shop), it functions to announce the sphere of usages to which the hammer as a simple item of equipment is put. Signs thus refer to the "world," in Heidegger's sense of the word, as the totality of Dasein's involvements. "Signs always indicate primarily 'wherein' one lives, where one's concern dwells, what sort of involvement there is with something" (BT, 111). Because signs refer in this way to the structure of Dasein's involvements, it is in and through signs that Dasein is capable of coming more explicitly to understand the worldhood of the world. Signs invoke the system of relations that constitutes the world as world. Thus Heidegger maintains that "the context of assignments or references, which, as significance, is constitutive for worldhood, can be taken formally in the sense of a system of Relations" (BT, 121).

To return to the theme of the dispositional field, what is important in Heidegger's analysis of worldhood is the way in which things are constituted in the light of the world and the world, in turn, is implicitly present in things. Precisely as we have described the constitutive effects of the dispositional field, the world of Dasein's concernful involvements serves to light up entities in characteristic ways. Moreover, like the ground of gestalt perception against which the figure stands out and like the dispositional field as we have described it, the worldhood of the world is never fully conscious or thematized. Dasein's sphere of everyday involvements and the way it determines things ready-to-hand in terms of the "in-order-to" and the "toward-which" cannot be followed out with perfect explicitness but rather implicate final purposes that remain only incompletely and vaguely articulated. Such final purposes constitute the problematic horizon of a "for-the-sake-of-which." The ultimate "for-the-sake-of-which," as the site at which the question of the meaning of life itself might be posed, retains an essentially indeterminate character. In this way, the "for-the-sake-of-which" toward which involvement tends is seen to bear special significance for Dasein's own being as Heidegger has defined it: that being for which its own being is a question. Thus Heidegger claims that

> the totality of involvements itself goes back ultimately to a "towards-which" in which there is no further involvement. . . .

This primary "towards-which" is not just another "towards-this" as something in which an involvement is possible. The primary "towards-which" is a "for-the-sake-of-which". But the "for-the-sake-of" always pertains to the Being of *Dasein*, for which, in its Being, that very Being is essentially an *issue*. (BT, 117)

Why, then, is Dasein's everydayness characterized by Heidegger as inauthentic? The answer is to be found in Dasein's tendency to flee its own essential openness to Being and to become caught up with and preoccupied by particular beings. For Heidegger, the vertigo of Dasein's radical openness constitutes the very essence of anxiety, to escape which Dasein tends to close off the horizon of its possibilities. In accordance with its own essence as *ek-sisting*, as exposed to the presencing of being, Dasein is that being for which, in its being, its own being is a question. For that very reason, however, Dasein seeks to constitute itself as a question that has already been answered. It does so primarily by taking refuge in the banal and thoughtless interpretation of the world proffered by *das Man*, the ubiquitous and anonymous "they." Allowing itself to be absorbed by the flattening discourse of the "they," Dasein enjoys the illusion of having anchored itself in a world of apparently stable and dependable things. In this way, Dasein seeks to staunch the hemorrhage of anxiety by losing itself in a reified world. The being of things ready-to-hand is reduced to the status of mere presence-at-hand. The world becomes a mere collection of objective facts. It is for this reason that the question of the ultimate for-the-sake-of-which of Dasein's involvements is usually more or less closed off and obscured. The fundamentally questionable character of existence disappears behind a reassuring absorption in particulars. "Because the phenomenon of the world itself gets passed over in this absorption in the world, its place gets taken by what is present-at-hand within-the-world, namely, Things" (BT, 168). For the question of existence to be reopened, for Dasein to reencounter its own ek-stasis, Dasein must be brought into some relation with the possibility of its own ceasing to be, its own being-toward-death.

The idea that Dasein falls away from its authentic potentiality-for-being in preoccupation with particular things obviously echoes a number of traditional doctrines stretching back through the history of thought to Plato. What is most interesting and original in Heidegger's view is the way in which his analysis is built around the notion of intimate relations between thing and world. The inauthenticity of Dasein's everyday comportment toward things is rooted in the forgetfulness of this very relation. In Dasein's inauthentic existence, things appear as *mere* things. However, Heidegger holds out the possibility of another, more authentic relation to the thing. This more authentic relation to the thing opens up with the realization that the thing is constituted only in and by the worldhood of the world and that the world and its mystery are made present in the thing. A good example is afforded by Heidegger's discussion of the peasant woman's shoes depicted in a painting of Van Gogh. These humble shoes body forth the entirety of the world to which they belong. Their worn and wrinkled leather testifies to the passage of many seasons of arduous labor. The dark clods of earth with which they are encrusted recall the fields over which they have trod. In effect, what these shoes *are*, their very being, is inseparable from the entirety of a world and of a life lived within it.

> From the dark opening of the worn insides of the shoes the toilsome tread of the worker stares forth. In the stiffly rugged heaviness there is the accumulated tenacity of her slow trudge through the far-spreading and ever-uniform furrows of the field swept by a raw wind. On the leather lie the dampness and richness of the soil. Under the soles vibrates the silent call of the earth, its quiet gift of the ripening grain and its unexplained self-refusal in the fallow desolation of the wintry field. This equipment is pervaded by uncomplaining worry as to the certainty of bread, the wordless joy of having once more withstood want, the trembling before the impending childbed and shivering at the surrounding menace of death. This equipment belongs to the *earth*, and it is protected in the *world* of the peasant woman. From out of this protected belonging the equipment itself rises to its resting-within-itself.[25]

The example of the peasant shoes invites a reflection on the essential nature of the thing, a topic to which Heidegger later returns in an essay called simply, "The Thing." Here, too, what is at stake is the complex relations between the thing and the larger world. Heidegger compares their relation to a form of "appropriating mirror-play" (*ereignende Spiegel-Spiel*), a metaphor that recalls the grainstacks in which we first recognized the constitutive effects of the dispositional field and that Monet referred to as "mirror-like objects in a kind of open thoroughfare where environmental influences . . . manifest themselves." The thing is what it is by virtue of the world in which it is placed. The world is gathered and sustained in the thing. In "The Thing," Heidegger develops an example as apparently simple and innocuous as the peasant shoes: the earthen jug. Composed of clay in order to receive the rain, the jug conjoins earth and sky. Offering to human beings the free dispensation of its outpouring in order to slake their thirst and to sustain their life, the jug sites the relation of mortals and divinities. In this way, the jug can be said to gather the fourfold of earth and sky, mortals and divinities. It is this drawing into oneness of the fourfold that is the mirror-play of the thing. Its effect is to enable the world to be experienced in its unity as world, to allow the "worlding" of world. Understood in this way, Heidegger proposes, the noun sounds itself as verb: the thing things. "The thing stays—gathers and unites—the fourfold. The thing things the world. Each thing stays the fourfold into a happening of the simple onehood of the world."[26]

When the thing genuinely "things the world," we are no longer in the presence of a mere object but are drawn from the locus of the thing into the expanse of the world in which the thing is located and meaningful. In the terms we have adopted, this mirror-play of thing and world revives awareness of the dialectical relation between the thing and the dispositional field. The movement of authenticity is therefore bound up with a fuller appropriation of the totality, a process in which it might be said that the world is appropriated by Dasein but equally well that Dasein is appropriated by the world. Such appropriation is not merely "added on" to things, as if the already existing facticity of things were simply to be augmented with the shading of a secondary coloring. Rather, the more authentic epiphany of the thing represents a return to a more truly original constitution of the thing. How, now, can we push further in understanding what is at stake in this more authentic posture?

It is not by accident that Heidegger finds his privileged example in the jug. The being of the jug is determined by the way in which its sides and bottom are wrapped around a central emptiness. The jug harbors a nothing. In fashioning the jug, the potter forms clay around a void. It is this central void that makes the finished jug useful. Heidegger makes a great deal of this point, aptly observing, for instance, that we do not pour into the sides or onto the bottom of the jug but rather pour deliberately into its open, waiting emptiness. In this theme of the Nothing, we find a thread that will open another approach to the question of authenticity. How so? What does this Nothing, contained and stabilized by the jug, have to do with the larger topic of the thing in general?

The course of our reflections on the dispositional field has already prepared an approach to these questions. Like the ground of the Gestalt figure that must recede from explicit awareness in order that the figural moment be elevated to prominence, the dispositional field is always and essentially subject to a kind of primordial negation. Precisely in order to promote the coming-to-presence of something within it, the field must withdraw into invisibility, it must absent or negate itself. Presencing of one thing is therefore fully correlative with a becoming and making-absent of something else. This insight is at the heart of Heidegger's meditation on the problem of Being. Every moment of revealment is ineluctably bound up with a moment of concealment. Presence is inseparable from concomitant absence. The openness of Dasein to being involves at the same time a closedness and loss.

> In the midst of beings as a whole an open place occurs. There is
> a clearing, a lighting. . . . [Thanks] to this clearing, beings are
> unconcealed in certain changing degrees. And yet a being can be
> *concealed*, too, only within the sphere of what is lighted. Each
> being we encounter and which encounters us keeps to this curi-
> ous opposition of presence in that it always withholds itself at
> the same time in a concealedness. The clearing in which beings
> stand is in itself at the same time concealment.[27]

There can be openness and disclosure only because there is closure and withdrawal. All emergence of truth thus occurs against a background of untruth. *Aletheia* presupposes a prior *lethe*, or primordial forgetting. Dasein is thus said to exist equally in truth and in untruth. In the terms we have evolved, what is at stake here is the negative moment, the *dis*-position, that is the condition of every positing. How are we to think of this power of negation and concealment, this archaic shadowing of being? In one sense, it seems necessary to attribute this power to Dasein itself, as if Dasein is able to encounter beings only by virtue of the fact that it also actively "nihilates" being. It is this point of view that dominates Sartre's early work and informs the guiding question of *Being and Nothingness:* "where does Nothingness come from?"[28] Sartre's answer is to locate the source of nothingness in the peculiar character of the human for-itself. For Sartre, "man is the being through whom nothingness comes to the world."[29] Accordingly, nihilation is understood as the defining activity of consciousness. In this way, "nihilation" assumes the force of a transitive verb, and it becomes possible for Sartre to compare the nihilating action of the for-itself to a form of "secretion." Consciousness "secretes" its own nothingness into the heart of being. Sartre develops this idea in terms now well familiar to us, referring the nihilating power of consciousness to the figure-ground structure of perception. He illustrates the point in a description of looking for a friend in a café. The example shows that the appearance of any being, its explicit positing for consciousness, is conditioned by a concomitant negation or nihilation of the ground, the totality of other beings that surround it. The passage in which it is described is worth quoting at length:

> We must observe that in perception there is always the construction of a figure on a ground. No one object, no group of objects is especially designed to be organized as specifically either ground or figure; all depends on the direction of my attention. When I enter this café to search for Pierre, there is formed a synthetic organization of all the objects in the café, on the ground of which Pierre is given as about to appear. This organization of the café as the ground is an original nihilation. Each element of the setting, a person, a table, a chair, attempts to isolate itself, to lift itself upon the ground constituted by the totality of the other objects, only to fall back once more into the undifferentiation of this ground; it melts into the ground. For the ground is that which is seen only in addition, that which is the object of a purely marginal attention. Thus the original nihilation of all the figures which appear and are swallowed up in the total neutrality of a *ground* is the necessary condition for the appearance of the principle figure, which is here the person of Pierre. This nihilation is given to my intuition; I am witness to the successive disappearance of all the objects which I look at— in particular of the faces, which detain me for an instant (Could

this be Pierre?) and which as quickly decompose precisely because they "are not" the face of Pierre. Nevertheless if I should finally discover Pierre, my intuition would be filled by a solid element, I should be suddenly arrested by his face and the whole café would organize itself around him as a discrete presence.

But now Pierre is not here. This does not mean that I discover his absence in some precise spot in the establishment. In fact Pierre is absent from the *whole* café; his absence fixes the café in its evanescence; the café remains *ground*; it persists in offering itself as an undifferentiated totality to my only marginal attention; it slips into the background; it pursues its nihilation. Only it makes itself ground for a determined figure; it carries the figure everywhere in front of it, presents the figure everywhere to me. This figure which slips constantly between my look and the solid, real objects of the café is precisely a perpetual disappearance; it is Pierre raising himself as nothingness on the ground of the nihilation of the café. So that what is offered to intuition is a flickering of nothingness; it is the nothingness of the ground, the nihilation of which summons and demands the appearance of the figure, and it is the figure—the nothingness which slips as a *nothing* to the surface of the ground. It serves as foundation for the judgment—"Pierre is not here."[30]

Although Sartre refers crucial points of his analysis to Heidegger and although it is possible to evince passages from Heidegger that seem to echo Sartre's active and transitive sense of nihilation,[31] the main thrust of Heidegger's own answer to the question of the origin of nihilation is to reject the subjectivist overtone adopted by Sartre. Does Dasein actively nihilate, or does it passively receive the effects of a nihilation that occurs in the heart of Being itself? Particularly in his later work, Heidegger puts the accent on the passive, receptive moment. The metaphor of *Eräugnung*, the lighting of Being by which a kind of primordial evidence is placed before one's eyes, gives way to that of *Ereignung*, the moment of appropriation. The force and effects of nihilation must be reckoned among the elemental and unalterable givens of Dasein's existence. The matter is put especially forcefully in the "Letter on Humanism"; indeed, settling the question of Dasein's agency in nihilation, and settling it in implicit cognizance of Sartre's position, are among the central concerns of that essay.[32] Heidegger insists that "nihilation occurs essentially in Being."[33]

> Nihilation unfolds essentially in Being itself, and not at all in the existence of man—so far as this is thought as the subjectivity of the *ego cogito*. Dasein in no way nihilates as a human subject who carries out nihilation in the sense of denial; rather, Da-sein nihilates inasmuch as it belongs to the essence of Being as that essence in which man ek-sists. Being nihilates—as Being.[34]

The gestalt paradigm of figure and ground illuminates the contending positions of Sartre and Heidegger on this point and reminds us that there is something to be said for both sides of the question. As a paradigm relevant primarily to acts of perception, the Gestaltist idea offers support for the Sartrian view. Must not the perceptual discrimination of the figure, always highly selective and often conspicuously idiosyncratic in character, be rightly counted as an *act*? Moreover, does the fact that different perceivers construe the same perceptual field differently not lead us to assert the role of subjective agency in the promotion of the figure and demotion of the ground? Indeed, we seem forced to grant credence to Sartre's subjectivist position if only to take account of the commonplace notion that perception is decisively influenced by the interests of the perceiver, the clichéd recognition that "a man sees what he wants to see." From another point of view, however, the figure-ground relation also lends support to the Heideggerian position. The very examples adduced by Gestalt psychologists to illustrate the figure-ground phenomenon seem to confront us with the operation of a pure automatism that precedes all subjective intention. One or another detail inevitably announces itself to perception as most salient, but generally with the accompanying sense that it is the detail itself, and no negating activity of our own, that has made it so. We seem on the contrary to be in a posture of pure receptiveness, passively impressed by such extraprominent features. Thus we recontact the observation of Nietzsche that "a thought comes when 'it' wishes, and not when 'I' wish. . . . It thinks, but that the 'it' is precisely the famous old 'ego' is, to put it mildly, only a supposition, an assertion, and assuredly not an 'immediate certainty.'" It is precisely this sense of the immediately convincing givenness of perception, the sense that what stands out most strikingly does so, as it were, by virtue of some force or power of its own, that underlies and seems to give warrant to our sense of what Husserl called the "natural attitude," that is, the deep and unreflective conviction that what is perceived is not our invention but is really "out there."

This discussion returns us to the theme of authenticity with greater understanding. The inauthentic absorption in things that obscures Dasein's open potentiality-for-being can otherwise be characterized as an obliviousness to the nothing. Remaining true to the essence of its being-there implies the necessity of Dasein's encounter with the nothing. Heidegger puts the matter in "What is Metaphysics?" in the following way: "Da-sein means: being held out into the nothing."[35] The movement toward authenticity thus necessarily passes by way of anxiety in the face of the nothing.

> In the clear night of the nothing of anxiety the original openness of beings as such arises: that they are beings—and not nothing. But this 'and not nothing' we add in our talk is not some kind of appended clarification. Rather it makes possible in advance the revelation of beings in general. The essence of the originally nihilating nothing lies in this, that it brings Da-sein for the first time before beings as such."[36]

The authentic existence of Dasein involves some lived relation to the question: why are there beings and not nothing? Authenticity reopens Dasein to the dimension of an indeterminacy of being. It reminds us that there are beings only because something else is primordially missing.

The Gestaltist Ontology of Merleau-Ponty

Having drawn the concept of the dispositional field from the example of Monet's Series, we sought first to show its resonance with the work of James, Bergson, and Nietzsche, then noted its corroboration in Gestalt psychology and phenomenonlogy, including Heidegger's existential analytic. This trajectory of ideas is focused and deepened by Merleau-Ponty. Over the entirety of his *oeuvre*—from his first book, *The Structure of Behavior*, through *The Phenomenology of Perception*, to the posthumously published text of *The Visible and the Invisible*—Merleau-Ponty was preoccupied with the basic discoveries of Gestalt psychology. Indeed, the whole course of his work attests to a deepening conviction that the implications of Gestalt theory have been insufficiently appreciated and that the guiding concept of figure and ground runs like a red thread through the phenomenological tradition. In his very last writings, a series of fragments written in the two years before his death and appended to the text of *The Visible and the Invisible* under the title "Working Notes," Merleau-Ponty sketches his own sense of a fundamental ontology centered on a series of immensely suggestive reflections on the paradigm of the figure and ground. "The figure on a ground," he insists, "the simplest '*Etwas*'—the *Gestalt* contains the key to the problem of the mind."[37] In this conviction, he regathers and radicalizes the lessons of his own earlier studies of perception and proposes that "what one might consider to be 'psychology' . . . is in fact ontology" (VI, 176). The "Working Notes" and the studies that lead up to them are especially valuable as a complement to Heidegger's analytic of Dasein as they locate the disposition of being described by Heidegger in a reappreciation of embodied existence, the phenomenon Merleau-Ponty calls "the Flesh." In doing so, they return us to our ultimate concern with a conceptual regrounding of psychoanalysis.

Let us begin with the monumental *Phenomenology of Perception*. The significance of Gestalt psychology for regrasping the basic structures of perception and embodiment is clearly announced in the opening pages. At every point, Merleau-Ponty insists on the Gestalt concept of configuration within an encompassing field.

> When Gestalt theory informs us that a figure on a background is the simplest sense-datum available to us, we reply that this is not a contingent characteristic of factual perception, which leaves us free, in an ideal analysis, to bring in the notion of impressions. It is the very definition of the phenomenon of perception, that without which a phenomenon cannot be said to be perception at all. The perceptual 'something' is always in the middle of something else, it always forms a part of a 'field.' . . . Suppose we construct, by the use of optics and geometry, that bit of the world which can at any moment throw its image on our retina. Everything outside its perimeter, since it does not reflect upon any sensitive area, no more affects our vision than does light falling on our closed eyes. We ought, then, to perceive

a segment of the world precisely delimited, surrounded by a zone of blackness, packed full of qualities with no interval between them, held together by definite relationships of size similar to those lying on the retina. The fact is that experience offers nothing like this, and we shall never, using the world as our starting point, understand what a field of vision is. Even if it is possible to trace out a perimeter of vision by gradually approaching the centre of the lateral stimuli, the results of such measurement vary from one moment to another, and one never manages to determine the instant when a stimulus once seen is seen no longer. The region surrounding the visual field is not easy to describe, but what is certain is that it is neither black nor grey. There occurs here an *indeterminate vision,* a *vision of something or other,* and, to take the extreme case, what is behind my back is not without some element of visual presence.[38]

In this and similar passages, we are reminded of Monet's attempt to evoke the invisible conditions of visibility. The visible floats in an indeterminate field, its meaning is shaped and sustained by what lies beyond the specific contour of the object. Monet would easily have recognized the aptness of Merleau-Ponty's observation that "the invisible is not the contradictory of the visible: the visible itself has an invisible inner framework (*membrure*), and the in-visible is the secret counterpart of the visible, it appears only within it, it is the *Nichturpräsentierbar* which is presented to me as such within the world" (VI, 215). The domain of the invisible is ineluctably dis-positional: it continually recedes from the very focus of the gaze that it serves to constitute. "One cannot see it there and every effort to *see it there* makes it disappear, but it is *in the line* of the visible, it is its virtual focus, it is inscribed within it (in filigree)—. . . the visible is pregnant with the invisible" (VI, 215–16). The invisible surrounds and embraces the visible, exerting upon it the force of a strange mode of presence. Thus "we must recognize the indeterminate as a positive phenomenon" (PP, 6).

If Merleau-Ponty returns us to Monet's effort to render the *enveloppe* of visibility, he also conceives the intercourse of objects with one another in a way that recalls the fusional cosmos of the Water Lilies. The field within which objects come to presence in perception is not only structured by the elevation of a figural moment and the corresponding withdrawal of the margin but is also crisscrossed by the mutual influence exerted by objects upon one another. Part of what enables me to see objects is the fact that, in a certain sense, the objects in the field of my vision "see" one another.

> In normal vision, . . . I direct my gaze upon a sector of the land-scape, which comes to life and is disclosed, while the other objects recede into the periphery and become dormant, while, however, not ceasing to be there. . . . The horizon, then, is what guarantees the identity of the object throughout the exploration. . . . To see is to enter a universe of beings which display themselves, and they would not do this if they could not be hidden behind each other or behind me. In other words: to look at an object is to inhabit it, and from this habitation to grasp all things in terms of the aspect which they present to it. But in so far as I see those things too, they remain abodes open to my gaze, and, being potentially lodged in them, I already perceive from various angles the central object of my present vision. Thus every object is the mirror of all others. When I look at the lamp on my table, I atttribute to it not only the qualities visible from where I am, but also those which the chimney, the walls, the table can 'see'; the back of my lamp is nothing but the face which it 'shows' to the chimney. I can therefore see an object in so far as objects form a system or a world, and in so far as each one treats the others round it as spectators of its hidden aspects which guarantee the permanence of those aspects by their pres-ence. Any seeing of an object by me is instantaneously repeated between all those objects in the world which are apprehended as co-existent, because each of them is all that the others 'see' of it. (PP, 68)

For Merleau-Ponty, the structure of the perceptual field provides the clue to the structure of thought itself. The process by which the contour of the perceptual figure is set apart from a background is discernible in the unfolding of all consciousness. Thought is the ongoing process in which the adumbration of determinateness is continually shifting in relation to a horizon of the indeterminate.

The unity of consciousness is thus built up step by step through a 'synthesis of transition.' The miracle of consciousness consists in its bringing to light, through attention, phenomena which re-establish the unity of the object in a new dimension at the very moment when they destroy it. . . . This passage from the inde-terminate to the determinate, this recasting at every moment of its own history in the unity of a new meaning, is thought itself. (PP, 30–31)

What is essential in this process is the dialectical relation in which the positing of a new focus subtly redisposes the entire field within which it comes to appearance, thereby seeding the ground of consciousness for the emergence of a new focus of attention. Without this transformative rever-beration of the object of thought in the larger horizon of the unthought, consciousness itself would be extinguished. "The whole life of conscious-ness is characterized by the tendency to posit objects. . . . And yet the absolute positing of a single object is the death of consciousness, since it congeals the whole of existence, as a crystal placed in a solution suddenly crystallizes it" (PP, 71).

In a manner reminiscent of Bergson, Merleau-Ponty shows that the figure-ground structure of the perceptual field enables us to conceptualize the relation between the body and the world with which it is actively engaged. He observes, in the first place, that the posture and attitude of the body is an implicit component of every registration of perceptual fig-ure and ground. The body is thus "co-present in every *Gestalt*. . . . [I]t is a component of every *Gestalt*. The *Gestalt* therefore implies the relation between a perceiving body and a sensible" (VI, 206). This co-presence of the body is especially clear in the case of visual perception, in every instance of which the body's position is implicitly registered in the figure-ground relation. "As far as spatiality is concerned, and this alone interests us at the moment, one's own body is the third term, always tacitly under-stood, in the figure-background structure, and every figure stands out against the double horizon of external and bodily space" (PP, 100–101). For these reasons, every moment of consciousness must be reckoned in relation to some incarnation. "Consciousness is being toward the thing through the intermediary of the body" (PP, 138). For this reason, "con-sciousness is in the first place not a matter of 'I think that' but of 'I can'"

(PP, 137). Yet the relevance of the body to the staging of consciousness is by no means limited to the perceptual registration of physical objects. For Merleau-Ponty, "my body is the fabric into which all objects are woven, and it is, at least in relation to the perceived world, the general instrument of my 'comprehension'" (PP, 235). The body's role as medium of comprehension extends beyond its relation to tangible objects to abstract ones. Thus "it is my body which gives significance not only to the natural object, but also to cultural objects like words" (PP, 235).

From another point of view, however, the body appears itself as the ground from which the focus of perception is projected. It is the means by which things are perceived (as, for example, when the mass and weight of a hammer are reckoned in relation to the force it exerts upon the hand and arm that holds it), yet it always tends to disappear in order for the "things themselves" to come forward into the light of awareness (when hefting the hammer, I am not aware of my hand and arm but of the hammer itself). It is in this sense that the body deserves to be called "the other side" of the mind, the necessarily unperceived ground of all perceiving, the unthought platform of thought. It is on the basis of this aspect of the body that Merleau-Ponty constructs his concept of "the flesh."

> *Define* the mind as the *other side* of the body—We have no idea of a mind that would not be *doubled* with a body, that would not be established on this *ground*. . . . The essential notion for such a philosophy is that of the flesh, which is not the objective body. . . . My body is to the greatest extent what every thing is: *a dimensional this*. It is the universal thing—But, while the things become dimensions only insofar as they are received in a *field*, my body is this field itself. (VI, 259–60)

The perceiving body absents itself in order to make things present, it makes itself invisible in order to found the realm of the visible. The body constitutes itself as a "zone of not being" in front of which beings can be presented to consciousness.

> Bodily space can be distinguished from external space and envelop its parts instead of spreading them out, because it is the darkness needed in the theatre to show up the performance, the background of somnolence or reserve of vague power against

which the gesture and its aim stand out, the zone of not being *in front of which* precise beings, figures and points can come to light. In the last analysis, if my body can be a 'form' and if there can be, in front of it, important figures against indifferent backgrounds, this occurs in virtue of its being polarized by its tasks, of its *existence towards them*, of its collecting together of itself in its pursuit of its aims. (PP, 100–101)

The way in which the body is itself dispositional, the way that it behaves exactly like the background of the visual field that recedes from awareness around a figural contour, is most clearly evident in the sense of touch. In running our fingers over the contours of a surface, we are aware only of the surface itself and not of the hand that feels it. This outer border of the body's dispositional character, the extremity of its sensate perimeter, can be artificially extended. Merleau-Ponty illustrates this point with the example of the blind person's cane.[39] The blind person does not experience the cane as an object intermediary between the hand that holds it and the pavement of the street with which it is in contact. Rather, the pavement, even the precise texture of its surface, is directly felt through the cane as if it were an elongated finger. The cane has become a pure extension, a genuine appendage of the body. The tip of the cane has become a sensible surface while the handle and shaft behind it, along with the hand and arm that wield the cane, cease to exert any claim on explicit awareness. The cane has been absorbed into the dispositional field that is the body itself.

The concept of the flesh, in which the body itself functions as dispositional field, enables Merleau-Ponty to reapproach psychoanalysis in a novel way, informed both by the figure-ground structure and by what he takes to be its more profound ontological implications. He thus asserts that "the philosophy of Freud is not a philosophy of the body but of the flesh—The Id, the unconscious—and the Ego (correlative) to be understood on the basis of the flesh" (VI, 270). In his last papers, Merleau-Ponty calls for the necessity to "make not an existential psychoanlaysis, but an *ontological* psychoanalysis." For such an "ontological" psychoanalysis, the unconscious becomes the constitutive background field out of which the figures of consciousness are adumbrated. "This unconscious is to be sought not at the bottom of ourselves, behind the back of our 'consciousness,' but in front of us, as articulations of our field. It is 'unconscious' by the fact that it is not an *object*, but it is that through which objects are possible..." (VI, 180). The unconscious discovered by psychoanalysis thus becomes an elaboration of the inescapable blind spot, the *punctum caecum* of all consciousness.

> Blindness (*punctum caecum*) of the "consciousness." *What* it does
> not see is what makes it see, is its tie to Being, is its corporeity,
> are the existentials by which the world becomes visible, is the
> flesh wherein the *ob*ject is born. It is inevitable that conscious-
> ness be mystified, inverted, indirect, in principle it sees the
> things *through the other end*, in principle it disregards Being and
> prefers the object to it, that is, a Being with which it has broken,
> and which it posits beyond this negation, by negating this nega-
> tion. (VI, 248)

The Unthought Ground of Thought in the Freudian Unconscious

The approach to our main objective of rereading psychoanalytic theory, circuitous though it has been, allows us to better grasp the underlying movement of Michel Foucault's project in *The Order of Things* and the reasons why it culminates in an appreciation of psychoanalysis. Indeed, our effort to elucidate the concept of the dispositional field has a great deal in common with the characterization of modernity offered in *The Order of Things*. Foucault, too, begins his book with discussion of a quintessentially modern painting, Velázquez's *Las Meninas*.

The painting's composition is emblematic of modernity for the self-consciousness of its mirror-play. This mirror-play is first engaged when we, the viewers who presumably stand in the position previously occupied by the painter himself, recognize that Velázquez has included in the painting another painter who looks back at us, the surface of his immense canvas invisible to us. In the face of this reversal, the ostensible focus of the painting—the luminous figure of the Infanta in the foreground, carefully posed as if it is she who is being painted—is suddenly displaced. We ourselves seem to be the subject painted by the artist who inhabits the painting. A second moment of reversal occurs, however, when our eye falls upon a mirror hanging at the back of the room directly across from us.

According to the spatial logic of the painting, it is our own reflection that we expect to see in this mirror. But, no, the distant mirror displays the image of the king and queen of Spain. Is the royal couple, then, the true subject of the painting? No sooner has the question formed itself than the dance of viewpoints shifts yet again, for the mirror occupied by the king and queen, the mirror in which we might otherwise glimpse ourselves, is equally well located to reflect the position from which the whole tableau is gathered and focused: the position of the true painter. Is it not Velázquez himself who should appear in this mirror? In this series of ingenious dislocations, *Las Meninas* effects a coincidence of the three positions that define the logic of representation: those of the painter, the painted subject, and the viewer of the painting. As if to emphasize these paradoxical invaginations of perspective, our eye is drawn finally to the mysterious figure at the back of the room who surveys the entire scene from a brightly lighted doorway that leads out upon some other space altogether.

Velázquez's painting exemplifies Foucault's central point about modernity as the self-consciousness of representation. Its own presuppositions made explicit, the concept of representation inevitably folds back upon the unrepresented position from which representation becomes possible. In *Las Meninas* "representation undertakes to represent itself . . . in all its elements, with its images, the eyes to which it is offered, the faces it makes visible, the gestures that call it into being. But there, in the midst of this dispersion which it is simultaneously grouping together and spreading out before us, indicated compellingly from every side, is an essential void: the necessary disappearance of that which is its foundation."[40] In evoking this necessarily unrepresented dimension that is the precondition of all representation, Velázquez's painting emblematizes what we have called the dispositional field.

Although announced in the opening discussion of *Las Meninas,* the overarching theme of Foucault's book is made fully explicit only toward the end in the section devoted to "The 'Cogito' and the Unthought." Across the main currents of knowledge in the modern period Foucault traces a common concern for the way in which thought borders upon the domain of the unthought, the varied ensemble of conditions that are intimately determinative for the structure of thought without being themselves masterable by reflection.

The modern *cogito* (and this is why it is not so much the discovery of an evident truth as a ceaseless task constantly to be undertaken afresh) must traverse, duplicate, and reactivate in an explicit form the articulation of thought on everything within it, around it, and beneath it which is not thought, yet which is nevertheless not foreign to thought, in the sense of an irreducible, an insuperable exteriority. In this form, the *cogito* will not therefore be the sudden and illuminating discovery that all thought is thought, but the constantly renewed interrogation as to how thought can reside elsewhere than here, and yet so very close to itself; how it can be in the forms of non-thinking. The modern *cogito* does not reduce the whole being of things to thought without ramifying the being of thought right down to the inert network of what does not think. (OT, 324)

It is with the theme of the unthought that we can grasp the meaning of Foucault's characterization of the concept of "man" as a recent and problematic coinage. Modernity clings to the category of "man" as way of refinding unity and stability in the encounter with the heterogeneity of the unthought. Thus "man and the unthought are, at the archaeological level, contemporaries" (OT, 326). Yet, even as the concept of man offers reprieve from the oceanic character of the unthought, the very heterogeneity of the beyond of the cogito threatens to wash away all unity and stability of definition "like a face drawn in sand at the edge of the sea" (OT, 387). The "human sciences" therefore constantly threaten to erase the very object of their research. All these sciences are founded on an uneasy tension, a mixed allegiance between the conditions of thought they investigate and the assertion of a coherent subject who performs the investigation. Phenomenology, for example, tends to waver between an insistence upon the fact that consciousness always opens out on an indeterminate horizon and a temptation to restablize the position of the knowing subject in the notion of a transcendental ego.

In view of these tensions endemic to the human sciences, a special privilege must be accorded to psychoanalysis for the fact that only in psychoanalysis is the exploration of the unconscious undertaken in and for itself. The other human sciences inevitably encounter the limits of representation, the points at which the realm of what is representable borders upon profound obscurity, but in psychoanalysis it is precisely those limits that remain the central concern.

> This means that, unlike the human sciences, which, even while turning back towards the unconscious, always remain within the space of the representable, psychoanalysis advances and leaps over representation, overflows it on the side of finitude, and thus reveals, where one had expected functions bearing their norms, conflicts burdened with rules, and significations forming a system, the simple fact that it is possible for there to be system (therefore signification), rule (therefore conflict), norm (therefore function). And in this region where representation remains in suspense, on the edge of itself, open, in a sense, to the closed boundary of finitude, we find outlined the three figures by means of which life, with its function and norms, attains its foundation in the mute repetition of Death, conflicts and rules their foundation in the naked opening of Desire, significations and systems their foundation in a language which is at the same time Law. (OT, 374)

The essential situation of psychoanalysis is well described in terms of "the cogito and the unthought," including its reference to Descartes. The point at which Freud will assert the reality of the unconscious is readily recognizable in the unfolding of Descartes's *Meditations.* In his second proof for the existence of God, Descartes demonstrates the necessity that at least one other being exist in addition to himself as a thinking thing. It is this other being who insures that the cogito, the very existence of consciousness, is maintained from moment to moment. Descartes goes on to argue that this other being who possesses the power to sustain my existence as conscious can only be God. The problem with this conclusion, of course, is that it remains unclear why the constitutive power that maintains my conscious existence must be attributed to God and not to the omnipotent Evil Genius hypothesized by Descartes earlier in his argument. Yet even if Descartes fails to win the conclusion he wants, the second proof succeeds in showing that consciousness is maintained by a power other than itself. Consciousness is dependent for every moment of its existence upon the activity of something that remains outside and beyond itself. What is this but the conclusion that consciousness arises from out of something *un*-conscious?

Psychoanalysis, the archaeology of the unthought, is a science of the dispositional field. Indeed, even before his invention of analysis proper, Freud had already arrived at what would remain his most fundamental guiding assumption: the idea that the psyche is always at work as a whole, that the mind has essentially the character of a *field*. It is this idea that underlies Freud's position in his 1891 paper "On Aphasia." Following the lead of Hughlings Jackson, Freud's argument militates against localizing psychical functions in particular regions of the brain. This rejection of localization bears broader implications for a grasp of the mind's operation as a total system, what Freud later called the working of the "psychical apparatus." In this and other ways, "On Aphasia" marks parallels between Freud's thinking and the figures and movements we have discussed. Freud's denial of the existence of "simple sensory impressions," for example, foreshadows the critique of empiricism later articulated by Gestalt psychology. This denial entails a rejection of the distinction drawn by the empiricist tradition between perception and association. Every increment of perception is already implicitly inflected with associations. There is no impression that is not already imbricated within an entire network of psychical content. Every increment of the psychical process is intrinsically complex, above all the processes that govern the comprehension of speech and language. The understanding of words involves simultaneous innervation of pathways in different functional modalities. Freud thus remarks that "from the psychological point of view the 'word' is the functional unit of speech," but he immediately goes on to emphasize that "it is a complex concept constituted of auditory, visual, and kinaesthetic elements."[41]

On the basis of this assumption of holistic functioning, Freud is able to ascribe the mechanism of aphasic disorders not to a breakdown of one or another functional "center" but rather to a failure of conduction between centers. He thus claims to "feel justified in rejecting the differentiation between the so-called centre or cortical aphasias and the conduction (association) aphasias, and we maintain that all aphasias originate in interruption of associations, i.e., of conduction." This suggestion contains in embryo the basic definition of pathology that will implicitly inform the whole of the psychoanalytic project. The pathogenic processes with which psychoanalytic therapy deals represent the breakdown of connections and of pathways of conduction. From this point of view, the psychical disorders treated by psychoanalysis can be characterized as malignancies of the dispositional field.

With the birth of the psychoanalytic technique, Freud's concern became even more directly focused on the dynamics we have attributed to positionality and dispositionality. From the very beginning, Freud was concerned with explaining the nature and function of "excessively intense ideas,"[42] a problem that offers a point of contact between psychoanalysis and phenomenology. The strangely compelling claims of certain memories, dream images, compulsive ideas, phobias, and fetishes in which the psychoanalyst discerns the workings of the unconscious are describable by the phenomenologist as the coming-to-presence of somehow exceptional or privileged appearances. The Freudian problematic particularly resembles Heideggerian phenomenology, for which every coming into appearance is correlative with a disappearance, every revealment conditioned by a concealment. It is what remains hidden in the heart of what is most manifest that interests Freud. Freud is attracted by the way presence is haunted by absence. There is always an unconscious staging, an invisible, conditioning ground out of which the conscious rises up. Yet it is at this point that the Freudian perspective goes beyond phenomenology and contributes something new by clarifying the motives and mechanisms that structure the dynamics of revealment and concealment. The processes of condensation and displacement and the whole theoretical construction of the unconscious of which they form a part serve to define the pathways by which excessively intense ideas may be traced back to their relations with previously undetected contents. In the terms we have evolved, psychoanalytic interpretation is concerned to revivify the links by which a given figure is produced from out of an immensely complex ground. From this point of view, psychoanalysis emerges as a method for the excavation of the dispositonal field, the aim of which is a recovery and restructuring of its constitutive network. The means by which this recovery is accomplished is the exercise of free association, the effect of which is not so much to forge connections where they are wholly lacking as to bring into play already existing connections that have been active only on the level of the unconscious. It is for this reason that the method and the aim of psychoanalysis coincide. The adequate employment of the method constitutes in itself the most crucial step toward the achievement of its objective.

To conceive Freud's essential problems in the terms we have been exploring is thus to suggest a parallel between psychoanalysis and phenomenology. And it is not difficult to make out what further shape this linkage will take. Psychoanalytic repression becomes comparable to the gestalt process by which a perceptual figure is adumbrated by means of a nihilating reduction of the surrounding background. As we will see in the following chapter, this idea can be discerned with striking clarity in key moments of Freud's work and can be drawn upon to integrate some of his most far-reaching theoretical formulations. The task of laying bare this link between psychoanalysis and phenomenology is a primary goal of this book. However—and we can hardly overestimate the importance of this qualification—at some point the analogy between psychoanalytic repression and the figure-ground relation breaks down. To identify repression and the unconscious with the unthematized margin of awareness would seem to account for the absence to consciousness of certain contents at any given moment but not for the enduring inability of retrieval that characterizes neurotic complexes and symptoms. Contents in the unthematized penumbra of awareness remain momentarily absent but can presumably be recalled to consciousness at some other moment. The phenomenological approach thus seems capable of accounting only for what Freud called "preconscious" processes. The model of the figure-ground distinction is further unable to provide an explanation for the highly structured character of unconscious mechanisms such as we find them in the elaborations of the dream-work or in the formation of symptoms. With its twofold structure of a more or less unified focus set against a relatively indistinct, "repressed" background, the figure-ground concept seems to offer a tempting analogy to the opposition between conscious and unconscious, but by itself the Gestalt concept tells us little about the structure of the ground from which the figure is distinguished.

Difficulties of this sort have foiled many attempts to translate psychoanalytic concepts into phenomenological terms.[43] But the imperfect analogy between repression and the figure-ground relation is related to another, even more fundamental, problem. Both Gestalt psychology and phenomenology offer analyses of the structure of consciousness for which perceptual experience provides a crucial, perhaps indispensable, paradigm. The question becomes whether any theoretical framework relevant primarily to the example of perceptual processes can do justice to the centrality of language in psychoanalysis. Anna O. was profoundly right to call analysis a "talking cure." The work of analysis is conducted in the medium of speech, and it is from speech and language that its transformative effects are derived. It is in reminding us of this fact that the Lacanian interpretation of Freud is especially challenging. The Freudian perspective faces us with the strange, almost unthinkable, proposition that the effects of language in the human being are more fundamental and far-reaching than the functions of perception that developmentally precede the acquisition of speech. How is the parallel we have begun to develop between the Freudian unconscious and the dispositional field explored by Gestalt psychology and phenomenology to be sustained in the face of this primacy of linguistic structure in the Freudian unconscious? How, indeed, are we even to conceive that primacy?

As we will see in what follows, the path toward an answer to these questions is to be found in what may well seem the least likely place. Freud, too, theorizes the dialectics of positionality and dispositionality that we have traced from Monet to Merleau-Ponty and does so in a highly original way. He thinks it in terms of the metaphor of psychical energy. This conclusion will no doubt sound strange. What could be more foreign to the categories of phenomenology than the crude mechanics of Freudian energetics? What, moreover, could be more unsuited to address the nature of language than the hydraulics of libido? What makes these pairings seem strange bedfellows is a misunderstanding of what Freud meant by energetics. As will become increasingly apparent in the discussions to follow, the Freudian sense of energy is less a concept of substance than of system. Far from being a crude vitalist notion, the supposition of a formless chaos, energetics is an essentially *structural* concept. It has less to do with the physical concept of force than the economic concept of value. Energetics concerns differential distribution within a total field. In this respect, Freudian energetics has less in common with nineteenth-century physicalism than with the postulates of Gestalt psychology. Energetics is the operative metaphor by which Freud conceives the dynamics of the dispositional field.

The basis on which Freud's thought can be compared with that of Husserl, Heidegger, and Merleau-Ponty is thus to be found where we might least suspect it. The whole edifice of energetic concepts, including the central notion of *Besetzung*, energetic investment or cathexis, has been almost universally taken to be a reductive and mechanistic throwback, the very point at which Freudian psychoanalysis is most completely inimical with philosophical reflection. Correctly interpreted, however, the energetic metaphor can be relied upon to locate subtle problems of perception and language. The goal will be to see how the energetic metaphor can be used to elaborate the concept of a dispositional field in a way that is equally applicable to the image and the word. Far from being inimical to the lessons of phenomenology or to the Lacanian emphasis on language in the unconscious, the guiding clue of energetics is precisely what is needed to show the integration of perceptual and linguistic dimensions in the psychoanalytic theory of the unconscious. If this goal can be accomplished, the result will be of inestimable value for reconceiving the groundlines of the psychoanalytic theory. At the same time, it will enable us to resituate psychoanalysis in relation to other movements of contemporary thought. It will allow us to demonstrate not only the internal connectedness of phenomenology and structuralism but will suggest the way in which psychoanalysis is crucially situated at the intersection of the two.

CHAPTER 2

Between the Image
and the Word

How, then, can the Freudian unconscious be adequately conceived on the model of a dispositional field? How, moreover, can the concept of a dispositional field, derived primarily from examples of perceptual experience, be applied to the nature of language and to the linguistic character of unconscious processes?

In what follows, we will first see the extent to which the psychoanalytic conception of the unconscious resonates with Gestaltist and phenomenological principles. We will trace Freud's royal road to the unconscious back to its point of departure in phenomena of perception and attention. But in addition, we will come not only to grasp the compatibility of the two different approaches to the unconscious, perceptual and linguistic, but to recognize that the real heart of psychoanalysis is located precisely at the intersection of imagistic and verbal functions. The result of these considerations will be to illuminate the foundations of psychoanlaysis in a new way, allowing us to glimpse the coherence of Freud's metapsychology as if for the first time.

In the Shadow of the Image

In his first seminar, Lacan offers a discussion of the patient's resistance to analysis that bears an unmistakably phenomenological resonance. Lacan's remarks center on those moments in which the progress of the patient's discourse and the unfolding of associations that sustain it are interrupted by a sudden and pronounced awareness of the *presence* of the analyst. All at once "the subject himself feels something like a sharp bend, a sudden turn which causes him to pass from one slope of the discourse to the other, from one aspect of the function of speech to another" (S.I, 40).

> Just when he seems ready to come out with something more
> authentic, more to the point than he has ever managed to come
> up with up to then, the subject, in some cases, breaks off, and
> utters a statement, which might be the following *I am aware all
> of a sudden of the fact of your presence.* (S.I, 40)[1]

Such derailments of the patient's speech tend to occur precisely when something important to the progress of the analytic work is about to emerge. The suddenly compelling sense of the analyst's presence functions to insure an absence. It usurps the place of an emerging revelation. The mechanism of resistance might thus be characterized as a substitution of one moment of presence for another, one revelation in the place of another. Taken generally, consciousness of one thing short-circuits the entry into consciousness of something else.

Similar processes of substitution are absolutely typical of the behavior of the unconscious and can be found repeatedly throughout Freud's writings. In his early essay on "Screen Memories," for example, Freud analyzes the memory of a bouquet of yellow flowers. Freud remarks about the curious vividness of the color—it appeared to be *überdeutlich*, or "ultra-clear"—and he compares it to a burlesque poster in which the women's breasts were accentuated in three dimensions by being padded from behind (SE, 3:312). In the course of the analysis, the yellow of the flowers is found to be a stand-in for other, less palatable thoughts. Elsewhere, Freud traces other experiences of "ultra-clear" ideas to parallel processes of substitution. In "The Psychical Mechanism of Forgetfulness," Freud recounts his inability to remember a street name but notes that the house number, "as if to jeer at me," was ultra-clear to his mind's eye (SE, 3:297).

In The Psychopathology of Everyday Life, a woman's extravivid memory of a dress worn while entertaining a visit from her brother is interpreted in terms of her fear for her brother's failing health: her overly intense experience of the visiting dress is revealed to be a substitute for the fearful alternative of funeral attire (SE, 6: 266-67).

In these few examples, we already encounter some of the most fundamental and perplexing questions posed by psychoanalysis. By what process are some ideas announced to consciousness with special force while others languish in darkness? By what law, principle, or structure is the economy of revealing and concealing ordered? We have already begun to see how these questions receive an answer from a phenomenological point of view. In every perceptual field, indeed, in every moment of consciousness whatever, some more focused, thematized, or foregrounded content or figure is separated from an environing background that remains less clearly or distinctly perceived. On analogy to this figure-ground structure, it is tempting to compare the action of repression to the process by which the background contents of awareness are relegated to the vague and indeterminate margin. But what warrant is there in Freud's own text for such a comparison?

An answer is provided in Freud's 1895 *Project for a Scientific Psychology,* the value of which for discerning the groundlines of Freud's thought can hardly be overestimated. As Lacan writes, "the *Entwurf* is very revealing of a kind of substructure of Freud's thought. Its obvious relationship to all the formulations of his experience that Freud was led to offer subsequently makes it especially precious."[2] In the *Project,* Freud attempts to provide an exhaustive account of psychical processes in terms of a purely quantitative apparatus composed of neurons differentially "facilitated" to allow passage of greater or lesser quantities of energy. Of key importance is the explanation of "primary defense," by which the psychical apparatus protects itself against a passage of energy (designated "Q" or "quantity") along pathways leading to a neuron associated with unpleasure. Primary defense blocks the movement of Q energy from an initial, perceptual neuron "a" to an unpleasure neuron "b," by means of a "side-cathexis" to a third neuron, designated "α" or alpha. In this way, energy is siphoned off from its original route and "bound" as a railway car might be drawn onto an auxiliary track. We immediately sense the relevance of side-cathexis to the substitutive process remarked upon above, in which, as

Lacan says, the subject feels "a sudden turn which causes him to pass from one slope of discourse to the other." We also begin to see better in Freud's own terms the link stressed by Lacan between the action of resistance and the structure of the ego. Side-cathexes, Freud says, are possible only when a mass of neurons adjunct to the path of conduction leading to unpleasure are permanently invested with energy. Precisely such a mass of permanently cathected neurons constitutes what Freud calls the "ego," the function of which is thus essentially defensive and inhibitory. Freud provides the following diagram and commentary to illustrate the role of the ego in the process of defense:

> Let us picture the ego as a network of cathected neurones well facilitated in relation to one another, thus:

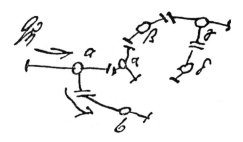

> If we suppose that a Qn enters a neurone a from outside ϕ then, if it were uninfluenced, it would pass to neurone b; but it is so much influenced by the side-cathexis a—α that it gives off only a quotient to b and may even perhaps not reach b at all. Therefore, if an ego exists, it must inhibit psychical primary processes. . . . It is easy now to imagine how, with the help of a mechanism which draws the ego's attention to the imminent fresh cathexis of the hostile mnemic image, the ego can succeed in inhibiting the passage [of quantity] from a mnemic image to a release of unpleasure by a copious side-cathexis which can be strengthened according to need. (SE, 1:323-24)

But is Freud's neurological concept of cathexis compatible with a phenomenological viewpoint? In fact, we are not as far from a phenomenological perspective as it may appear. Initially presented as cellular way stations for the transmission of energies, the neurons of the *Project* are also clearly taken by Freud to represent moments of lived experience. The initial neuron "a" is referred to as a *hostile mnemic image*. The process of defense is thus conceivable in phenomenological terms as the substitution of one image for another or, as Freud says of it, "the emergence of another object in place of the hostile one" (SE, 1:322). Far from precluding a phenomenological orientation, the mechanistic concepts of the *Project* must be completed by a phenomenological reading, especially with reference to the function of images and attention, for the full meaning of Freud's text to emerge. Lacan is alert to this necessity and insists that his own conception of the imaginary ego and its function of *méconnaissance*, or alienating misrecognition, compared by him to the lessons of Gestalt psychology, can already be discerned in the *Project*. "Freud isn't a Gestaltist," Lacan remarks, "one cannot give him credit for everything—but he does sense the theoretical demands which gave rise to the Gestaltist construction" (S.II, 107). Referring to the inhibiting, filtering function of the ego as Freud envisages it in the *Project*, Lacan proposes that "the imaginary must indeed be here" (S.II, 107).

The Gestaltist distinction between figure and ground clarifies a key issue that remains incompletely resolved in Freud's text: if neurons *a* and *alpha* are taken to be images or ideas, what is the relation between them? Freud's own text gives an initial clue: the substitutive idea, the idea in the position of neuron alpha, is *die nächste Einfall*, the next or closest association. What, then, is meant by "the next closest association"? Might it not refer first of all to a *perceptual* association? *Die nächste Einfall* would then point to the most immediate and primitive movement of association: a movement across the space of the perceptual field. The closest association would be something immediately to the side of the gestalt figure, a position in the phenomenal background. In the text of the *Project*, a clinical example provided by Freud suggests precisely that.

The case concerns a woman who suffered from a terror of entering shops alone, a fear that she attributed to an incident in which a pair of shop assistants had *laughed at her clothes*. The details of the laughter and clothing stood out to her memory in high relief. But why? Analysis revealed an earlier scene in which another shopkeeper had grabbed at her genitals through her clothes. Freud then offered the following reconstruction: the earlier scene and its sexual content had remained unavailable to the woman's consciousness, but certain details of the original episode were retained with special intensity and formed an associative bridge to the second incident; namely, the *laughlike grin* of the shopkeeper and the memory of her *clothes* being grabbed at. In this instance, therefore, we again find a process of substitution in which the central element of a painful experience was occluded by an overintense perception of some ancillary detail. We are led to suppose that the sexual object of the shopkeeper's gropings, the actual point of his contact with the woman's body, was obscured from her consciousness because its place in the focus of attention had been taken by two peripheral details—his grin and the clothes that prevented his grabbing hands from fully reaching their aim. The figure of the phenomenal field was lost only by virtue of being displaced by details from the environing background.

The instances of substitution reviewed earlier can be interpreted similarly in terms of a gestalt shift. In the example from "Screen Memories," the *yellow* of a girl's dress was substituted for the girl herself and the troubling feelings she aroused. In the instance of the forgotten street name, the *house number* (which would stand just next to the street name in a written address) was ultra-clear. For the woman worried about her brother's health, a whole complex of ideas associated with a funeral (the corpse, the casket, the mourners, etc.) was lost to consciousness to the extent that a single element of the funeral scene—the image of the *dress*—dominated the subject's awareness. The same approach also explains the situation of resistance described by Lacan in which the patient is suddenly distracted by the presence of the analyst. On the verge of saying something uncomfortably revealing, the patient's attention is drawn to a point in the periphery of his field of awareness: that is, to the person of the analyst sitting behind him.

In all of these instances, the substitutive element is selected by perceptual contiguity. The focus of conscious attention is overtaken by an element in the periphery of the perceptual field. Freud points to a similar mechanism in his account of the origin of the fetish. The choice of the fetish object is guided by a specifically perceptual process in which the approach to the site of the maternal phallus is arrested just short of the fearful revelation of its absence. The fetishistic interest then centers upon what it finds there. Freud notes with some surprise that this process is not metaphorical, that a substitute for the absent phallus is not chosen from among typical symbols of the phallus. Rather, the process of substitution is *metonymical*. The choice of fetish object is made in a lateral movement across the field of the perceptual tableau of the maternal body. His remarks on this process are worth quoting at some length.

> One would expect that the organs or objects chosen as substitutes for the absent female phallus would be such as appear as symbols of the penis in other connections as well. This may happen often enough, but is certainly not a deciding factor. It seems rather that when the fetish is instituted some process occurs which reminds one of the stopping of memory in traumatic amnesia. As in this latter case, the subject's interest comes to a halt half-way, as it were; it is as though the last impression before the uncanny and traumatic one is retained as a fetish. Thus the foot or shoe owes its preference as a fetish—or a part of it—to the circumstance that the inquisitive boy peered at the woman's genitals from below, from her legs up; fur and velvet— as has long been suspected—are a fixation of the sight of the pubic hair, which should have been followed by the longed-for sight of the female member; pieces of underclothing, which are so often chosen as a fetish, crystallize the moment of undressing, the last moment in which the woman could still be regarded as phallic. (SE, 21:155)

The preceding instances, including that of the fetish, prompt us to seek a role for the figure-ground relation in the activity of repression in general and thus suggest a link between the Gestalt concept and the dynamics of *cathexis* and *anticathexis*—the terms in which Freud sought to offer a metapsychological account of repression. We are led to suppose that what Freud called cathexis and anticathexis correspond, at least in part, to the perceptual process by which a figure is separated from its surrounding background. Cathexis, as an investment of energy that focuses attention and interest, becomes identifiable with the adumbration of a perceptual figure. Correlatively, anticathexis is linked with the activity by which the periphery or margin of the sensory field is suppressed and rendered less obtrusive. Looked at from this point of view, repression is linked to the workings of an absolutely fundamental automatism that guides and structures all perceptual activity—an advantage that would no doubt have appealed to Freud. At the same time, these considerations lead us back to the Lacanian concept of the imaginary as a way of integrating the various points of our discussion. A key aspect of the imaginary function, perhaps its very essence, consists in the capacity to adumbrate the unitary contour of perceptual objects, the very activity so central to the Gestalt psychologists. It is the imaginary function that grounds the relative stability of perceived objects, lending to them their "attributes of permanence, identity, and substantiality" (E:S, 17). Yet precisely correlative with the power of the Gestalt is an effect of misrecognition, or *méconnaissance*.

The Unconscious Play of the Signifier

The preceding discussion highlights parallels between Freud's theory and the basic concepts of phenomenology, yet there remains a wealth of instances in which the workings of the unconscious seem better explained not by phenomenology but by linguistics. Rereading many of Freud's analyses of dreams, slips, and symptoms, we are forcefully reminded of Lacan's dictum about the unconscious structured like a language. Few more singularly instructive examples could be offered than the fragment of Freud's self-analysis recounted in his essay on "The Psychical Mechanism of Forgetfulness." The example is especially valuable for our purposes as it puts into high relief a dynamic of substitution, staging anew the question of why one presentation appears in the place of another. Chatting with a stranger on his way to Herzegovina, Freud was unable to recall the name of the painter of the famous frescoes at Orvieto. Two names occurred to him—"Botticelli" and "Boltraffio"—but were immediately rejected as incorrect. Why did the sought-after name "Signorelli" remain inaccessible, while two other names obtrusively announced themselves?

In explaining his lapse of memory, Freud suggests that the painter's name became entangled in a complex web of secondary associations, relevant to the topic of conversation immediately preceding the discussion of the Italian frescoes. That conversation had concerned the local customs of the region in which Freud and his companion were traveling—the area around Bosnia-Herzegovina—and in particular the conspicuous deference shown by the Turks of that region to their doctors. Even when told of the impending death of a loved one, family members might be heard to say: "*Herr* [Sir], what is there to be said? If he could be saved, I know you would help him" (SE, 3:292). A second thought occurred to Freud at the time but remained unspoken. It had to do with the overriding importance attributed by the Bosnians to sexual enjoyment. As one man had expressed it: "*Herr*, you must know, that if *that* comes to end then life is of no value" (SE, 3:292). The interwoven themes of death and sexuality called up by these two thoughts resonated with the topic of the frescoes, which dealt with similarly disturbing themes in their depiction of the Antichrist, the End of the World, and the Last Judgment. By means of this associative link, the urge to suppress what was uncomfortable in the conversation about the Turks, an urge rooted in matters of deep personal concern to Freud but redoubled by the demands of politeness with a stranger, was carried over to the topic of the frescoes. This general unease was then given specific focus by another associative bridge. The "Herr" of the anecdotes about the Turks was brought into association with the "Signor" of the artist's name by way of a translation between German and Italian, a circumstance made more likely by the fact that Freud had continually been speaking Italian over the previous few days of his journey. The promotion of the "Herr" fragment to special status was further favored by its presence in the place-name "*Herzegovina*." A last and decisive association knotted together thoughts of death and sexuality: the memory of a former patient of Freud's who had committed suicide in despair over a sexual dysfunction. Under the influence of this memory—no doubt an occasion for self-recriminations about Freud's own role as a doctor—the "Signor" in question might well have borne a reference to Freud himself, a reference all the more readily suggested by the way in which the missing fragment echoed the initial syllable of Freud's own name. Drawn into the nexus of these associations, the "Signor" of Signorelli was split off and remained unavailable to Freud's consciousness. Only the last fragment of the name survived, finding its way into consciousness as the last portion of the name Bottic-*elli*.

If the Signorelli episode provides an especially clear window on the workings of repression, it also demonstrates with equal distinctness the return of repressed to consciousness. This process issued in the two fragments "Bo" and "traffio" that completed the substitute names "*Bo*-tticelli" and "Bo-l-*traffio*." The "Bo" element derived from *Bo*-snia in a fashion precisely parallel to the selection of "Herr" from *Her*-zegovina, although its psychical function was exactly the opposite. While the "Herr" fragment provided the crucial linkage in a process of repression, the "Bo" reappeared in its place as a kind of proxy, as if to mark the site of repression with a delegate of the repressed. So, too, the "traffio" element pointed back to the nucleus of repressed ideas, as it was at "Trafoi" that Freud received the news of his patient's suicide. Freud provides the following diagram (Fig. 3) to illustrate the entire process of forgetting and substitute formation.

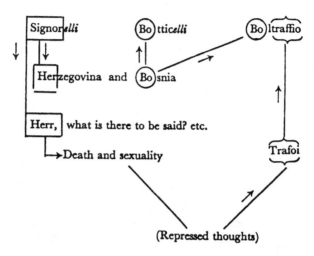

Figure 3

Freud's analysis of the Signorelli example strikingly illustrates the Lacanian thesis that the unconscious is structured like a language. The painter's name was rendered unavailable to consciousness through a two-stage process in which a series of associations was strung together by repetition of a common phonemic element (Herr), then translated from one language to another (Signor). This evidence suggests an alternative model of the mechanism of repression, less as a shift of attention than as a failure of translation. Repression is effected less as a failure to *see* what remains in the shadows than a failure to *read* what has been inscribed in a different manner. Lack of conscious access to the repressed becomes analogous to the inability to read words from an unknown language that have been inserted into an otherwise familiar text.

Although the Signorelli episode appears in this way to support Lacan's linguistic conception of the unconscious, a question might yet be raised about whether the process of repression can be fully accounted for in terms of the play of the signifier. The question arises because the circuits of the signifier that mark the fault lines of repression (in the "Herr-Signor" complex) also provide the pathways by which the repressed contents make their return toward consciousness (in the "Bo" and the "traffio"). If the symbolic system provides the matrix for both repression and the return of the repressed, if the signifier becomes the vehicle for both the disappearance and reappearance of the repressed, must there not be another factor involved in the mechanism of repression? Where is such an additional factor to be sought? Returning to Freud's discussion, we find an intriguing clue that leads us back to the phenomenon of "ultra-clear" ideas. Freud notes that his inability to recall the painter's *name* was accompanied by an overintense experience of his *visual image,* included in one corner of the fresco as a kind of signature. In recalling the episode in *The Psychopathology of Everyday Life,* Freud remarks that

> in the Signorelli case, so long as the painter's name remained inaccessible, the visual memory that I had of the series of frescoes and of the portrait which is introduced into the corner of one of the pictures was *ultra-clear* [*überdeutlich*]—at any rate much more intense than visual memory-traces normally appear to me. (SE, 6:13)

With the discovery of the name, the overintensity of the image dissipated.

> I had for several days to put up with this lapse of memory . . . until I fell in with a cultivated Italian who freed me from it by telling me the name: Signorelli. I was myself able to add the artist's *first* name, *Luca.* Soon my ultra-clear memory of the master's features, as depicted in his portrait, faded away. (SE, 3:291)

This detail suggests that the psychic process at work in the forgetting of the name involved a conflictual interplay of visual *and* verbal functions. It was in similar terms that Freud later came to describe the mechanism of repression as a disturbance in the relation between *thing-presentations* and *word-presentations.* As he put it in his 1914 essay "The Unconscious," "the conscious presentation comprises the presentation of the thing plus the presentation of the word belonging to it, while the unconscious presentation is the presentation of the thing alone" (SE, 14:201). According to this view, the work of repression thrusts ideas into unconsciousness by somehow splitting apart the thing- and word-presentations that belong to them. What, then, are we to understand by "thing-presentation" (*Sachvorstellung*) and "word-presentation" (*Wortvorstellung*)? Despite the importance of the issues at stake, Freud offers only the briefest remarks on the distinction between them. He does make it clear, however, that of the two forms of presentations, thing-presentations represent the more elemental function. Thing-presentations are said to be *older* (as mental life operates upon thing-presentations before the acquisition of language), they are more deeply rooted in *perceptual* mechanisms ("if not of the direct memory-traces of the thing, at least of remoter memory-traces derived from these" [SE, 14:201], and they are simpler in their basic structure (in contrast to the complexity of word-presentations as Freud emphasizes, for example, in his 1891 monograph *On Aphasia*). Thinking in thing-presentations is *imagistic* thinking.

Are the Freudian concepts of thing- and word-presentations assimilable to the Lacanian categories of imaginary and symbolic? If this link can be sustained, the process of repression becomes conceivable at the intersection of imaginary and symbolic functions. Precisely such a view is suggested by the most fundamental schema of Lacan's work: the Schema L (Fig. 4).

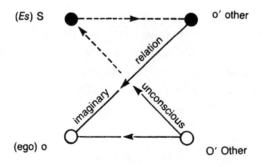

Figure 4

At the four corners of the schema the following are represented: the ego (o) and the pole of its identifications (o'), the locus of the code or symbol system (O), and the position of the subject of the unconscious beyond the ego (S). Between the ego and its objects stretches the axis of imaginary relations. Between the Other of the symbolic order and the Subject determined by it lies the symbolic axis. The significant point for our present purposes is the way in which the two axes cross each other, suggesting a conflictual relation. It is a conflict between the demands of the narcissistic ego, formed in the mirror phase and always tending toward the reestablishment of an imaginary coherence, and the resources of the symbolic system, in which is circuited the unconscious desire of the subject. The intersection between the two axes can therefore be taken to represent the necessity of symbolic castration; the necessity, that is, that the narcissistic bond of the ego and its objects must give way before the emergence of a speaking subject determined by its reliance on a symbolic code, a discourse of the Other. But the work of castration that installs the subject in a symbolic function is never complete. The narcissistic substructure of the personality forever exerts its own gravity, drawing the symbolic process into the orbit of imaginary formations. This essential incompleteness of the submission to the symbolic function is represented in the schema by the way the line extending from the locus of the code at "O" to the position of the subject "S" remains broken in its upper portion. What the subject receives from the symbolic system is always interrupted and broken up under the influence of the imaginary.

In his second seminar, Lacan compares the interference exerted upon the symbolic by the force of the imaginary to the passage of electrons in a vacuum tube. To position this analogy on the structure of the Schema L, we must imagine the locus of the symbolic system at "O" as a cathode and the subject "S" as an anode. The passage of current between O and S thus represents the fact that "the unconscious has its own dynamic, its own flow, its own paths. It can be explored according to its own rhythm, its own modulation, its own message, quite independently of whatever interrupts it" (S.II, 120). Yet the transmission of material from the unconscious, the flow of the primary process, is subject to interruption, pulsation, or oscillation, exactly as the beam of electrons in the vacuum tube is bent and broken by a second current directed across its path. "That," says Lacan, "is what resistance, the imaginary function of the ego, as such, is,—it is up to it whether the passage or non-passage occurs of whatever there is to transmit as such in the action of analysis" (S.II, 120).

By relating the distinction between thing- and word-presentations to the two modalities of the psychical process, imaginary and symbolic,

Lacan militates against a crude reification of Freud's concepts. When repression occurs, it is not because an entity called a thing-presentation is split off from the complex of an idea and cast into the pit of the unconscious, as if word- and thing-presentations could be taken as two separable halves of the body of an idea. On the contrary, repression occurs in the conflictual interplay of two essential psychical functions. It corresponds to a shift of valence from the symbolic to the imaginary axis. The unconscious is therefore not a state but a process, not a receptacle into which an idea might be closeted away but rather a kind of cross-wiring of functions in which an idea is structurally transformed. That "the unconscious presentation is the presentation of the thing alone" means that a psychical process that might otherwise pass along the circuits of the signifying system has become caught up in an imaginary formation.

This view explains a great deal. It explains, for example, why the processes of resistance and repression characteristically leave behind an unusually intense image. The presence of the image is not merely a byproduct of the process but rather represents an essential aspect of its operation. In repression, the unfolding of a symbolic process has been submitted to the force of an imaginary effect. A special investment of attention has occurred that now functions to obstruct the further play of associations. The psychical process has become bound to a particular representation. In the language of Freud's concepts, thought has come under the influence of a "fixation." Beyond the point of such imaginary interference, however, the structured network of the symbolic system remains intact. Although truncated and distorted by the influence of the imaginary, the articulations of the symbolic organization never fully cease to function, and it is precisely for that reason that the return of the repressed is able to seek its way back to consciousness along the tendrils of the signifier.[3]

From this perspective, too, we can explain and integrate the two models of repression we have offered. Along the imaginary axis we can recognize the gestalt function of our earlier discussions, and we can once again assert the role played by the figure-ground structure in the differentiation of conscious and unconscious. There is, indeed, a sense in which repression pivots upon the valencing of a specially invested figure by means of which consciousness is distracted. And yet, as we noted before, the properly *un*conscious aspects of repression that account for the subject's inability to voluntarily reverse its effects cannot be derived from the figure-ground function alone. This is so because repression is brought about not simply by a gestalt shift between figure and ground on the level of perception, but by the way that shift is accompanied by a certain dislocation of symbolic relations that remain beyond the reach of perception. Retrieval of contents submitted to repression is impeded by the fact that they have been distributed across two psychical functions, each governed by different laws. In the same stroke, we understand why the process of repression cannot be fully explained solely in terms of linguistic linkages. The linguistic elements indeed provide the switching points around which the formations of the unconscious turn, yet it remains necessary for an imaginary component to enter into the process. If the unconscious is structured like a language, it remains no less the case that the pivot point of its process lies on the unstable fault line between the symbolic and the imaginary.

The preceding points are remarkably illustrated by the Signorelli episode; indeed, nearly everything we have discussed from the outset can be discerned in the details of Freud's analysis. The painter's image, like the other substitute ideas discussed earlier, represents a moment of resistance to the surfacing of a threatening revelation. The Signorelli example also exhibits the structure of side-cathexis as we saw it before, in which a peripheral element usurps the focus of awareness. It is not incidental that the painter's portrait, which occupies the lower left-hand corner of the fresco in question, stands to the side of the central and more disturbing scenes depicted in the painting as a whole. But that is not all. We also see how the choice of the perceptual element, the painter's image, is caught up in a symbolic network. In fact, we can see the precise point at which the nexus of associations carried by the signifier "Herr" is abruptly shunted into the imaginary. The painter's portrait is the translation into imaginary terms of the signifier "Herr." It is the "Signor" of the fresco itself. As long as Freud's consciousness is dominated by the imaginary presentation (the thing-presentation), the linguistic equivalent (the word-presentation) will not appear.[4] Lastly, we see how it is only at this confused intersection of imaginary and symbolic, this point of crossed signals, that Freud's ability to remember is impeded. Other points of access into the same network of associations remain available to him, as is evidenced by the emergence of the "Bo" and the "traffio" fragments.[5]

From Image to Sign

Freud's analysis of the Signorelli episode reveals an elemental dynamic of presence and absence in which the theater of consciousness is staged by processes that remain unconscious. Lacan recasts this dynamic of presence and absence in terms of the play of imaginary and symbolic functions. Can we now understand more precisely what this dialectic of imaginary and symbolic means? How must imaginary and symbolic be conceived that such a dialectic is possible at all?

In providing an answer to this crucial question, it will be useful to refer again to Freud's distinction between thing- and word-presentations. Here, as elsewhere, Freud's theorizing is guided by the assumption of psychic energy. Of key importance is the way in which energetic cathexis is susceptible of two different modes of distribution. On the one hand, energy may be invested in a focused concentration. It is this function of cathexis that we earlier linked to the activity of attention and to the investment of particular images with interest. Such focused cathexis is the process that issues forth "thing-presentations." On the other hand, however, cathexis may be spread over a highly diffuse field of psychical relations that never register in perception or consciousness. In this second aspect of its function, cathexis becomes virtually identical with the Freudian concept of association. It is in terms of such a dispersion of cathexis across an immensely complex web of associations that Freud explains the psychical process by which words assume meaning. Precisely such dispersed and complex patterns of cathexis underlie "word-presentations." The distinction between these two modalities of cathexis, though not explicitly conceptualized by Freud, is clearly implicit everywhere in his theorizing. It is already discernible, for example, in his 1891 paper *On Aphasia*.

It is easy to recognize the two modalities of cathexis in the interplay of visual and verbal elements of the Signorelli episode. Economically speaking, the process of repression that we related to a dynamic of thing- and word-presentations is conceivable as a precisely structured redistribution of cathexis, in which the focal overinvestment in a perceptual element (the painter's portrait) siphons off cathexis from a whole series of associative linkages (the death-sexuality complex surrounding "Herr-Signor").

This view of the matter implies an essential paradox. The investment of cathexis in a perceptual figure describes the very mechanism of attention and is thus intimately bound up with the function of consciousness. But any investment of cathexis in one system necessarily implies a disinvestment elsewhere. For this reason, perceptual cathexis must be considered to be an indispensable moment in the constitution of the unconscious and the maintenance of repression. This paradox is part of the central enigma brought to light by psychoanalysis: it is in and through consciousness that the unconscious maintains itself.

It is not difficult to imagine how the Freudian distinction between focal and diffuse cathexis might be brought into line with the Lacanian categories of imaginary and symbolic. By "imaginary" let us designate the process of focal cathexis by which a perceptual figure is disembedded from a background and held before consciousness. In this definition, the imaginary presents an essentially twofold structure: isolation and promotion of the figural content along with suspension or suppression of the environing ground. Such a conception does justice to Lacan's often acknowledged debt to the Gestalt psychologists and highlights the process by which the unitary contour and relative stability of objects are constituted. It is on the model of such perceptual unities that the primitive ego is formed. The ego, Lacan insists, is itself an object.

If the imaginary corresponds to Freud's focal cathexis, the symbolic is comparable to diffuse cathexis. By "symbolic," we refer above all to the way in which the meaning of linguistic signs is imbricated within a broad system of other signs and associations that remain the unconscious possession of every speaker. It is at this point that Lacan follows the teaching of structuralist linguistics in conceiving of language as a network of differences in which the meaning of each element is determined by its relation of difference to the other elements in the system. From this point of view, the difference between the imaginary and symbolic functions aligns itself with a distinction between the perceptual and the nonperceptual. Unlike the imaginary, which distinguishes figure and ground within a perceptual field, the symbolic is always conditioned by its relation to a network of signifiers that is not and in fact *cannot* be made an object of perception. We perceive speech and writing but not the symbol system that makes them possible. Let us briefly expand upon this perspective with reference to structuralist linguistics and in particular to the problematic status of linguistic units.

The question concerning the proper unit of linguistic investigation is among the most fundamental problems raised by Saussure's *Course in*

General Linguistics.[6] For Saussure, the fundamental linguistic unit is, of course, the sign. Yet by Saussure's definition, the sign immediately shows itself to be a unity of a strange sort, first of all because it brings together two essentially different dimensions into a single entity. The sign consists of the fusion of a sound image (or signifier) and a concept (or signified). The fuller import of the problem of the sign's unity only appears, however, with the realization that both signifier and signified are constituted by their opposition to other elements in a system or network of differences. In its aspects of both sound and meaning, the specific character of any sign—say, for example, the word "bed"—consists in its distinctness from other sounds (bad, bid, bode, bet, beck, bell) and from other meanings (chair, table, couch). But this means that the unity of the sign, even in its perceptual registration, is internally conditioned by its relations to other and different elements. Linguistic unity is pervaded by otherness. This participation of otherness in the very heart of the linguistic unit is expressed by Saussure's concept of linguistic "value," and it is with reference to value that he states the enigmatic character of the sign-unit most provocatively.[7] Inasmuch as "language is only a system of pure values," Saussure insists, "in language there are only differences *without positive terms.*" In an important sense, then, the units of language turn out not to be units at all. The linguistic sign is less a discrete unit than a kind of reverberation in a system of pure relations. For the sign to fulfill its signifying function, it must activate the network of the code the way a wriggling fly shakes a spider's web.

The paradoxical character of linguistic units is even more impressively apparent when we turn from Saussure's *Course* to Roman Jakobson's analysis of the structure of all languages in terms of a table of twelve pairs of differential features (voiced vs. unvoiced, rounded vs. unrounded, tense vs. lax, etc.). The phoneme, previously taken by many linguists as the most elemental linguistic entity, is shown by Jakobson to be "a bundle of differential elements."[8] "*Phonemes,*" he insists, "*are complex entities*" (SM, 99). In this way Jakobson demonstrates with even greater precision and concreteness than did Saussure how the sign is structured by difference and opposition down to the level of its microconstituents. Jakobson's view thus shows more strikingly how the perception of any sign must simultaneously innervate a network of opposing elements or features that remains absent to perception in the moment but nevertheless provides the indispensable condition for the sign's functioning as a sign. Jakobson stresses that the oppositions embodied by differential features "are real binary oppositions, as defined in logic, i.e., they are such that each of the terms of the opposition *necessarily* implies its opposite" (SM, 81). To which he adds "what logic teaches us on the subject of oppositions. The opposed terms are two in number and they are interrelated in a quite specific way: if one of them is present, the mind educes the other. In an oppositive duality, if one of the terms is given, then the other, though not present, is evoked in thought" (SM, 76).

By clarifying the way in which the sign is internally conditioned by the system of differences that make up a given language, the structuralist conception of the sign serves to explain two striking features of linguistic signification, two dimensions of meaning in language, that Lacan particularly emphasizes. These two dimensions correspond to the functions of simultaneity and succession, or what Saussure calls synchrony and diachrony. With respect to synchrony, the question concerns how the meaning of any linguistic sign is structured at any moment in accordance with its relations to a whole network of differences. Lacan thus asks us to "see from what radiating center the signifier sends forth its light into the shadow of incomplete significations" (E:S, 152). It is this penumbra of "incomplete significations" that allows for the fact, as Lacan puts it, that "all discourse is aligned along the several staves of a score. There is in effect no signifying chain that does not have, as if attached to the punctuation of each of its units, a whole articulation of relevant contexts suspended 'vertically', as it were, from that point" (E:S, 154). The diacritical constitution of the sign also provides the inner principle of its diachronic dimension. The succession of signs that comprise a complex utterance is guided in large part by the structure of the code itself. The unfolding of a chain of signifiers, the stringing together of a discourse, is structurally conditioned by the totality of the signifying system as it is carried in the minds of individual speakers. Lacan points to this phenomenon when he notes the way in which the enunciation of any signifier, by extending before itself a web of connections to other signifiers, sets up a palpable expectation of meaning to come.

The signifier, by its very nature, always anticipates meaning by unfolding its dimension before it. As is seen at the level of the sentence when it is interrupted before the significant term: 'I shall never . . . ', 'All the same it is . . . ', 'And yet there may be . . . '. Such sentences are not without meaning, a meaning all the more oppressive in that it is content to make us wait for it. (E:S, 153)

To return to our main concern, this brief and schematic characterization of imaginary and symbolic functions is valuable for specifying the structured relations between them. The essential point is, in one sense, extremely elementary. Although the symbol system as a whole remains in principle imperceptible, every entrance into the system, every specific act of signification, requires some perceptual registration. The linguistic signifier must initially be registered upon perception as an auditory or visual gestalt. Like any gestalt figure, the sign must be perceptually construed as a unit distinct from its environing background. The sound image of the phoneme must be picked out from the cacophony of other sounds and must be abstracted from idiosyncracies of dialect and pronunciation. The body of the written sign must be disengaged from the confusion of marks in which it is embedded and its specific identity discerned from among the chance variations of a handwritten script or the stylistic peculiarities of a machined font. To insist in this way upon the registration of the signifier as a perceptual gestalt is to remind ourselves of an absolutely elemental necessity— although one easily overlooked for the fact that it is operative on the level of the microstructure of signification. Nevertheless, it forces us to recognize something surprising as it points us toward what might be called the necessarily imaginary moment at the heart of linguistic signification.

This recognition invites us to reappreciate the special property of the signifier. Only when we hold fast to the perceptual moment ingredient to every event of signification, the moment in which the signifier is construed as a microgestalt, do we become aware of a remarkable feature of the signifier: the linguistic sign must necessarily register upon perception as a gestalt, yet in order to function *as a signifier* the gestalt of its perceptual presence must immediately dissolve itself. Precisely contrary to the relatively enduring presence of the imaginary form, the gestalt of the signifier must make itself instantaneously *disappear*. It must evacuate its own perceptual materiality. This perceptual exacuation of the linguistic signifier is related to a profound paradox of speech and language, the paradox provisionally attested to by the simple fact that the very nature of the sign is to indicate something *other than itself*. The sign must be recognized as an image, yet can only fulfill its signifying function when we cease to see the image as such. The imaginal body of the sign must become transparent to its meaning. The pointing finger becomes a sign precisely when we no longer look at the finger but turn away from it in the direction it indicates. A spoken word only delivers us over into the domain of its meaning when we cease to attend to the auditory element by which the word is first announced. The printed page conducts us into a virtual world only to the extent that we lose sight of the print itself. In his 1957-58 Seminar, "The Formations of the Unconscious," Lacan remarks on this self-evacuating character of the signifier. Lacan compares the signifier to a "melting pot," in the sense that "there is always a passage, namely something which is beyond each one of the elements which are articulated, and which are of their nature fleeting, vanishing, that it is the passage from one to the other which constitutes the essential of what we call the signifying chain. . . . [O]ne of the fundamental dimensions of the signifier is to be able to cancel itself out."[9] From this point of view, linguistic signification is characterized by a special kind of continuously shifting presence and absence.[10] The functioning of the signifier, the very heartbeat of signification, is bound up with a constant oscillation of appearance and disappearance, a continuous formation and breakdown of perceptual gestalten. It is this oscillation that distinguishes the linguistic signifier from the relatively enduring contours of imaginary forms and inaugurates a new and properly symbolic process.

Comparing the function of the signifier in this way to the gestalt form points us toward an utterly fundamental structure, a kind of elemental ontological matrix, underlying both imaginary and symbolic functions. It is in order to name the two essential dimensions or gradients of this structure that we have offered the terms of positionality and the dispositional field. Within the structure of this ontological matrix, the imaginary corresponds to the valence toward the promotion of a positional contour. The essence of the imaginary function is related to the capacity to sustain the contour of an object even through changes of its position or shape. Such a power of adumbration, innate to the mechanisms of human perception and perhaps especially to visual perception, obviously represents a profoundly primitive endowment. It would be indispensable, for example, for the task of tracking an animal scurrying across a variegated background. Where the imaginary gathers perception toward the definition of a central position, the essential tendency of the symbolic is a return to the dispositional field, but a field of a special kind. Even without the contribution of a symbol system, we can imagine the possibility of casting away from the imaginary focus toward the periphery, a dispersal of the positional figure into the dispositional field. The distinguishing characteristic of the symbolic return to the field lies in the fact that the field is elaborately pre-structured according to rules of a closed order. Perception of the gestalt of the signifier immediately gives way to a second moment of semiosis that is to be distinguished in terms of the way in which it is *internally articulated in accordance with rules belonging to the code.*

For readers familiar with Lacan's writings, it will be clear that I have defined the concepts of imaginary and symbolic in a far more abstract and limited sense than Lacan's own rich and polyvalent usage allows. My approach seems to me valuable, if only because it forces us to be more precise about some of Lacan's most central formulations, among them that of the *signifier* itself. Is it not reasonable to ask, for example, what relation obtains between the Lacanian signifier and the two registers of imaginary and symbolic? Although ostensibly an inheritance from Saussure and thus of relevance first of all to the category of the symbolic, Lacan's concept of the signifier often seems strikingly ambiguous, in clinical analyses as well as in theoretical discussions. Indeed, it is not difficult to conclude that the Lacanian notion of the signifier harbors an intentional ambiguity and that it serves Lacan's purposes so well precisely because it occupies the unstable juncture between imaginary and symbolic functions. To locate what Lacan calls the "signifier" in the Schema L, we might well place it in the exact center, at the "X" of the crisscrossing imaginary and symbolic axes.[11]

The functioning of this intersection of imaginary and symbolic axes is neatly illustrated in the example of the shop phobia we have already considered. As Freud is careful to point out, the details of the laughter and clothes functioned as *symbols*. This is so, first, because they form the link between the original scene with the older shopkeeper and its later repetition, and second, because the laughter and clothes serve to symbolize the sexual content of the two experiences. Moreover, in being repeated from one occasion to the next, the two elements display a key feature of the primitive signifier identified by Roman Jakobson in his analysis of the phonemic repetitions characteristic of the child's first naming of its parents: "ma-ma" or "pa-pa." Parallel to the function of these reiterated phonemes, the repetition of which sets up a kind of minimal condition for signification, the second appearance of the laughter and clothes establishes their earlier memory image *as signifiers*. In these ways, the laughter and clothes behave like linguistic signifiers. Yet the two elements are obviously not fully linguistic in the structuralist sense. What distinguishes the function of the signifier from any mere image is its imbrication within a diacritical system of other elements. The linguistic signifier must participate in the embracing synchrony of *la langue*. Yet the existence of such a system is missing in this instance. The laughter and clothing thus appear to occupy a curious halfway point between images and signs. On the basis of this observation, are we not invited to suppose that their power to constitute a symptom resides in their very liminal character? On their way to becoming signifiers, the laughter and clothes are somehow stuck in the register of the imaginary.

Our discussions have led us to the following point: far from being wholly distinct and separate, the imaginary and symbolic functions are internally linked to one another. We now understand how and why the imaginary registration of a particular psychical content may function to obstruct the unfolding of the symbolic potential of the same representation. It is precisely the overintense image that prevents a potential for signification from being realized. This view finds remarkable confirmation in one of Freud's analyses.

In keeping with our other examples, this instance also concerns the emergence of an "ultra-clear" idea. For all its brevity, it perfectly emblematizes the process of repression as a slippage between symbolic and imaginary axes. The example concerns a young woman who, discussing the life of Christ with a small gathering of university people, struggled to remember the name of an English novel she had recently read. Freud notes that while "the name of the work refused to come to her mind . . . the visual memory she had of the cover of the book and the appearance of the lettering in the title was excessively clear (*überdeutlich*)" (SE, 6:41). A number of unconvincing substitute names occurred to her—including "*Ecce homo*," "*Homo sum*," and "*Quo vadis?*" She also realized that she had forgotten the correct name because, as she put it, "it contains an expression that I (like any other girl) do not care to use—especially in the company of young men." Nevertheless, the title refused to appear. The mechanism of the memory lapse precisely replicates that of the Signorelli incident, in which the sought-after name was connected by a train of associations to a complex of unacceptable thoughts. The title of the novel, *Ben Hur*, bore a painful resemblance to the German words "*bin Hure*" ("I am a whore"). What makes this example remarkable is that the ultra-clear idea, the imaginary element, *is the signifier itself*. The young woman saw before her the title page of the book in question and even remarked the excessive clarity of the lettering of the title itself. *Yet she failed to read it.* In this instance, *it was the very body of the signifier itself that was turned into an image.* A more striking example could hardly be found to demonstrate the way in which the mechanism of repression, the very pivot-point of an unconscious process, turns upon a transposition from a symbolic to an imaginary register.

The Ratman's Phantasy

Our main interest has centered on the relation between imaginary and symbolic, and we have evolved a new vocabulary—that of positionality and dispositionality—to help articulate that relation. The *Ben Hur* example effectively displays what we might call the negative, or "abductive," function of positionality, by which the perceptual figure obscures the background over and against which it is distinguished. The abductive power of positionality tends to close off access to pathways into the dispositional field. Abduction is the blinding effect of fascination, the effect by which the focus of attention throws the periphery of awareness into shadow. But the same example also illustrates the movement correlative to abduction, that by which specific factors in the dispositional field guide and shape what emerges into positional awareness. The perceptual intensity of the book's cover that contributed to the inability to recall its title was produced by a conjunction of signifiers—*Ben Hur* and *bin Hure*—that constituted part of a constellation of unperceived dispositional factors. Correlative with the abductive moment, then, is the positive, or "productive," aspect. It is under the influence of elements in the field that a particular content may be promoted to positional awareness. In this section, we will examine this positive or productive aspect in which the excessive intensity of perception is generated by a particular configuration of dispositional factors.

In highlighting the productive moment of disposition, we will have occasion to underline the main point of the preceding discussions: the dispositional field is articulated in two dimensions—perceptual and linguistic. The two dimensions and their productive effects are well illustrated by Freud's analysis of the fetish. We first encountered the fetish in the course of an attempt to situate gestalt concepts in Freud's theory, taking note of the way in which primary defense arrives at the substitute idea simply by traversing the perceptual field. The threatening object is replaced by an element drawn from the environing sensory field. Thus the prototype of the fetish object is found in the immediate periphery of the missing maternal phallus or is located at a site contiguous with it (hair, lace, garters, etc.). In this case, the dispositional field is perceptual, and the production of the positional element is determined simply by substituting one portion of the perceptual field for another. As we have now seen, however, the dispositional field is not limited to perceptual contents but comes to include the diacritical network of the signifying system. Our interest thus turns to instances in which the perceptual vividness of positional investment is conditioned by the linguistically mediated dimension of the dispositional field.

In the same paper in which Freud describes the election of the fetish object by perceptual contiguity with the site of the mother's genitals, he also offers an example of a fetish derived from a conjunction of purely linguistic signifiers. The fetishistic interest centered upon a certain "shine on the nose," or "*Glanz auf der Nase.*" But from where did this peculiar interest originate? The course of the analysis revealed its source in a verbal phrase from the patient's childhood. What emerged in German as a *Glanz auf der Nase* was originally spoken in the English of the patient's mother tongue: *a glance at the nose*. The fetish in this case was thus constructed around an accident of the signifier—the ambiguous *Glan(z)ce.*

Other of Freud's analyses offer parallel examples in which the perceptual intensity of a symptomatic element is determined by a conjunction of factors in the imperceptible system of the signifier. Few are as remarkable as the case of the Ratman. The clinical picture presented by the Ratman is unmistakably dominated by the electrifying phantasy of the rat torture. It is not accidental, of course, that Freud seized upon this element in naming the case; it focused what Freud called "the great obsessive fear" and formed, as he remarked in the original record of the treatment, the "nodal point" of the case (SE, 10:292). Just after having lost his pince-nez while on army maneuvers, an event that was to trigger an immense proliferation of obsessional behaviors, the patient was introduced to the idea of a hideous torture by a captain whom the patient described as "obviously fond of cruelty" (SE, 10:166). The torture victim is bound, and a pot containing starving rats is placed upside down on his buttocks. The rats proceed to gnaw their way into the victim's anus. The recounting of this torture, however horrifying in itself, was made more objectionable for being accompanied by another idea that immediately passed through the patient's mind upon hearing it: "this was happening to a person who was very dear to me" (SE, 10:167). "A person," or better *two* persons: his ladylove and his father. In thus imagining the torture applied to the lady and the father, the Ratman locates the central axis of his life conflicts around the question of a love relation and especially around the choice of the love object. What is of special interest for our purposes is the way in which the immense tangle of associations surrounding this central conflict is embodied and intensified in the image of the rats. The analysis of the rat idea is exemplary for showing how an enormously intense perceptual registration is produced by an imperceptible confluence of signifiers. As we will see in what follows, the rat image is lit up by a signifying matrix. It is the *becoming perceptible* of the overdetermined morpheme "rat."

The indispensable background for interpreting the rat idea resides in the relation between the patient's father and mother. Of paramount importance was the mother's higher social status. The implication, reinforced by the mother's behavior, was that the father married her for her money. The mother had been brought up in a wealthy family that owned a successful industrial concern into which the father had been introduced at the time of their marriage. The question of the father's more humble origins remained an unsettled one in the mind of the patient, continually recalled by the father's penchant for coarse language. His vulgarity, Freud notes, was a result of the father's experience as a noncommissioned army officer prior to his marriage. It was during that period that a key event occurred in the father's life that would decisively influence his son's obsessional disorder. Entrusted with the regimental funds, the father recklessly gambled them away and was forced to borrow money from a friend in order to cover the loss. Significantly, the debt was never repaid. In this way, the father's relation to the mother was tainted, both in its general outline and in relation to a specific detail of his past. The father was a gambler or *Spielratte*, literally a "play-rat." His figure was negatively colored by the incurring of debts, *Raten*. In a profound sense, it was this indebtedness that the Ratman inherited from his father. The elaborate series of doubts, recriminations, false starts, and misapprehensions—in short, the whole obsessive machinery in which the Ratman was caught up—represented a repetition of the father's unresolved debt.

These elements of the father's history, forming a web of what Freud called a "complexive sensitiveness," prepared the stage for the precipitating cause of the Ratman's illness (SE, 10:210). Overhearing a discussion between his parents, the patient had become aware that, not long before meeting his mother, his father had pursued an attractive but penniless girl—a fact that seemed only to confirm the compromised nature of the father's marriage. Sometime after his father's death, the details of this history were revivified by his mother's attempt to arrange for him a marriage to a wealthy cousin. By means of this advantageous union, the son might be brought into the family firm as his father had been. Indeed, the mother's plan brought the Ratman's situation into precise alignment with that faced earlier by his father, as it presented him with the choice between the poor girl he loved and the more materially promising match arranged for him by his mother. The father's troubled legacy had directly insinuated itself into his own love life. The father's taint of debt, or *Raten*, now contaminated the son's own marriage—his *Heirat*.

It was in this context, then, that the Ratman heard the cruel captain's story. As the patient's own preface to the captain's story makes clear, the issue of a conflict of social status, parallel to that involved in his father's choice of spouse, was immediately relevant to the situation in which the story was told. He notes that he "was keen to show the regular officers that people like me had not only learnt a good deal but could stand a good deal, too" (SE, 10:165). That is to say, he was anxious to show that he, the educated son of a moderately well-to-do family, could nevertheless accept the rigors of army life as well as any hardened soldier of humbler birth. In this way, he was concerned to bring together the two poles of rich and poor, higher and lower social status, that had divided his own family history.[12]

Yet higher and lower could not be conjoined so easily. The effort to do so was frustrated by the encounter that led up to the story of the rat torture: when the captain enthusiastically defended the practice of corporal punishment, the Ratman "had been obliged to disagree with him very sharply" (SE, 10:166). The captain then described, as if throwing down his trump card, the horrible torture that would crystallize the Ratman's obsessional system. Not only did the drama with the cruel captain reenergize the essential polarity that governed the Ratman's family history, but the story of the torture with rats—*Ratten*—repeated the key signifier of the underlying tension: the phonemic concatenation of *Raten* and *Heiraten*. In this way, an immense web of associations, shot through with powerful ambivalences, was suddenly knotted at the point of a "complex stimulus word" (SE, 10:216). The signifying link between the indebtedness and the rat torture was reflected in the verbal formula that sprang to his mind when the Ratman accepted Freud's fee for treatment: "So many florins, so many rats" (SE, 10:213). So, too, the connection was underlined by his persistent mispronunciation of the two words, sounding both *Ratten* and *Raten* with a short *a*.

We could easily continue to unfold the complexity of associations bound together in the rat idea. We might point, for example, to the connection between the gnawing rats of the torture scene and a childhood memory in which the Ratman *bit* someone. Beaten by his father for this childhood transgression, the Ratman is said to have responded with an enraged series of curious epithets: "You lamp! You towel! You plate!" (SE, 10:205). How, in the light of the subsequent course of his illness, can we not suspect that the meaning of this strange outburst lies in precisely what is missing from it: "You rat!"?[13] But we will keep to the main point: what is most remarkable about the torture phantasy is the way in which a phantasmatic experience of tremendous intensity is produced by a conjunction of signifying elements. The function that Freud collects under the term "complex stimulus word" points in fact to an intricate lacing of associations that are, in the most literal way, "structured like a language." What he has in mind is a synchrony of linkages, strung together at privileged points by the repetition of the morpheme "rat," that produces an image-spark of blinding brilliance—so blinding, in fact, that it serves to conceal the very factors that gave rise to it. A complex of signifying tendrils conditions the emergence of an electrifying image, but remains itself invisible. The network of the signifier thus acts in a fashion that is precisely parallel to the luminous *enveloppe* explored by Monet's paintings: it is the unseen source of illumination that brings an object to visibility.

The Specimen Dream of Psychoanalysis

If dreams provided Freud with the royal road to the unconscious, we ought to be able to demonstrate our basic thesis with special clarity by means of their example. The famous dream of "Irma's Injection," offered by Freud as the prime illustration of his dream book, offers an ideal opportunity.

Freud's dream and his analysis of it are well known. Greeting guests in a large hall, Freud meets his patient Irma, who complains to him of pains in her throat, stomach, and abdomen. "It's choking me," she says. Freud counters that Irma's continuing pains are really her own fault as she has not yet accepted his "solution"—presumably referring to a psychoanalytic interpretation. Yet he worries that he may have overlooked some organic trouble. Irma resists his effort to look down her throat, "like women with artificial dentures," but when she "then opened her mouth properly" Freud discovers "a big white patch" with "extensive grey scabs upon some remarkable curly structures which were evidently modelled on the turbinal bones of the nose." A trio of colleagues, Dr. M, Leopold, and Otto, suggest an infection, but Dr. M is optimistic: "There's no doubt it's an infection, but no matter; dysentery will supervene and the toxin will be eliminated." The cause of the infection then seems obvious to everyone: "my friend Otto had given her an injection of a preparation of propyl, propyls . . . proprionic acid . . . trimethylamine (and I saw before me the formula for this printed in heavy type)." The dream concludes with the thought that "injections of that sort ought not to be made so thoughtlessly . . . And probably the syringe had not been clean" (SE, 4:106).

What is immediately striking about this dream is that, like other examples we have examined, it culminates with an element that is presented to awareness with exceptional clarity and intensity—the formula for trimethylamine. And like the ultra-clarity of the lettering that served to obviate the reading of *Ben Hur*, the extra-intense registration of the formula, its mesmerizing "heavy type," conceals much more than it reveals. But what exactly does it conceal? To see further into the dynamics of this nodal point of the dream, poised at the juncture of imaginary and symbolic functions, we must dig deeply into the meaning of the dream.

The conclusion of Freud's own analysis of the dream is to locate its motive in his wish to be exonerated of blame for Irma's continuing pains. This end is accomplished by multiple means, like the defense of the man charged by his neighbor with returning a borrowed kettle in damaged condition: "The defendant asserted first, that he had given it back undamaged; secondly, that the kettle had a hole in it when he borrowed it; and thirdly, that he had never borrowed a kettle from his neighbor at all" (SE, 4:120). In like fashion, the dream presents three different reasons, each incompatible with the others, yet any one of which suffices to acquit Freud of responsibility for Irma's continuing pains: (1) Irma refused to accept his solution, therefore her continuing distress is really her own fault; (2) Irma's condition was organic, not hysterical, and therefore lay outside the sphere of psychoanalytic treatment, and (3) Irma's pains were caused by Otto's injection, probably made with a dirty syringe. In any one of these ways, the dream fulfills the wish to vouchsafe Freud's "professional conscientiousness" (SE, 4:120).

Given the privileged place accorded to the Irma dream by Freud himself, it is not surprising that it has attracted the attention of the most astute commentators. Erik Erikson, for example, reads the dream against the background of professional anxieties Freud faced as a lone investigator on the verge of making a genuine discovery, as a Jew in a predominantly Catholic culture, as a maverick in psychiatry committed to a new and controversial theory of hysteria, and as a middle-aged man whose professional status had been painfully slow in coming and whose wife was entering her sixth pregnancy.[14] These themes are reflected in the central anxiety of the dream: the fear that he had overlooked an organic diagnosis in his eagerness to characterize Irma's difficulties as psychologically determined. The dream turns the tables on a circle of older colleagues, revealing them to be inept bunglers who may themselves be responsible for Irma's condition.

Max Schur's commentary on the Irma dream serves to underline many of Erikson's points by focusing on connection between the figure of Irma and that of another of Freud's patients, Emma Eckstein, whose case was reported in his *Studies on Hysteria* and whose health had been gravely threatened when Freud's intimate friend and confidant, Wilhelm Fliess, operated on her nose.[15] Consulting another physician some two weeks after Fliess's operation on Eckstein, Freud discovered to his horror that the persistent swelling, putrid odor, and massive hemorrhages in her nose were caused by "at least a half meter of gauze" that Fliess had accidently left in her nasal cavity.[16] We are led to wonder whether it is not this length of gauze that reappears in the "remarkable curly structures" Freud finds in

Irma's throat. Schur thus reveals a basis in reality for Freud's fear of having overlooked something in the treatment of one of his female patients. He also demonstrates the way the dream exculpates not only Freud but also Fliess, on whose opinion so much of Freud's own confidence depended.

Erikson and Schur both point to the role of ego anxiety in the Irma dream: Erikson emphasizes conflicts relevant to the cultural context and to Freud's own position in a scheme of psychosocial development, Schur focuses on determinants in reality of Freud's anxiety about his professional responsibility. Lacan's treatment of the dream radicalizes this concern for the integrity of the ego, identifying the very essence and function of the Irma dream with a certain disintegration of the ego. The crucial thing, Lacan suggests, is to recognize that "in the dream of Irma's injection, the subject decomposes, fades away, dissociates into its various egos" (S.II, 176). The Irma dream concerns a fragmentation of the ego under the force of the unconscious, where the notion of the "unconscious" is taken to be "that of the acephalic subject, of a subject who no longer has an ego, who is outside the *ego*, decentered in relation to the *ego*, who is not the *ego*" (S.II, 167, translation corrected).

This process of ego disintegration is discernible around two key moments, two fundamental images: first the mysterious and disarming white structures in Irma's throat and later the chemical formula of trimethylamine, which appears before the dreamer "printed in heavy type."

> The phenomenology of the dream of Irma's injection led us to distinguish two parts. The first leads to the apparition of the terrifying anxiety-producing image, to this real Medusa's head, to the revelation of this something which properly speaking is unnameable, the back of this throat, the complex, unlocatable form, which also makes it into the primitive object *par excellence,* [at once] the abyss of the feminine organ from which all life emerges, this gulf of the mouth in which everything is swallowed up, and no less the image of death in which everything comes to its end. (S.II, 163-64)

> The dream, which culminated a first time, when the ego was there, in the horrific image I mentioned, culminates a second time at the end with a formula. (S.II, 158)

These two nodal moments of the dream represent an initial disintegration of the ego effected by the vision of an imaginary violation, followed by the production of a new form in which the contribution of a symbolic function is conspicuously present. In the first of these two moments, the sight of Irma's throat triggers in the dreamer an irruption of something dreadful and uncanny, a rupturing of imaginary coherence that stages a revelation of the Real. This encounter with the Real constitutes the unspeakable vortex around which the entire dream turns. Gazing into Irma's throat,

> there's an anxiety-provoking apparition of an image which summarizes what we can call the revelation of that which is least penetrable in the real, of the real lacking any possible mediation, of the ultimate real, of the essential object which isn't an object any longer, but this something faced with which all words cease and all categories fail, the object of anxiety *par excellence*. (S.II, 164)

> [What takes place in Irma's throat is] a horrendous discovery. . . . Spectre of anxiety, identification with anxiety, the final revelation that *you are this—You are this, which is so far from you, this which is the ultimate formlessness*. (S.II, 154-55)

In confrontation with the horrifying vision in Irma's throat, Lacan suggests, the greatest anxieties of Freud's life, "his relations with women, his relations with death, are telescoped." However, this initial vision of imaginary abomination gives way to the final epiphany of the trimethylamine formula. Like a sort of oracle, "the formula gives no reply whatsoever to anything. But the very manner in which it is spelt out, its enigmatic, hermetic character, is in fact the answer to the question of the meaning of the dream" (S.II, 158). On Lacan's reading, therefore, the dream's "last word" is significant precisely because it is *a word*. The wish behind the dream, as Freud had said, was a desire to discover the secret of dreams. That wish is fulfilled in "trimethylamine." The dream tells us, as it also told the dreamer: "[T]here is no other word, no other solution to your problem, than the word" (S.II, 158). For Lacan, the Irma dream well deserves its status as a paradigm of all dreams because it illustrates that the secret of the dream process, and of the unconscious in general, is the power of the signifier.

But if Lacan is right that "trimethylamine" is the master signifier of the Irma dream, perhaps even the crucial clue to Freud's whole theory of dreams, we still have yet to know what it signifies. It is Lacan himself who most clearly articulates the need to delve further, simply by observing that Freud's interpretation of the dream, which may be fair enough as far as it goes, fails to satisfy Freud's own criteria. The wish Freud evinces to explain the dream's motivation is not, as Freud claims it must finally be, an *unconscious* wish. Lacan prompts us to ask:

> How is it that Freud, who later on will develop the function of unconscious desire, is here contented, for the first step in his demonstration, to present a dream which is entirely explained by the satisfaction of a desire which one cannot but call preconscious, and even entirely conscious? (S.II, 151)

Freud is by no means unaware that his analysis of the dream is incomplete. Though he remarks that the Irma dream was the first dream he submitted to a "thorough" (*eingehend*) interpretation, he admits in conclusion that "I will not pretend that I have completely uncovered the meaning of the dream. . . . I myself know the points from which further trains of thought could be followed" (SE , 4:121). He then claims that "considerations which arise in the case of every dream of my own restrain me from pursuing my interpretative work," and he challenges the reader "to make the experiment of being franker than I am" (SE, 4:121). We are left to wonder about the "points from which further trains of thought could be followed" and can only conclude that they were of an even more highly sensitive nature than the many personal details he does divulge in the analysis of the dream. In prefacing the dream text, Freud points to the inherent difficulties of self-observation, but adds that he had

> other difficulties to overcome, which lie within myself. . . . There is some natural hesitation about revealing so many intimate facts about one's mental life; nor can there be any guarantee against misinterpretation by strangers. I have probably been wise in not putting too much faith in my reader's discretion. (SE, 4:105)

By Freud's own admission, then, we can be sure that his interpretation of the Irma dream is incomplete and may be continued along specific lines. But what lines are these? Of course, Freud's own theory leads us to expect that they concern sexuality. It comes as no surprise, therefore, to find Erikson conclude that the Irma dream permits "a complete sexual interpretation alongside the professional one—an inescapable expectation in any case."[17] An examination of the verbal trends in the dream

> induces us to put beside the accusation of medical carelessness (the dispensation of a "solution") and of a possible intellectual error (the solution offered to Irma) the suggestion of a related sexual theme, namely, a protest against the implication of some kind of sexual (self-) reproach.[18]

But though Erikson points to a second, sexual, meaning of the Irma dream, and though he gives some grist for such an interpretation by pointing to the way Freud's childhood memory of urinating in his parents' bedroom stands behind the imagery of Otto's dirty syringe, he never elaborates this suggestion of a sexual interpretation. Schur likewise points toward a sexual meaning of the dream, but fails to develop it. "That the Irma dream . . . had sexual connotations," Schur maintains, "is self-evident." But he then adds that "I have deliberately refrained from attempting any such reinterpretation of the 'deeper' sources of the dream, and restricted myself to the use of material presented in Freud's own words."[19] Erikson and Schur both point to a sexual interpretation of the Irma dream, yet fail to produce one. The situation is not much different with Lacan. Though he insists on the necessity of an unconscious wish, he chooses to work out the implications of Freud's own interpretation rather than trying to plumb anew the motivating forces behind the production of the dream.

Other investigators have similarly evoked the possibly sexual meaning of the Irma dream, but also failed to pursue it very far. Thus in *Sigmund Freud's Dreams,* Alexander Grinstein proposes that "we may conjecture whether and to what extent Freud projected upon Otto his own feelings of a libidinal countertransference nature."[20] Yet Grinstein does not develop any further his own suggestion. Didier Anzieu, in his monumental *Freud's Self-Analysis,* notes several key pointers toward a sexual interpretation but generally leaves them to one side in his discussion. He observes, for example, how easily the amusing story of the borrowed kettle, drawn upon by Freud to illustrate the basic exculpatory function of the dream, can be translated into sexual terms: "The story takes on a particular piquancy if the kettle is replaced by an object that its shape suggests, i.e. a woman's belly. The man accused of having 'borrowed' his neighbor's wife or daughter and of having returned her 'in a damaged condition' defends himself in three ways: no, I returned her undamaged; she already 'had a hole' in her; I did not lay a finger on her."[21] Anzieu also remarks in passing upon the undoubtedly erotic tone of the countertransference in the case of Irma, who was in reality the young Anna Hammerschlag-Lichtheim, said by Freud to have been one of his favorite patients. Yet despite these clues, none of the five "other interpretations" Anzieu offers to supplement the analysis supplied by Freud himself attempts to develop the question of sexual desire in any detail.

A notable exception to this tendency to overlook a sexual interpretation of the Irma dream is an article by Barbara Mautner in which she extends the associative material surrounding the dream to postulate a childhood sexual scene between the young Sigmund and his sister Anna.[22] Mautner pointedly remarks the lack of attention devoted by its many reinterpreters to the sexual and infantile determinates of the Irma dream, and claims that Freud's own approach, which concentrates on the manifest content of the dream, has become a virtual dogma. Ironically, Mautner says, "attempts to approach the Irma dream in more Freudian terms were met by intimations of betrayal. So effective was the call for fidelity that Irma has become virtually locked away in the realm of the manifest. Even would-be revisionists have launched their rebellion on details of the day residue."[23]

In the Navel of the Dream

To take up the material of the dream where most writers leave off, we need only attend to the dream's sexual imagery and associations. These indications of sexual meaning are centered on the pivotal idea of a "solution" (*Lösung*), which in both German and English possesses the same ambiguity between an answer to a problem and a fluid. Our suspicion that it refers in part to the fluids of love is reinforced by the way the dream is centrally concerned with Irma's unwillingness to accept it.[24] This "recalcitrance" takes the form of a reluctance to "open her mouth properly" and contrasts markedly with a friend of Irma's of whom Freud confesses he "had a very high opinion, a woman" who "would have been wiser, that is to say she would have yielded sooner. She would have opened her mouth properly and told me more than Irma."[25]

The double meaning of the word "solution," referring both to the resolution of a puzzle and to the fluids passed in the sex act, forms a kind of linchpin on which the meaning of the dream hangs.[26] It is, in Freud's terms, a "switch word." In the idea of a solution the two main concerns of the dream intersect: the search for the truth (the correctness of Freud's diagnosis of Irma and, more generally, the truth of his theory of hysteria) and sexuality (an expression of Freud's personal relation to Irma). But to appreciate its function and significance, it is necessary to enter more deeply into the dream's tangle of associations. First and most importantly, we ought to observe that the "solutions" of the dream, around which proliferate suggestions of maleness and masculine potency, are complemented by two feminine images: those of the mouth and the nose.

The status of the mouth as a representative of the female genitalia requires little comment. Nevertheless, it is interesting to note Freud's remark in a letter to Fliess (January 1899) that the identification of the mouth with the vagina was an especially typical feature of the hysterical processes he was then investigating (CL, 340). In the context of the Irma dream, however, the nose is an equally potent sexual symbol. During the years of his correspondence with Freud, nasal anatomy and function constituted Wilhelm Fliess's primary research interest, which focused especially on the close connection he claimed to exist between the nose and the female sexual organs—an interest that found a certain resonance in Fliess's correspondent. Only one month after the date of the Irma dream, Freud suggested that Fliess turn his notes into a pamphlet on "The Nose and Female Sexuality" (CL, 141). Further, Freud had Irma examined by Fliess, as he did Emma Eckstein, "to see whether her gastric pains might be of nasal origin" (SE, 4:117). Finally, Fliess associated the turbinate bone in particular, which appears so prominently in the Irma dream, with the female genitals. He maintained, for example, that "the swelling of the turbinate bone during menstruation is to be observed by the naked eye."[27] All of this points to the sexual significance of the reference to the nose in the Irma dream. Carrying her turbinate bone in her throat, Irma appears, quite literally, to be a woman whose sexual organs are in her mouth.

There is, then, no shortage of sexual overtones in the Irma dream. Yet Freud doesn't make very much of them. Indeed, in the account offered in

The Interpretation of Dreams, he seems positively resistant to a sexual interpretation. By contrast, when he reported the dream in a letter to Fliess shortly after it occurred, it was the sexual theme that was most prominent: ". . . [In a dream of my own]," Freud writes, "R. has given an injection of *propyl* to A. I then see *trimethylamine* before me very vividly, hallucinated as a formula. Explanation: The thought simultaneously present . . . is the sexual nature of A's illness . . ." (SE, 1:341–42). In the published version of 1900, Freud's interest in the sexual themes in the dream has taken a backseat to that of professional competence. When sex is alluded to, Freud seems anxious to get off the topic as quickly as possible. Indeed, it is when he begins to explore the connection between Irma and her friend about whom Freud "had a very high opinion," who "would have yielded sooner," and whom Freud "should have *liked* to exchange [for Irma]," that Freud claims to encounter the impenetrable navel of the dream (SE, 4:110). "I had a feeling," he confesses, "that the interpretation of this part of the dream was not carried far enough to make it possible to follow the whole of its concealed meaning.

> If I had pursued my comparison between the three women, it would have taken me far afield.—There is at least one spot in every dream at which it is unplumbable—a navel, as it were, that is its point of contact with the unknown. (SE, 4:111n)

Given the conspicuously sexual character of the dream's central imagery, Freud's apparent resistance to sexual themes only serves to increase our suspicions that sexuality constitutes one of the basic conflicts at work in the dream. However, the manifest symbolism of the dream is not the only indication that sexuality played a key role in its formation. The dream occurred during the period of Freud's most intense involvement with his "seduction theory" of hysteria. Freud had become convinced, especially by his experience with female patients, that hysterical symptoms were invariably traceable to traumatic sexual experiences in childhood. Understood against this background, the pivotal tension in the dream over the question of Irma's diagnosis—hysterical or organic—becomes equivalent to a question about the presence or absence of sexual trauma. The point of contention in the dream between Freud and his colleagues, as it actually had been in his collaboration with Joseph Breuer on the *Studies on Hysteria*, is whether or not the role of sexuality in the production of Irma's symptoms would be recognized and admitted.[28] Freud's committment at the time of the Irma dream to his sexual theory of hysteria makes it almost certain that the "solution" that Irma refused to accept concerned some aspect of her sexual life. Yet the solution to Irma's problem admits of a sexual meaning in a much more literal sense. Taken at the letter of his text, Freud's conclusion is that Irma's problems stem from her failure to accept a man's *seminal* solution. In explaining the significance of trimethylamine, Freud remarks that

> this substance led me to sexuality, the factor to which I attributed the greatest importance in the origin of the nervous disorders which it was my aim to cure. My patient Irma was a young widow; if I wanted to find an excuse for the failure of my treatment in her case, what I could best appeal to would no doubt be the fact of her widowhood. (SE, 4:116-17).[29]

This statement, typical of Freud's view during this period that sexual abstinence may produce neurosis, reveals how the Irma dream is crisscrossed by a contradictory tension: on the one hand, Irma's hysterical symptoms may be traced to childhood seduction, on the other hand, her problems may stem from lack of sexual activity. Sexuality assumes the double role as both cause and cure. But what manner of sexual activity is at issue here? The evidence of the dream points in the direction of oral sex, and in particular to the act of fellatio. Fellatio, of course, would be the appropriate means of intercourse for a woman whose sexual organs are lodged in her throat. Could the horrifying "white patch" that Freud finds in Irma's throat be the shockingly graphic evidence that she refused to swallow his solution? Were the "remarkable curly structures" covered by "whitish grey scabs" modeled not only on the turbinal bones but on the ropy consistency of seminal ejaculate?[30] This interpretation is supported not only by the facts of the dream itself but also by the way it echoes Freud's theoretical concerns at the time he produced the Irma dream. When his seduction theory turned his attention to the sexual abuse of young girls by fathers, uncles, and brothers, Freud was especially concerned with fellatio.[31] In 1897, for example, Freud made the following comments about the case of a young woman who suffered from an hysterical facial tic accompanied by oral lesions:

As a child she suffered greatly from anxiety. . . . A conspicuous tic; she forms [her lips into] a snout [from sucking].

She is suffering from ecxema around her mouth and from lesions that do not heal in the corners of her mouth. During the night her saliva periodically accumulates, after which the lesions appear. (Once before I traced entirely analogous observations to sucking on the penis). (CL, 220)

In 1896, Freud argued that symptoms identical to those of Irma in the dream were to be attributed to oral and anal violations.

Another set of exceedingly common hysterical phenomena—painful need to urinate, the sensation accompanying defaecation, intestinal disturbances, choking and vomiting, indigestion, and disgust at food—were also shown by my analyses (and with surprising regularity) to be derivations of the same childhood experiences and were explained without difficulty by certain invariable peculiarities of those experiences. For the idea of these infantile sexual scenes is very repellent to the feelings of a sexually normal individual; they include all the abuses known to debauched and impotent persons, among whom the buccal cavity and the rectum are misused for sexual purposes. (SE, 3:214)

How can the sexual meaning of the Irma dream be further specified? The obvious hypothesis is to suppose a sexual attraction to Irma on the part of Freud himself. Irma was, after all, an attractive young widow who was "on very friendly terms" with Freud and his family.[32] In his Preamble, Freud explicitly points to the way that "a mixed relationship such as this may be a source of many disturbed feelings in a physician and particularly in a psychotherapist." We can scarcely doubt that what Freud later called transference and counter-transference were especially intense in his treatment of Irma. Nor can we doubt that Freud was already well aware of the sexual nature of the transference relation and painfully familiar with its potentially disastrous results. Not so very long before Freud's dream of *Anna* Hammerschlag, Breuer had been terrorized by the development of an hysterical pregnancy in one his patients, the very patient whose case appears in *Studies on Hysteria* under the pseudonym *Anna* O. However, the best confirmation of the sexual meaning of the dream is the way it enables us to make sense of the dream itself. It helps clarify three main points.

1. Though Erikson rightly links the Irma dream to the anxiety Freud felt in defending a controversial theory before an unreceptive community of peers, the anxiety in the dream is obviously not simply an expression of Freud's fear that his work would be rejected by the medical establishment. The dream is centrally concerned not just with fear but with *guilt*. The dream presents the possibility, not only that Freud might have been wrong about the diagnosis of Irma's symptoms, but that he might have been in some way to blame for them.

Schur's article is helpful here as he relates the dream of Irma to the bungled case of Emma Eckstein. We might also point to other instances in which Freud's intervention led to disastrous results; Freud himself mentions two of them in his analysis of the Irma dream. In both cases—that of Freud's friend Ernst Fleischl von Marxow and that of another female patient, Mathilde—Freud recommended a "solution" (cocaine for Fleischl, sulphonal for Mathilde), which, when administered by injection, resulted in a fatality. These two tragedies, along with the Emma Eckstein debacle, were certainly ingredient to the Irma dream. But we might well ask whether the memory of these cases was sufficient to produce the sense of culpability present in the dream. With Emma, after all, it was clearly Fliess, not Freud, who was to blame. With Fleischl, Freud's provision of cocaine was intended to help rid the man of a more dangerous addiction to morphine; further, Fleischl disregarded Freud's instructions about the quantities of cocaine to be taken and the method by which it was to be administered.[33] In the case of the unfortunate Mathilde, Freud notes that the dosage of sulphonal he had prescribed "was at that time regarded as a harmless remedy" (SE, 4:111). If, on the other hand, Freud felt some sexual attraction to Irma, his unconscious sense of his own culpability would understandably have been greatly increased. This is so in part, of course, because Freud would have found the idea of using the privilege of his position for sexual advantage to be repugnant in the extreme.[34] But more than that, Freud was convinced at the time that hysteria was caused by a premature or unwilling exposure to sexual advance, especially by an older person or by a person in authority.[35] To the extent that he felt attracted to Irma himself, therefore, he could readily have feared that his own relation with her might inadvertently contribute to her disturbance.

Behind this consideration lies a much more general issue. A sexual interpretation of the Irma dream does not deny the validity of the other approaches we have examined but merely opens up an additional dimension. The conclusion, in a nutshell, is to show how Freud's anxieties about his own sexuality lay beneath and in important ways reinforced his anxiousness about his professional status. This was so, quite simply, because Freud's psychiatric innovations were focused on the psychical effects of sexual desire and sexual experience. It is almost impossible not to think that Freud found it difficult, especially during the early, lonely years of his researches into hysteria, to separate his professional concern with sexuality from his personal sexual life. We know from his letters to Fliess that Freud experienced such a crossover between the professional and personal in a particularly painful way. At the height of his committment to the seduction theory—precisely the period during which he had the Irma dream—Freud several times expressed to Fliess his conviction that hysterical symptoms in his brother and sisters must be attributed to the perversions of his own father.[36] On at least one occasion, he even implicated himself, finding evidence in a dream of his sexual attraction to his daughter (CL, 249). We will return to this last point in a moment.

2. Of the two solutions that appear in the dream, Freud's and Otto's, it is at least certain that the second, the trimethylamine, admits of a sexual meaning. Freud himself points this out, remarking that according to Fliess, trimethylamine was "one of the products of sexual metabolism" (SE, 4: 116). It is instructive, however, to see how this sexual connotation works in the structure of the dream as a whole. The principal question around which the dream is structured concerns who is responsible for Irma's continuing pains; Freud or Otto? As we have seen, this question is an extension of another, more basic one: were Irma's complaints attributable to a psychical disturbance related to sexuality or to an organic condition? By supposing the sexual nature of the "solutions" in the dream, we recognize the ingeniousness of the dream's wish fulfillment. If Otto's reckless injection has no sexual meaning, then Freud is absolved of guilt for Irma's pains, yet only at the price of giving up his theory of the sexual etiology of hysteria. Irma's symptoms would have been shown to be purely organic. Only if the trimethylamine solution functions to represent both a doctor's prescription and a lover's fluid can Freud win both his battles in a single stroke: the dream shows Otto to be at fault (Irma's pains are

organic) and also vouchsafes the validity of Freud's own diagnosis (Irma's pains are hysterical, i.e., related to a sexual violation). The detail of the dirty needle only serves to reinforce both sides of this double signification. On the medical side, Otto not only injected "an unsuitable drug" but did so in the most careless possible way; on the sexual side, the image of the "dirty little squirter," as Erikson calls it, suggests the theme of sexual perversion that was central to Freud's own theory of hysteria.

3. By asserting the sexual content of Otto's injection, the dream confirms Freud's hypothesis that hysteria is produced by sexual trauma: an injection of trimethylamine is, in effect, an injection of seminal fluid. If, in addition, we assume the sexual significance of Freud's "solution," the dream is revealed to contain a perfectly symmetrical structure. Otto's blameworthy injection is juxtaposed to Freud's offered but refused solution. The crucial point of difference between the two is that where Otto's solution was injected, Freud's was to be accepted *orally*. The importance to Freud of this difference is revealed in his association to the dream fragment concerning Otto's injection. After recalling that Otto had in fact given an injection to someone at a neighboring hotel during his stay with Irma's family, Freud relates these *injections* to the case of his friend Fleischl cited above and points out that "I had advised him to use the drug internally [i.e., orally] only, while morphia was being withdrawn, but he had at once given himself cocaine injections" (SE, 4:115). Two pages later, Freud returns to this point, underlining the importance of the distinction between an oral solution and an injected one: "As I have said, I never contemplated the drug being given by injection" (SE, 4:117).

We can thus see how elegantly the dream achieves the fulfillment of the dreamer's wish at two levels, professional and sexual, both neatly signified by the ambiguity of the word "solution." With respect to the medical meaning of the "solutions" in the dream and bearing on the issue of Freud's professional conscientiousness and his anxiety about the correctness of his new theory, the dream shows how wrong it was of Otto to treat Irma with an injection; that is, to treat her as if she were suffering from an organic condition. The correct treatment—and here we come upon an ambiguity of Freud's solution as an *oral* solution—would have been to pursue, as Freud recommended, an oral cure, a cure through speech. ("Irma seemed to me foolish because she had not accepted my solution. Her friend would have been wiser. . . . She would then have *opened her mouth properly,* and have told me more than Irma.") In so far as the dream points to sexual "solutions," Freud is able to take revenge on Irma ("it's really only your fault") for preferring Otto's solution to his own (some women patients "change their doctors as often as their lovers").

Our sexual interpretation of the Irma dream receives a striking, if indirect, confirmation when it is compared with another of Freud's dreams. In his commentary on the Irma dream, Freud pointed out that his daughter Mathilde was implicated in the condensations around the figure of Irma. "In so far as Irma appeared to have a diphtheritic membrane," he said, "which recalled my anxiety about my eldest daughter, she stood for that child" (SE, 4:292). Mathilde had in fact suffered from diphtheria twice during her childhood and had caused Freud a great deal of anxiety. He wrote to Fliess in 1897 that he had "given her up for lost" (CL, 232). How does the parity between Irma and Mathilde contribute anything to the supposition that the dream about Irma was centrally concerned with a sexual attraction? A year after the Irma dream Freud reported to Fliess another dream in which he had "overaffectionate feelings" for Mathilde. The astonishing thing is the parallel structure exhibited by the two dreams: both dreams culminate with the vision of a word "printed in heavy type."

> Recently I dreamed of [having] overaffectionate feelings for Mathilde, only she was called Hella; and afterward I again saw "Hella" before me, printed in heavy type. Solution (*Auflösung*): Hella is the name of an American niece whose picture we have been sent.
>
> Mathilde could be called Hella because she recently shed bitter tears over the defeats of the Greeks. She is enthralled by the mythology of ancient Hellas and naturally regards all Hellenes as heroes. The dream of course shows the fulfillment of my wish to catch a *Pater* as the originator of neurosis and thus [the dream] puts an end to my ever-recurring doubts. (CL, 249)

Freud never returned to this dream. Were it not for the evidence of the Fliess correspondence preserved by Marie Bonaparte against Freud's insistence that she destroy them, we would know nothing of it. It is, however, relevant to the discussion of the Irma dream. The remarkable formal homology between the two dreams—both dreams of a young woman followed by a vividly hallucinated word printed in heavy type—suggests a shared content: that of a sexual attraction for a forbidden partner, a daughter in the one case, a patient in the other.[37] In addition, both dreams are explicitly set against the background of Freud's emerging theory of hysteria, in which such illicit sexual liaisons were thought to produce hysterical symptoms. In the Irma dream, concern about the origin of symptoms forms the very spine of the dream. The theme of illness is absent in the Mathilde dream, but not from the situation of the dreamer's life. At the time the dream occurred, Mathilde Freud was in fact recovering from a diphtheritic infection—the very symptom that linked her to Irma in Freud's earlier dream. Nine months earlier, Freud had reported to Fliess that Mathilde, like the girl whose symptoms he would trace to "sucking on the penis," was suffering from a facial tic (CL, 196).[38] These parallels between the dream of Irma and that of Mathilde prompt a suspicion that both dreams may have been essentially sexual in content.

The Dream's Solution

The preceding discussions invite some general conclusions about dreams and their interpretation. The extra-intense image of the Irma dream reminds us of the most basic point of Freud's theory of dreams: the fact that dreams are essentially imagistic. "The waking mind produces ideas and thoughts in verbal images and in speech," says Freud, "but in dreams it does so in true sensory images" (SE, 4:51). Oneiric consciousness fuses a massive quantity of psychical material into the body of an image. The term chosen by Freud to name this fusional process—*Verdichtung*, or condensation—is an interesting one as it connotes not only the process by which something is thickened and gathered, as water droplets coalesce from vapor, but also the process by which light is focused into a concentrated beam, as by the condenser of a photographic enlarger. Freud compares the process to the production of an image in a telescope. Somewhere in the arrangement of lenses, a new and unique entity—an image—is brought into being. The analogy is an especially suggestive one for our purposes because the birth of the image within a complex apparatus readily recalls the way in which the objects of consciousness are generated in a dispositional field. The telescope analogy suggests that the images of dreams are wholly virtual entities that do not exist at all outside the apparatus that produces them. If the image is ultimately related in some way to an object beyond the telescope, the specific character and qualities of the image are decisively determined by the construction of the instrument itself.

The comparison to a telescope is offered by Freud to flesh out another idea, borrowed from Gustav Theodor Fechner, that bears even greater resemblence to the concept of a dispositional field. Fechner's key insight, the most important of his contributions to the theory of dreams, says Freud, was to recognize "that *the scene of action of dreams is different from that of waking ideational life*" (SE, 4:48). Freud remarks that no one, including Fechner himself, had known exactly what to make of this reference to an other scene, *ein anderer Schauplatz*. Freud reformulates it by saying that the dream is produced in a different "psychical locality." Both formulas echo the spatial metaphor that informs the concept of the dispositional field, a concept that we evolved in discussions of Monet's concern for the luminous *enveloppe* and for what he called "the moment of landscape." Similar analogies to a landscape continued to shape Freud's thinking throughout his career and especially his mature theory of the mind as a *topography*. This spatial-topographical conception can be said to be relevant in a special way to the phenomenology of dreams. The phenomenal experience of dreams is primarily that of a special dream-*space* within which the dreamer seems to find himself or herself. Freud remarks upon this characteristic of dreams by pointing to their tendency to *dramatize* thoughts, to place thoughts in the context of an entire situation of experience. Thus dreams differ from waking consciousness not only for the fact that they hallucinate thoughts by turning them into images but also because dreams go on to "construct a *situation* out of these images; they represent an event which is actually happening . . . they 'dramatize' an idea" (SE, 4:50). This situational character of the dream, what might be called the dream's *topos*, is not only registered in terms of a visual horizon but also and often more importantly in terms of the dreamer's implicit understanding that one or another state of affairs obtains in the dream. Dreams are very typically pervaded by such global understandings and the emotional tonality that accompanies them. Such encompassing understandings establish the experiential context of the dream and color the events that occur within it in a way that readily recalls Monet's concept of the *enveloppe* of illumination.

Freud's concept of psychical locality describes the phenomenology of dreaming, but it also helps to explain the process by which dreams are formed. As Freud is careful to point out, the notion of psychical locality is not meant to designate a specific anatomical site in the brain but rather a distinct psychical system that operates according to a particular set of laws. That dreams show us an alternative reality, that they stitch together a variety of materials in the fabric of an entirely new location of experience, is due to a departure from the psychic system that governs the consciousness of the waking ego. During sleep, investment in the bound matrix of the ego undergoes a far-reaching alteration as a result of which the potentialities of consciousness are opened to a wider and alternative field of influences, that of the primary process. Freud thinks of this shift between psychical systems in terms of an altered relation between the register of images and the register of words. Freud's best explanation of this process is to be found in his "Metapsychological Supplement to the Theory of Dreams." What enables the mnemic traces of the day residues to fuse with repressed material in the unconscious and what, furthermore, allows this fusion to emerge in the manifest dream in the form of images is "the easing of communication between the *Pcs.* [preconscious] and the *Ucs* [unconscious]" (SE, 14:226). This bringing of the preconscious and unconscious contents into intimate exchange constitutes a topographical regression. Its effect is to bring about a kind of short circuit between the verbal formations of the preconscious and the imagistic thing-presentations of the unconscious. "In dreams there is free communication between (*Pcs.*) word-cathexes and (*Ucs.*) thing-cathexes. . . . [F]or a dream all operations with words are no more than a preparation for a regression to things" (SE, 14:229).

This account of the dream-work in terms of a slippage between systems of verbal and imagistic presentations tallies exactly with our discussions of the dispositional field. As we have seen over the course of this chapter, the notion of the dispositional field can be drawn upon to reveal a profound homology between perceptual and linguistic cognitions. Perceptual orientation toward an object, which implies the registration of a figure distinct from an environing ground, was shown to be structurally akin to the reverberation of a signifying element in the diacritical system that comprises a language. In both cases, the underlying structure is one of positional adumbration and dispositional configuration. We were careful to point to the differences that separate the movement of semiosis from imaginary formation, differences that can be traced along two main lines.

There is, first, the temporal inertia of the positional moment. In the mediation of the psychical process by linguistic forms, the duration of the perceptual identity in recognition of the signifier is reduced to the vanishing point. For the imaginary presentation, by contrast, the positional moment is held in suspense. Secondly, there is the fact that the dispositional field of linguistic cognition, composed of the interlaced network of relations that Saussure called the "floating kingdom" of the signifier, is structured by rules determined in large part by convention. Nevertheless, in both cases mental activity is essentially configurational. Whether fixed upon a figural contour or slid along the line of discourse, the psychical process remains implicitly oriented in the compass of an embracing field. In a certain sense, then, both perceptual and linguistic fields share the integrated structure of a world. It is along the lines of a parallel supposition that Merleau-Ponty many times suggested a deep affinity between the structures of perceptual experiences and the organization of speech and language. The network of relations that make up the system of signifiers constitutes a virtual world. Now, it is among the primary purposes of normal, waking consciousness to distinguish these two levels, to ensure that the subject does not mistake words for things. Failure to make this discrimination threatens the subject with descent into psychosis. During sleep, however, this discriminating function is abrogated in some degree. For the dreaming subject, as for the psychotic, linguistic forms offer themselves as immediately transposable into the register of image perception. Dreaming thus arises from a kind of hemorrhage in the strictures usually applied to the dispositional field that defines waking awareness. The dreamer might be said to actually dwell in the world of words and verbal residues as the waking subject moves about in the perceived environment. It is along the plane of this slippage between perceptual and verbal dimensions of the dispositional field that the dream-work effects its miraculous transformations.

The primary distinguishing characteristic of the dream process in comparison with the waking state therefore involves an alteration in the dispositional field out of which the objects of consciousness are generated. Dreaming represents a more labile and fluid process of positional adumbration. Correlative with this alteration in the conditions of image production, however, the images of dreams exhibit a more pronounced effect of abduction. The dream image more completely obscures the constellation of factors that gave rise to it for the simple reason that the return to wakefulness recongeals the organization of the dispositional field appropriate to the waking state. Recalled upon awakening, the images of dreams are therefore liable to exert an even greater imaginary density and mesmerizing quality than the objects of waking consciousness. The metaphor of the telescope by which Freud seeks to illustrate the production of the dream image also suggests this intensification of the abductive moment. Like the telescope's series of lenses, the psychical apparatus that performs the dream-work remains transparent to the objects it labors to produce. The complex matrix of conditioning structures in which the image is brought forth, though precisely articulated, may itself never become conscious.

The increase of the abductive power of the image in the dream makes a special effort of interpretation necessary. At the same time, it determines the basic course such interpretation will take. The aim of Freud's method of dream interpretation is to look beyond the image itself toward the web of conditioning structures that has brought it into being. To do so, interpretation must resist the totalizing appeal of the image. If the dream-work functions to fuse the tangle of unconscious thoughts into the body of an image, the labor of interpretation must move in the opposite direction. Above all, the manifest dream cannot be taken *as a whole*. The dream cannot be accepted as it presents itself to the dreaming consciousness, precisely because it appears in imagistic form. The essence of Freud's innovation consists in the effort to pulverize the dream, to split it into its constitutive elements. The dream is first dismembered into individual image fragments, then each fragment is further atomized by the effects of free association. Only in the retrospective regathering of the material gleaned from free association can the meaning of the dream as a whole be deciphered.

From this perspective, we are able to regrasp the very essence of the method of free association as a resistance to the fusional power of the image and its abductive effects. The exercise of free association presupposes a suspension of the demand for coherence that is at the heart of the imaginary process. Free association becomes the royal road to the interpretation of dreams precisely because it seeks to put out of play the motive force of imaginary agglutination.

With these points in mind, we rediscover the sense in which Freud's method is rightly called an *analysis* of dreams. His aim is to split apart what the dream work has synthesized. In this way, we find ourselves in agreement with Lacan that the dream of Irma's injection deserves its status as the inaugural dream of psychoanalysis, that this dream is, in part at least, a dream about the theory of dreams. Freud's method of dream interpretation sets out to splinter the imaginary body of the dream, to atomize its "heavy print." The dream of Irma is thus a worthy exemplar of Freud's method, not only because the dream culminates in a word—not only, that is, because it suggests that the meaning of dreams must be traced back into a network of unconscious thoughts that are structured like a language—but also because the solution to the dream lies in its solution. The Irma dream is truly a dream of *Auflösung*. The action of interpretation puts the dream into solution, it dissolves the dream, decomposes its image nuggets, melting them into the ocean of associations out of which they were composed. The interpretation di-gests what the dream work has con-gested. In the terms we have evolved, the dream images are pulverized in order to trace them back into the dispositional field out of which the dream arose.

Circulation in the Psychical Apparatus

The discussions of this chapter have brought into view a structured interplay of perceptual and linguistic functions, in terms of which it is possible to regrasp some of the most basic concepts of psychoanalysis. This imaginary-symbolic interplay recalls William James's conception of the stream of consciousness as a succession of substantive and transitive moments. James compares the flow of awareness to "an alternation of flights and perchings"—a process that is reflected in the rhythms of speech "where every thought is expressed in a sentence, and every sentence closed by a period." He explicitly points to the imaginal character of the substantive moments.

> The resting-places are usually occupied by sensorial imaginations of some sort, whose peculiarity is that they can be held before the mind for an indefinite time, and contemplated without changing; the places of flight are filled with thoughts of relations, static or dynamic, that for the most part obtain between the matters contemplated in the periods of comparative rest. *Let us call the resting-places the 'substantive parts,' and the places of flight the 'transitive parts,' of the stream of thought.* It then

appears that the main end of our thinking is at all times the attainment of some other substantive part than the one from which we have just been dislodged. And we may say that the main use of the transitive parts is to lead us from one substantive conclusion to another. (P, 1:243)

Reminiscent of the substantive and transitive moments described by James, Lacan's distinction between imaginary and symbolic functions is closely bound up with different relations to time. The formations of the imaginary are characterized by the temporal perdurance of perceptual registrations. The gestalt unity characteristic of the imaginary, the coherence and stability of the imago, displays a special kind of temporal inertia. By contrast, the function of the signifier is distinguished by a particular evanescence of perceptual forms. Every symbolic process must take its point of departure from a perceptual registration but proceeds along the trajectory of signification only by evacuating the initial investment of attention in the perceptual contour of the sign. Following from this characterization of the differing temporalities of the imaginary and symbolic functions, we are led to envisage an ongoing interaction between them, a dynamic process of intrapsychic "circulation."[39] We are given to suppose a continual exchange between the two axes in the intersection of which the progress of thought and discourse unfolds. A good model for such a theory of circulation is offered by the activity of reading, during which the mind's progress along the trail of written marks alternately calls up images that function like stopping points or way stations in which thought and feeling take their bearings even as the reader is pulled on toward subtleties of meaning that escape imagistic representation. In its most elemental terms, this theory would envision a dialectic of identity and difference, a shifting play of unity and multiplicity that is effected by the interaction of imaginal forms in tension with subtler and more diffuse effects of meaning. Such a conception of imaginary-symbolic circulation provides the basis for a Lacanian account of what Freud called the "psychical apparatus."

The metaphor of circulation informed the basic assumptions of Freud's metapsychology throughout the whole trajectory of his career and can be discerned in his earliest theoretical efforts. In the *Project* Freud bases his conception of mental activity on the notion of "quantity in a state of flow" (SE, 1:295). As an attempt to conceive mental activity in analogy to the physical laws of rest and motion, the *Project* lays down "neuronic inertia" as the first law governing the psychical system. Modeled on the example of a reflex arc, it supposes a perfectly untrammeled flow of quantity from the reception of sensory stimulus to its discharge in motor activity. The need for another mode of functioning intervenes in the event that flight from the stimulus is impossible. This circumstance arises primarily in the case of endogenous stimuli originating from the interior of the organism itself—what Freud will later call the energy of the drives. Faced with the buildup of such endogenous energies, the system must tolerate a constant level of quantity. In this way, a second guiding principle of psychical activity is introduced, that of the principle of constancy, in accordance with which a degree of stasis and inhibition is introduced into what would otherwise be an unimpeded flow. This second principle is equivocal. On the one hand, it runs counter to the basic tendency toward immediate discharge. On the other hand, the energies stored up and held in suspense by the second principle allow for the accomplishment of specific actions by means of which discharge might be achieved at some later point in time. The essential function of the constancy principle thus becomes that of delay. In this formulation we readily see the outline of Freud's later distinction between the pleasure principle, here represented by the original tendency toward immediate evacuation, and the reality prinicple, in which the original tendency is modified under the pressure of "the exigencies of life" (SE, 1:297). Even under the restraining influence of the reality principle, drive energies struggle toward discharge. The opposition of perfect flow and impediment thus underlies the distinction between primary and secondary process. It is by means of structures of defense and inhibition that the architecture of the personality will be erected. Moreover, it is only as a result of the impeding of a primary flow that consciousness will become possible. In every case, however, the circuit of flow and discharge will eventually be completed, even if it is forced to escape by way of the symptom. Even at this early stage of his thinking, Freud conceives the psychical apparatus as a circulatory system in which defensive structures function as buffers and checkpoints between the entry of energy into the system and its eventual evacuation.

The concept of an imaginary-symbolic circulation quite naturally suggests a spectrum of possible adjustments between the two functions in which one of the two may dominate or in which a variety of breakdowns or malformations of the relation between them may occur. Over the range of such a spectrum, we might locate the forms of psychopathology recognized by psychoanalysis. Lacan proposes something similar in his article on the mirror stage when he finds "the most extensive definition of neurosis" in the fixity of imaginary schemata, the effects of what he calls "the inertia characteristic of the formations of the *I*" (E:S, 7). Indeed, it is not difficult to recognize many of the typical signatures of neurosis—the phobia, the compulsive idea, the hysterical identification—as situations in which the fluid potentiality of the symbolic has been pooled and frozen in the hollows of imaginary formations. At the same time, we might conceive the psychological equilibrium of everyday life, compared by Freud to a kind of low-grade neurosis, as a more or less stable economy in which the symbolic is oriented within a relatively fixed landscape of predictable and routinized perceptions. In the grip of everydayness, discourse becomes mere "empty speech," a discourse of the defensive ego that closes down the more open and potentially threatening horizon of the symbolic.

Extending the same logic in the opposite direction, the onset of psychosis becomes comparable to an uncontrolled slippage of the signifier, compensated for by delusional overgrowths of the imaginary. In psychosis, as Freud had already suggested, the relation between words and things breaks down with the result that words are mistaken for things. The problem for the paranoid psychotic is that *everything* has become meaningful, everything appears to be addressed to the subject himself or herself. The result is a state of complete alienation in which nothing is any longer meaningful. Having lost its anchorage in the imaginary, the play of the signifier rushes over the falls of cascading associations.

We are thus led to envisage two forms of distortion correlative with the malignancy either of the symbolic or of the imaginary. It is a two-sided picture evoked by A. J. Greimas: "Paraphrasing Lacan, we can say two kinds of madness await mankind: on the one side, schizophrenia, the exaltation of total freedom in communication, ending in noncommunication; on the other side, a completely socialized and iterative speech, Queneau's 'you talk, you talk, that's all you know how to do,' which is also the negation of communication, discourse deprived of information."[40] To this brief typology of psychopathologies, we may add a note on "normality" from a psychoanalytic viewpoint. From the perspective we have developed, it should be clear that there is no definitive state of normalcy, as if the varieties of pathology could be taken as so many forms of descent from the summit of a perfect psychological health. Normalcy is rather at best a steerage between the alternatives of neurosis and psychosis, a balance struck between the claims of imaginary fixity and symbolic fluidity.

The progress and effects of analysis can also be reposed in terms of an imago-semic circulation. To the extent that various clinical syndromes represent interrupted or truncated circulation between imaginary and symbolic functions, the work of analysis becomes a matter of promoting a realignment or redistribution between the two. As Lacan says of it, the labor of psychoanalysis is fundamentally one of *repunctuating* the patient's discourse.[41] The work of analysis in "making the unconscious conscious" does not require the import of something from outside the patient's discourse, something altogether missing from it, but rather demands a certain redistribution of what has already emerged into the analytic space. The trick of analytic interpretation thus consists in locating those points in the space of the transference at which the effects of a symbolic process have been short-circuited by the imaginary. This point is illustrated by the example of resistance with which we began the first chapter. The imminent emergence of something significant in the patient's discourse gives way to resistance as the patient is distracted by an overwhelming sense of the analyst's presence. Faced with this surfacing of resistance, the aim of analysis is not to reduce or dissolve the moment of resistance, as if to find something else beneath or beyond the resistance, but to act in and with the resistance itself in order to promote the potential signification that remains impacted within it. Such a repunctuation of the moment can be accomplished by a number of means, including accentuating a key element of the patient's discourse or even terminating the session. Theoretically, the important point is that "the transference, simultaneously resistance and motor of the analysis, can only be understood within the dialectic of the imaginary the symbolic" (S.I, 284). Lacan thus opposes those analysts who see in resistance and defense only the necessity "of lifting them, in so far as they constitute an obstacle to a beyond, a beyond which is nothing more than a beyond" (S.I, 285). The real action of analysis consists rather in "analysing the symbolic character of the defences, of bringing the subject to realize the dimension at stake on the plane of the symbol" (S.I, 285-86).

The notion of a dialectical circulation of imaginary and symbolic functions liable to various forms of breakdown or arrest readily offers itself as a theoretical translation for many of Freud's most basic ideas. We have already pointed to the parallel between Freud's concept of object cathexis and that of imaginary identification. So, too, what Lacan calls "capture" (*captation*) in the imaginary is comparable with the process of fixation. For Freud, fixation involves an attachment of the energy of the drives to a particular, stage-specific "representative." The imaginary character of this process is suggested by the history of the very term "*fixieren*," which contains a reference to hypnotic fascination, particularly with a visual stimulus. Moreover, Freud's concept of fixation, like the Lacanian imaginary, is closely related to the process of character formation and to the genesis and stability of the ego. What remained implicit in Freud is thus made explicit by Lacan: the ego itself is formed by a process of fixation precisely parallel to the mechanism involved in symptom formation. As Lacan says of it, "the ego is structured exactly like a symptom. At the heart of the human subject, it is only a privileged symptom, the human symptom *par excellence*" (S.I, 16). Belonging to the same complex of ideas and equally resonant with the Lacanian imaginary is the concept of regression. As the theoretical chapter 7 of *The Interpretation of Dreams* presents it, regression characteristically displays a return to perceptual immediacy, a tendency that fits well with the fact that the psychic life of children, like that of aboriginal peoples, is predominantly imagistic. In general, Freud assumes that the progress of psychical development tends to move away from the highly specific, perceptual orientation of the primitive drives toward a broader horizon of symbolically mediated behaviors and attitudes characteristic of sublimation. Under the pressure of challenging life experiences, however, the psychic organization reverts to older and simpler patterns established by perceptual residues and memory traces.

The Metaphoric and Metonymic Poles

We have provisionally conceived a process of psychical circulation in terms of a fundamental opposition between perceptual and linguistic organizations, an opposition that is discernible both in the Freudian distinction between thing-presentations and word-presentations and in the Lacanian categories of imaginary and symbolic. In the following chapter, we will continue to rely on this dichotomy of image and sign to lay bare the foundations of psychoanalysis in a new way, a strategy that will reilluminate the dualistic tendency of Freud's thought. Throughout our discussions, however, we have sought to articulate the opposition of image and sign along the lines of a second dualism, that of positionality and the dispositional field. It is now possible to determine more precisely the relation of these two pairs of terms to one another and thereby to see more clearly the value of our new construction. If the couplet image-sign is in important ways comparable to that of positionality-dispositionality and if our discusssions at times allow a near identification between the two pairs of terms, they must nevertheless be theoretically distinguished. The language of positionality and dispositionality is intended to designate a dynamic more fundamental than the distinction between image and sign, a dynamic that is operative in both the perceptual and linguistic domains. To underline this point, let us conclude the present chapter with some remarks about the role of positionality and dispositionality as ordering principles of speech and language.

Consider, first, the way in which the semantic field of words displays a structure that is unmistakably reminiscent of positionality and dispositionality. For most linguistic terms, any fully adequate account of their meaning must take note of two dimensions. On the one hand is the more discrete and definite moment of determinate indication by which reference can be made to an object in the world. On the other hand, there is a more vague and diffuse horizon of subtle hints and shadings that escape explicit registration yet may decisively color the term's total meaning. This distinction between the semantic nucleus of a term and the nebula of associative linkages that surround it is especially (though by no means exclusively) applicable to nouns. It roughly corresponds to the grammarians' distinction between denotation and connotation. It is precisely such a distinction that James sought to highlight in his concept of the psychical "fringe" attached to every word. It is this penumbra of tacit meaning that makes possible the process, absolutely essential to the functioning of language yet rarely noted in and for itself, by which the utterance of a word or series of words shapes an incompletely determinate yet palpable expectation of words to follow. "In our feeling of each word," James observes, "there chimes an echo or foretaste of every other" (P, 1:281). We earlier quoted Lacan making the same point:

> The signifier, by its very nature, always anticipates meaning by
> unfolding its dimension before it. As is seen at the level of the

sentence when it is interrupted before the significant term: 'I shall never . . .', 'All the same it is . . .', 'And yet there may be . . .'. Such sentences are not without meaning, a meaning all the more oppressive in that it is content to make us wait for it. (E:S, 153)

It is entirely typical, then, that words possess primary meanings that are girt about by a range of incomplete tendrils of inchoate significance the way that the yolk of a fried egg is surrounded by its spreading skirt of white. On the basis of this observation, we can sketch the outlines of a general theory of metaphor. Metaphor generates a new experience of meaning by overlapping the associative penumbra of one term with that of another substituted for it. When we say that "it's raining cats and dogs," for example, two systems of semantic relations are laid over one another as we might superimpose transparencies to produce a double image. In accordance with their primary and objective meanings, the terms of the metaphoric conjunction are obviously distinct. Yet a measure of identity is achieved in the dimension of a common associative background: pelting rain and scrapping cats and dogs share something frenzied and staccato, a blur of speeding parts. The excitement created by metaphor depends upon this play of identity in difference: a conjunction that is simultaneously interpenetration and collision. The result is to illuminate a latent dimension in the meaning of the metaphorized term.

This metaphoric process can be described in the terms we have adopted. Precisely because the positional moment of a relatively objective meaning is elided, its place marked by another term that has been substituted for it, aspects of the term's dispositional dimension are brought forward in unexpected ways. Metaphoric substitution effects a measured suspension of positionality—at times brought about by an almost violent clash between the core meaning of one term and that of another—with the result that previously hidden strata of meaning are freed from the domination of the primary signification.

This account of metaphor agrees well with Lacan's definition of the metaphor as "the substitution of signifier for signifier . . . [by means of which] an effect of signification is produced that is creative or poetic" (E:S, 164). He illustrates his view with an example from Victor Hugo's "Booz endormi": "His sheaf was neither miserly nor spiteful" (E:S, 156). It is precisely the lack of any objective similarity between Booz and his sheaf that establishes the gap across which the poetic spark will fly. In the noncoincidence of their positional contents, a strange and novel experience of meaning will resonate in the dispositional properties of the two terms. The metaphor thus succeeds in awakening aspects of the terms it conjoins by means of playing upon "language insofar as it carries within itself its moments of meaningful creation but in a non-active, latent state."[42]

> Metaphor presupposes that a meaning is the dominant datum
> and that it deflects, commands, the use of the signifier to such
> an extent that the entire species of preestablished, I should say
> lexical, connections comes undone. Nothing in any dictionary
> usage can suggest for one instant that a sheaf is capable of
> being miserly, and even less of being spiteful. And yet it's clear
> that the use of language is only susceptible to meaning once it's
> possible to say *His sheaf was neither miserly nor spiteful,* that is to
> say, once the meaning has ripped the signifier from its lexical
> connections.[43]

As the Surrealists knew, the power of metaphor derives from strategic dislocation and recombination. The paradigm of metaphor could thus be found in "the fortuitous encounter upon a dissecting table of a sewing machine and an umbrella."[44] Everything depends, as Max Ernst put it, on "the exploitation of the chance meeting of two remote realities on a plane unsuitable to them."[45] So reliable is this effect of metaphoric cross-fertilization that the random transposition of words can be sufficient to produce it, a fact observed by Lacan in the one-act comic play of Jean Tardieu, *Un mot pour un autre,* in which two women address one another with strangely evocative absurdities. "*My dear, my dearest, how many pebbles is it since I have had the apprentice to sugar you?*" asks the first. "*Alas, my dear,*" answers the other, "*I myself have been extremely unvitreous my three littlest oil-cakes*" (S.III, 226). In this exchange, the insertion into the discourse of wholly unexpected and irrelevant words creates strange and subtle resonances of meaning, effects that are unable to transcend nonsense yet do not fail completely to produce an odd and indescribable feeling of significance.

Returning to Hugo's metaphor, we can further specify the dynamics at work. When "Booz" is replaced by "his sheaf," where, we might ask, has Booz gone? For the metaphor to be effective, the absent figure of Booz must tacitly inform the sheaf. And what does this mode of implicit presence mean but that Booz has been taken up into the dispositional field attaching to the word "sheaf"? Booz himself has become part of the total field, the conditioning environment of influences, that determine the meaning of "sheaf." But now we come to the crucial point: inasmuch as Booz has been drawn into the dispositional field associated with "sheaf," he is brought into communication with the range of connotative resonances attached to that word. Among those resonances, and appropriate for a term whose primary meaning refers to the gathering of grain stalks into a bundle for the purposes of storage, is a hint of possession and even of positive acquisitiveness. But if this is so, we immediately recognize the real achievement of the metaphoric substitution: by means of the metaphor, Hugo's line deftly expresses a primary signification of generosity (the sheaf is neither miserly nor spiteful) but also, by virtue of dipping the figure of Booz into the waters of indirect association that swirl about the word "sheaf," creates the subtlest hint to the contrary. The metaphor manages in a single stroke to allude to Booz's admirable magnanimity yet also suggests that Booz is no fool, that he watches out for himself. Indeed, his magnanimity is all the more laudable for shining out against the background of a basic practicality and concern for what is rightfully his. With these considerations in mind, we can make sense of the commentary Lacan devotes to Hugo's metaphor—a passage that would otherwise be challenging indeed to interpret.

> It is obvious that in the line of Hugo cited above, not the slightest spark of light springs from the proposition that the sheaf was neither miserly nor spiteful, for the reason that there is no question of the sheaf's having either of these attributes, since the attributes, like the sheaf, belong to Booz.

> If, however, his sheaf does refer us to Booz, and this is indeed the case, it is because it has replaced him in the signifying chain at the very place where he was to be exalted by the sweeping away of greed and spite. But now Booz himself has been swept away by the sheaf, and hurled into the outer darkness where greed and spite harbor him in the hollow of their negation.

> But once *his* sheaf has thus usurped his place Booz can no longer return there; the slender thread of the little word *his* that

binds him to it is only one more obstacle to his return in that it links him to the notion of possession that retains him at the heart of greed and spite. So *his* generosity, affirmed in the passage, is yet reduced to *less than nothing* by the munificence of the sheaf which, coming from nature, knows neither our reserve nor our rejections, and even in its accumulation remains prodigal by our standards. (E:S, 157)

The capacity for metaphor depends upon the achievement of positional substitution between terms whose primary semantic contents are different. This achievement presupposes the ability to disengage the primary meaning from a halo of secondary and tertiary resonances. It presupposes on the level of linguistic form an act of separation and isolation that is parallel to the disengagement of the gestalt figure from its ground in perception. It is a capacity that must be developed in the course of language acquisition and one that Lacan will associate with the resolution of the Oedipus complex. Very young children are unable to understand metaphor, he insists, a fact that is evidenced by their inability to follow Surrealist poetry.

We are told that children understand surrealist and abstract poetery, which would be a return to childhood. This is stupid—children detest surrealist poetry and find repugnant certain stages in Picasso's painting. Why? Because they're not yet up to metaphor, but only metonymy. And when they do appreciate certain things in Picasso's paintings it's because metonymy is involved. (S.III, 228)

How, then, is metonymy distinct from metaphor? The distinction between the two tropes can be somewhat confusing because both metaphor and metonymy result from the substitution of one thing for another. What differs is the means by which the substitution is arrived at. The capacity for metaphor is predicated upon the achievement of positional substitution. Metonymy, by contrast, is effected by one or another mode of slippage across the dispositional field. The metonymic link is made not by insertion of a new content into the positional locus but by a kind of lateral movement—a process that is accomplished most primitively by movement in space. It is therefore typical of metonymy, Lacan therefore claims, that "one thing is named by another that is its container, or its part, or that is connected to it" (S.III, 221). The difference is illustrated by the following pairs: a series of very elementary metaphors gives us "canoe-rowboat," "car-truck," "house-nest," "jacket-wrapper." Metonymic substitution for the same four items yields "canoe-river," "car-road," "house-garage," "jacket-pants." The metaphoric substitutions bring about a virtual transubstantiation, the positing of an equivalence between dissimilars. The metonymies merely shift the positional focus across the field of experience. In the cases cited, the metonymy is achieved by a spatial movement, a shift to what is adjacent or contiguous with the point of departure. It might otherwise move, as in synecdoche, from the whole to a part—"canoe-thwart," "jacket-sleeve," etc.—but that case, too, would fit the same description of a dispositional slippage. The same can be said of thematic shifts—"canoe-paddling," "car-traveling"—for which the field of movement is not spatial but semantic.

In showing the relevance of positionality and dispositionality to the semantic field of words and to the functions of metaphor and metonymy, the way is open for discerning general styles of speech, thought, and behavior for which one or the other dimension is predominant. One example is the distinction between what psychologists call field dependence and field independence.[46] Field independence designates the capacity readily to perceive and judge objects in isolation from their environing contexts. If a frame surrounding a vertically suspended rod is rotated slightly to one side, an observer who is field independent will continue to perceive the rod as perfectly vertical. The field dependent observer, on the other hand, unable to disintricate the rod from its surrounding frame, tends to be misled into thinking that the rod has itself tipped to one side. The field independent observer, able more effectively to disembed the figure from the influence of its context, shows a greater capacity for grasping positional autonomy.

Another example concerns the metaphoric and metonymic poles identified by Jakobson in his study of two types of aphasia. Jakobson associates the former, the so-called similiarity disorder, with an incapacity of selection and substitution. Like the field dependent observer, patients suffering from similarity disorder tend to be bound to the context. Unless prompted by features of the immediately present situation, they become confused and uncertain. As a result, these patients are typically able to complete sentences once they have been presented with fragments but find it difficult to begin one of their own. They may be unable to utter phrases like "It's raining" unless they see that it is actually raining. Significantly, similarity disorder implies not only a forced reliance on the context but correlatively involves a positive inability to focus explicitly upon an object in and for itself. This inability shows itself in an incapacity to name things. "Thus Goldstein's patient never uttered the word *knife* alone, but, according to its use and surroundings, alternately called the knife *pencil-sharpener, apple-parer, bread-knife, knife-and-fork*; so that the word *knife* was changed from a free form, capable of occurring alone, into a bound form."[47] Other aphasics of this type may drop the attempt to produce specific names altogether; everything becomes a mere "thing," "*chose*," or "*Stückel*." Similarity disorder thus evidences a disabling of the metaphoric capacity, an inability to produce positional equivalence. At its most extreme, the disability seems to affect not only the positing of an equivalence between two dissimilar things but even an equivalence of a word or thing with itself. When asked to repeat the word "no," one patient replied "No, I don't know how to do it." As Jakobson goes on to remark: "While spontaneously using the word in the context of his answer ("No, I don't . . . "), he could not produce the purest form of equational predication, the tautology *a = a*: 'no' is 'no'."[48] A further example recalls a phenomenon we have already twice encountered in Freud: the inability to recall the name of an object while confronted with its image.

> The same difficulty arises then the patient is asked to name an object pointed to or handled by the examiner. The aphasic with a defect in substitution will not supplement the pointing or handling gesture of the examiner with the name of the object pointed to. Instead of saying "this is [called] a pencil", he will merely add an elliptical note about its use: "To write". . . . Likewise, the picture of an object will cause suppression of its name.[49]

If the similarity disorder centers upon a disabling of the positional function and a correlative reliance on the context, the second type of aphasia, called by Jakobson "contiguity disorder," is precisely the opposite: the patient is unable to hold on to the context and can produce nothing but a series of disconnected positings. While the first type of aphasia can subsist only in the tissues of the dispositional field, the second, as if seeking to cross a swamp by hopping from one stone to another, sustains itself by continually regenerating the positional moment. Whereas the speech of patients suffering from similarity disorder may be constructed almost entirely from connectives and dependent words or phrases, speech under the influence of the contiguity disorder becomes disjointed and "telegraphic." The words most dependent upon the context of the sentence tend to be omitted while words well suited to stand on their own are retained. The result is less a coherent stream of discourse than a mere "word heap." While the patient with similarity disorder talks on and on without coming to the point, the subject of contiguity aphasia tends to make one-sentence or even one-word utterances. Where the capacity to produce metaphor is almost absent in the similarity disorder, metaphoric equivalences, or something approaching them, are constantly produced by the sufferer of contiguity disorder. As we might expect of a subject unable to tolerate immersion in the dispositional field, however, these equivalences tend to remain on the level of *mere* substitutions, mere trading of positional contents that fails to generate a significant exchange of latent meaning. "*Spyglass* for *microscope*, or *fire* for *gaslight* are typical examples of such QUASI-METAPHORIC EXPRESSIONS, as Jackson terms them, since, in contradistinction to rhetoric or poetic metaphors, they present no deliberate transfer of meaning."[50]

Both the example of field dependence and independence and that of the aphasic types described by Jakobson suggest general styles or orientations that can be correlated with the terms we have attempted to outline. Field dependence and similarity disorder both evidence a reliance on the context that results from a disabling of the capacity for positional equivalence. By contrast, field independence and contiguity disorder have in common a marked preference for positional stability and a tendency to sever connectedness to a larger field of relations. The relevance of these distinctions for psychoanalytic concepts was not lost on Jakobson, who likened the metaphoric and metonymic poles to the processes of condensation and displacement identified by Freud in the dream-work—a comparison taken up and greatly expanded upon by Lacan.

CHAPTER 3

The Freudian
Dialectic

In the previous two chapters we surveyed a series of predominantly dualistic formulations based on the paradigm of figure and ground, expanded and generalized in the terms of positionality and dispositionality. In this chapter, we will continue along similar lines—a strategy warranted by the deeply dualistic character of Freud's own thought. If our constructions do any justice to Freud's essential insights, we can rightly expect them to account in new ways for Freud's dualist tendency, and above all for its culminating expression in the primal drives of Eros and Death. Yet even as we carry further this binary approach, we need to acknowledge in advance that it will eventually be necessary to complicate it significantly. What we have conceived up to now dualistically will have to be recast in the frame of a triadic and finally a quadrilateral structure. That task will occupy us in the fourth and fifth chapters. For the moment, however, keeping in mind its provisional character, let us continue to unfold the logic of a bipolar dialectic and spell out its implications for rereading some of Freud's most basic concepts.

The Formative Power of the Image

Lacan's signal contribution has been to highlight the pivotal importance of language in psychoanalysis. In the wake of that contribution, however, there has been a temptation among his followers to become preoccupied with the linguistic signifier to the exclusion of the register of images. If psychoanalysis is aptly described as a "talking cure," it is also well characterized as a science of phantasy, an archaeology of the image. Indeed, Lacan's most valuable contribution consists not simply in putting the "function and field of speech and language" back into the talking cure but of complementing the category of the symbolic with that of the imaginary and in locating the essential subject matter of psychoanalysis in the dynamic relation between the two. A major concern of this book is a careful mapping of that relation. Toward that end, we begin this chapter with a closer examination of the Lacanian imaginary.

Lacan was most preoccupied with the imaginary during the earliest period of his work. In subsequent decades he turned greater interest toward the symbolic and the real. This evolution has led some commentators to suppose that the Lacanian concern for the signifier can be neatly separated from the imaginary. In view of this trend it is necessary to remind ourselves of Lacan's insistence upon the absolutely integral relation of the three registers, which he likened to the three interlocking rings of a Borromean knot. Far from leaving the imaginary behind in the course of an increasing involvement with linguistics, Lacan remains at every point in dialogue with it. Philippe Julien is right to say that "the teaching of Lacan is, from start to finish, a debate with the imaginary."[1] Only by returning to the concept of the imaginary can we adequately grasp the distinctive contribution of the linguistic signifier and, in turn, chart the relation of the first two registers to that of the crucial third category, the real.

The path to Lacan's conception of the imaginary passed through Henri Wallon's theory of the infant's mirroring relation to the other. In fact, Lacan borrowed the term "mirror stage" from Wallon.[2] Yet Lacan clearly took over Wallon's idea for his own purposes, radicalizing many basic points in the process. Like Wallon, Lacan emphasizes the prematurity of the human newborn and the lack of motor coordination that continues throughout the first half year of life. But Lacan adds a reference to the findings of the Gestalt psychologists and places greater stress on the unifying function of the image. What the prematurely born human being discovers in the imaginary gestalt is above all a mobilizing and enabling schema of unity.

> What I have called the *mirror stage* is interesting in that it man-
> ifests the affective dynamism by which the subject originally
> identifies himself with the visual *Gestalt* of his own body: in
> relation to the still very profound lack of co-ordination of his
> own motility, it represents an ideal of unity, a salutory *imago*; it
> is invested with all the original distress resulting from the child's
> intra-organic and relational discordance during the first six
> months, when he bears the signs, neurological and humoral, of a
> physiological natal prematuration. (E:S, 18-19)

Directly or indirectly, the unifying power of the imaginary gestalt is the central point around which turns everything else in Lacan's concep-tion of the imaginary function. It is in respect of this function of unity that the imaginary assumes a status in the human being that it does not have in animals. As Lacan points out, the work of Konrad Lorenz, Nikolaas Tinbergen and others have shown the influence of imaginary mechanisms on the behavior of animals up and down the evolutionary ladder. Among many species of fish, birds, and mammals, behaviors of parade, territoriality, attack, courtship, and mating are regulated by the perceptual image of the other member of the species. Likewise, a quasi-imaginary function is strikingly present in many species of insects whose forms and colors play critical roles in triggering behaviors necessary for the completion of the life cycle. In human beings, however, the imaginary function of the fellow creature is subject to a profound alteration because of the prematurity of human birth. For the animal, the perceptual machinery of the imaginary is firmly rooted in instinctual automatisms. In the human neonate, by contrast, the integrated operation of instinctual schemata is lacking. In the face of this deficit of instinctual organization, the activity of perception is detached from the regulating influence of innate endowments. The elementary functions of perception, the whole battery of imaginary potentialities, are effectively orphaned. This separa-tion of human perception from instinctual guidance implies an ascen-dency of form over content at a very elementary level. The unity of the perceptual object assumes decisive importance over the particularities of the image. This difference accounts in part for the greater range of objects on which the imaginary function can be deployed in the human being. The imaginary tropisms of the animal can be deceived (the maturing pigeon, for example, whose reproductive organs will develop only with the perception of another member of its own species, can be adequately stimulated by its reflection in a mirror), but the latitude of stimuli remains extremely limited. For the human being, however, the imaginary function effects a kind of elemental, preconceptual abstraction. Perception feeds less on specific qualities of the object than on its *objectality*, its unity and stability *as an object*. Paradoxically, it is precisely this detachment of the imaginary from specific perceptions in favor of purely formal attributes that grounds the radical variability of human desire.

The imaginary seeks perceptual unities but also seeks to preserve them over time. Unlike the chimpanzee, for which an initial interest in the mirror image quickly fades, the human infant displays an ongoing fascination. Lacan compares the fixity and inertia of the formative imago of the mirror phase to a "formal stagnation (similiar to the faces of actors when a film is suddenly stopped in mid-action)" (E:S, 17). In and through this stabilizing relation to the enduring image, the path is opened to objects in general. It is for this reason that Lacan claims that the mirror phase "discloses a libidinal dynamism, which has hitherto remained problematic, as well as an ontological structure of the human world. . . . [T]he mirror-image would seem to be threshold of the visible world" (E:S, 2-3). The imaginary relation establishes the mold in which the human relation to objects assumes a permanence and stability that are not present in animals. Indeed, in comparison with the imaginary structure in which fixed and stable objects are given to human perception, the animal cannot be said to relate itself to discrete objects at all. The functioning of the imaginary in the human being is therefore said by Lacan to be

> akin to the most general structure of human knowledge; that which constitutes the ego and its objects with attributes of permanance, identity, and substantiality, in short, with entities or 'things' that are very different from the *Gestalten* that experience enables us to isolate in the shifting field, stretched in accordance with the lines of animal desire.

In fact, this formal fixation, which introduces a certain rupture of level, a certain discord between man's organization and his *Umwelt*, is the condition that extends indefinitely his world and his power. (E:S, 17)

Lacan's conception of the imaginary recasts key points in the Freudian theory of the drive. It helps clarify, for example, the liminal character of the drive, located on the threshold between the somatic and the properly psychological. Freud carefully distinguished between the pure force of the drive (*Drang*) as an upsurge of biological forces or excitations (*Reizen*) and the mental representation in which those forces become psychically operative. Without attachment to the *Triebrepräsentanz*, or instinctual representative, the force of the drive remains utterly unknowable. It becomes psychically effective only by means of a psychical proxy or delegate. Thus Freud claims that

> the antithesis of conscious and unconscious is not applicable to instincts. An instinct can never become an object of consciousness—only the idea that represents the instinct can. Even in the unconscious, moreover, an instinct cannot be represented otherwise than by an idea. If the instinct did not attach itself to an idea or manifest itself as an affective state, we could know nothing about it. (SE, 14:177)

The chaotic impulses of the prematurely born human infant, particularly the forces of sexual energies, are organized for the first time in imaginary formations. Thus Lacan asserts that "the libidinal drive is centered on the function of the imaginary" (S.I, 79). Yet in being fixed in relation with an imaginary presentation, the force of the drive becomes subject to a radical contingency and can no longer be said to correspond to a naturally occurring need.[3] In view of this primordial denaturalizing of impulse in which somatic energies become subject to representation in the imaginary, the drive in the human being can no longer be compared to the predetermined responses to stimuli that characterize animal instincts. For that reason, the common translation of Freud's *Trieb* as "instinct" is more than misleading, it misses the real point of Freud's concept altogether. "What [Freud] calls *Trieb*," argues Lacan, "is quite different from an instinct" (E:S, 236). When it is a matter of referring to the innate character of animal behaviors, Freud uses the term *Instinkt*, not *Trieb*. What differentiates the Freudian *Trieb* from any animal behavior is its detachment from biological need and from any naturally designated object of satisfaction. Indeed, Freud went so far as to claim that, for the *Trieb*, the choice of object is finally a matter of indifference. It is in this sense that the entirety of human sexuality may be said to be perverse. By virtue of its insertion into the imaginary, the sexual impulse is deviated from any purely natural aim and object. At one point, Lacan proposes to translate the Freudian Trieb by "*dérive*," thus Frenchifying the English "drive" with a word that connotes a deflection and turning-aside, but also a sense of continual drift. The life of human desire, contrary to the specificity of animal need, moves *à la dérive*: having been loaded aboard the imaginary, it floats off down the river.

Our review of the Lacanian concept of the imaginary helps to clarify another point in the Freud's theory of the drive and of the unconscious in general: what Freud called its timelessness. As we have seen, the imaginary remains distinct from its function in animals owing to the temporal inertia of its objects. The "formal stagnation" of the human imaginary distinguishes it from the "shifting field . . . of animal desire." What differentiates the drive discovered by psychoanalysis from any biological function is its *constancy*.

> What exactly does Freud mean by *Trieb*? Is he referring to something whose agency is exercised at the level of the organism in its totality? Does the real qua totality irrupt here? Are we concerned here with the living organism? No. . . . [T]he characteristic of the drive is to be a *konstante Kraft*, a constant force.
>
> The constancy of the thrust forbids any assimilation of the drive to a biological function, which always has a rhythm. The first thing Freud says about the drive is, if I may put it this way, that it has no day or night, no spring or autumn, no rise and fall. It is a constant force. (FFC, 164-65)

The central value of Lacan's conception of the imaginary consists in retrieving the genuine meaning of Freud's theory of the ego. The principle features of Lacan's approach, which seeks to recapitulate "the fundamental fact which analysis teaches us . . . that the ego is an imaginary function," are already present to a remarkable extent in Freud's text on narcissism. Thus Lacan remarks that the very choice of the term "narcissism," with its reference to erotic enthrallment with the mirror image, "reveals in those who invented it the most profound awareness of semantic latencies" (E:S, 6). The theory of the mirror stage enables Lacan to make new sense of Freud's insistence that "a unity comparable to the ego cannot exist in the individual from the start; the ego has to develop" (SE: 14:76-77). The libidinal investment in the primitive ego carves an enduring organization out of the polymorphous perversity of infantile impulse. Lacan's theory of the mirror stage precisely explains this process by revealing the origin of the ego as a transcendence of the primal chaos of prematurity. The idea that the primitive ego coalesces around the perceptual gestalt of the other makes new sense of Freud's claim that "there must be something added to auto-erotism—a new psychical action—in order to bring about narcissism" (SE, 14:77).

If the Lacanian concept of the imaginary coincides in these ways with the general outline of Freud's account of the ego's origin and nature, many of the particulars of Lacan's idea are also reflected in Freud's text. The prematurity of human birth is a case in point. Freud, too, accorded crucial significance to the "unfinished state" in which the human infant is born into the world. In seeking to identify the factors that predispose the human being to neurosis in *Inhibitions, Symptoms, and Anxiety*, Freud offers three considerations: one phylogenetic, one psychological, and one biological. The phylogenetic factor concerns the supposition of an inherited propensity to guilt, the legacy of the murder of the primal father of perhistory. The second, psychological factor is the formation of the ego itself as distinct from the id and in conflict with it. The third factor, relevant to the genesis of the ego, is the biological fact of the unparalleled helplessness and dependency of the human infant.

> The biological factor is the long period of time during which the young of the human species is in a condition of helplessness and dependence. Its intra-uterine existence seems to be short in comparison with that of most animals, and it is sent into the world in a less than finished state. As a result, the influence of the real external world upon it is intensified and an early diffentiation between the ego and the id is promoted. (SE, 20:154-55)

Lacan's stress on the privileged role of the body image is also an echo of key points in Freud's own description of the origin of the ego. Freud related the function of the ego, always centered on defense, to the protective integument of the body and to its role in demarcating the boundary of self and world. Yet the visual sense of the body's wholeness clearly comes to play the decisive role in establishing the groundlines of subjective identity. In *The Ego and the Id*, Freud puts the emphasis on this visual aspect. "The ego," he says, "is first and foremost a bodily ego, it is not merely a surface entity, but is itself the projection of a surface" (SE, 19:26).

The Lacanian notion of the imaginary illuminates the deep correspondence of ego and object that must be counted among Freud's most basic working assumptions. What is at stake is the bipolarity of the ego and its objects, from one point of view a relation of mutual exclusion, from another viewpoint a relation of co-constitution. We glimpse this bipolar relation in Freud's notion of a seesaw of libidinal investment between the ego and the object, the dynamic he compares at one point to an amoeba's extension of pseudopodia. Libido may be pooled in the ego itself or thrust outward to invest objects in the world. The ego and the object thus form the twin loci of the most basic economy of cathexis. This polarity opens up the possibility of a whole series of psychical acts, such as turning round upon the self, in which an affective disposition toward an object is reversed upon the ego itself; or projection, in which something belonging to the subject is disowned by the ego and attributed to the object outside it.

Lacan's conception of the imaginary expresses another point in Freud that tends to be less explicitly spelled out but that remains central to the underlying assumptions of psychoanalysis: the resistance of the ego to change. As the system around which the stability of psychic identity is maintained, the ego strives by its very nature to remain unaffected by changing circumstances. Indeed, both before and after the introduction of the theory of the dual drives, Freud associated the ego with the self-preservative drive. Lacan, too, emphasizes the recalictrance of the imaginary ego to change. "One cannot stress too strongly," he suggests, "the irreducible character of the narcissistic structure" (E:S, 24). The process of psychical maturation cannot eliminate but can at best produce a transformation in this narcissistic substructure. "The narcissistic moment in the subject is to be found in all the genetic phases of the indivdual, in all the degrees of human accomplishment in the person" (E:S, 24).

Imaginary Alienation

The imaginary identification of the mirror stage is formative and enabling but also deeply alienating. Paradoxically, the subject is estranged from itself in the very moment in which it achieves a measure of self-representation. Alienation is not merely an effect or by-product of the imaginary identification, it is its very essence. "Alienation is constitutive of the imaginary order," says Lacan. "Alienation is the imaginary as such" (S. III, 146).

> The first effect which appears from the *image* in the human being is an *alienation* of the subject. It is in the other that the subject first identifies and makes certain of himself—a phenomenon that is less surprising when we remember the fundamentally social conditions of the human *Umwelt*—and if one evokes the intuition which dominates the entire speculation of Hegel.[4]

Lacan's notion of alienation is absolutely fundamental to everything in his thought. Indeed, it is no exaggeration to say that the alienating character of the narcissistic ego is the foundation on which the Lacanian reappropriation of psychoanalysis is based. "Psychoanalysis alone," says Lacan, "recognizes the knot of imaginary servitude that love must always undo again, or sever" (E:S, 7). This labor of love, as Freud taught, is realized in and through the transference, itself a form of love, but only insofar as it is mediated by the act of speech. It is the contribution of the symbolic that counters the alienating effect of the imaginary. The keynote of Lacan's sensibility is therefore audible in his claim that "imaginary incidences, far from representing the essence of our experience, reveal only what in it remains inconsistent unless they are related to the symbolic chain which binds and orients them."[5] The following series of passages well illustrate this point:

> What is my desire? What is my position in the imaginary structuration? This position is only conceivable in so far as one finds a guide beyond the imaginary, on the level of the symbolic plane, of the legal exchange which can only be embodied in the verbal exchange between human beings. (S.I, 141)

> The relation of the subject to his *Urbild*, his *Idealich*, through which he enters into the imaginary function and learns to recog-

nize himself as a form, can always see-saw. Each time the subject apprehends himself as form and as ego, each time that he
constitutes himself in his status, his stature, his static, his desire
is projected outside. From whence arises the impossibility of all
human coexistence. . . . But, thank God, the subject inhabits the
world of the symbol, that is to say a world of others who speak.
That is why his desire is susceptible to the mediation of recognition. Without which every human function would simply
exhaust itself in the unspecified wish for the destruction of the
other as such. (S.I, 171)

Speech is that dimension through which the desire of the subject is authentically integrated on to the symbolic plane. (S.I,
183)

What, then, is alienating about the imaginary? The standard explanatory reference is to Hegel's dialectic of lordship and bondage. For both
Lacan and Hegel, the pathway to the first objects of desire is inevitably
oriented by the desire of the other. "The object of man's desire," claims
Lacan, "and we are not the first to say this, is essentially an object desired
by someone else."[6] The primoridal confusion of self and other supposed by
this view seems well evidenced by the phenomenon of infantile transitivism. Transitivism refers to the tendency of many young children to mistake the other's experience for their own. After hitting another child, for
example, the two-year-old may complain of being hit. The same child may
burst into tears at the sight of another child falling down.

But the usefulness of the reference to Hegel has its limits. The
Hegelian model relates the dawn of self-consciousness to the struggle for
recognition between competing subjects. It is an alienation of the individual in the social other. This perspective is well summed up by Anika
Lemaire: "Alienation is the fact of giving up a part of oneself to another.
The alienated man lives outside of himself."[7] But there is another aspect
of alienation that is not well accounted for in this picture. As Lacan says
of it,

it may be no bad thing to see what the root of this celebrated
alienation really is. Does it mean, as I seem to be saying, that
the subject is condemned to seeing himself emerge, *in initio,*

only in the field of the Other? Could it be that? Well it isn't. Not at all—not at all—not at all. (FFC, 210)

Consideration of the alienation between two individuals must be supplemented by recognition of a more fundamental alienation of the subject from itself. We must make sense of the fact, as Lacan puts it, that "the spatial captation of the mirror-stage, *even before the social dialectic,* [is] the effect in man of an organic insufficiency" and that the imaginary form "situates the agency of the ego, *before its social determination,* in a fictional direction" (E:S, 4 and 2, emphases added). "It is clear," claims Lacan, "that the structured effect of identification with the rival is not self-evident, except on the level of fable, and can only be conceived of by a primary identification that structures the subject as a rival with himself" (E:S, 22). This internal dimension of alienation is the distance that separates the form of the *ego* from the desire of the *subject.*

The form [of the imago] situates the agency of the ego, before its social determination, in a fictional direction which will always remain irreducible for the individual alone, or rather, which will only rejoin the coming-into-being (*le devenir*) of the subject asymptotically, whatever the success of the dialectical syntheses by which he must resolve as I his discordance with his own reality. (E:S, 2)

Lacan's stress on the opposition between the ego and the subject can be understood as a strong reading of Freud's view of the ego as essentially inhibitory, that of "an organized, progressive filtering," the purpose of which is to select and diminish the stimuli impinging upon the psychic apparatus, from within the organism as well as from without (S.I, 107). An essential characteristic of the imaginary thus consists in its capacity to represent only a portion of the organism's vital energies. When we compare the imaginary form to the totality of the living being, Lacan claims, we are forced to conclude that "everything limits [the ego] with respect to the being which it represents, since almost the whole of the life of the organism escapes it, not only in so far as that life is normally misrecognized by the ego, but in that for the most part it doesn't have to be known by the ego" (E, 179-80). An effect of alienation is produced insofar as the formations of the imaginary must positively exclude some portion of the pulsional energy that animates the body. "The *Urbild* of this formation is alienating . . . by virtue of its capacity to render extraneous" (E:S, 21). "The ego makes itself manifest there as defense, as refusal" (S.I, 53). Lacan thus compares the ego to a fundamental constriction, a kind of bottleneck, in the impulse life of the organism.

> The original notion of the totality of the body as ineffable, as lived, the initial outburst of appetite and desire comes about in the human subject via the mediation of a form which he at first sees projected, external to himself, and at first, in his own reflection. . . . Man knows that he is a body—although he never perceives it in a complete fashion, since he is inside it, but he lives it. This image is the ring, the bottle-neck, through which the confused bundle of desires and needs must pass in order to be him, that is to say in order to accede to his imaginary structure. (S.I, 176)

For Lacan, the imaginary ego remains by its very nature inimical to desire. The ego is characterized by "its essential resistance to the elusive process of Becoming, to the variations of Desire."[8] Two important consequences accrue from this opposition between the ego and the desire of the subject. The first concerns the influence of the ego on perception and consciousness. As a result of the ego's defensive posture, the subject's perceptions of itself, others, and the world around it are submitted to a systematic distortion. Perception by the ego is continual misperception or *méconnaissance*. "That the ego hasn't a clue about the subject's desires," says Lacan, ". . . is called misrecognition (*méconnaissance*)" (S.I, 167). The imaginary sees in order not to see. The ego continually devotes itself to a stereotyped picture of reality, indeed, the tendency toward stereotypy belongs to the very essence of the imaginary function.

Correlative with this effect of systematic distortion is a second consequence that involves the economy of the subject's drives and impulse energies. The formation of the ego effects a primordial bifurcation in the field of the organism's vital energies. Psychical identity is established only at the price of a splitting of the subject, in accordance with which an organized unity is opposed to an anarchic and heterogeneous remainder. Thus Lacan claims that the entire dialectic which I have given you . . . under the name of the *mirror stage* is based on the relation between, on the one hand, a certain level of tendencies which are experienced—let us say, for the moment, at a certain point in life—as disconnected, discordant, in pieces—and there's always something of that that remains—and on the other hand, a unity with which it is merged and paired. It is in this unity that the subject for the first time knows himself as a unity, but as an alienated, virtual unity. (S.II, 50)

The importance to Lacan of this opposition between the structure of the ego and the heterogeneous pulsionality of the organism, the very ground of its being, can hardly be overestimated. As he says of it, "this discordance between the ego and being will be the fundamental note which will be retained in the whole harmonic scale which, through the phases of psychic history, will function to resolve it by developing it" (E, 187). The fixed and constant structure of the ego, a structure that in Lacan's view has appropriately been called a "character armor," inevitably becomes an impediment to the free discharge of incipient drive energies. Lacan thus claims that the imaginary ego "turns the I into that apparatus for which every instinctual thrust constitutes a danger, even though it should correspond to a natural maturation" (E:S, 5-6). In this way, the establishment of imaginary identity alienates the subject from its own future. With respect to the desire of the subject, the influence of the ego always puts time "out of joint." Referring to the imaginary unity of the ego, Lacan asks "how can one not conceive that each great instinctual metamorphosis in the life of the individual will once again challenge its delimitation, composed as it of a conjunction of the subject's history and the unthinkable innateness of his desire?" (E:S, 19-20).

It is not difficult to see that the Lacanian distinction between the ego and the subject's desire parallels the Freudian dichotomy between the ego and the id, in which a partial and specialized organization is split off from a larger chaos of pulsional energies. So why not stick with the Freudian terms? The first part of the answer lies in Lacan's polemic against the ego psychological tradition that centers the personality upon the ego and equates the adaptive functions of the ego with the "self." "[Freud] wrote *Das Ich und Das Es*," Lacan claims, "in order to maintain this fundamental distinction between the true subject of the unconscious and the ego as constituted in its nucleus by a series of alienating identifications" (E:S, 128). By linking the Freudian *Es* with the subject, an association betokened for Lacan by the way the German word is heard in the first letter of "*sujet*," Lacan reemphasizes the fundamental scandal discovered by psychoanalysis, namely, that the core of our being (*die Kern unseres Wesens*) is unconscious. The being of the subject, far from being exhausted by the system of its compromises with the reality of the world outside it, remains a perpetually unanswered question, a task to be completed, a path the origin of which recedes with each step taken along its course. But in addition, Lacan is leery of the way in which Freud's description of the id as a seething cauldron of instinctual energies tempts us to postulate a vitalist substratum at the motive origin of subjectivity. What prohibits such a vitalist appeal is Lacan's insistence that human desire is radically distanced from any organic determination by virtue of its dependence upon the signifier. The Freudian *Es* might thus be compared homophonically not only with the initial letter of *sujet* but also with the "S" of the signifier, whose slippage along the signifying chain describes for Lacan the very essence of the primary process.

If Lacan distances himself somewhat from the Freudian terminology of the id, it nevertheless remains crucial for Lacan, as it was for Freud, to locate the pulsional sources of the subject's desire in some dimension beyond the bounds of the ego. In Freud's idiom, this dimension was designated by energtics, and in particular by the notion of free or unbound energy in contrast to the bound cathexis of the ego. Although he does not often utilize the language of energetics, Lacan is far from failing to appreciate its significance for Freud's theory. "Freud's innovation," Lacan writes in his dissertation on paranoid psychosis, "seems to us capital in that it brings to psychology an *energetic* notion, which provides a common measure to very diverse phenomena. In fact," he continues,

> the notion of *libido* reveals itself in Freud's doctrine as an
> extremely broad theoretical entity, which far outstrips the spe-
> cialized sexual desire of the adult. It tends to identify itself
> rather with desire, the eros of antiquity taken in a very extended
> sense, namely as the ensemble of appetites in the human being
> which surpass the strict limits of conservation. . . . For all the

relative imprecision of the concept of libido, it seems to us to retain its value.[9]

The energetic metaphor allows psychoanalytic theory to postulate the transmission of psychical value between very different representations and to conceptualize a surplus of excitation forever excluded from the system of representations. It is this double function of the energetic metaphor that grounds Freud's project of metapsychology but at the same time makes energetics an essentially metaphysical idea. Energy is a wholly indeterminate quantity, a pure factor "X," which serves to mark a source of motion and activity that cannot be otherwise specified.

> That becomes completely mysterious—we are absolutely igno-
> rant as to what it might mean, to say that there's an equivalence
> of energy between the internal pressure, tied to the equilibrium
> of the organism, and what results from it. So what use does it
> serve? It's an X, which, after having been used as a starting
> point, is totally abandoned. (S.II, 106-7)

The energetic assumption, or something like it, must be assumed, says Lacan, because "to draw the rabbit out of the hat, you always have to have put it in beforehand. . . . That is the principle of energetics, and that is why energetics is also a metaphysics" (S.II, 61). Yet talk of psychical energy opens the door to a reified organicism, leaving us prey to "the need we have . . . to confuse the *Stoff*, or primitive matter, or impulse, or flux, or tendency with what is really at stake in the exercise of the analytic reality."[10] Why, then, must we speak of energy at all? The problem is one of knowing how to refer to the reality of the drives before they are symbolically represented. "If, for lack of representation, [the *Trieb*] is not there," asks Lacan, "what is this *Trieb*? We may have to consider it as being only *Trieb* to come" (FFC, 60). "I am not at all trying to deny here that there is something which is before," Lacan says elsewhere, "that, for example, before I come into being, there was something, the It was. It is simply a matter of knowing what is that It."[11]

In order to avoid the pitfalls of Freud's metaphor of energetics yet do justice to its conceptual necessity, Lacan thinks the basic issues at stake in his own terms: that of the real. The real is a notion of pure force that remains wholly unknowable in itself. The real is precisely what is never fully assimilable in the imaginary or in the symbolic. The real, says Lacan, is the impossible. It bears a special, inverse relationship to the imaginary. In the primordial partitioning of inner and outer effected by the imaginary, the real is the primitively excluded, the rejected, the spit out, the *Aufgestosst*. In the establishment of the primitive ego, "the distinction is drawn between what is included in the narcissistic structure and what isn't. It is at the seam where the imaginary joins the real that the differentiation takes place" (S.II, 98). Imaginary and real thus stand to one another in a relation of mutual exclusion. Indeed, the very function of the imaginary is to institute a boundary of inclusion and exclusion. "In so far as one part of reality is imagined," says Lacan, "the other is real and inversely, in so far as one is reality, the other becomes imaginary" (S.I, 82). The real and the imaginary therefore become comparable to the noncoincidence of mathematical sets for which "the conjunction of different parts, of sets, can never be accomplished" (S.I, 83). What is excluded, remaindered, and alienated by the imaginary is in the first place something of the subject's own being, a portion of the vital energies that animate the living organism. Lacan will therefore claim that "psychoanalysis involves the real of the body and the imaginary of its mental schema" (E:S, 302).

If the real is radically unknowable, if it remains forever unimageable and unsymbolizable, in what way can we speak of it at all? The question recalls our earlier discussion of Heidegger's reflection about the role of the Nothing in metaphysics. On the level of abstract discussion, the notion of the real, like that of Heidegger's Nothing, can only generate paradox and aporia. But, like the Nothing, the actuality of the real is attested to by a fundamental human experience: that of anxiety. In fact, Heidegger and Freud define anxiety in a remarkably similar way. For both thinkers, anxiety is distinct from fear because it has less to do with the approach of a threatening object than it does with the *lack* of an object. Moreover, both Heidegger and Freud assert the primacy of anxiety. Anxiety is transformed into fear, says Freud, "if it has found an object" (SE, 20:105). For Heidegger, "fear is anxiety, fallen into the 'world,' inauthentic, and, as such, hidden from itself" (BT, 234). In the context of our present discussion, we may add a crucial point with the help of Lacanian categories. It is in anxiety that the subject comes closest to a pure experience of the real. But according to the most basic of Lacan's definitions of it, the upsurge of anxiety occurs in the breakdown of imaginary coherence. "This illusion of unity," says Lacan of the imaginary, "in which a human being is always looking forward to self-mastery, entails a constant danger of slipping back into the chaos from which he started; it hangs over the abyss of a dizzy Assent in which one can perhaps see the very essence of Anxiety."[12] We have only to put these two points together to arrive at an essential insight that we will further develop in subsequent discussions: the real erupts in the disintegration of the imaginary. The real affords no direct engagement and no positive characterization but is encountered only in the negation of the imaginary. The real is experienceable only in the loss of an imaginary unity, a collapse into the *corps morcelé*.

Lacan playfully evokes the real in his fable of the *lamelle*. Lacan's answer to the creation myth of Aristophanes retold in Plato's *Symposium*, the *lamelle* is "intended to embody the missing part," that is, to embody that portion of the real that escapes organization in the imaginary. Lacan compares it to the placenta or to the fluids that burst forth when an egg is opened. "Let us imagine," he says, "that each time the membranes are ruptured, by the same issue a phantom flies off which has a form infinitely more primary than life" (E, 845). In Freudian terms, this phantom-being that slips away at the birth of the imaginary subject is a pure extract of undifferentiated drive energies. The *lamelle*, says Lacan, "is the *libido, qua* pure life instinct, life that has need of no organ, simplified, indestructible life" (FFC, 198). Divided and separated from the ego, utterly undifferentiated and inarticulate, the *lamelle* remains foreign and uncanny. Yet it continues to haunt the subject, indeed, like the slip of feathery tissue surrounding the main body mass of certain molluscs from which it takes its name, the *lamelle* remains tethered to the subject by a strange attachment. Lacan compares it to an organ, albeit a "false organ," a paradoxical organ whose "character is not to exist" (FFC, 197-98). "This organ ought to be called irreal, in the sense in which irreal is not imaginary, and precedes the subjectivity that it conditions by being in direct contact with the real" (E, 847). Lacan pictures the *lamelle* as active and seeking, like the "Blob" of cut-rate horror movies or, as Lacan suggests, like "a large crêpe which spreads out like an amoeba, ultra-flat in order to pass under doors, omniscient as it is guided by the pure instinct of life, immortal as it is capable of splitting itself" (E, 845). That this ontological slime tends to revisit the subject whose very identity was established by rejecting it provides a parable of the way the real is excluded by the imaginary, yet inevitably returns in the upsurge of anxiety. "Here's something," says Lacan, "you wouldn't want to feel silently slipping over your face while you're sleeping" (E, 845).

Aggressivity and the Death Drive

Closely linked with imaginary alienation is a fundamental human predisposition to aggression and destructiveness. Part of what Lacan has in mind are the fantasies of bodily dismemberment, amply evidenced across a spectrum of experiences, from the most murderous atrocity to childrens' play, which display spectacular violations of the bodily gestalt. The opening and mutilation of the body fascinates even as it horrifies. The stream of motorists slows down in the vicinity of a serious car accident—to see what? Plato cites the antique equivalent of such "rubbernecking" in the *Republic*. Passing by the place of execution where the bodies of slain criminals were laid out in the open, Leontius found the scene repulsive but could not resist gaping at it. "With wide, staring eyes, he rushed up to the corpses and cried, 'There, ye wretches, take your fill of the fine spectacle.'"[13] It is with these sorts of examples in mind that Lacan envisages "a *Gestalt* proper to aggression in man . . . the images of castration, mutilation, dismemberment, dislocation, evisceration, devouring, bursting open of the body, in short, the *imagos* that I have grouped together under the apparently structural term of *images of the fragmented body*" (E:S, 11-12).

Imaginary aggressivity is attracted to the *scene* of dismemberment, yet, properly understood, this propensity to aggression is ultimately less an urge to destroy the other than it is an impulse to destroy oneself. It results from the tension between the ego and the subject of the unconscious that follows upon the imaginary structuring of identity. Aggressivity is thus said to be "a correlative tension of the narcissistic structure in the coming-to-be (*devenir*) of the subject" (E:S, 22). Lacan insists that "the aggressiveness involved in the ego's fundamental relationship to other people . . . is based upon the *intra-psychic* tension we sense in the warning of the ascetic that 'a blow at your enemy is a blow at yourself.'"[14] Sadism must ultimately be traced back to a more fundamental masochism. "For a sadistic fantasy to endure, the subject's interest in the person who suffers humiliation must obviously be due to the possibility of the subject's being submitted to the same humiliation himself. . . . It's a wonder indeed that people could ever think of avoiding this dimension and could treat the sadistic tendency as an instance of primal aggression pure and simple."[15]

Positing the essential link between the imaginary and aggression, and bringing to light its essential self-destructiveness, Lacan regrasps the meaning of the Freudian death drive. "The point emphasized by Freud's thought, but [that] isn't fully made out in *Beyond the Pleasure Principle*," he suggests, "[is that] the death instinct in man [signifies] that his libido is originally constrained to pass through an imaginary stage" (S.I, 149). For Lacan, the disintegrating force of the death drive is aimed not at the integrity of the biological organism, as Freud had concluded, but rather at the imaginary coherence of the ego. "Freudian biology," says Lacan, "has nothing to do with biology" (S.II, 75). It is not simply a biological force but rather the alienating character of the ego, the *distance* between biological force and psychical structure, that sets in motion the obscure impulse toward self-immolation. "This life we're captive of, this essentially alienated life, existing, this life in the other, is as such joined to death, it always returns to death" (S.II, 233).

Lacan's reworking of this essential point of Freud's theory avoids many of the paradoxes and near contradictions of Freud's supposition of an elemental tendency, inherent in all organic matter, to return to an inorganic state.[16] It also allows Lacan to find in the desire for death the paradigm of all desire. The emergence of desire is always linked with a certain disintegration of imaginary coherence, the breakdown of the narcissistic ego and a challenging of its boundaries. "The function of desire," claims Lacan, "must remain in a fundamental relationship to death" (S.VII, 303). "[Freud] questioned life as to its meaning and not to say that it has none . . . but to say that it has only one meaning, that in which desire is borne by death" (E:S, 277). It is for this reason that Lacan asserts a paradoxical identity between the death drive and the realization of a fuller vitality. The path toward a fuller access to the desire of the subject necessarily passes by way of a deconstruction of its imaginary anchorage. The concept of the death drive thus harbors a basic ambiguity. "It is not enough to decide on the basis of its effect—Death. It still remains to be decided which death, that which is brought by life or that which brings life."

As a moment's reflection shows, the notion of the death instinct involves a basic irony, since its meaning has to be sought in the conjunction ot two terms: instinct in its most comprehensive acceptation being the law that governs in its succession the cycle of behavior whose goal is the accomplishment of a vital function; and death appearing first of all as the destruction of life. (E:S, 101)

The Lacanian interpretation of the death drive makes new sense of key elements of Freud's conception. It makes explicable, for example, why death remains only indirectly capable of representation. There is no positive and particular representation of death, not only because the time and manner of our own demise is unknowable, but because death in the Freudian sense is essentially the breaking apart of an imaginary unity, the disintegration of an organized whole. It is for this reason that the death drive is rightly said to be mute. Where Eros conspicuously displays itself in a parade of lures, the work of the death drive is evidenced only in impinging destructively upon the formations of Eros. It is its purely negative character that links the death drive to anxiety. "If it is difficult to conceptually grasp the death drive," Serge Leclaire has remarked, "at least we have in anxiety the experience of being grasped by its force."[17]

Lacan's reconception, which relates the death drive to the alienating character of the imaginary structure, furnishes a simple and elegant explanation of a further, crucial point of Freud's thinking. Freud unambiguously conceived the death drive as a self-destructive impulse whose ultimate aim was utter dissolution of the individual. Yet Freud also insisted that aggression and destructiveness aimed at others are attributable to the operation of the death drive. To have it both ways, it was necessary to suppose a mechanism by which the self-directed force of the death drive could be turned outward toward someone or something else. Freud supposed that the destructive potential of the death drive was turned from its original aim under the influence of the self-protective motive of the erotic drive. Accordingly, sadism could be understood as a projecting outward, in the interests of self-preservation, of an original masochism. The Lacanian conception of the imaginary as an essentially binary, mirroring relation, supplies a ready means by which Freud's notion of projection outward can be understood. Because the gestalt unity constitutive of the imaginary organization is originally found in the body of the other, the phantasmatic dismemberment of the other inevitably implicates the subject itself. On the level of infantile transitivism, murder and suicide amount to the same thing. The imaginary relation binds the subject to an "other which isn't an other at all, since it is essentially coupled with the ego, in a relation that is always reflexive, interchangeable" (S.II, 321).

But we have yet to draw the most important consequence of Lacan's shifted perspective. For the Lacanian approach fulfills Freud's intention to offer the dialectic of the two primal drives as the twin poles which structure the entirety of the psychic field. The challenge of Freud's original hypothesis of the death drive was to conceive the life of the mind as an ongoing interaction between the two great tendencies of binding and unbinding. Eros is the great builder, the force of agglutination by which self and object are constituted. The death drive, by contrast, effects the disintegration of what Eros has bound together. The theoretical couplet of binding and unbinding thus forms the very spine of Freud's metapsychology, comparable to the Empedoclean dualism of Love and Strife. But to what exactly do the dynamics of binding and unbinding refer? In Lacanian terms, psychical binding is identifiable with the structuring power of the imaginary. It is by means of the imaginary that fixity and constancy are introduced into the psychic system. Correlatively, the unbinding force of the death drive represents the disintegrating return of the real against the strictures of the imaginary. This reformulation has two main advantages.

1. While it requires rejecting Freud's biologizing of the death drive, the Lacanian view makes new sense of Freud's insistence that the relation of the two primal drives represents an absolutely elemental conflict. The conflict that activates the death drive is not to be situated between the living and the non-living, but between what is psychically bound and what remains to be organized by binding. The conflictual dynamic of the life and death drives is thus rooted in the dichotomy of ego and the id. The death drive is set in motion, not by an obscure tropism toward the inorganic, but by the alienating institution of psychical identity in the ego. It is for this reason that Lacan remarks that *Beyond the Pleasure Principle*, far from being "a mere sideshow . . . is precisely the prelude to the new topography respresented by the terms *ego, id,* and *super-ego*" (E. 44-45).

2. When the life and death drives are reconceived in terms of the binding power of the imaginary in active tension with the unbound excess of the real, the interaction of the two primal drives becomes more readily discernible in every increment of the psychic process. The metabolism of

the psychical apparatus becomes identifiable with a ceaseless cycle of formation and deformation. Unities are continually crystallized by the action of imaginary fusion, broken apart by the effects of the death drive, and congealed once again in new forms. In this way, the underlying dialectic discovered by psychoanalysis, compared by Freud to the Empedoclean struggle of *Philia* and *Neikos*, comes even more suggestively to resemble Anaximander's meditation on the dialectic of the Limited and the Unlimited, the *Peras* and the *Apeiron*. In the vision of Anaximander, the coming-into-being and passing away of all things is attributed to the intercourse of these two great governing principles. Like the death drive, said by Freud to constitute the more primordial of the two basic drives, and like the Lacanian real, whose status as a dark origin is never exhausted either by the imaginary or the symbolic, the Unlimited is for Anaximander more elemental and archaic than the principle of Limit. Determinate beings are carved out of the Unlimited by the defining action of Limit, only to be reclaimed, in the fullness of time, by the maelstrom of the Unlimited. The famous fragment of Anaximander thus declares that "the Unlimited is the first-principle of things that are. It is that from which the coming to be of things takes place, and it is that into which they return when they perish, by moral necessity . . . according to the order of time." Toward the end of *Civilization and Its Discontents,* Freud refers to the epochal struggle between the life and death drives by citing Goethe's paraphrase of the Anaximander fragment: "For all things, from the Void called forth, deserve to be destroyed" (SE, 21:120).

The Agency of Death in the Signifier

In the preceding discussion, we located the Freudian death drive in the pressure of the real against the alienating structure of the imaginary. The "death" at stake is the death of the imaginary ego. The impact of the real on the imaginary organization constitutes, in Lacanian terms, the very essence of trauma. To this account, we must now add another crucial point, according to which the death drive is associated with the agency of the symbolic. In his 1953 "Discourse at Rome," Lacan claims to "have demonstrated the profound relationship uniting the notion of the death instinct to the problems of speech" (E:S, 101). In his seminar on the psychoses, he remarks that "the nature of the symbol remains to be clarified," but adds that "we have come close to its essence by locating its genesis at the same point as that of the death instinct" (S.III, 215). Elsewhere, the death drive is said to be "only the mask of the symbolic order."

> The symbolic order is simultaneously non-being and insisting to be, that is what Freud had in mind when he talks about the death instinct as being what is most fundamental—a symbolic order in travail, in the process of coming, insisting on being realized. . . . This is the point where we open out into the symbolic order, which isn't the libidinal order in which the ego is inscribed, along with all the drives. It tends beyond the pleasure principle, beyond the limits of life, and that is why Freud identifies it with the death instinct. . . . The symbolic order is rejected by the libidinal order, which includes the whole of the domain of the imaginary, including the structure of the ego. And the death instinct is only the mask of the symbolic order." (S.II, 326)

In what sense can the function of symbols be identified with death? There are several important points to be made here.

1. The symbol is tied to death, first, because it implies the absence of the thing it represents. It is in this sense that Lacan cites Hegel's remark that "the word is the murder of the thing." "The being of language," as Lacan puts it elsewhere, "is the non-being of objects" (E:S, 263). The capacity for linguistic cognition presupposes a letting-go of the object. The ability to offer a signifying substitute implies the achievement of a certain distance and independence from the thing signified. This achievement involves a loosening of the imaginary bond to the perceptual presence of the object. The most elementary act of symbolization thus enacts an essential negation with respect to the thing symbolized. All cognition of symbols requires a concomitant awareness that the symbol is not the thing. This negative relation implied by every symbolic substitution is especially relevant for psychoanalysis to the extent that the anxiety of separation from the mothering figure becomes bound up with the process by which language is acquired. According to Lacan, it is not by accident that, along the path of his approach to the hypothesis of the death drive, Freud remarks upon the efforts of his grandson to symbolize the departure and return of his mother by means of throwing away a spool—"Fort!"—and

retrieving it—"Da!" Although Freud is unable to draw out all the implications, what Freud discovers in this drama of presence and absence is the negativity of the signifier and its relation to separation and loss.

> It is in so far as the symbolic allows this inversion, that is to say cancels the existing thing, that it opens up the world of negativity, which constitutes both the discourse of the human subject and the reality of his world in so far as it is human. Primal masochism should be located around this initial negativation, around this original murder of the thing. (S.I, 172-74)

2. The function of signification is also tied to death in another sense, relevant to a point made in the previous chapter about the special properties of the linguistic sign. Unlike the perceptual gestalt, which offers to consciousness an enduring and unitary form in the midst of a surrounding field, the linguistic sign must evacuate its own status as an image in order to fulfill its signifying function. The perceptual body of the sign is merely the point of entrance, the jumping-off point, for a structured reverberation across the network of relations that constitutes the sign system. The power of the sign to signify thus requires that the sign not be seen as an image. The life of the sign is predicated upon the death of its own image.

3. These first two points tying the symbolic function to death—that the sign implies both the murder of the thing and the death of its own image—both hinge upon the fact that the symbolic order constitutes a system. As we have already seen, it is the systemic character of the symbolic that most distinguishes it from the order of the imaginary. Produced in response to an innate endowment of sensation, the adumbration of a perceptual unity in the imaginary gestalt requires no contribution from a convention code or system of the sort that makes up a language. By contrast, the linguistic sign functions only by virtue of participating in a precisely articulated network of differences, a system of conventionally fixed relations. This imbrication within a system affects the very being of the sign. As Saussure had already remarked, not only is it exceedingly difficult to circumscribe the unity of the sign, in an important sense the sign cannot be said to be a unit at all, but must rather be understood as a selective network of relations contained within the still larger web of a language. The sign is less a unit than a system within a system.

Consideration of the sign as system leads us to a central paradox of speech and language: it is the precisely structured and lawful character of language that allows for the emergence in speech of something new and unexpected. Because language is a synchronic totality that transcends the consciousness of every speaker, to enter into the labyrinth of signs inevitably exposes the speaking subject to the possibility of an unintended consequence. It is with this in mind that Lacan claims that "what the structure of the signifying chain discloses is the possibility I have, precisely in so far as I have this language in common with other subjects, that is to say, in so far as it exists as a language, to use it in order to signify *something quite other* than what it says" (E:S, 155). Lacan would have us think here of the way in which the voice of the unconscious makes itself heard, as it does in a slip of the tongue, even in the course of the most ostensibly deliberate speech. But the point at stake can also be made in a more general manner. Even if the movement of discourse is oriented toward the unity of a single topic or perspective, a unity in which the influence of the imaginary is discernible, discourse authentically comes into its own precisely when it is not possible for the speakers to fully control its path and outcome. In accordance with its very nature, genuine discourse includes an openness to an unexpected result. Every entrance into language, every sounding of the word's call, implicitly invites the eruption of something uncalled for. Symbolically mediated exchange is therefore very aptly called "dis-course," if we hear in this word a possibility of losing or being diverted from the track of any preconceived course. Genuine discourse includes an openness to wandering, to getting lost or waylaid. This essential waywardness of the signifier, linked to what Lacan calls the "incessant sliding of the signifier," binds the functions of speech to the experience of death. Carried along by the stream of signifiers, the speaking subject can at any moment be delivered over the falls. Entrance into the signifying chain replays the essential paradox of the encounter with death: the only certainty is the presence of uncertainty.

We now see clearly the link Lacan draws between the function of speech and language and the operation of the death drive. What is "deathly" about the subject's relation to the symbolic is precisely the way in which it tends to frustrate the dream of simple coherence promised by the imaginary. In the symbolic register, there is always something further to be said, for every position there is always another reply. Every entrance into the symbolic function results in an essential incompleteness and exerts over the subject a fragmenting influence. As Lacan says of it, "life is only caught up in the symbolic piece-meal (*morcelé*), decomposed. The human being himself is in part outside life, he partakes of the death instinct" (S.II, 90). In accordance with the essential complexity of its structure, the system of signifying elements that compose a language inevitably draws every act of speech beyond the intention that animates it.

> The symbolic system is extraordinarily intricate, marked as it is by this *Verschlungenheit, property of criss-crossing,* which the translation of the papers on technique has rendered as complexity, which is, and how, much too weak. *Verschlungenheit* designates linguistic criss-crossing—every easily isolable linguistic symbol is not only at one with the totality, but is cut across and constituted by a series of overflowings, of oppositional overdeterminations which place it at one and the same time in several registers. This language system, within which our discourse makes its way, isn't it something which goes infinitely beyond every intention that we might put into it, and which, moreover, is only momentary? (S.I, 53–54)

The symbolic system forms a totality that transcends the being of every subject even as it assigns the subject its place and destiny. This system governs the unfolding of the subject's desire in a way that leads the subject beyond itself and up to the limit of its own death.

> Symbols in fact envelop the life of man in a network so total that they join together, before he comes into the world, those who are going to engender him "by flesh and blood"; so total that they bring to his birth, along with the gifts of the stars, if not with the gifts of the fairies, the shape of his destiny; so total that they give the words that will make him faithful or renegade, the law of the acts that will follow him right to the very place where he is not yet and even beyond his death; and so total that through them his end finds its meaning in the last judgement, where the Word absolves his being or condemns it—unless he attain the subjective bringing to realization of being-for-death" (E:S, 68).

We have, then, evolved two accounts of the death drive from a Lacanian point of view, first as the force of the real excluded by the imaginary economy of the ego and later as the action of the symbolic. Yet the two accounts can be neatly integrated. In both cases, it is the alienating effect of the imaginary that sets the death drive in motion. The "death" sought by the destructive drive is that of the subject's imaginary identity. But the splintering of the imaginary can be effected on either of two levels. On the one hand, it can occur wholly on the level of the imaginary. This is the brute violence of dismemberment and evisceration. Violence effects a deconstruction of the imaginary in its own terms. On the other hand, the work of death is carried on through the influence of the symbolic. The entrance of the subject into a symbolically mediated process of exchange submits the imaginary organization of the ego to a continuous pressure toward re-formation. Extended over time and regulated by the structure of the symbolic system through which it moves, the agency of the signifier accomplishes the ultimate aim of the death drive in dissolving the encrustations of the imaginary. To paraphrase Clausewitz's famous remark about war and politics: the symbolic function is the dismemberment of the imaginary by other means. This functional equivalence of violence and symbolization allows us to clarify a number of points:

1. What is mortified in the accession of the subject to language is the imaginary ego and its claim to a self-contained wholeness. The action of the death drive is thus identifiable with the force that propels the human being beyond the imaginary. It is the answer to the question "why does man get out of narcissism. Why [in the narcissistic position] is man dissatisfied?" (S.I, 131). The coming-to-be of the subject beyond the imaginary entails the enactment of a certain primordial masochism that for Lacan is concomitant with the accession of the subject to a symbolic mediation. Thus Lacan claims that "we cannot understand [the masochistic outcome] without the dimension of the symbolic. It is located at the juncture between the imaginary and the symbolic" (S.I, 172).

2. The fixity of the imaginary stabilizes a restricted economy of energies by posing an impediment to unlimited discharge, the ecstatic release Lacan calls *jouissance*. It is in this sense that *jouissance* remains "beyond the pleasure principle." *Jouissance* thus requires the deconstruction of the imaginary, but can occur in either of two ways, either by the violence that tears the imaginary form asunder or by the submission of the subject to the

law of the signifier. For the human being, bound by the alienating effects of its imaginary identity, the pathways to the realization of desire pass either through murder or signification. Prior to the evolution of symbolic competence, the only opening to the real of desire is presented by violation of the imaginary. "So when we wish to attain in the subject what was before the serial articulations of speech, and what is primordial to the birth of symbols, we find it in death, from which his existence takes on all the meaning it has" (E:S, 105). With the installation of the subject in a symbolic order, however, a new mode of access to *jouissance* is established. By means of the signifier, the barrier of the pleasure principle is breached.

> If the living being is something at all thinkable, it will be above all as subject of the *jouissance*; but this psychological law that we call the pleasure principle (and which is only the principle of displeasure) is very soon to create a barrier to all *jouissance*. . . . [T]he organism seems to avoid too much *jouissance*. Probably we would all be as quiet as oysters if it were not for this curious organization which forces us to disrupt the barrier of pleasure or perhaps only makes us dream of forcing and disrupting this barrier. All that is elaborated by the subjective construction on the scale of the signifier in its relation to the Other and which has its root in language is only there to permit the full spectrum of desire to allow us to approach, to test, this sort of forbidden *jouissance* which is the only valuable meaning that is offered to our life.[18]

3. The work of the signifier is a form of sublime violence. This point illuminates Lacan's understanding of the symbolic foreclosure that issues in psychosis. When foreclosure impairs access to the symbolic function, the essential work of castration collapses onto the level of the imaginary. This result is spectacularly demonstrated in the vignette Lacan cites from Freud's analysis of the Wolfman. Seated by his nanny in the garden, the Wolfman is suddenly horrified by the hallucination of his severed finger. As Lacan interprets this episode, what emerges on the level of phantasmatic dismemberment represented a failure on the level of symbolic mediation. "Castration," Lacan remarks, "which is precisely what didn't exist for him, manifests itself in the form of something he imagines—to have cut his little finger, so deeply that it hangs solely by a little piece of skin" (S.I, 58).

4. Distributing the activity of the death drive in this way between the imaginary and the symbolic enables us to illuminate the commonplace observation that violence is best avoided by an act of symbolization, an attempt to "talk things through." "It is clear," says Lacan, "to recall very obvious things, that violence is indeed what is essential in aggression, at least if we situate ourselves on the human plane. It is not the word, it is even exactly its contrary, it is violence or the word which can appear in an interhuman relationship, if violence is something in its essence which is distinguished from the word."[19] Lacan reveals how violence and the signifier can function as alternatives to one another because they are, at bottom, deeply akin in bringing about the breakup of imaginary unities.

5. We can now reprise, with regard to the action of the signifier, Lacan's point that the action of the death drive is fatal in one sense but revitalizing in another. To the extent that the death drive is identifiable with the submission of the subject to the movement of the signifier, to the extent, as Lacan puts it, that "the signifier . . . materializes the agency of death," it does so by giving voice to what has been excluded by the restricted economy of the ego.[20] "Of course, as it is said," remarks Lacan, "the letter killeth while the spirit giveth life . . . but we should also like to know how the spirit could live without the letter" (E:S, 158).

In the following section, we will consider the implications of these points for Lacan's rereading of the Oedipus complex. Before turning to that task, however, let us add a note about their impact on Freud's metapsychology. We have argued that the process Freud called unbinding finds its translation into Lacanian concepts in terms of a breakup of imaginary coherence and, in addition, that some form of imaginary unbinding, some challenge to the narcissistic integrity of the ego, can occur alternately in violence or in signification. The fusional power attributed by Freud to the erotic instinct that seeks "to establish ever greater unities and to preserve them thus" (SE, 19:148), identifiable with the perceptual tropism of the imaginary toward unitary forms, now appears assimilable to what we earlier called "positionality." A second fundamental drive is set in motion by the alienating effects of positionality. This second drive of unbinding seeks to break apart what the imaginary has fused together. The death drive thus represents the tension of a subject at odds with itself. Like the aggressive and destructive fury that provides its most visible representative, the death drive aims to undermine and pull asunder every unitary position. But unlike brute violation of the imaginary form, symbolic transformation of the image is conditioned by the operation signs within an ordered system. In order to characterize this circumstance in metapsychological terms, we are forced to say that symbolic competence, even as it makes possible an ongoing process of unbinding of imaginary forms, is itself dependent upon a kind of bound structure. In effect, the system of the symbolic code comprises a second order of binding.

This conclusion is paradoxical, for it implies the existence of an order of binding the very function of which is to promote a measured activity of unbinding. Indeed, the more securely the symbolic system is bound, the greater is its capacity to facilitate effects of imaginary unbinding. We can neatly characterize these two orders of binding, imaginary and symbolic, by relying again upon the distinction between positionality and the dispositional field. Binding on the level of the imaginary involves a fixation of the positing function. Imaginary binding consists in a determination of positionality, the adumbration of a perceptual form that is rendered distinct from a background and can be repeated in various contexts. What is bound in the symbolic function, by contrast, are dimensions of the dispositional field itself. Built upon a diacritical network or system of relations, symbolic competence not only shares the *form* of the dispositional field, it also shares its function. Just as the dispositional field of perception provides a tacitly co-present manifold that informs whatever enters the positional locus, the degree and kind of the subject's symbolic competence direct the flow of discourse in varying directions. Both the selection of signifiers and the order of their combinations are decisively influenced by the synchronous totality of the language system possessed by a given speaker at a given moment. The learning of a language thus enacts the binding of an ever more complex and articulated system on the basis of which the subject may be said to cultivate a disposition to speech.

When the disintegrative, antipositional force is linked to the function of the signifier, the result is especially satisfying on theoretical grounds because it enables us to envisage an ongoing process in which psychical unities are continually generated, broken apart, and reassembled. The stream of linguistic articulation forms a continuous process in which the action of the dual drives is operative at every turn. As speech unfolds over time, attention is continually drawn to ever-shifting loci of attention, unities momentarily cast up by a moving stream. But such islands of relative stability in the current of speech are immediately washed again into the general flow. The focus cannot be held fixed but must be open to change in accordance with laws belonging to the system itself. From this point of view, the capacity for speech emerges as the privileged instance of what Freud called the "fusion" of the instincts, in which the two great drives are brought into mutual interpenetration. In the unfolding of the speech chain, the forces of binding and unbinding function in an on-going dialectical exchange.

Language Acquisition and the Oedipus Complex

Perhaps Lacan's single most important innovation is to place the Freudian theory of the Oedipus complex on a new foundation, as he finds in the Oedipal drama, together with the castration complex that is its pivot, the critical moment in which the child's relation to language is crystallized. Relying upon the theoretical clarifications of the preceding discussion, we can better understand Lacan's innovation on this crucial point.

Despite his insistence upon the centrality of the Oedipus complex in psychical development and upon its status as a structural constant of human experience, Freud was never able to conceive its underlying dynamics independently of contingent factors. Particularly in case of the little boy, the onset of the Oedipal period remained closely bound up with the child's perception of a threat of castration announced by parents or caretakers. If the Oedipal dilemma corresponded to the emergence of new instinctual pressures, it was nevertheless necessary in Freud's view that intrapsychic conflicts be related to external ones. As Freud remarked in the *Outline of Psycho-analysis*, "an instinctual demand is, after all, not dangerous in itself; it only becomes so inasmuch as it entails a real external danger, the danger of castration" (SE, 20:126). At the same time, Freud himself recognized the inadequacy of leaving so fundamental a point of the theory prey to chance factors, and it was to answer this challenge that he went on to speculate that the fear of castration might form part of the genetic inheritance of human beings.

Like Freud, Lacan views the Oedipal crisis as triggered by the upsurge of a new current of libido toward the mothering figure. This new and more properly genital libido challenges the pre-Oedipal organization.

The libido which is related to the genital object is not on the same level as the primitive libido, whose object is the subject's own image. That is a crucial phenomenon. . . . If the primitive libido is relative to prematuration, the nature of the second libido is different. It goes beyond, it responds to an initial maturation of desire, if not of organic development. . . . Here there is a complete change of level in the relation of the human being to the image, to the other. It is the pivtoal point of what is called maturation, upon which the entire Oedipal drama turns. It is the instinctual correlative of what, in Oedipus, takes place on the situational plane. (S.I, 180)

But here we encounter this difference: where Freud saw the flowering of libido in the Oedipal period as triggering the father's prohibition (stay away from your mother or I'll cut it off!), Lacan recognizes the upsurge of Oedipal libido as precipitating a conflict internal to the subject itself: it challenges the structure of the imaginary ego. The Oedipus complex corresponds not only to tensions between the child and parent but also to a fundmental shift in the child's psychical economy: the transition from a predominantly imaginary mode of functioning to a predominantly symbolic one. For Lacan, "the Oedipus complex means that the imaginary, in itself an incestuous and conflictual relation, is doomed to conflict and ruin" (S.III, 96). The ruin at stake is, very literally, that of the integrity of the ego image itself. In this way, the Oedipal child is predisposed to phantasies of dismemberment even without the prompting of a parental threat of punishment. Accordingly, the fear of castration and the psychological transformation it ushers in emerge in the child's phantasy life for essential reasons. Castration is thus said to be a "radical function for which a more primitive stage in the development of psychoanalysis found more accidental (educative) causes" (E:S, 320). Because the coherence of the infantile ego coalesced around the image of the body's wholeness, the emergence of new drive energies quite naturally issues in a tendency toward imagining the partitioning of the body. Children of four to seven years of age display a marked interest in the breaking apart of the body's wholeness, a kind of anxious but fascinated enthrallment with the image of the *corps morcelé*. These children will gleefully threaten their caretakers and peers with all manner of bodily atrocity: plucking out eyes, pulling off heads and limbs,

Figure 5   **Figure 6**

cutting someone in half. This intense interest in bodily dismemberment, not infrequently enacted upon dolls or even small animals or insects, also readily shows itself in children's drawings and paintings.

The following series of drawings by a young boy demonstrates this phenomemon. The first two drawings (Figs. 5 and 6), made at the age of three-and-a-half-years, display very deliberate concern for the wholeness of the body, a concern that is in fact typical of children at this age. Indeed, the artist of these drawings is so anxious not to overlook any of the body's appendages that he has supplied each hand with eight or ten fingers and each foot with a similar surfeit of toes.

In subsequent drawings (Figs. 7–14) from age five, however, something very different appears. In this series—which is in fact a proper *series* of drawings, all drawn over a very short time in a sheaf of pages bound together—anxiety over the completeness of the body image seems to have given way to a no-holds-barred impulse to violate it. In Figures 7 and 8, for example, we are surprised to find one eye flying out of the face. The proximate inspiration for these drawings was a toy called a Madball. A

Figure 7

Figure 8

Figure 9

Figure 10

Figure 11

Figure 12

Figure 13   Figure 14

popular gimmick of the mid-1980s, a Madball is a rubber ball fashioned in the form of a distorted and disfigured face, complete with lolling tongue, gouged-out eye, stitched wounds, bulging veins, and so on; in short, a toy whose prime attraction consists in its capacity to generate the squirmy excitement of "grossing people out." The first picture of this series repeats the familiar Madball face. That image is followed, however, by a parade of body parts, each of which was baptised with a name. Figure 9 is fairly recognizably "Fingerman." Figure 10, with eyes planted in a forest of hairs, was dubbed "Hairman." Figure 11 is recognizable if one imagines a figure bending over and viewed from behind with a face inscribed on the buttocks; he is, of course, "Bottom-man." In Figure 12, "Scrotum-man," the previous drawing is repeated but with male genitals suspended from it instead of legs. Figures 13 and 14 are "Handman" and "Footman," drawn as rough tracings of the artist's own hand and foot.

In a striking way, these drawings present a phantasmagoria of what Lacan calls the *corps morcelé*. They make up a veritable encyclopedia of the body in bits and pieces. But equally striking, each of the body parts is outfitted with a face, making it possible to ascribe to each a name. Especially when compared with the earlier drawings, which so conscientiously protect the body's wholeness, these drawings suggest a deliberate experimentation with the body's fragmentation, as if the challenge were to see how far the body could be cut up and still retain a sense of self. It is difficult not to conclude that an important developmental task was being worked out by means of this series of drawings, a conclusion that is all the more tempting in view of the peculiar energy with which they were undertaken and the large number of drawings produced.

The Oedipal phantasy of castration must be understood, at least in part, against this background of the child's general interest in bodily fragmentation.[21] Castration, after all, is a species of dismemberment. In this way, castration anxiety is recognized to be a privileged moment of a more general testing of bodily integrity. The castration complex is part of a fundamental restructuring of the child's imaginary identity for which the unity of the body image provides the basic template. But why this particular form of dismemberment? Even if it can be maintained that the Oedipal child is predisposed toward phantasies of bodily violation, what privileges the violation of the male genital?

Although a crucial part of the answer to this question must be postponed until the following chapter, we can already recognize how and why the penis becomes the pivot point for the psychical transformation that occurs during the Oedipal period. If the essential task of the Oedipus complex involves the transition from an predominantly imaginary to a symbolic mode of functioning, the phantasy of castration provides the perfect emblem of this transition. It does so for two reasons, one appropriate to the breakup of the infantile organization of the imaginary, the other relevant to child's accession to the function of the linguistic signifier. On the side of the imaginary, the penis readily marks for the little boy a site of vulnerability to bodily loss or amputation. The penis is the only bodily appendage unsupported by bone, it is highly sensitive and easily injured, and the upright posture exposes it conspicuously to possible damage. The penis, says Lacan, bears "the mark of the cut." The little boy's sense of natural vulnerability for the penis is multiplied by discovery of its absence in the little girl, the sight of which calls up the possibility of losing it himself. Yet the presence and absence of the penis has consequences on the level of the imaginary for both sexes, as it introduces a variable factor, a basic line of cleavage in the wholeness of the body gestalt. It is this structural fault, discovered in the unity of the body schema, that the narrative constructions of the Oedipal period seek to explain (the father must have cut it off, the mother is to blame for its absence, etc.). At the same time, the variability of the penis between the two sexes serves to provide a support, figured in the imaginary, for the emergence of the symbolic function. Present in the male and absent in the female, the penis models the structure of the signifier by displaying a fundamental binary opposition. Genital difference functions on the level of anatomy like the differential feature discovered by Jakobson at the basis of all languages. The penis and its absence can readily be offered as a primitive registration of what Jakobson has called the "marked and the unmarked."

Noting the role of the penis in representing the Oedipal transformation alerts us to the signifying function of other parts of the body. Indeed, the partial objects discovered by psychoanalysis—including for Lacan not only the penis, breast, and feces, but also the voice and the gaze—assume the status of primitive signifiers. In effect, the parts of the body supply the material for the first acts of signification. Nor should this be surprising. The body gestalt offers the frame of unity around which the imaginary identity of the primitive ego is mobilized. With the further unfolding of cognitive development, parts of the body are traded off against the whole with novel signifying effects. The breast and feces may thus come to signify different aspects of the child's relation to its own needs and to the mother who satisfies or frustrates them. Moreover, if the parts of the body offer themselves as the most primitive signifiers, the body itself becomes the unifying field in which they are correlated. The body becomes the original matrix of signification, the ground upon which the synchrony of the most elemental signifying system will be oriented. It is no mere accident of phrasing that leads us to refer to the "body" of a discourse or a text.

The Lacanian account of the Oedipal crisis inevitably invites a simple but important question. What sense does it make to say that children accede to language during the Oedipal period? After all, the four-to-seven-year-old child has already been speaking and responding to language for a long time. What exactly is acquired at the Oedipal period? The answer to this question is crucial not only for Lacan's interpretation of the Oedipus complex but also for his view of the nature and function of representation in general. What occurs at the Oedipal stage is a change in the child's relationship to language. The child may come for the first time to appreciate puns and verbal jokes, to embroider his or her own stories with greater flair and imagination, or even to take a positive pleasure in telling lies and "tall tales." Where the pre-Oedipal child typically demands that stories be repeated exactly (and will complain if, for reasons of expediency, a page is skipped in a favorite book), the Oedipal child can enjoy novelty and surprise. These changes are accompanied by a corresponding shift in the style of the child's self-reference. Where the infant child typically refers to herself or himself as "me" ("me want a drink," "me go too"), around the time of the Oedipal period the children begin to refer to themselves with the pronoun "I," thereby acquiring mastery of linguistic "shifters," those pronouns whose reference changes depending upon which of the partners in dialogue utters them. These new capacities result from a shift in the child's relation to the symbolic function. For the pre-Oedipal child, speech is largely characterized by repetition and mimicry. The toddler speaks, but its use of language tends to be dominated by the presence of imaginary factors. The passage through the Oedipal period brings the child's thought process more completely under the sway of the symbol system. Thought is guided by structures belonging not to the perceptual register of imaginary forms but to the system of signifiers and the rules that govern it. These observations recall Heidegger's description of the authentic relation of the human being to speech: it is not man who speaks language but language that speaks man. As Lacan interprets it, what is at stake in the Oedipus complex is the moment during which the child is appropriated by this more determinative relation to language—the moment, as he puts it, "in which desire becomes human is also that in which the child is born into language" (E:S, 103). During the Oedipal period, it is less a matter of language being acquired by the child than of the child being acquired by language.

Lacan's crucial innovation is to view the Oedipus complex not thematically but structurally. Less important than any particular intention to marry the mother and murder the father is an underlying transformation in the child's capacities of representation, a shift in the means by which intentionality is formed in the first place. The child's accession to language requires a measure of escape from anchorage in the imaginary, an escape that results in a general qualification of the force of images in favor of signs and the system in which they are imbricated. This shift is effected by an alteration in the imaginary registration of subjective identity. In the course of the Oedipus complex the imaginary ego is confronted with a revived specter of the *corps morcelé*. For Lacan, then, the phantasmatic projection of bodily dismemberment is anything but incidental to the psychical sea change of the Oedipal period. The imagining of the fragmented body that issues in castration anxiety is therefore not merely the threatening inducement to the Oedipal transformation, it is itself a prime constituent of that transformation. Castration is no longer a fearsome possibility to be avoided but rather a psychical task to be achieved.

With this emphasis on the necessary deconstructing of the imaginary body, the Lacanian account reveals the link between the unfolding of the Oedipus complex and the activity of the death drive. The passage through the Oedipal period is internally motivated by the death drive itself, the profound impulse that impels the subject beyond imaginary identification. It is a linkage that Freud was prevented from making, in large part as a result of the biological frame to which his conception of the death drive remained tied. In other respects, however, Freud's own thinking pointed toward a similar confluence between his two most basic theoretical constructions. For Freud, too, the Oedipal drama involved the encounter with a mortifying wound to the child's narcissism, indeed the assimilation of such a wound into the psychical economy lay at the very heart of what Freud called the dissolution of the Oedipus complex. Moreover, when Freud approached the question of the representability of death, he did not hesitate to privilege the phantasy of castration. Freud thus concluded that "the mechanism of the fear of death can only be that the ego relinquishes its narcissistic libidinal cathexis in a very large measure." Such relinquishing is "possible to regard the fear of death, like the fear of conscience, as a development of the fear of castration" (SE, 19:58).

From a Lacanian viewpoint, the Oedipus complex is recognizable as a labor of the death drive. But if the specter of violence is ingredient to the psychic transformation of the Oedipal period, it is also in and through the accomplishment of symbolic castration that violence is transcended. Thus Lacan associates passage through the Oedipus complex with a pacifying of imaginary aggressivity. "The Oedipal identification," he claims, "is that by which the subject transcends the aggressivity that is constitutive of the primary subjective individuation" (E:S, 23). This "pacifying" function of passage through the Oedipal period, he maintains, was under-appreciated by early theorists who tended to evaluate the function of the Oedipus complex solely in terms of the sadistic character of the superego that issues from it. Thus "the emphasis that was placed at first in psychoanalytic theory on the aggressive turning around of the Oedipal conflict upon the subject's own self was due to the fact that the effects of the complex were first perceived in *failures* to resolve it" (E:S, 25). To the extent that the Oedipal drama succeeds in achieving its basic function of stabilizing the subject's relation to the symbolic order, it serves to divert the action of the death drive from its more archaic deployment on the imaginary plane and to reengage it in the symbolic process itself. This virtualization of imaginary dismemberment in the agency of the signifier may properly be called an effect of sublimation, indeed what is accomplished by this process can be said to constitute the necessary precondition for any sublimation whatever.

The same series of reflections enables us to recast essential points of the theory of the superego. It enables us, for example, to identify two moments ingredient to the genesis of the superego, one imaginary and the other symbolic. As the psychical agency by which the symbolic function is installed in the child, the very seat of the symbolic imperative, the superego is consolidated around the experience of the voice. The superego is therefore the precipitate of a shift from a visual to an auditory register—a shift that is deeply appropriate for the accomplishment of the primary function of the Oedipal crisis as a pivot between the imaginary order of infancy and the establishment of the symbolic function. Yet equally appropriate to its ultimate function of breaking the spell of narcissism is the fact that the ground lines of the developing superego are laid down in terms of an imaginary threat. The father's voice and the call of conscience that will be modeled upon it are typically prepared for by the menacing image of the ferocious punisher whose power is wielded on the imaginary level. The punishment *imagined* by the naughty child is often a good deal more spectacular than what is actually meted out.

In taking note of the severity of the superego in mistreating the ego, a mistreatment that may assume a truly mortifying aspect in the depths of melancholia, Freud characterized the superego as containing a "pure culture of the death instinct." This association of the superego with the death drive is especially well illuminated by a Lacanian interpretation. If it is above all the imaginary form of the ego that is the object of the dis-integrating influence of the death drive, then the virulence of superego's attacks upon the ego become straightforwardly explicable as an exten-sion of the "self-destructive" drive. Moreover, if, the death drive is taken to represent the return of the real against the alienating strictures of the imaginary, then much of what Freud says of the superego becomes understandable in a new way. We readily understand, for example, why Freud claims that the superego everywhere "displays its independence from the conscious ego and its intimate relations with the unconscious id" (SE, 19:52). Contrary to the naive view that simply opposes the activity of the superego to the expression of desire, Freud stresses the proximity of the superego to the id. Freud thus claims that "the *cathectic energy* does not reach these contents of the superego from auditory per-ception (instruction or reading) but from sources in the id" (SE, 19:52-53). In this way, the superego may be said to be "always close to the id and can act as its representative *vis à vis* the ego. It reaches deep down into the id and for that reason is farther from consciousness than the ego is" (SE, 19:48–49).

The theoretical importance of the more intimate association of the superego with the death drive made available from a Lacanian point of view is hard to overestimate. Freud had struggled to understand how and why, contrary to the rule of the pleasure principle, the superego visited such torments upon the guilty ego. Indeed, he felt the necessity of addi-tional constructions in order to explain why a third psychical agency arose at all. In response, he offered the theory of an inherited predisposition to guilt, the legacy of primal patricide. By placing greater emphasis on the alienating character of the imaginary ego, an emphasis that makes a psy-chological reading of the death drive seem immensely more plausible than Freud's biologizing of it, Lacan is better able to present the internal moti-vations at play in the origin of the superego and thereby to suggest the role of the superego in the realization of desire. For Lacan, the law by which the pretensions of the narcissistic ego are brought up short, far from being simply inimical to desire, signifies a possible expression of desire. "The true function of the Father," Lacan insists, ". . . is fundamentally to unite (and not to set in opposition) a desire and the Law" (E:S, 321). "Nothing forces anyone to enjoy, except the superego. The superego is the impera-tive of *jouissance—Jouis!*"[22]

Psychoanalysis and the Theory of Sacrifice

In concluding this chapter, let us make the experiment of using a Lacanian perspective to shed new light on a very old problem: the phenomenon of blood sacrifice. It was a problem that attracted Freud's attention. Midway through the text of *Totem and Taboo*, Freud quotes a description of a fourth-century Bedouin ritual of sacrifice.

> The victim of the sacrifice, a camel, 'is bound upon a rude altar
> of stones piled together, and when the leader of the band has
> thrice led the worshippers round the altar in a solemn proces-
> sion accompanied with chants, he inflicts the first wound . . .
> and in all haste drinks of the blood that gushes forth. Forthwith
> the whole company fall on the victim with their swords, hacking
> off pieces of the quivering flesh and devouring them raw with
> such wild haste, that in the short interval between the rise of the
> day star which marked the hour for the service to begin, and the
> disappearance of its rays before the rising sun, the entire camel,
> body and bones, skin, blood and entrails, is wholly devoured.'
> (SE, 13:138)

Already in this picture of ecstatic savagery, itself a kind of primal scene, we are brought up short before one of the central mysteries explored by psychoanalysis, that in which an elemental fulguration of desire is released amid spectacular violence. Yet what is most challenging about the Bedouin killing-feast is that it is less the exception than the rule for many ancient or aboriginal cultures. In a similar rite among the African Dinka, a cow is tied to a stake and surrounded by a chanting throng who take turns hurling insults at the beast and raining blows down upon it. In a cli-mactic rush, the animal is trampled and crushed by a stampede of the young men of the tribe, after which the carcass is carved and eaten.[23] Elaborate sacrificial rites are familiar to us from classical Greece and Rome, and were central to Vedic Hindu traditions, indeed the word *vedi* designates the site of the sacrificial altar.[24] The Hindu rites included veg-etative sacrifices, in which stalks of the soma plant were cut and ground up, but the linkage to earlier animal and even human sacrifice is made clear by the use in both instances of the verb *hanti*: "to slay" or "kill." Bears were a special object of sacrifice among both the Ouataouak tribe in North

America and the Aino of Japan, as were dogs among the Iroquois and African Minyanka, sheep among the Zulu, Thonga, and Lovedu, and black oxen among the Swazis.[25] Despite Islamic injunctions against blood sacrifice, the ritual slaughter of sheep, goats, and camels continues in such quantity among pilgrims to Mount Arafat that Saudi authorities have used bulldozers to remove the carcasses.[26] The practice of human sacrifice among the Aztecs takes its place among this litany, though admittedly distinguished by the horrible particulars of the killing ritual, by the vast quantities of its victims and, of course, by its shocking choice of object.[27]

These ritual killings enact, in particular locations of culture, a drama of violence that is repeated countless times in other human communities. Indeed, the near ubiquity of traditions of ritual slaughter may prompt us to reconsider the very definition of the human being, not as the two-legged animal, not as the rational, speaking, or laughing animal, nor even as the animal that is cognizant of its own mortality, but rather as the animal for whom ritual killing is an essential moment of its self-constitution, the animal that ceremonially butchers living things, at times other animals, at other times members of its own species. The enigma of this ritual bloodletting is only deepened as we take note of the frequency with which the entrails of victims are carefully laid open and rummaged for the auguries of human destiny before being shared out among the gathering to be eaten. How, then, to explain it? From a psychoanalytic point of view, the obvious response is to link ritualized killing with the activity of the death drive.

But perhaps we cannot make this linkage so easily. By no means all sacrifice involves the dramatic violence displayed by the Bedouin ritual; indeed, it has been argued that the record of it with which we began may be exaggerated or even apochryphal.[28] More importantly, a great many practices categorized as sacrificial involve no overt violence whatever. In anthropological literature, the theory of sacrifice is uncomfortably divided between practices of ritual killing and the many instances of less spectacular sacrifice in which a variety of objects are simply left upon the altar in a gesture of oblation. Sacrificial practices thus seem to confront us with two classes of phenomena: one centered on the enigma of ritual killing and dismemberment, the other concerned with practices of voluntary wasting or expenditure that generally do not involve violence. Interpreters of sacrifice accordingly fall into two main camps, depending on which of the two faces of sacrifice is given greater emphasis, offering or immolation, donation or destruction. For some theorists, these two aspects of sacrifice are sufficiently distinct as to render illegitimate the usage of a single term to describe them. For others, an attempt is made to reconcile the two by supposing a general evolution away from rituals centered upon an actual killing toward those in which death and dismemberment are merely symbolic. How, then, is a psychoanalytic approach to the phenomenon of sacrifice to proceed in the face of this divided judgment among anthropologists?

In what follows, we will seek an answer to this question by way of the reinterpretation of psychoanalytic theory offered by Lacan. One of the prime values of a Lacanian contribution lies in its capacity to close the gap between the votive and violent aspects of sacrifice and to reveal the inner relation that binds them together. In this way, the resources of psychoanalysis are put to the task of clarifying a lacuna of anthropological theory. At the same time, however, a Lacanian approach returns us to key Freudian concepts with renewed precision, enabling us not only to compare the dynamics of sacrifice with the machinations of the death drive, but also to glimpse the centrality of sacrifice for the theory of the unconscious in general. Let us prepare the way for appreciating that contribution by making a brief survey of anthropological theories of sacrifice.

The potential fruitfulness of a psychoanalytic approach to sacrifice has been stunted by Freud's reliance on the conclusions of Robertson Smith, whose attempt to trace the origin of sacrifice to totemism has been largely discredited. Leaving aside Smith's emphasis on the totemic animal, however, there are features of his conception of sacrifice that were appreciated by Freud and that continue to hold currency among anthropologists. Particularly for practices of blood sacrifice, for example, other observers have corroborated Smith's supposition of an identification between the sacrificer and the victim. Not infrequently, the victim is treated as a relative whose kinship with the sacrificer is reinforced by elaborate speeches and behaviors. Smith also clarified the way in which communal consumption of the sacrificial victim functions to establish social solidarity and cohesion. Even without assuming a common origin in totemism, therefore, sacrifice can be fairly said to play a vital role in bonding together the members of a community by staging a shared participation in ritual killing and a calculated distribution of the victim's body in a ceremonial meal.

Although subject to successive waves of criticism and revision, E. B. Tylor's theory of sacrifice has enjoyed more enduring and far-reaching influence than that of Robertson Smith.[29] For Tylor, the enigma of sacrifice centered upon the giving up of a valuable object, which he sought to explain not as pure wasting but as exchange, a means by which human beings ingratiate themselves with heavenly and chthonic powers in hopes of receiving something in return for what is sacrificed. In one way or another, sacrifice enacts the formula of Roman ritual: *do ut des:* I give in order that you may give. From this original meaning of sacrifice evolved traditions of self-abnegation and renunciation in which expectation of recompense was increasingly deferred. A main problem with Tylor's approach, however, was its reduction of the religious posture to market values and of sacrifice to a form of bribery. In response to this problem, Wilhelm Schmidt assigned paradigmatic value to the offering of the first fruits common among many agrarian cultures and construed sacrifice less as an attempt to secure return on investment than as a symbolic gesture of pure homage and thanksgiving.[30] Yet another mode of approach returns to the model of sacrifice as a mode of exchange but conceives the offering of gifts as a way of reseeding cosmic energies of creation. For Gerardus van der Leeuw, for example, sacrificial practices presuppose a conception of the world as animated by *mana*.[31] The bloodletting of sacrifice functions to stimulate the circulation of generative forces. What is accomplished by sacrifice is no mere exchange of goods but rather a more fundamental transfer of force: not *do ut des* but *do ut possis dare*, "I give you power in order that you can give it back to me."

The theory of Henri Hubert and Marcel Mauss, too, can be understood on the model of sacrifice as exchange, though less as a matter of exchanging particular goods than of establishing the two dimensions of existence between which such exchange can take place. Seeking in sacrificial practices a unifying schema that cuts beneath traditional distinctions between rituals of expiation, thanksgiving, and request, Hubert and Mauss locate the purpose of sacrifice in the regulation of a cyclical economy between domains of the sacred and the profane. The sacrificial system that sets up this economy is essentially triangular. Between the generative power of the sacred and the human being who seeks to come into relation with it is inserted a mediating object, the sacrificial victim, whose immolation at once stabilizes the personality of the sacrificer and engages the potentially dangerous force of the sacred. Indeed, it is in and through repeated destruction of the sacrifical object that the untamed and impersonal powers of the sacred come to be conceived as a personal diety who requires propitiation. The sacrificial victim becomes the hinge between the realms of the mundane and the uncanny, the profane and the sacred. Also central to the theory of Hubert and Mauss is their insistence that the conduct of sacrifice does not merely orient the sacrificer in relation to immanent and transcendent dimensions but also alters the sacrificer's very person. This internal transformation of the sacrificer is given prominence in their most general definition of sacrifice as "a religious act which, through the consecration of a victim, modifies the condition of the moral person who accomplishes it."[32]

The theory of sacrifice put forward by Georges Bataille in *The Accursed Share* departs radically from the model of sacrifice as exchange or contract. For Bataille, the real function of sacrifice is an exercise of pure expenditure in which the order of utility is subjected to an ecstatic destruction. Bataille's view enables him to contrast archaic, heroic cultures, characterized by apparently gratuitous expenditure, from industrial modernity organized in the service of production. In this way, Bataille's view retrieves a more authentic sense of the religious posture in which the offering of sacrifice is purified of any expectation of compensation. However, it is a view that is ultimately understandable only on the basis of a series of fundamental assumptions, both about the essential character of natural processes and about the fate of human beings inhabiting an artificially constructed world of objects. As Bataille envisions it, the creation of a world of stable and independent "things," governed by the rule of utility, entails the loss of that immediate and ecstatic vulnerability to being that Bataille calls "intimacy." Energy that would otherwise be poured out in a limitless and indefinite exuberance of vitality is harnessed and stabilized in the restricted economy of human artifacts. But this fixed structure, in which human beings are alienated from the law of pure squandering that governs natural processes, must be continually tested and periodically overthrown. The order of utility is inevitably challenged by the three great "luxuries of nature"—eating, death, and sex—but is also ceremonially challenged by practices of sacrifice. If sacrifice "destroys that which it consecrates," it does so to ensure "the return of the *thing* to the *intimate* order."[33]

If the paradigm of offering and exchange informs the profusion of theories from Tylor to Bataille, a second current of theoretical construction responds to the other great mystery of sacrificial practices: that in which the object is not just donated but positively destroyed. Interest in the violence of sacrifice was spurred by the work of Adolph Jensen, whose attempt to interpret sacrifice as a repetition of a primordial killing of the diety in some ways parallels Freud's theory in *Totem and Taboo*. For Jensen, sacrifice demonstrates the necessity of killing in order to live, while at the same time channeling, controlling, and civilizing the killing impulse. The argument of Walter Burkert in *Homo Necans* echoes this line of thinking as it traces the function of sacrificial practices to the control of aggressiveness among hunting peoples. In the interests of group harmony and solidarity, the community must innoculate itself against the violence inherent to a life based on hunting and does so by ritualizing the central elements of the chase, the kill, and the consumption of the quarry.

Most challenging and far-reaching among recent theories of sacrificial violence, however, is the work of René Girard. For Girard, the human disposition to violence, far from being limited to the aggression of the hunt, is an unavoidable consequence of the nature of human social interaction. He bases this conclusion on the analysis of what he calls the "mimetic character of desire." In Girard's view, a view much more conspicuously Hegelian than Girard seems to acknowledge, objects become desirable not for their intrinsic qualities but because they are desired by someone else. Conflict and competition thus become inevitable. The impulse to murderous violence is rekindled with every new incitement to desire. The calamitous specter of a "war of all against all" is averted only by selection of a scapegoat upon whom the full force of collective envy and hatred is focused. With the killing of this scapegoat, the group discharges the force of its aggression and reestablishes the bonds of its solidarity. In Girard's view, the formula which best expresses the structure of the group process in human beings is "unanimity-minus-one."[34]

This underlying function of sacrifice as discharge of competitive aggression is typically obscured by the fact that the identity of the original scapegoat, a member of the human group, is disguised by substituting another victim for it, an outsider or an animal. In this redoubling of the victim, the true function of the entire ritual, its origin in murderous envy, is masked. In its most radical implication, this dynamic of surrogacy not only creates an essential blind spot behind which the inevitable murderousness of human desire remains hidden, but also establishes the basic pattern for all symbolic competence. Sacrificial practice thus becomes for Girard the prototype of all religiosity and effects the original act of sublimation. "The origin of symbolic thought," Girard insists, "lies in the mechanism of the surrogate victim."[35]

There is a great deal in Girard's theory that is reminiscent of Freud; indeed, Girard suggests that *Totem and Taboo* "is directed toward a general theory of sacrifice."[36] Nevertheless, Girard spends a great deal of energy distancing himself from psychoanalysis. He insists that the systematic misrecognition produced by substitution of the sacrificial victim has nothing to do with the psychoanalytic unconscious. In Girard's view, the Oedipus complex, illegitimately universalized by Freud, must be limited to the cultural context of modernity, that is, to "a society in which the father's authority has been greatly weakened but not completely destroyed."[37] Moreover, Freud misunderstood the underlying dynamic of the Oedipal period, as he assumed a quasi-natural desire for the mother as the basis for rivalry with the father instead of tracing conflict back to the mimetic nature of desire: that the child is bound to grasp for any object desired by the father. We would do better, Girard claims, to abandon the Oedipal paradigm altogether. The one thing Freud appears to have gotten right is the supposition of an actual event of patricide long lost in the mists of prehistory. Girard wants the actuality of such an originary event in order to ground his theory of the substitute victim.

The example of Girard returns us to psychoanalysis, though not along the lines Girard himself would like. Upon reflection, Girard's whole relation to psychoanalysis appears decidedly problematic. On a very general level, Girard's theory of the scapegoat clearly echoes the analysis offered by Freud in *Civilization and Its Discontents,* according to which group solidarity is achieved by the projection of aggression onto a convenient outsider. Yet Girard never mentions this text. Nor does he ever seem aware of the parallel between his concept of misrecognition in the substitute victim and the structure of the Freudian symptom. Far from having nothing to do with the Freudian unconscious, the false consciousness produced by Girard's sacrificial substitution could readily be identified with the very essence of symptom formation, in which an unacceptable impulse is simultaneously repressed and satisfied. Worse still, Girard's overliteral reliance on the notion of primal parricide is problematic. Girard wants to find an ally in Freud concerning the assumption of an actual event of primal violence, but appears miss the irony of Freud's calling his own hypothesis a "just-so" story. When *Totem and Taboo* is read carefully in relation to the greater trajectory of Freud's theoretical formulations, it is not difficult to connect the entire drama of the primal horde with that enigmatic but absolutely central theme of Freud's psychology: the theory of deferred action or *Nachträglichkeit*. Apparently unaware that the event at once symbolized and obscured by the substitute victim might be less real than desired, Girard overlooks the assumption of psychical reality that lies at the heart of Freud's theoretical innovation. For precisely this was the enduring lesson of Freud's earliest encounter with the pathogenic legacy of the trauma: that the unfolding of psychic life may be decisively influenced by an event that never occurred, a lost object that was never possessed, a primal scene whose formative power is constituted retroactively.

Girard's mishandling of psychoanalytic theory is most glaring in relation to Lacan, whose potential contribution to the problem of sacrifice Girard dismisses in a few lines midway through *Violence and the Sacred.* This dismissal is all the more fantastic for Girard's addressing it to "the mimetic nature of desire which Lacan, too, failed to discover."[38] What is Girard talking about? How can we fail to notice the likeness of Girard's concept of mimetic desire to the Lacanian definition of desire as the desire of the other? But there is another point to be made, in the light of which Girard's dismissal of Lacan seems, at the very least, a missed opportunity. At the core of Girard's thesis is a theory that can be recognized as deeply akin to that of Lacan. Girard insists that the establishment of symbolic competence, the installation of the signifying function and the domain of cultural transubstantiations opened up by it, is somehow profoundly bound up with practices of sacrificial violence. The link to Lacan emerges clearly when proper emphasis is laid upon a key element of ritual killing: the action of bodily dismemberment. The crucial point is that, literally or figuratively, practices of blood sacrifice are centered upon the act of cutting up the body. It is a point that is spectacularly demonstrated by Aztec practices or by the dismemberment of the bull in the Greek *Bouphonia* but is also readily discernible in more metaphoric guises, as in the careful cutting up of the Vedic soma or in the breaking of the Eucharistic loaf. The way in which a more archaic practice of sacrificial dismemberment is symbolically focused and concentrated in the rite of circumcision, as if efficiently reduced to the absolute minimum of disfigurement, the pure trace of the cut, only serves to return us with greater force to the Lacanian theory. For if practices of blood sacrifice center in a particularly poignant way upon bodily dismemberment, and if, as Girard wants to argue, such practices serve above all to launch the symbolic function, how can we fail to link the function of sacrifice with Lacan's rereading of castration as the gateway through which the subject comes to language?

Toward a Lacanian Theory of Sacrifice

With these background remarks in mind, we can sketch the outlines of a distinctively Lacanian approach to sacrifice in which the key points of the theories surveyed earlier can be regrasped and integrated. Indeed, from a Lacanian vantage point, other attempts to explain sacrifice fall into place as so many facets of single account, the underlying unity of which emerges for the first time. Briefly stated in Lacanian terms, the general function of sacrificial practices is to establish the operation of the signifier. This interpretation takes its clue from the likeness of blood sacrifice to the dynamics of castration, in which the installation of the symbolic function is conditioned by a violation of the body's imaginary wholeness. But Lacanian interpretation also accounts for the other, oblative aspect of sacrificial practice. Sacrifice releases the unthinkable force of pure animation from its capture in the sacrificial body and allows it to circulate in an economy of symbolic elements. We can develop this view in six points:

1. A Lacanian conception of sacrifice makes new sense of the function of identification that underlies the relation of the sacrificer to the body of the victim. The basis of that identification is the imaginary equivalence that structures the most primitive contour of the ego in the mirror phase. The role of such imaginary identification, elaborately staged and enacted in a ritual for which the *sight* of killing is absolutely central, is especially well displayed in every step of ancient Greek sacrifice. Great care is taken, for example, to ensure that the animals prepared for sacrifice, most often bred and raised specifically for the purpose, are completely free from visible mar or blemish. The crucial moment of the ritual is, of course, that in which this perfect specimen, a flawless exemplar, will submit to the knife. Up until the very climax of the ceremony, the knife is hidden beneath a basket. Now approaching the victim with it, the officiant slices a tuft of hair from the animal's brow, as if deliberately to mark the last moment at which the body

integrity of the animal remains intact. With this final preparatory gesture, the women in the assembly raise the shrill cry of the "sacrificial scream" or *ololygé*. The scream marks the emotional apotheosis of the ritual, the moment at which a second and decisive blow at the neck brings forth the gush of blood. Special care is taken that its flow not touch the ground but is rather directed onto the altar or into a designated pit. From this point on, the ceremony assumes a different, almost clinical aspect, in which the carcass is carefully dismembered and the internal organs are exposed and inspected. The heart, sometimes still beating, is placed on the altar stone, and the lobes of the liver are meticulously interpreted by a seer. Immediately afterward the organs and flesh are roasted and eaten. The bones are partially burnt and, with particular attention to the thigh bones and the pelvis still bearing the tail, are reassembled "in proper order," as if in an attempt to reconstruct the body of the victim in a new and consecrated form. The remains are finally consumed by the purifying fire.

2. Blood sacrifice forms a kind of pivot between the imaginary and the symbolic. Sacrificial dismemberment not only enacts a violation of imaginary integrity but also functions to support the installation of a system of signifiers. Ritual killing is followed, very literally, by a reading of the entrails. The victim's body is opened like a book. Indeed, the analogy is not a trivial one, for can we resist placing the book itself in a symbolic lineage with this moment of the sacrificial act? Pulling aside the folds of the book to consult the secrets inscribed therein, do we not repeat this ancient, mantic practice? For centuries, the outer bindings of books were made from animal skins and their pages from dried and flattened viscera. The place of the sacrificial animal is thus taken over by scripture. One swears oaths on The Book as one earlier pledged troth over the disemboweled animal. The sacred Scripture housed by the Hebrew tabernacle is very literally identifiable with the sacrificial body, as its replacement by the body of the god in the Christian Eucharist only serves to underscore.

In providing a space of reading, a site for the exercise of decipherment, the sacrificial body furnishes the very material of the signifier. The partitioning of the body and the ritual operations to which the parts are subjected offer the elements for a complex matrix of binary oppositions. Sacrifice incessantly rehearses such oppositions both in its grander dimensions, the mortal and the divine, the sacred and the profane, as well as in the microtexture of its details, describing alternatives that are subject to strict cultic observance: raw versus cooked, flesh versus blood, meat versus smoke, meat versus bones, boiled versus roasted, etc. In manifold ways, the cleaved body of the sacrificial victim offers itself as an originary lexicon, a primal alphabet of tissues and organs.

On the basis of these considerations, we are led to extend and generalize the basic point of Tylor's theory of sacrificial exchange: what is accomplished by sacrifice is less the engagement of any particular exchange than the establishment of the very law of exchange itself. In the same way, we are also reminded of the substitutive character of sacrifice and are able to explain it more satisfactorily. Practices of symbolic substitution so typical of sacrifice across a wide range of traditions—offering an animal for a human victim, a cucumber for an ox, etc.—are not merely indications that sacrifice bends to the demands of utility but are reflections of the essential function of sacrificial practices, that of establishing a range of equivalences across chasms of undeniable difference. There is no contradiction or incoherence when sacrifice continually resparks the gap between incommensurable domains, offering mere beans and beasts to the infinite powers, because what is founded by sacrifice is that function of fertile incommensurablity that operates at the very heart of language, the incommensurablity that results, that is, from the fact that the signifier substitutes only the barest trace of sound or scrawl for the presence of the thing itself. From this point of view we may recast the famous Hegelian expression: the word is not merely the murder of the thing, it is more precisely the *sacrifice* of the thing.

3. We were prompted to recognize the altar of sacrifice as a springboard of the signifier by noting the homology between sacrificial violence and the phantasy of dismemberment that Lacan takes to be the pivot of the Oedipus complex. A Lacanian viewpoint allows us to recognize very precisely how sacrifice is an exercise of castration. Along the line of this correspondence we rediscover the parallel between phylogeny and ontogeny that formed the spine of Freud's thinking about the origin and function of culture. Sacrifice replays on the level of cultural formations the process of symbolic structuration accomplished in the individual by the Oedipus complex. In the light of this discussion, we can recast the thesis of Hubert and Mauss that sacrificial practice brings about an alteration internal to the sacrificer. The one who sacrifices demonstrates a distance from brute need and suspends any immediate expectation of its fulfill-

ment. But sacrifice not only enacts the deferral of need but also transforms the sacrificer's relation to the Other from whom fulfillment might come. In Lacanian terms, the Other—the so-called "big Other"—is the locus of the code, the treasury of signifiers that constitutes the symbolic system. Understood from the point of view we have adopted, the example of sacrifice allows us to see with special clarity what this big Other is doing there. The big Other of sacrifice is, first of all, the deity in whose name the ritual is performed and to whom sacrificial offerings are extended. This Other establishes the third point of a triangle between sacrificer and victim. There is something uncanny about this triangulating point, standing off the dual axis of imaginary relation. It is an unlocatable and perpetually eccentric point, a purely supposed locus of subjectivity that stands behind the unfolding stream of discourse. It is the function of sacrifice to prepare the array of objects and events—the products of the harvest, the outcome of battles, the course of weather, the fertility of women—by which this Other will evidence itself.

4. In tracing the relevance of Lacanian theory to sacrificial practices, we cannot fail to be struck by the presence in those practices of something like the Lacanian real, that uncanny and unrepresentable dimension, beyond all capacity to image or to name, that is touched upon by the experience of the trauma. The real bursts forth in sacrifice above all in the substance of blood. In sacrifice, as also in tales of war and taboos concerning menstruation, blood is a privileged embodiment of the traumatic real contained and concealed by the forms of the imaginary. Not in itself an object, but produced precisely by the object's being torn asunder, blood is a kind of anti-entity, not object but abject. At the moment of the sacrificial cut, the rush of crimson spouts forth, a throbbing jet, brilliant and steaming, apparently animated with an energy of its own. And how alarming must be the contrast between the stable form of the victim's body just prior to the moment of sacrifice and the sudden eruption of fluid when its integument is breached. But if blood is the sap of the body, the source of its vitality, it is also a fluid and thus readily represents the very substance of symbolic circulation: easily gathered, pooled, and shared out. We may readily suppose that it is for the same reason, concerning their fitness as material embodiment of the circulating signifier, that a variety of fluids— wine (the blood of the grape) or milk, water, oil, honey—so typically figure prominently in sacrificial ritual.

It is at this point that we can recall the profound ambiguity of the sacred, at once nurturing and potentially annihilating, sustaining and destructive, that has been remarked by many theorists of sacrifice. It is an ambiguity that is central to Rudolf Otto's classic study of the holy.[39] It is also a duality already discernible in Lacan's conception of the imaginary as a formative influence that is indispensable for the establishment of identity, yet whose alienating effects issue in the disposition to aggressivity. What is at stake in this essential tension is the relation to the real that is unstably contained by the imaginary constitution of objects. It is precisely such a conception that we find in Bataille's understanding of sacrifice. The basic idea is especially clear in the context of his pithy monograph, *Theory of Religion,* in which he characterizes religion as the search for lost intimacy, and intimacy as above all the immediate reality of pure flow. The animal, fully enmeshed in an immanent order, is said to be "in the world like water in water."[40] For the human being, by contrast, the world is fractured into the discontinuity of discrete and stable objects. It can thus be said that the human being "does not eat anything before he has made an object of it." The deep purpose of sacrifice is to acknowledge the object character of the human world but also, by submitting the sacrificial object to destruction and wasting, to tear asunder its very being as object. Bataille can therefore claim that "the first fruits of the harvest are sacrificed in order to remove the plant and the animal, together with the farmer and the stock raiser, from the world of things. The principle of sacrifice is destruction, but though it sometimes goes so far as to destroy completely (as in a holocaust), the destruction that sacrifice is intended to bring about is not annihilation. The thing—only the thing—is what sacrifice means to destroy in the victim."[41]

5. A Lacanian interpretation also sheds significant light on the idea, proposed by Tylor but shared by many other theorists, that ritual killing is the most archaic form of sacrifice, both historically and psychologically, and that sacrificial practices have generally undergone an evolution from blood sacrifice to practices of offering and oblation and finally to traditions of self-denial and asceticism in which violence has no explicit part. From a Lacanian viewpoint, an evolutionary trend of this sort is favored by dynamics internal to the process of signification itself. The launching of the signifier, conditioned by the staging of imaginary violation, is coterminous with the founding of the gift, in as much as the birth of the signi-

fier establishes the very possibility of exchange. The cultural condition for the development of nonviolent practices of pure oblation is a high degree of symbolic stabilization and, perhaps in particular, the establishment of writing. It would be no coincidence, therefore, that explicit critique of blood sacrifice emerged prominently among the ancient Hebrews, whose achievement of a phonetic alphabet well entitles them to be called the People of the Book.

From a Lacanian point of view, sacrifice emerges as a ritual machinery for the demotivation of the signifier. What is sacrificed is immediate access to the objects of desire. One repeats the gesture of giving up in order to rehearse the possibility of regaining in a new form, just as one must give up the seed, defer eating it, in order to sow and cultivate it for the harvest. Sacrifice thus serves to establish the kingdom of signification in which the objects of desire can circulate in an unending economy of substitutions.[42] This interpretation brings the function of sacrifice into line with the dynamics of the Oedipus complex as it recapitulates on the level of ritual practices the original sacrifice made by every human being—that of separating from the mother by renouncing the security, comfort, and satisfaction of her body.

6. Unlike anthropological theories of sacrifice, which have been hobbled by reliance on one or another kind of thematic analysis—of the gift, of homage, of expiation, etc.—a Lacanian approach has the advantage of offering a properly structural account, based on consideration of the conditions of representation. The superiority of a Lacanian view is especially clear in comparison with the theory of Girard. By forcing sacrifice to conform to the thematics of the scapegoat, it is almost impossible for Girard to bridge the gap between sacrificial violence and oblation. A Lacanian interpretation reveals the hidden continuity between violent and votive sacrifice. The destruction of the sacrificial body serves to launch the function of the signifier. Rising from the ashes of the sacrificial fire, like the simulacrum of the victim's body reconstructed on the altar from its charred and fleshless bones, is a phantom double of the slaughtered creature, a kind of virtualization of the sacrificial object. The destruction and loss of the object thus opens up a symbolic dimension in which what was lost might be recovered in a new form. In this dimension, the space of signification itself, the movement of discourse will be continually renewed. The process of the transformation effected by sacrificial ritual, pivoted on the

shock of violence and loss, thus functions less simply to offer a gift than to found the very being of the gift by establishing the dimension in which the cycle of giving and receiving will be enacted. This cycle is consubstantial with the operation of the signifier. The promise of the gift is continually called up by the shuttle of signification but forever escapes from it. By establishing the scaffold of binary relations upon which the system of the signifier is constructed, while at the same time setting in motion the virtual object with which discourse is continually haunted, sacrifice serves to constitute the very matrix of desire. The essential function of sacrifice is less *do ut des,* I give so that you might give, than *do ut desidero*: I give in order that I might desire.

CHAPTER 4

The Freudian Thing

We now come to a crucially important crossroads at which the basic approach of the preceding chapters must be significantly complicated. The first imperative is to reconsider the dualistic character of our discussions, centered as they have been on the conceptual couplet of positionality and dispositionality. In many ways, of course, a dualistic approach was called for by the binary tendency of Freud's own theorizing. Yet it now remains to show how this dualism can be unfolded into the triadic conception implied by Lacan's imaginary, symbolic, and real. In much of what has been said up to this point, we have acted as if the imaginary and the symbolic could be understood in a dialectic of their own, independent of the real. To allow this idea to go unqualified, however, would lead to a complete misconception. The three categories must be rigorously integrated in a fashion that does justice to Lacan's comparison of the three registers to the interlocking rings of a Borromean knot. The ultimate objective is not simply to clarify Lacanian theory but rather to demonstrate how Lacan develops his theory in a genuine reading of Freud's text. The task will be to see how familiar Freudian dualisms *require* development into triadic structures as an unfolding of their own inner logic.

Our discussions to this point face another equally fundamental challenge. In addition to retracing a series of binary oppositions, our inquiry has centered upon problems of representation. While we have sought to repose that problem by articulating structural continuities underlying both imagistic and linguistic processes, this approach tends to assume a representing subject *for whom* such structures exist. For an examination of psychoanalytic theory, it is precisely the identity of such a subject that cannot be taken for granted. The force of these considerations becomes especially compelling in relation to Lacan, who inserts a dimension of radical otherness into the heart of the human subject. For Lacan, the most truly revolutionary and unsettling discovery of psychoanalysis, the discovery that justifiably begs comparison with that of Copernicus, concerns the way in which the human subject is found to be eccentric to itself. The human subject is a split subject, a subject that is always and forever outside itself, ineluctably bound up with an opaque and unencompassable Other. If we are to take seriously Lacan's characterization of the unconscious as "structured like a language," we cannot fail to consider the companion characterization of the unconscious as "the discourse of the Other." It is the evidence of psychoanalysis above all that forces us to ask: "Who, then, is this other to whom I am more attached than to myself, since, at the heart of my assent to my own identity it is still he who agitates me?" (E:S, 172).

The business of the present chapter is to address both of these deficits, showing how the dynamics of the unconscious escape any simple dualism and how the locus of the subject discovered by psychoanalysis lacks the unity attributed to it by a long philosophical tradition. As we will see in what follows, these two problems are intimately bound up with one another. Psychoanalysis reveals that every relation of subject and object is triangulated by a third position, the locus of the Other. Indeed, it is precisely such a triangle of subject, object, and Other that is at stake in the Oedipus complex. By clarifying these issues, however, we will be drawn to consider a final and decisive Freudian theme: the wrinkled temporality of deferred action, or *Nachträglichkeit*. Not only does the question of *Nachträglichkeit* go to the heart of Freud's theory of the unconscious, it also bears very significant consequences for the assessment of Freud's work for philosophy.

A Love Triangle

If our task now is to move beyond dualism and to introduce the Lacanian concept of the Other, there is no better place to begin than with the Oedipus complex and, more particularly, with the pivotal role played by the phallus. In the previous chapter, we treated the question of the phallus in terms of the imaginary dismemberment at stake in the phantasy of castration. From that point of view, what is crucial about the male genital is the way in which it is situated on the threshold between the imaginary and the symbolic: its presence in the male and absence in the female renders it both a privileged site at which the wholeness of the body gestalt is threatened and an anatomical marker of signifying difference. But this account tells only half the story. For the phallus derives its special status in the child's imagination not only for its role in staging the question of imaginary identity and symbolic difference but also for the way that it provides an answer to the question of the mother's desire. It is at this point that Lacan's perspective most conspicuously shows its indebtedness to the Hegelian analysis of desire. The child's relation to its primary caretaker, when it begins to transcend the barest fulfillment of physical need, becomes caught up in the question of what the mother desires. For Lacan, it from this angle that the father enters the Oedipal complex. The question arises in the child's mind of what outfits the father to warrant the mother's interest—the question, in short, of what the father has that the mother lacks.

In order to appreciate adequately what is at stake in this formative moment and to see why it implicates the phallus, it is essential to grasp not only the inevitability of the child's underlying question but also the primitiveness of its capacity to answer it. The child is led to the male genital by a judgment that is distorted by the evidences of an imaginary anatomy. According to the primitive logic of infantile thinking, a logic rooted in the brute givens of perception, something, anything, is always better than nothing. Take any two grade-schoolers and ceremoniously give one of them something to hold—it might be an ice-cream cone or a tarantula—the other child will clamor to have one, too. When the Oedipal child unconsciously seizes upon the phallus in answer to the question of the mother's desire—that is, when the child frames that question in terms of the question of what the mother *lacks*—it is obeying a similarly elementary logic. Biologically there is nothing missing in the female, but it *looks* like there is. The child is impressed by that so-apparent, extra something possessed by the father. By the same path of perceptual reasoning, my four-year-old son was led to proclaim that Mommy has a vagina and Daddy has a penis *and* a vagina. Having heard my wife and I explain that Mommy doesn't have a penis but she *does* have a special something of her own, he quite naturally concluded that the vagina in question must be the pubic hair—the only thing visible to him. *Ergo*, Mommy has a vagina and no penis, but Daddy has both.

Lacan's insistence that the penis offers an imaginary answer to the question of the mother's desire in no way denies the fact that the symbolic value of the male member is also signaled by a whole range of phallic representations endemic to the cultural context in which the child grows up. Indeed, the Lacanian categories readily offer themselves to explain the three levels on which the privilege of the penis/phallus is announced: real, imaginary, and symbolic. The penis is an important object in the real: it is an organ conspicuous for its functions in generation and elimination, to say nothing of its potential as a source of pleasurable stimulation. It also claims a special imaginary status: aside from the breasts, it is the most *visible* mark of differentiation between male and female. And it is a symbolic object par excellence: its form is mimicked in all manner of cultural icons, especially in representations of power and prestige. By locating its function on each of these levels—biological, psychosocial, and symbolico-cultural— and by suggesting how the three levels are interconnected with one another, the Lacanian rereading of the psychoanalytic doctrine of the phallus illuminates its role in the Oedipus complex much more effectively than did Freud's more limited focus on fears of castration.

If the father's *penis* offers the imaginary hook on which the question of the mother's desire is hung, it is the *phallus* that is symbolically at issue, insofar as question of the other's desire is inevitably posed on the limen between the imaginable and unimaginable. The distance between the penis and the phallus opens up when the penis begins to function properly as a signifier, that is, when it refers beyond itself to an open horizon of desirability. The difference can be illuminated by reference to Lacan's distinction between need, demand, and desire. To return to our grade-schooler begging for an ice-cream cone: what is asked for has very little to do with any service of organic need. The ice-cream cone is an object not of need but of demand. Need is raised to the level of demand simply by being put into words. A determinate quantity will satisfy hunger on the level of an organic need, but the very fact of having been put into words— "I want ice cream!"—effectively opens the door to a limitless demand, a hunger beyond all hunger. What, then, is the relation of demand and desire? We get a clue when the child is given the coveted confection and immediately begins whining that it is the wrong flavor, or that what he or she really wanted was a shake, a candy bar, etc. The parent who tries to meet these new demands may succeed only in stimulating a new series of demand. The reason is that what appears as demand for an object is in fact a demand for love, a demand to monopolize the desire of the other.

What, then, is the relation of demand to desire? When the insatiability of the demand for love is posed, as Hegel might say, explicitly in and for itself, when the force of demand is detached from particularity and passes into the open circuit of signifiers, the stubborn fixity of demand gives way to the movement of desire. Demand seizes upon the most obvious token of value in an effort to anchor the relation to the other's desire with a privileged exchange.[1] From a Lacanian point of view, that the assumption of desire is tied to the acceptance of castration means that the literality of the male organ must accede to the function of the phallus as a pure signifier. The phallus becomes the privileged object of desire precisely when it stands for what cannot be given literally, when it represents what remains forever beyond one's grasp.

Already in the dialectic of demand and desire—the way in which desire brings forward the unlimited character of demand, the way that desire re-circuits, we might say, the very demand of demand—we begin to recognize how psychical dynamics in the child unfold in accordance with a paradoxical, retroactive temporality. Desire is in one sense the *telos* of the whole movement it and, in another sense, the point of departure. Keeping sight of this point means refusing to conceive of psychical development as a linear process. Without taking this retroactive effect into account, the child's approach to the Oedipus complex appears to be a simple progression, and—we have to admit—it is largely in these terms that we have presented it up to now. This point of view supposes that the unitary ego is first formed in the mirror phase, modeled on the imago of the other. Only later does the child come to realize that the mother's desire gravitates toward some third position, and the child begins to ask, "What is it that the mother desires when she desires something other than me, the child?"[2] Thus begins the search for the privileged object of the mother's desire—a search that will lead to the phallus as signifier of desire. But this two-stage, linear account proves inadequate to the extent that the narcissistic ego is produced not merely by the perception of the mother's object-body, but also by the formative influence on the child of the mother's adoring gaze. The infant comes to experience its own unity through the eyes of the other. The infantile ego is formed as an object offered to the other's desiring look. Lacan especially emphasizes the child's wish to be itself the phallus of the mother. "If the desire of the mother is the phallus, the child wishes to be the phallus in order to satisfy that desire" (E:S, 289). The theroetically challenging point is that such a wish to be the phallus of the mother cannot be taken as a subsequent add-on or extension of the narcissistic ego, rather this wish constitutes in itself the very essence of narcissism. The formative role of the phallus is there from the very start.

Let us be clearer about what this means. Up to now, we have presented the formation of the imaginary ego as a precipitate of the gestalt properties of perception, the unity of the primitive ego being based on a mirror relation with the perceived object. The point we are now making does not invalidate that perspective but does qualify it in an important way. The Lacanian theory maintains that the signifier of the phallus is retroactively insinuated into the process by which the narcissistic core of the personality is formed, but does so in such a way that it not only comes to occupy the very core space of the narcissistic identification, but must be said to be, in accordance with a strange temporality, the motive for that identification. It is as if the phallus had been, from the very beginning, the cause and agent of the entire process of the ego's formation. We are thus faced with a paradox: the phallus, as the supposed object of the mother's desire, is the last object to be registered in the child's mind, the last stop in the train of infantile discoveries, and yet it is always already in play, motivating the entire development of the ego.

It will now quite reasonably be asked what makes such a paradoxical formulation necessary. Is this merely a gratuitous complication of theory? Admittedly, the issues involved are complex and obscure; we will require the remainder of this chapter to develop a better sense of them. Yet there can be no doubt about the importance of the theoretical issues at stake. It concerns the priority of imaginary and the symbolic. From one point of view, the perceptual register of the imaginary claims priority. As we have been at pains to point out, the capacity for gestalt recognition is a necessary precondition for the functioning of language. Moreover, the formation of the ego in the mirror stage is already well under way by the time the child gains any significant degree of competence in speech and language. On the other hand, however, Lacan insists that the child's sense of self, even at the most primitive level, will be formed along the lines laid down for him or her by the parent's desire—a desire that will be borne by key signifiers. The clearest example is the influence of the proper name. Most frequently chosen not only before the drama of the mirror phase, but before the child is even born, the name exerts a formative influence over the very foundations of the emerging ego. As Lacan points out,

> language and its structure exist prior to the moment at which
> each subject at a certain point in his mental development makes
> his entry into it. . . . Thus the subject, too, if he can appear to be
> the slave of language is all the more so of a discourse in the uni-
> versal movement in which his place is already inscribed at birth,
> if only by virtue of his proper name. (E:S, 148)

The human child is bathed in currents of the parents' desire that are set in motion even before birth and are transmitted to the child by means of signifiers. This Lacanian point is aptly illustrated by the example of Anita Nall, the young American swimmer who won three medals at the 1992 Olympics. Sixteen years earlier, in 1976, her mother lay in the hospital, distracting herself from the trials of her birth labor by watching . . . the Olympic Games. She was delighted, as was the rest of the world, with the magical performance of a Romanian gymnast named Nadia Comaneci. The motion of desire excited by that experience was passed along to her unborn daughter, inscribed in the portion of her name that is most often left unpronounced: *Nadia* Anita Nall.

Whatever the claim of the imaginary to primacy, Lacan insists that "in the beginning was the Word." The human being is born into a nexus of signifiers that will preside over its destiny, indeed, will direct even the minutest increments of that destiny. Lacan is not unaware of the nearly contradictory character of the resulting situation, but nevertheless he holds his ground. It is this commitment to a curiously retroactive temporality, equally unthinkable by the standards of common sense and mechanistic science, that stands behind Lacan's polemical rejection of psychologies of "development." What such theories overlook is precisely this enigmatic, yet absolutely essential, feature of the human being that is simultaneously behind and ahead of itself.

Perhaps, it may now be objected, the *Lacanian* subject is characterized by such retroactive temporality, folded back upon itself by the effects of the signifier, but with what right does Lacan make this claim for the subject theorized by Freud? The answer to this question is admittedly incomplete in Freud's *oeuvre*, to the extent that he never fully articulated the concept of *Nachträglichkeit*. There can be no doubt, however, about the importance to Freud of the concept. Arrived at early in his experience and discernible in the foundations of his later theoretical elaborations, the idea was prompted by the experience of the trauma that is everywhere at the core of the mystery of the unconscious. Investigating cases of childhood seduction, Freud repeatedly found that the pathogenic impact of the trauma arose, not during the period in which the traumatic incident actually occurred, *but only at some time after the original trauma.* The effects of the trauma were thus deferred, *nachträglich*, triggered by a revival of the memory of the original incident. The point is remarkably illustrated by the case of the woman's shop phobia, recounted in the *Project for a Scientific Psychology*, to which we have already referred more than once.

The Thing about the Other

For all its brevity, described by Freud in just a few pages midway through the *Project*, the case vignette of Emma remains immensely rich and suggestive. This fragment of analysis will allow us to place a whole range of crucial concepts in close coordination with one another.

We have already considered the basic outline of the case: a young woman is afflicted with a crippling fear of going into shops alone. In explaining her fear to Freud, she first recalled an incident that occurred during her early puberty: she entered a shop and saw two shop assistants laughing together, whereupon she fled from the shop in a panic. She had the impression that the two assistants were laughing at her clothes, and she recalled that one of the two had aroused a feeling of sexual attraction in her. Her discussions with Freud led her to a second memory of an incident that had occurred some four years earlier: she had gone into a shop to buy some candy, and the shopkeeper had grabbed at her genitals through her clothes. The two scenes were linked by the element of the clothes and also (as she realized in thinking back on it) by the laughing of the two shop assistants, which reminded her of the grin of the shopkeeper in the earlier incident. What Freud found significant in this case was that the traumatic effect of the shopkeeper's assault was produced only later, when elements of the original incident were repeated in the second scene involving the two shop assistants. After the original experience, far from fleeing the shop and staying away from it, she returned a second time a little while later. By contrast, the second, ostensibly more innocent scene with the two shop-assistants produced a severe attack of anxiety and triggered a lasting phobia of going alone into shops. The question, obviously, was how to explain the mechanism of this deferred effect.

To grasp Freud's answer, we need to go back to the beginning. He offers the case of Emma to illustrate a point of absolutely general interest for the theory of the unconscious: the occurrence of excessively intense ideas. Neurosis typically manifests itself in the force or frequency with which particular ideas emerge into consciousness. Freud points out that such excessively intense ideas also occur normally, indeed they undergird key elements of character structure: "They lend the ego its individuality" (SE, 1:347-48). What distinguishes psychopathological ideation is above all the nonsensical, intractable, and incongruous character of the thoughts involved. These traits of unintelligiblity derive from the relation of the neurotic compulsion to acts of repression. Behind every compulsive idea A, the intensity or effects of which seem out of keeping with its actual content, stands another, more significant and justifiably upsetting idea, B. "The subject does not know why he weeps at A," for example. Analysis then discovers that "there is an idea B, which justifiably gives rise to weeping" and that "B stands in a particular relation to A" (SE, 1:348-49). Neurotic complusion can thus be explained by assuming that

> there has been an occurrence which consisted of B+A. A was an incidental circumstance; B was appropriate for producing the lasting effect. The reproduction of this event in memory has now taken a form of such a kind that it is as though A had stepped into B's place. A has become a substitute, a *symbol* for B. Hence the incongruity: A is accompanied by consequences

which it does not seem worthy of, which do not fit in with it. (SE, 1:349)

Freud contrasts the neurotic outcome with more normal circumstances in which a relatively trivial idea is strongly cathected by virtue of being a substitute for another (e.g., the soldier who dies for the flag that represents his homeland, the knight who fights for his lady's glove). In order to distinguish the two cases, Freud begins by supposing that the original idea can be consciously retrieved in the normal case where in the neurotic, owing to the effects of repression, it cannot. How, then, does this repression of the original idea work? Freud insists that two criteria must be met: unacceptability to the ego and connection to sexual life. "Repression is brought to bear invariably on ideas which evoke a distressing affect (unpleasure) in the *ego*, secondly on ideas[s] from sexual life" (SE, 1:350). But this consideration is still inadequate to fully resolve the issue, for it can be stated as a general rule, by no means limited to the sexual sphere, that "we avoid thinking of what arouses only unpleasure, and we do this by directing our thought to something else" (SE, 1:351). There must be an additional factor, but where is to be found? The question is all the more puzzling because, contrary to what his theorizing to this point would lead us to expect, the neurotic person can sometimes bring the repressed idea B to consciousness with relative ease. "This is a surprise," he says, "for it might well have been supposed that B was really forgotten, that no memory trace of B remained" (SE, 1:351). The path to a new answer is opened by considering the fact that the repressed idea is not a simple presentation, but a *complex*. If the original idea is in some way internally divided between different levels, one part of it may be easily recalled to consciousness while some other aspect of the idea remains inaccessible. Thought tends to get caught up in conflicts pertaining to an initial level of the complex and never reaches a second, more deeply hidden one. "If, as is usual, B is a complex of cathexes, then a *resistance* arises, which is uncommonly large and hard to defeat, against activity of thought with B. . . . resistance is directed against thought being in any way concerned with B, even if it [B] has already been made partly conscious" (SE, 1:351).

We are now in a position to appreciate how exactly the case of Emma illustrates the theory Freud is putting forward. Freud offers a diagram (Fig. 15) that makes the points of connection especially clear:

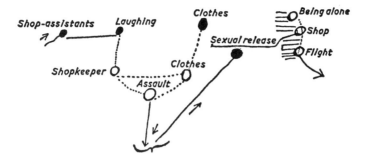

Figure 15

The diagram shows us, in the upper right, the unintelligible and incongruous features of the neurotic compulsion—the phobia of entering shops alone. If this cluster is taken as the compulsive idea or response that Freud designates "A," then the idea "B" for which it has been substituted, the justifiably upsetting idea for which which A is a more or less unintelligible symbol, is the whole range of material to the left concerning her visits to shops, and most especially the original incident in which the shopkeeper groped for her genitals. Significantly, however, B is itself internally complex. It consists, on the one hand, of the elements of the clothes and laughter, both of which are fairly readily accessible to consciousness, but also of the event of the original assault, which is clearly more deeply repressed. The problem, Freud says, is that "the whole complex is represented in consciousness by the one idea of clothes" (SE, 1:355). Freud thus pictures the formation of the phobia as a two-stage or two-level process. The real core of the repressed remains at a double remove from the symptomatic manifestation. The shop phobia was triggered by the assistants' laughter at her clothes, but clothing was already a symbolic disguise for the repressed content of the original assault. The phobic symptom was therefore only indirectly related to the repressed. The phobia was effectively a symbol of a symbol.

The notion that the repressed idea lies hidden behind at least two layers of symbolic substitution helps significantly to understand the mechanism by which the sympton is produced. But still Freud is not satisfied. He is convinced that there is yet another, and most crucial, factor to be put in place: the di-phasic onset of sexuality. Sexual experiences may occur in early childhood that become understandable as such only at puberty. The case of Emma is a perfect illustration. The true meaning the shopkeeper's attack when she was eight years old appeared only later, with the development of sexual feelings of her own. It was this time delay that made possible the traumatic effect of the second incident. Ordinarily, Freud argues, incoming perceptions that would arouse unpleasure are readily dealt with by means of primary defense, the mechanism of which we examined in an earlier chapter. Attention to the threatening perception sets in motion a side-cathexis that succeeds in derailing the sequence of neuronal activation that would otherwise lead to a full-blown experience of unpleasure. But in cases like the present one, in which the traumatic potential is attached not to a perception but to a memory, the idea may slip by the usual lines of defense (the structures of the secondary process) and precipitate a serious overload of the system (a discharge on the level of the primary process). In effect, some content is smuggled into the psychic apparatus under the guise of a memory—it presents itself, that is, as an idea that has already been well worked over and "tamed" by the secondary process—but this content then turns out, in the light of knowledge about sexuality acquired at puberty, to involve an unexpected power of excitation and as a result brings about an uncontrolled sexual release (e.g., the feeling of sexual attraction that Emma felt in relation to one of the two shop assistants). The ego draws its conclusions, as it were, from a false premise, a kind of original lie, or *proton pseudos*.

> Thus it is the ego's business not to permit any release of affect, because this at the same time permits a primary process. Its best instrument for this purpose is the mechanism of attention. If a cathexis releasing unpleasure were able to evade this, then the ego would come into action against it too late. Now this is precisely what happens in the case of the hysterical *proton pseudos*. Attention is [normally] adjusted towards perceptions, which are what ordinarily give occasion for a release of unpleasure. Here, [however, what has appeared] is no perception but a memory, which unexpectedly releases unpleasure, and the ego only discovers this too late. It has permitted a primary process because it did not expect one. . . . *The retardation of puberty makes possible posthumous primary prcocesses.* (SE, 1:358-59)

Freud especially emphasizes the sexual nature of the original lie, or *proton pseudos*. The effect of deception is possible because of the delay between infantile experiences and the later revelations of puberty in the light of which the earlier experiences assume their specifically sexual meaning. What is crucial, therefore, is the *prematurity* of the original experience. This prematurity prepares the way for a release of sexual feeling sometime after puberty that the subject didn't experience at the time of the original experience. Because virtually every human being passes through this di-phasic unfolding of sexuality, everyone is liable to the development of the *proton pseudos*. "Accordingly," says Freud, "every adolescent must carry the germ of hysteria within him" (SE, 1:356). Every human being is subject to the effects of traumatic *Nachträglichkeit*.

Keeping in mind these aspects of the assumption of sexuality at puberty, we can resolve what might at first sight appear to be a contradiction in our account. In our first dealings with the case of Emma (in chapter 2), we offered it as an illustration of primary defense, in which a threatening overcharge in the neuronal network was shunted to a side-cathexis. The clothes-laughter complex was substituted for the shopkeeper's gropings. We now recognize, however, that the case interests Freud most as an example of the *failure* of primary defense. So which is it? The answer is that it is both, but at different times. Primary defense succeeded in the first scene with the shopkeeper: unpleasure was avoided by virtue of the assault on the subject's own body being deflected by a side-cathexis to the ancillary details of the clothing and laughter. The substitution accomplished the basic aim of defense by providing "the emergence of another object in the place of the hostile one" (SE, 1:322). The success of the whole strategy was attested to by the fact that Emma found no difficulty in returning to the shop a second time. But defense failed in the second, later scene with the shop assistants. Why? Because the side-cathexis that had adequately defended against an *external* stimulus failed to protect against an *internal* one. In this point, the whole thrust of Freud's analysis is summarized. A primary process leading to unpleasure was unleashed (where it would have been prevented by successful primary defense) because the clothing-laughter complex, itself already structured by the secondary process of the ego, unexpectedly triggered a sexual release in the subject herself that was not possible at the time of the original incident. Everything depends on the distinction between outer and inner dangers. The situation of the second incident and the deferred trauma effected by it is analogous to a country that has deployed its army exclusively against invasion from without only to be suddenly overwhelmed by a rebellion from within.

Lacan's contribution to this case can be located at precisely this point. What Freud conceived mechanistically as a difference between sources of excitiation that are either internal or external, Lacan reconstrues in terms of the subject's relation to the Other. In reviewing the case, Lacan draws the conclusion concisely: the deferred traumatic effect accrued from a memory that "*echoes the idea of a sexual attraction experienced in the other*" (S.VII, 74, emphasis added). In the original experience of the old shopkeeper's gropings, a key element remained unknown and unknowable, forming a kind of hard kernel that resisted representation, *because it belonged to the desire of the other*. Lacan calls this hard kernel, that portion of the desire of the other that outstrips all capacity to represent it, "the Thing"—*das Ding*. It is, he says, "a primordial function which is located at the level of the initial establishment of the gravitation of the unconscious *Vorstellungen*" (S,VII, 62). Like the Kantian *Ding-an-sich*, or thing-in-itself, an oblique reference to which is included in Lacan's choice to retain the German word, *das Ding* designates an unencompassable aspect of every representation, a kind of ungraspable center of gravity that lends coherence to the various manifestations of an object while remaining itself ineluctably out of reach.

From a Lacanian point of view, the shop phobia described by Freud points back to the traumatizing potential of the otherness of the Other, absorbed at a time when it could not be understood. The nucleus of Emma's trauma was her inability to comprehend the *motive* of the old shopkeeper's groping. What was he after? What did he want? The central point of the trauma was a question concerning the shopkeeper's desire. In this sense, there was something unknown and unknowable in the original confrontation. It was an encounter with the real. In Lacanian terms, the "germ of hysteria" related by Freud to the delayed unfolding of sexuality is thus rooted not only in the wrinkle of organic maturation by which puberty occurs some ten or twelve years after birth, but in the originary dependence of the human being upon the Other that even precedes birth. The human child comes into possession of its own sexual impulse only with the onset of puberty, but the pathway by which the child arrives at the assumption its own desire inevitably passes under the shadow of the desire of the Other, the dimension of *das Ding*. In the encounter with *das Ding* the subject thus comes into relation with an aspect of the real that is at once outside and inside itself. *Das Ding* functions to site, to hold the place of, something that will emerge at the heart of the subject itself. It will establish the originary object that all subsequent longing will strive to refind, but in doing so serves to orient the subject with respect to its own innermost longings. It can therefore be said of *das Ding* that

> what is involved is that excluded interior which, in the termi-
> nology of the *Entwurf*, is thus excluded in the interior. In the
> interior of what then? Of something that is precisely articulated
> at that moment as the *Real-Ich*, which means then the final real
> of the psychic organization, a real conceived of as hypothetical,
> to the extent that it necessarily presupposes the *Lust-Ich*. (S,VII,
> 101)

Is this business of the Thing just a Lacanian invention? What warrant can be found in Freud's own text for it? In fact, Lacan's innovation is a gloss on very text of the *Project* that we have been examining. The vignette of the shop phobia is presented in the context of Freud's own theorization of the Thing. The problem is among the most basic taken up in the *Project* and concerns the nature of imaginal presentations, or *Vorstellungen*. One of the most elemental functions of the psychic apparatus is to seek identity between the first and subsequent registrations of images, a coincidence between memory and perception. But there is always something that escapes this coincidence, there is always a failure of identity. It is in the space of this failure that Freud locates the function of the "Thing." The process by which identity is sought, according to Freud, is judgment, and "what we call *things* are residues which evade being judged" (SE, 1:334). The fact of such noncoincidence, and the retention of an unassimilable remainder in the form of the Thing, are of prime importance for Freud's conception of the way the mind works, for it is the failure of identity between memory and perception that provides the motive for thought: "their non-coincidence gives the impetus for the activity of thought, which is terminated once more with their coincidence" (SE, 1: 328).

As we have already seen, the analysis of the shop phobia pivots on the notion that the repressed idea forms a complex. It can now become clear that the question of the complex is none other than the question of the Thing. Perceptual images are typically complexes, and the first activity of judgment is that of resolving the complex into two components: on the one hand, the portion that matches up with previous mnemic traces and, on the other hand, the portion—identifiable only as the Thing—that does not coincide with previous experience. As Freud puts it, "perceptual complexes are divided into a constant, non-understood, part—*the thing*—and a changing, understandable, one—the attribute or movement of the thing" (SE, 1:383). Freud's discussion of the Thing thus rejoins the classical notion of judgment as distinguishing the subject and predicate of a proposition. Yet questions of wish and satisfaction are also integral to his analysis. The search for identity between a mnemic image and a perception—the process Freud calls "cognizing" the image—is typically a matter of a search for satisfaction in which the upsurge of a mnemic trace is motivated by a wish and the achievement of identity with perception indicates a reliable situation for action and discharge. To the extent that the activity of cognizing is set in motion by wishes, he suggests, "the eminently practical sense of all thought-activity would in this way seem to be demonstrated" (SE, 1:332).

Freud develops the concept of the Thing in way that is applicable to any and all *Vorstellungen*, but it is relevant in a privileged way to the appearance of the fellow human being, the *Nebenmensch*. It is at this point that it is most relevant for the case of Emma. The perception of the *Nebenmensch* is unique, first and foremost, because "the object that furnishes the perception resembles the subject." Moreover, "an object *like this* was simultaneously the [subject's] first satisfying object and further his first hostile object, as well as his sole helping power. . . . For this reason it is in relation to a fellow human-being that a human-being learns to cognize" (SE, 1:331). It is on the basis of this text that Lacan evolves his own conception of *das Ding* as the originary uncanniness of the Other. Freud points out that "the complex of the fellow human-being falls apart into two components, of which one makes an impression by its constant structure and stays together as a *thing*, while the other can be *understood* by the activity of memory—that is, can be traced back to information from [the subject's] own body" (SE, 1:331). How can we fail to recognize in Freud's description (of what is "traced back to information from the subject's own body") the mirror relation of the imaginary ego? In Lacanian terms, the complex of the *Nebenmensch*, divided between what is reflected of one's own body and something that remains opaque and enigmatic, is nothing else but the presence in the Other of both the imaginary and the real. Looking back on the diagram of the shop phobia and its mechanism, it seems that Freud has already located the horizon of the real, ambiguous between what is unknown in the other and unknown in oneself, at the very bottom of the schema. There we find a curious, undesignated bracket that marks the intersection of two arrows, one that descends from the complex of ideas retained from the original experience ("shopkeeper-clothes-assault"), and another that ascends to the sexual release of the second scene during puberty. It is entirely fitting that this bracket lacks any specifying designation, as it is marks the point at which the whole structure turns around something unsymbolized and unsymbolizable. Beneath this bracket, in the space of what is as-yet uncognizable, is the stuff of the real, the body of *das Ding*.

Whatever the first impression of novelty in Lacan's discussion of *das Ding*, his treatment is in fact an explication of Freud's text. It is an excellent example of Lacan's method. He brings to light a less well known text of Freud and seizes upon a little remarked distinction in it, but thereby succeeds in framing a conception that reaches far beyond the particular text in question and touches on the very foundations of the psychoanalytic theory. We can recognize the extent of its implications especially clearly in the relation of *das Ding* to the notion of a *complex*. It is by no means a distortion to read back into this term of the *Project* the full weight of its later usage in psychoanalytic theory—in relation, that is, to the subjective inscription of family dynamics that Freud later called the Oedipus and castration complexes. Just as the Thing designates an uncognizable surplus in perception, the two great developmental complexes concern the child's coming to terms with what is originally unmasterable in the family: the desire of the mother and the elusive object toward which it points.

With this notion of the complex in hand, it is also possible to clarify a key point in the psychoanlaytic concept of trauma. In particular, it allows us to separate the truly Freudian conception of trauma from a cruder, more naive and commonsensical one. According to that cruder notion, trauma results from a kind of brute shock, the influence upon the psyche of a massive, formless charge. This view invites us to picture the psychic organization as a homeostatic unity that is suddenly impinged upon by an overwhelming outside force. What makes things somewhat confusing is that Freud's conception is by no means wholly unrelated to this more common conception. We see it appear, for example, in his description of trauma in *Beyond the Pleasure Prinicple* as an unmasterable influx of energy that breaches the protective integument of the psychic vesicle. Nevertheless, the real heart of Freud's notion of trauma is more subtle. Trauma is not merely a shapeless and inarticulate mass that enters the psychical system like a great and indigestible bolus. The psychoanalytic sense of the trauma must rather be understood along the lines of the view we have taken of energetics as an essentially structural concept. The trauma is not a brute shock but is always imbricated within a complex structure. Moreover, we can see how Freud maps this complexity in the schemata we have examined. The impingment from without of the quantity Q is complex, in so far as the subject is presented with an image one aspect of which aligns itself with mnemic traces while some additional aspect exceeds the bounds of the image—the excess Freud associates with the Thing. What is most problematic about this excess, and what serves to establish its traumatic potential, is the way in which it implicates something emerging from the unknown interior of the subject itself. In the context of the *Project*, Freud calls it the emergence of endogenous energies. Later he will refer to it as the unbound or untamed pressure of the drives. It is inscribed in the diagram of the shop phobia in the mysterious bracket at the bottom of the schema. At this point something in the original experience with the groping shopkeeper is seen to touch upon a hidden depth of the subject's own impulse life. Out of this hidden confluence emerges the experience of a sexual excitation, marked higher up in the schema as "sexual release."

For Freud, then, trauma results not simply from a brute impact but from an unresolved perceptual complex that outstrips the subject's capacity for representation and excites an unrepresentable dimension of the subject's own desire. Far from supposing a unified subject that is split by traumatic experience, Freud's conception of trauma thus implies an original split within the subject. Trauma results from the unmasterable encounter with the Thing, but only insofar as that encounter touches upon that aspect of the subject's own being that remains uncognizable, the internal Thing that Freud eventually calls *das Es*, the id. From this perspective, we can see clearly how Freud's conception of trauma is related not only to the formation of a symptom (as the means by which the uncognizable is marked) but also to his definition of the ego as a defensive formation, tantamount to a kind of master symptom, the symptom of all symptoms. Freud's analysis of defense against the trauma in the *Project* thus contains in embryo his mature doctrine according to which the bound organization of the ego is always in some measure a misrecognition of the intersubjective complex of the family structure, even as its dynamics are encoded symptomatically within the ego's pattern of identifications. The unity of the ego is a refusal of the essential complexity of the subject's involvement with the Other.

Thing or No-thing

The case of the shop phobia has led us to a discussion of *das Ding*, but we earlier drew upon the same case to illustrate the role of positionality and the dispositional field in the dynamics of repression. How do these two treatments stand in relation to one another? Our earlier commentary focused on the process of primary defense, specifically on the pathway by which resistance to a threatening image results in a side-cathexis to a substitute idea. This process of substitution, we said, typically replaces the focus of awareness with an element taken from the periphery of the perceptual field. Defense effects a gestalt reversal in which the figure is traded for some detail of the background. In Emma's memory of the shopkeeper's grabbing at her gentials, what is remembered is not the touch of his hand on her body but rather the image of her clothing accompanied by a grin or laughter. We compared this arresting of attention at a point perceptually adjacent to an unacceptable focus with the process by which the fetish is established at some point along the path leading to the mother's missing phallus—the pubic fur, the lace of undergarments, etc.

In the light of our most recent discussions, however, we can see much more deeply into the structures at issue. In evolving the concepts of positionality and the dispositional field, we had in mind the activity by which a zone of focal attention is disembedded from its environing context in the manner of the figure-ground relation described by Gestalt psychology. The notion of *das Ding*, along with Freud's insistence that every perceptual content forms a complex, now enables us to see how the positional focus is liable to an internal articulation, indeed, how it is always and necessarily internally divided. In order to maintain consciousness of an object of attention, the Gestaltist act of detaching a figural contour from a sur-rounding background is necessary but not sufficient. The activity of per-ception in a moving, changing world must additionally rely on an ongoing process of discrimination by means of which small changes in the figure—of color, shape, texture, and lighting, in the case of visual object—are related to an virtual locus of unity. Such a virtual unity is a pure regulatory idea that allows for an overall impression of object-identity to be main-tained. In viewing a sculpture, for example, while it is necessary to distin-guish the form of the sculpture itself from the background elements of the park or gallery in which it is situated, it is also necessary continuously to collate the succession of views as we walk around the sculpture, relating them all to the unity of the whole. At no single point is the sculpture vis-ible as a totality. In fact, its totality exists only as a pure, regulatory idea to which the succession of views are related and in which they are integrated. A quick review of Freud's discussion shows that the function of such a regulatory idea is an essential aspect of what Freud calls *das Ding*.

Freud's account in the *Project* emphasizes two related aspects of the Thing: its unknowability and its constancy. On the one hand, the Thing is identified with that portion of the perceptual complex that remains unas-similable to any previous experience, that part of the perception that can-not be matched with memory. The Thing is the ungraspable kernel, the core of the unknown. On the other hand, the Thing is relevant to a con-sideration of time. Freud points out repeatedly that the Thing is an aspect of the complex that remains constant and unchanging in relation to fea-tures of the perceptual complex that display changes over time: "perceptual complexes are divided into a constant, non-understood part—the *thing*—and a changing, understandable, one—the attribute or movement of the thing" (SE, 1:383). But these two features of the Thing ultimately come to the same: the Thing remains unchanging precisely because it cannot be given any definite content. The Thing is thus a pure posit, an empty and ideal locus of being amid a shifting whirl of other aspects of the percep-tual complex that are more familiar to memory. The function of this posit-ing is to establish a staging area in which memory and perception can be matched. In effect, the Thing is an utterly virtual outline that marks the site of a failure of identity between memory and perception. The Thing provides a unifying topos within which memories and perceptions can continue to be worked on, or as Freud says, "cognized," until an identity is reached. Until that happens, however, there remains something strange and unassimilable at the heart of the object. The Thing is the provisional matrix by which memory and perception are held together, but so long as identity between them remains elusive, the Thing remains a kind of unencompassable and resistant kernel. We therefore have this paradox: what makes future cognition possible is the very locus of the Thing that marks its present impossibility.

In Lacan's view, the radical thing about Freud's notion of *das Ding* is the way that it implies a locus of absence. "At the level of the *Vorstellungen*," Lacan suggests, "the Thing is not nothing, but literally is not. It is characterized by its absence, its strangeness" (S.VII, 63). It is this concern with absence and negativity, for example, that most interests Lacan in Heidegger's essay on "The Thing," in which the relations of earth and sky, mortals and divinities are seen to intersect in the hollow of the most humble jug. Negativity is at the center of Heidegger's analysis, focusing as it does on the way in which the walls of the jug enwrap an emptiness, the manner in which the jug bodies forth a pregnant void. Lacan reads Heidegger's meditation on the Greek temple in "The Origin of the Work of Art" in the same fashion, finding in the temple "a construction around emptiness that designates the place of the Thing" (S.VII, 140).

More significant for our immediate purposes than its philosophical resonances, however, are the consequences of the Thing for our understanding of Lacan's own categories. Up until now, we have taken the unity of the perceptual object to be a product of the imaginary. Indeed, the power to establish such unity is offered by Lacan, especially in his early papers, as the essential feature of the imaginary function. Yet with the introduction of *das Ding*, we see a kernel of the real come to inhabit the very heart of the imaginary. Indeed, *das Ding* is the real core around which the unity of the imaginary contour is wrapped. What, then, is the imaginary itself? If it falls to the real to provide the unifying kernel of imaginary unity, a kind of central vortex that must be perpetually approached precisely because it can never be overtaken or occupied, if it is something of the real that forms the inner cohesion of the imaginary, then how are we to conceive the specific contribution of the imaginary as such?

How else but to assume that it is the imaginary that gives the illusion of fullness, of substance, of filling-out what cannot be filled? The imaginary becomes the power by which the skin of appearance is stretched over the empty skull of the real. The imaginary is the power of the veil, the power of seduction *par excellence*. Here again we see how Lacan provides a general theory along the path opened up by Freud's more special theory: for Freud the hysterical *proton pseudos* is a particular mistranscription of ideas. Yet the explanatory potential of the *proton pseudos* far exceeds the passing reference Freud makes to it. Far from merely illuminating a minor point in the argument of the *Project*, the concept of the *proton pseudos* retraces the broadest outline of the psychoanalytic theory of the human subject and reveals the radicality of the psychoanalytic meaning of the object. From a Lacanian point of view, the *proton pseudos* is linked with the register of the imaginary as such. We see it clearly operating in the case of Emma. If, in the experience with the shop assistants, the psychical process is set off in the wrong direction by the clothing and laughter as by a mistaken first premise or "first lie," the power of the clothing/laughter complex to mislead is based on an even more archaic "lie" that was laid down in the original scene with the shopkeeper. In that original scene, imaginary presentations—of the clothing and grin—congealed over what remained ungraspable behind the shopkeeper's behavior. The clothing-grin became the representative of something otherwise unrepresentable: the invisible source and meaning of his desire. As Lacan says of the case "the path of truth is suggested in a masked form, in the deceiving *Vorstellung* of her clothes" (S.VII, 74).

> In an opaque way, there is an allusion to something that did not happen on the occasion of the first memory, but on the second. Something that wasn't apprehended in the beginning is apprehended retroactively, by means of the deceitful transformation—*proton pseudos*. Thus in that way we have confirmation of the fact that the relationship of the subject to *das Ding* is marked as bad—but the subject can only formulate this fact through the symptom. (S.VII, 74)

We grasp the real significance of the *proton pseudos* when we recognize that its falsity is less a matter of mere exchange of images or objects than of the constitution of the object-image as such. In the *proton pseudos* a discrete and bounded unity is substituted for an original complexity. The images around which the subject first mobilizes its own identity and in which it first positions itself with respect to its desire are fraught with an essential misrecognition. The Freudian subject is always already bound up with a battery of formative images that fall short of the reality of the Thing. The unity of the image is a falsification of an original complexity that cannot be represented. As we saw it in the case of shop phobia, the sound image of the laughter and the visual image of the clothing is substituted for a total intersubjective situation that remained ungraspable for the child exposed to it. That this original complexity sets in motion an effort to seek "a state of identity" then implies an effort to refind an object that was never in fact possessed.

Not long after introducing the notion of *das Ding* in his seventh seminar, Lacan illustrates the relation of imaginary and real at which we have arrived in the example of the Lady of courtly love. This figure—the woman whose beauty mesmerizes the knight who serves her yet whose service may demand his death—perfectly incarnates the absent-presence of the real concealed in the wrappings of imaginary fascination. To begin with, the attraction of the Lady is obviously bound up with an effusion of narcissism. Thus Lacan remarks that "the element of idealizing exaltation that is expressly sought out in the ideology of courtly love has certainly been demonstrated; it is fundamentally narcissistic in character" (S.VII, 151). Yet this narcissistic object that organizes a powerful imaginary force field ultimately derives its charge from the way that it secretly embodies *das Ding*. Behind the dazzling surface of her beauty lies a kind of abyss, a deadly emptiness. The poetry of courtly love evokes an object, Lacan says "that I can only describe as terrifying, an inhuman partner" (S.VII, 150).

> The idealized woman, the Lady, who is in the position of the
> Other and of the object, finds herself suddenly and brutally
> positing, in a place knowingly constructed out of the most
> refined of signifiers, the emptiness of a thing in all its crudity, a
> thing that reveals itself in its nudity to be the thing, her thing,
> the one that is to be found at her very heart in its cruel empti-
> ness. That Thing, whose function certain of you perceived in the
> relation to sublimation, is in a way unveiled with a cruel and
> insistent power. (S.VII, 163)

There is, and must be, something inaccessible about the beloved object of courtly love. Thus "it is impossible to serenade one's Lady in her poetic role in the absence of the given that she is surrounded and isolated by a barrier" (S.VII, 149). It is this very conjunction of a continually regenerated fascination with an essential inaccessibility that marks courtly love with the character of sublimation, indeed, that makes courtly love "an exemplary form, a paradigm, of sublimation" (S.VII, 128). What makes the Lady a fitting emblem of the work of sublimation is her relation with the Thing. "In every form of sublimation," Lacan claims, "emptiness is determinative" (S.VII, 130). For Lacan, all art worthy of the name achieves a similar contact with *das Ding*, making it at once present and absent, present *in* its absence. "All art is characterized by a certain mode of organization around this emptiness" (S.VII, 130). "Freudian aesthetics, in the broadest meaning of the term—which means the analysis of the whole economy of signifiers—reveals that the Thing is inaccessible" (S.VII, 159). In the very heart of artistic mimesis, precisely in the struggle to achieve a more telling representation of the object, something of *das Ding* rises up as the unrepresented beyond of all mimesis. If Lacan defines sublimation as "raising an object to the dignity of *das Ding*" (S.VII, 112), that definition is inseparable from the creation of a sense of distance between the object and the Thing. Art draws nearer into intimacy with the object precisely in order to stimulate an experience of the Thing that continually escapes from that encounter. The dimension of the Thing is "extimacy," the dimension of something called up in the heart of intimate proximity yet continually slipping away, continually withdrawing.

The space of the drives is opened up in the distance between the object and the Thing. Here again, we encounter a function of retroactivity. In one sense, sublimation effects a redeployment of a "natural" aim of the drive. Sublimation presumably transforms something on the level of primary process under the influence of the secondary process. Yet the limitlessness of striving in the sphere of sublimation serves to bring the force of the drive into its own proper element as if for the first time. The Thing toward which sublimation moves is the most prehistoric object, the primordially lost object. "The sublimation that provides the *Trieb* with a satisfaction different from its aim—an aim that is still defined as its natural aim—is precisely that which reveals the true nature of the *Trieb* insofar as it is not simple instinct, but has a relationship to *das Ding* as such, to the Thing insofar as it is distinct from the object" (S,VII, 111).

The distinction between the object and the Thing describes the essential structure around which the whole development of the human being, the very essence of desiring, will come to operate. It is this relationship between the imaginary object and the real of *das Ding* that structures the engine of desire, the real oscillating in the sleeve of the imaginary like a piston in a cylinder. As we will see more completely in what follows, it is the function of the Oedipus complex to stabilize the moment of separation between the object and *das Ding*. Passage through the Oedipus complex assigns to the Thing its proper place beyond every object of satisfaction, thereby insuring that the mere object, if it is sometimes raised to the dignity of the Thing, is never allowed to replace it. Lacan's discussion is explicit on this point, as it closely associates *das Ding* with the figure of the mother and the prohibition of incest with the establishment of the proper distance from it.

It is in the non-equivalence of the object and the Thing that a space beyond the pleasure principle is opened up. Pleasure and unpleasure, the whole economy of *Lust* and *Unlust* on which the most primitive valuations are based, belong to the relation to the object and its imaginal clothing. By virtue of standing outside this economy, the dimension of the Thing becomes the locus into which is projected the idea of an ultimate or sovereign Good, and likewise the possibility of a radical Evil.

> There is good and bad, and then there is the Thing. The good and the bad already belong to the order of the *Vorstellung*; they exist there as clues to that which orients the position of the subject, according to the pleasure principle, in connection with that which will never be more than representation, search for a privileged state, for a desired state, for the expectation of what? Of something that is always a certain distance from the Thing, even if it is regulated by the Thing, which is there in a beyond. (S.VII, 63)

> Well now, the step taken by Freud at the level of the pleasure principle is to show us that there is no Sovereign Good—that the Sovereign Good, which is *das Ding*, which is the mother, is also the object of incest, is a forbidden good, and that there is no other good. Such is the foundation of the moral law as turned on its head by Freud. (S.VII, 70)

Speaking of the Thing

We have yet to account for the most significant, and most difficult, aspect of Lacan's concept of *das Ding*—its relation to speech and language. Lacan is gratified to find a trace of this relation in the *Project*: Freud centers the child's discovery of the Thing on the perception of the other's *voice*—its scream (SE, 1:331). Yet Lacan develops the idea far beyond the letter of Freud's text, in part because he is able to draw upon the resources of structuralist linguistics that were unavailable to Freud.

How is the Thing related to language? Lacan claims, first, that the Thing is approachable only in and through language. Thus Lacan maintains that "the Thing only presents itself to the extent that it becomes word" (S.VII, 55). The Thing is not identical with the law of the symbolic, and yet it is somehow made accessible by the subject's relation to the law. "Is the Law the Thing? Certainly not. Yet I can only know of the Thing by means of the Law" (S,VII, 83). However, the relation of language and the Thing is by no means a merely external one. The Thing animates the very essence of language to the extent that it provides an originary orientation, a kind of primordial directionality toward the signified. "*Das Ding*," he says, "is that which I call the beyond-of-the-signified" (S.VII, 54).

But what sense are we to make of this obscure connection between the Thing and the Word? Let us begin at the simplest level with the Thing as that portion of the perceptual complex that remains uncognizable, unassimilable to any memory trace. The signifier serves to mark this unrepresentable moment, holding the place of the Thing as we say that "*X* marks the spot." Neither do we know what exactly is marked, nor does the mark itself have any intrinsic meaning. On this level, then, the appearance of the signifier requires an imaginary staging in order to perform its function. What is involved is an utterly primitive indication, a kind of verbal ostension. The signifier serves to designate something that overflows the imaginary economy; it says, in effect, "there is something extra here, I know not what." At this level we get a first glimpse of what Lacan means by identifying Freud's concept of *Vorstellungsrepräsentanz* with the signifier: the signifier serves to mark something that escapes representation. "It is less a representative representative than a *non-representative representative*" (FFC, 218). Not merely *Vorstellung* but *Vorstellungsrepräsentanz*, the signifier represents what has no *Vorstellung*.

Insofar as it marks the place of *das Ding* as a locus of unrepresentability, the signifier functions to mark an absence. With this result, we seem to have arrived at the truism that the power of language derives from its capacity to call to mind something that in fact remains absent. But the Lacanian view is more radical. Language is related to absence not only as the capacity to indicate that an object that was present a moment ago is now gone, but rather as the capacity to bring the speaker into relation with something that is essentially missing, something that is absent as such.

"But what an absurdity," the voice of common sense will now object, "it is no ghost of absence but rather the flesh and blood presence of objects that moves us to speech." Such would be the judgment of Hobbes, whose mechanistic empiricism so pervasively informs the implicit metaphysics of common sense. For Hobbes, the movement of speech, like every other movement in the apparatus of thought, must finally be traceable to the impact of sensible impressions. The Lacanian view could not be more opposite. Lacan follows Saussure in utterly rejecting the commonsensical view that identifies the paradigmatic operation of language with naming. But Lacan goes further: far from being a mere tagging of objects, a one-to-one correspondence of words and things, the innermost essence of language functions to evoke something that is missing in the object. In its most primordial function, language serves to name the no-thing. What most profoundly sets speech in motion is a dimension of absence in perception, a lack that haunts perceptual presence, a dimension of perception that remains uncognizable. The deepest motive origin of speech resides not in the highlight of the object but in the shadow of the Thing.

The preceding remarks about the capacity of speech to evoke what is absent illuminate an elementary characteristic of language: the fact that speech is about something, yet addresses this something without necessarily specifying what it is. Speech revolves around a topic, a subject matter of interest or concern, yet typically leaves the topical focus to some extent indeterminate. The stream of words may flow around or toward an objective without ever fully attaining or even defining it. Such an asymptotic approach to the topic of speech is what characterizes an authentic conversation. The most genuine dialogue is one in which neither of the partners fully grasps beforehand what the dialogue is really about but rather, like hunters tracking an elusive quarry that fleetingly appears and disappears through the thicket of undergrowth, must be content with an imperfect, tentative, and provisional hold on the topic of dialogue. The participants in this sort of conversation must apply themselves to the effort of continually renewing their sense of the discussion and must remain open to revising their estimate of its object. In a measured and partial way, dialogue of this kind is in touch with something of the order of the Thing.

The fact that speech is capable of referring to something that remains more or less indeterminate, indeed, that speech is most genuinely realized in such indeterminate reference, derives from a feature of the human relation to language that is as absolutely basic as it is mysterious. We can further characterize this power of language by relying again on the terms of positionality and dispositionality. For how can we fail to be struck by their relevance in this context? What is accomplished by speech is the projection of an indeterminate positionality, the establishment of a positional unity that remains open with respect to its content. The movement of speech can be said to generate a pure anticipation, a horizon of meaning that is at once focused and in-suspense, directed toward an object or end that remains as-yet-to-be-specified. Such open or indeterminate positionality is the unique contribution of language. The special power of language lies in its capacity to project a purely virtual positionality, that is, the capacity to set forward a figure of attention without "filling in" its content.

Let us summarize the implications of such virtual positionality. We have already begun to see how Freud's analysis of cognition and judgment helps to clarify the inner structure of positionality. In effect, the activity of positional determination is at work on two levels. In addition to an initial separation of figure from ground there must also be an ongoing operation in which changing aspects of the figure are regathered in relation to an unknowable kernel. This second operation can be thought of as a repetition of the first, but interior to the outline of the object itself. What is sought is a kind of figure of the figure, a positionality of the positional moment itself. Let us call the first stage "positional adumbration." It is on this level that a gestalt figure is distinguished from a background. The second stage achieves something more than mere adumbration. Within the space demarcated by adumbration, it performs what we may call "positional articulation." In this second operation, changes in the figure are collated in relation to a virtual unity, analogous to the locus of the Freudian Thing. Considered from a purely formal point of view, what most distinguishes these two components of the perceptual act is their relation to time. Where the definition of the perceptual figure from the ground is achieved all at once, the second level of the process is unfolded over time. The adumbration of figure and ground simultaneously structures the manifold of the perceptual field. Positional articulation, by contrast, concerns a process that is by its very nature extended through time, during which a succession of changes in the figure of attention are continually reoriented with respect to an open locus of identity.

When we notice the way in which a virtual positionality is projected ahead of the shifting play of perceptual traces, we suddenly recognize how the speech stream, the linearity of the signifier so emphasized by Saussure, makes up an analogous process. The flow of speech presents a series of continually changing sound images over and beyond which is projected a play of meanings, the evocation of the signified. Shunted along ahead of the wave of shifting sense traces that constitute speech is a partly circumscribed, partly open space of meaning. Parallel to the example of the sculpture we referred to earlier, in which the play of contours is referred to a totality that transcends all particular views, the speech flow continually reestablishes the space of positional articulation, it continually reposes the question as to what the discourse is actually about.

But what is really happening here? We can take a further step in understanding the process by which the movement of speech regenerates a relation to the Thing only by moving to another level of complexity. The signifier is able to mark the locus of the unrepresented, to hold the place of the Thing—a kind of absence—because the structure of the signifier is itself predicated upon absence. If the signifier holds the place of what lacks representation, if the signifier functions as *Vorstellungsrepräsentanz* to represent the unrepresented, it does so by virtue of the function of absence that constitutes its own binary structure. "The *Vorstellungsrepräsentanz*," says Lacan, "is the *binary* signifier" (FFC, 218, emphasis added).

The power of the sign to make present what is absent is ultimately related to the play of presence and absence that is at work in the binary microstructure of speech. The binarism of the signifier means that each enunciation of the sound image of the signifier can serve its function as signifying only by virtue of its coupling with at least one other element, an element from which it is *different* and that remains unspoken. For Lacan, the unique contribution of the symbolic consists in its capacity "to give absence a name," a capacity that is founded upon the functioning of the binary signifier as an alternation of presence and absence. "Through the word—already a presence made of absence—absence gives itself a name" (E:S, 65). The linguistic sign operates only "in so far as it connotes presence *or* absence, by introducing essentially the *and* that links them, since in connoting presence or absence, it establishes presence against a background of absence, just as it constitutes absence in presence" (E:S, 234).

It is the moment of absence constitutive for the functioning of the linguistic signifier that enables it to reach toward the absent Thing. The signifier is capable of touching upon the negative, unrepresented moment of the perceptual complex because it is itself a complex, a couplet of presence and absence. It is a point that is well illustrated in the example of the child's game of "gone and back again" from *Beyond the Pleasure Principle*. The sounding of the *Fort* implicates the absent *Da* and vice versa. "Fort is the correlative of *Da*. *Fort* can only be expressed as an alternative derived from a basic synchrony. It is on the basis of this synchrony that something comes to be organized, something that the mere play of *Fort* and *Da* could not produce by itself" (S.VII, 65). It is by virtue of always regenerating a constitutive moment of absence that the alternation of *Fort* and *Da* functions to signify something otherwise ungraspable. And what is that? Not, of course, something about the spool that the child throws over the bedside with an "Ooooo" and retrieves with an "Aaaaa," but rather something about the mother. And not simply the figure of the mother, as the object that serially appears and disappears, but at bottom something less palpable in this object: not merely the fact of her comings and goings, but the *motive* behind them—the question of her desire. Said otherwise, the *Fort-Da* bears less on the mother as a mere object of perception than upon the mother as *das Ding*.

"But hold on," someone will now object. "Your aim from the outset has been to reveal the intersection of perception and language, to map the crossroads of the image and the word in such a way as to bring out both analogies and differences of structure between them. It was for this reason that you introduced the vocabulary of positionality and dispositionality: the system of differences constitutive of a language functions in a manner that is in some respects comparable to the dispositional field of perception. The concept of the Thing then allowed you to propose the notion of positional articulation, a process of differentiation internal to the positional moment. So far, I follow your argument tolerably well. But now you claim, with warrant in Lacan, to associate positional articulation with the functions of speech and language. Language, you want to say, brings to perception a new dimension of absence by means of which the space of *das Ding* is opened up beyond the object. This novel power of the linguistic signifier to represent something that otherwise escapes representation is what makes possible the movement that leads beyond mere adumbration (the mere outlining of the figure of attention) and relates the play of figural aspects to a unifying yet indeterminate locus of the Thing. But surely this explanation can't satisfy us. In your earlier explanation of the Thing as a regulatory ideal, internal to the perceptual figure, you offered a purely perceptual example, that of walking around a sculpture. Doesn't this example belie the special status you now want to attribute to language? Doesn't it suggest that the differentiation of object and Thing is already at work on the level of perception independently of the influence of language? And if that is so, what is it that is distinctive about language?"

The objection is a fair one to the extent that we have not yet fully succeeded in resolving the relation of the word and the Thing. Indeed, our discussion thus far has oriented us to key issues, but without more careful development they finally leave us with no more than suggestive correspondences. Further, there is probably some truth in the idea that the rudiments of the distinction between object and Thing are native to the mechanisms of perception. Perhaps that is what Lacan means when he says that "the world of *Vorstellung* is already organized according to the possibilities of the signifier as such" (S.VII, 61). Nevertheless, from a Lacanian point of view the basic thrust of the objection must be countered with a flat assertion: the process that opens relation to *das Ding*—the process we have called positional articulation—is fundamentally the achievement of linguistic competence. The example of viewing a sculpture invites a confusion so long as we give in to the temptation of thinking of it as an instance of perception that is "pure" and unmediated, perception that is somehow free from the structuring influence of language. But according to Lacan such purity is an illusion. So radical is the relation of the human being to language that subjection to the law of the signifier may be said to be the condition, the structural principle, the underlying and implicit formative power of all human perceiving. We must reckon with the fact that perception itself is fundamentally altered in the speaking being. Indeed, this alteration of "innocent" perception in the human being is the most basic form of the *Nachträglichkeit* introduced by the acquisition of language. It is an alteration that can be crudely indicated in the distinction between perceiving *that* and *what* something is. Positional adumbration, we can say, makes possible the assertion *that* something exists. It is only with the second operation of "positional articulation" that the question can be sustained as to *what* that something is.

With these abstruse distinctions, we have not strayed as far from Freud as it might appear. Freud makes a similar distinction between judgments of existence (*that* something exists) and judgments of attribution (*what* it is, whether it is good or bad, etc.) in his essay on "Negation." It is in precisely this essay, with its evocation of a primordially lost object, that Lacan discerns an echo of the concept of *das Ding*. Nor is the idea of a retroactive restructuring of perception by language foreign to Freud's text. The theory of the Oedipus complex supposes precisely such a radical retro-formation of the child's powers of representation. This transformation is responsible for the production of infantile amnesia precisely because the store of pre-Oedipal memories is reordered in accordance with it. If we follow Lacan on this point, we must associate the pre-Oedipal period with predominantly imaginary formations and place the key moment of that Oedipal transformation in the acquisition of language. In the retroactive effect of the Oedipus, perception is harnessed to the law of language.

Yet the problem remains to distinguish precisely the function of positional articulation in perception and language. How are we to proceed? The problem at issue cannot fail to remind us of the guiding idea of Hegel's philosophy, that of the dialectical movement by which what is implicit and in itself (*an sich*) becomes explicit and for itself (*für sich*). We have allowed that the power of positional articulation is in some sense implicitly operative on the level of immediate perception but we insist that it emerges more decisively on the level of language. In his *Encyclopedia* Hegel develops very suggestively parallel ideas. In the section of the *Logic* devoted to Essence, for example, Hegel seeks to show how the immediacy of being must be subjected to a further dialectical movement of reflection-into-self. This movement, by which determinate being will be opened out on the categories of Essence, is centered on the examination of "existence" and of "the Thing." At stake is precisely the issue of concern to Freud: the necessity to distinguish all attributes and relations of determinate existence from a wholly abstract and purely posited nucleus: the Thing. "The thing-by-itself . . . ," Hegel asserts, "is the empty substratum for these predicates of relation."[3] It is this aspect of the perfectly empty and abstract Thing that was seized upon by Kant, who stressed its unknowability. "If to know means to comprehend an object in its concrete character," Hegel goes on to say, "then the thing-by-itself, which is nothing but the quite abstract and indeterminate thing in general, must certainly be as unknowable as it is alleged to be" (L, 181).

What enables the abstract nucleus of the Thing to be differentiated from the varying play of its perceptual features? Remarks in the third volume of the *Encyclopedia*, the treatise devoted to *Philosophy of Mind*, point to the key role played by the function of the linguistic sign. The passage entitled "Imagination to Thought" again stresses the necessity to conceive the Thing independently and for itself in opposition to the array of concrete attributes. Of crucial importance, however, is the creation of signs, the special property of which consists precisely in their capacity to mark the purely ideal dimension of the thing. "The name is thus the thing so far as it exists and counts in the ideational realm" (L, 219). By means of the sign, the thing is given over from imagination to thought by virtue of being freed from its moorings in intuition. "Given the name lion, we need neither the actual vision of the animal, nor its image even: the name alone, if we understand it, is the unimaged simple representation. We *think* in names" (L, 220). Only with the assignation of the name does thought gain access to the inner reality of the thing. "Just as the true thought is the very thing itself, so too is the *word* when it is employed by genuine thinking. Intelligence, therefore, in filling itself with the word, receives into itself the nature of the thing" (L, 221).

Hegel then turns to the question of what enables the sign to give access to the Thing. His answer anticipates the key insight of Saussure. It is arbitrary relation between the sound image of the linguistic sign and the thing that it signifies. The distinguishing characteristic of the linguistic sign, and the source of its power for enabling thought, consists in what Hegel calls "the arbitrary nature of the connection between the sensuous material and a general idea." (L, 212). What is crucial is the arbitrary relation between the sound image of the linguistic sign and the thing it signifies. Freed from every specific datum of sensation, the sign can become "the pyramid into which a foreign soul has been conveyed, and where it is conserved" (L, 213).

The sign is different from the symbol: for in the symbol the original characters (in essence and conception) of the visible object are more or less identical with the import which it bears as symbol: whereas in the sign, strictly so-called, the natural attributes of the intuition, and the connotation of which it is a sign, have nothing to do with each other. (L, 213)

If Hegel points us to the general form of a solution to the problem of positional articulation in perception and language, we must bring additional resources to bear in order to resolve it completely. We must turn to the structuralist linguistics that was available to neither Hegel nor Freud.

Freud avec Jakobson

The task before us is to show how linguistic competence is the uniquely privileged condition for positional articulation. We want to see more clearly into the means by which language makes possible the projection of an open horizon of meaning, how it sustains a relation to an indefinite locus of attention, what Lacan calls the "beyond-of-the-signified." If language plays a privileged role in this process, its capacity to do so is presumably related to what is most distinctive about language, what sets it apart not only from the figure-ground dynamics operative in perception but also from other sign systems. To determine that distinctiveness, we will accept the clue of Roman Jakobson. The essence of Jakobson's innovation in linguistics is to insist that language differs from other sign systems in being founded upon a level of differential structure that is not by itself meaningful. This differential function is centered upon the phoneme. The significative value of the phoneme consists solely in marking the difference between words. By itself the phoneme has no signified. It refers to nothing in the world but only to the system of signifiers itself. Jakobson's own remarks on this point are worth quoting at length.

So the phoneme, this cardinal element on which everything in the linguistic system hinges, stands in contrast to all the other integral parts of this system, and has a completely exceptional and distinctive character, a character which is not to be found in any entity analogous to the phoneme in the other sign systems. . . . Only the phoneme is a purely differential and contentless sign. The phoneme's sole linguistic content, or more generally its sole semiotic content, is its dissimilarity from all the other phonemes of the given system. . . . Language, in the narrow sense of the word, is distinguished from other sign systems by the very basis of its constitution. Language is the only system which is composed of elements which are signifiers and yet at the same time signify nothing. Thus the phoneme is the element which is specific to language. Philosophical terminology tends to call the various sign systems *languages* and language properly so-called *word language*. It would perhaps be possible to identify it more accurately by calling it *phoneme language*. This phoneme language is the most important of the various sign systems, it is for us language *par excellence*, language properly so-called, language *tout court*, and one might ask whether this special status of the phoneme language is not due precisely to the specific character of its components, to the paradoxical character of elements which simultaneously signify and yet are devoid of all meaning" (SM, 66-67).

With this discussion of the phoneme, it is tempting to think that we are already able to answer our guiding question. Positional articulation implies an open and indeterminate locus of meaning, a meaning without meaning, a meaning-in-suspense. Is this not precisely what is accomplished by the phoneme, insofar as it is a signifier that signifies nothing, a signifier whose only function is to establish the possibility of signification? But not so fast! In order to appreciate the distinctiveness of the phoneme and its role in language, we must pause to lay out Jakobson's view more carefully.

Jakobson begins with the essential teaching of Saussure: the linguistic sign is structured by binary opposition. The stabilization of meaning in language, and ultimately the capacity of linguistic elements to refer the mind along the path of signification, is rooted in the way in which the poles of such oppositive dualities are bound together by a force of necessary implication such that, as Jakobson says, "if one of the terms is given then the other, though not present, is evoked in thought" (SM, 76). This principle of oppositive implication is operative in the field of the signified, as it structures binary meanings that codetermine one another. Thus, "to the idea of white there is opposed only that of black, to the idea of beauty that of ugliness, to the idea of large that of small, to the idea of closed that of open, and so on. Opposites are so intimately interconnected that the appearance of one of them inevitably elicits the other" (SM, 76). The same force of necessary implication structures grammatical categories. So, for example, "the idea of an indirect object of an action necessarily evokes that of a direct object ; in short the meaning of the dative implies that of the accusative" (SM, 71). Hegel relied on the same basic principle in order to trace the interlocking architecture of concepts in his *Logic*. The great breakthrough of Saussure was to discern a similar oppositive structure in the domain of the signifier, defining the sound image of the sign, too, as organized around binary relations. Thus Saussure insists that "phonemes are above all else oppositive, relative, and negative entities" (SM, 76). When Saussure speaks of the two floating kingdoms of signifier and signified, what binds them together as kingdoms are the structuring effects of binary opposition. Binarism is what enables the two kingdoms to be coordinated with one another, allowing semantico-logical relations to be quilted on to the level of vocal-acoustic relations.

The entire edifice of Saussurian linguistics had thus been built on the notion of binary opposition and on the concomitant idea of a relation of necessary implication between the opposing binary terms. It is at this point that Jakobson introduces a key revision to Saussure's perspective and thereby brings the distinctive character of the phoneme into high relief. Jakobson notes that the phoneme, up until then taken to be the most elementary constituent of language, *does not fulfill this criterion of binary necessity*. In fact, the phoneme is precisely unlike an oppositive duality that is bound by necessary implication. In the case of *Fort* and *Da*, for example, the phonemic alternation of "Oooo" and "Aaaaa" contains no necessary connection. By this route, Jakobson is led to question the foundations of the Saussurean conception of language.

> The idea of expensiveness is necessarily opposed to that of
> cheapness. But the idea of the phoneme *a* in no way anticipates
> that of the phoneme *u*. There is no necessary connection
> between these two ideas. Should we conclude then that we have
> simply made a mistake in referring to the relation between
> phonemes as one of opposition, that in fact in this case it is

matter of simple differences, simple contingent dualities and not of real oppositions? (SM, 77)

Jakobson resolves this problem and rejoins Saussurean binarism by identifying another level of structure beneath the phoneme, that of differential features. Jakobson demonstrates that language is structured at the most elementary level by twelve sets of binary oppositions (tense versus lax, open versus closed, rounded versus unrounded, back versus front of the buccal resonator, etc.). Unlike phonemes, the differential features are binary oppositions in the strong sense of being mutually determining. When Jakobson refers to "real binary oppositions, as defined by logic, . . . such that each of the terms of the opposition *necessarily* implies its opposite" he is referring specifically to the oppositions between *differential features*. Phonemes are related to differential features as chemical compounds are related to elements. The phoneme is essentially a complex, a concatenation of more basic constituents. It is "a bundle of differential elements" (SM, 82). "Thus, for example, the Turkish phoneme *i* is a complex entity composed of the three following differential elements: closed, front, unrounded" (SM, 81).

The result of Jakobson's view is to recognize three basic levels of structure in language: first, the level of differential features; second, that of phonemes; and third, the level of morphemes and the larger units of words and sentences. Only on the third level can we speak of meaning proper, in the sense of reference to some positive semantic content. Yet the first two levels are indispensable in enabling the third level to function. Up this stair of structural levels, says Jakobson, ascends a scale of greater and greater freedom in language. On the level of differential features, relations are absolutely determined in fixed oppositions. On the phonemic level, particular languages select from among the repertoire of possible phonemes, but communication quickly breaks down if individual speakers stray from the constellation of phonemes that defines the parameters of the langauge they speak. It is only on the level of morphemes and the higher order units composed from them that speakers are able to exercise the functions of combination and selection that Jakobson associates with the full realization of speech.

Only when the phoneme is understood in the context of this three-tiered organization of linguistic structure does it fully emerge as an answer to the question before us concerning the relation of language and the Thing. By drawing out the implications of Jakobson's analysis, we will be able to show both how we can read "Freud with Jakobson," revealing the deep correspondence between Freud's concept of *das Ding* and the insights of linguistics, and also how the concepts of positionality and disposition-ality find privileged application in the phoneme. Let us make three basic points.

1. Like the Freudian Thing, the phoneme organizes a level of structure that transcends the form of the body-schema.

Jakobson refers to the phoneme as the "cardinal element on which everything in the linguistic system hinges" (SM, 66). What is "hinged" by the phoneme are, on the one side, the level of differential features and, on the other side, the semantically substantive level of morphemes. The ques-tion, then, is what function is performed by this mediating role of the phoneme. The answer is related to the fact that both of the levels hinged by the phoneme are structured by binary opposition, but of different kinds. On the one hand, there are the primary oppositions constitutive of differ-ential features. The variety of differential features (front and back, closed and open, compact and diffuse, voiced and unvoiced, and so on) represent alternate arrangements of the speech organs (closer to the surface versus deeper in the interior of the body, greater versus lesser vacuity of the res-onating chamber of the mouth, more versus less restricted release, active engagment of breath in the voice box versus mere passage of air over the structures of the buccal opening, etc.) In this way, the range of differential features are strictly correlative to structures of embodiment. On the other hand, as we have already noted with references to Saussure and to Hegel, there are the logical oppositions that organize the semantic universe opened up on the level of morphemes and the higher units of language. The system of meaning is shot through by a plurality of dualisms by means of which the dimensions of logical space are limned: up and down, here and there, now and then, subject and object, active and passive, etc.

The question now becomes: what relation obtains between these two layers of binary oppositions? Are we not led to suppose that semantic polarities are in some way based upon the phonological oppositions that structure the most elementary building blocks of linguistic structure, the differential features? This prospect would accord with the most general thrust of Jakobson's approach to language, which is to insist that in the analysis of linguistic structure sound and meaning can never be entirely separated. The semantic architecture of language, organized around conceptual oppositions, would be based in part upon the deeper oppositions of differential features. This would mean that the dynamics of logico-semantic space marked by words are to some degree rooted in the vocalic-anatomical oppositions that constitute the most primitive discriminations of speech sounds. In that case, the right and left of the body's bilateral symmetry, the up and down established by its stance, or the front and back of its relation to objects around it—in short, the whole structure of what Merleau-Ponty called the body's spatiality—not only reverberates in the binary form of the signifier but also informs the structure of the signified.

It is not difficult to adduce examples in support of this idea. Linguists have observed, for instance, that the first and second person pronouns in most Indo-European languages display a correlation with the physiological locus of their enunciation. The first person pronouns (*I, ich, je*) are sounded more deeply in the interior of the body, the second person pronouns (*you, du, tu*) are pronounced closer to the opening of the mouth. In each case, the site of sound production reflects the semantic task the sound performs. The same point is illustrated by Freud's *Fort-Da* example. The sound used to signify "away"—"Oooo"—is appropriately pronounced at the rounded opening of the mouth, further toward the boundary between the body and the world outside it, where the signifier of "back again"—"Aaaa"—is sounded deeper in the speaker's throat. Similarly, many linguists have noted the frequency with which higher-pitched, or "bright," vowels that are pronounced toward the roof of the mouth occur in words connoting lightness, mildness, softness, delicacy and related ideas. By contrast, the heavier and more sonorous "dark" vowels, pronounced deeper in the buccal cavity, predominate in words that connote weight, mass, force, roughness, etc. Such associative linkages between sound and meaning have been observed since antiquity. They figure prominently in the argument of Plato's *Cratylus* and were more systematically developed in the so-called "theory of roots."[4]

Examples like these suggest the way in which linguistic signification retains deep structural correspondences with the axes of the body-schema. The deep binarisms of language, and therefore the matrix upon which the most primitive signifying material is organized, are based on cleavages of the body gestalt. Vestiges of this bodily basis of meaning exert a discernible influence on the semantic level. At the same time, however, we must reckon with the *lack* of perfect correlation between the two levels and the oppositions that structure them. Indeed, coordination between the two levels is more the exception than the rule. The semantic field is by no means exclusively or exhaustively structured by binary opposition, let alone by binarisms derived from the organization of the body. Whatever the explanatory power of the theory of roots and whatever the validity of the linkages between sound and meaning it brings to light, it cannot supercede the Saussurean doctrine of the arbitrariness of the signifier. This point is especially indispensable for a discussion of Lacan's appropriation of the theory of language. For Lacan, the distinctiveness of language in the human being, the mark of its break from any natural or instinctive symbolism and therein the source of its transformative power, resides in the openness of the signifier, its capacity to assume new and wholly unprecedented significations.

These considerations lead us immediately to the unique role played by the phoneme. Given the two spheres of distinctive oppositions, a primitive level of purely binary oppositions that are correlative with postures of the speech organs, and a higher level of semantic oppositions that are influenced but not wholly determined by binary relations, the phoneme falls into neither class. As Jakobson is at pains to point out, phonemes do not differ from one another in the strongly and strictly binary fashion of differential features. But neither are phonemes the bearers of any semantic content. To make clear what this means in the perspective we are unfolding is to go beyond the letter of Jakobson's text and also beyond anything Lacan explicitly says about the matter. But the implication is not far to seek. The phoneme functions, exactly as Jakobson says, like a kind of hinge; it both joins and separates two universes of binary oppositions. As a bundle of differential features, every phoneme necessarily bears within itself a registration of the strong, binary oppositions that compose them. Yet by virtue of establishing a new unity in the structure of language, a novel form that must be registered by the auditor of speech in order for still more complex unities of speech to be understood, the phoneme also establishes a margin of independence from the organization of differential features. The phoneme thus embodies an exemplary instance of Hegelian *Aufhebung*: in the phoneme, the system of elementary oppositions operative on the level of differential features is both preserved and cancelled. The function of this *Aufhebung* is to launch speech into an altogether new orbit. The phoneme bears within itself the force of opposition constitutive for the level of differential features and redeploys it, so to speak, in a novel system of relations. But the phoneme also introduces a disjunction, a break and departure from that more primitive underlying binarism. A new domain is thereby opened up, one in which the structuring influence of binary opposition is still operative but tensed with new complexities and capable of infinitely greater extension.

Of crucial significance is the fact that the institution of the phoneme retains a certain resonance of bodily spatiality but also establishes a new margin of independence from the body. The substructure of language revealed by Jakobson is essentially a system of embodiment, the set of differential features being strictly correlative with the positioning and action of the speech organs. On the level of differential features, the most primitive signifying matrix is provided by binary aspects of the body. Moving up the ladder of linguistic structure from the order of differential features and that of phonemes thus involves a movement away from a body-relative organization. Viewed in this way, the *Aufhebung* introduced by the phoneme is seen ultimately to bear on the rootedness of linguistic symbolization in the form of the body.

It is at this point that the function of the phoneme can be linked with Freud's concept of the Thing. As Freud describes it, the Thing is not merely a failure of identity between memory and perception. In the pivotal case of the subject's relation to the *Nebenmensch*, the Thing is projected into the space beyond what can be understood on the basis of the reflection of the subject's own body. The Thing marks the discrepancy between that portion of the image of the other that can be identified with movements of the subject's own body and another portion that cannot. Thus, Freud says,

> the perceptual complexes proceeding from this fellow human-
> being will in part be new and non-comparable—his *features*, for
> instance, in the visual sphere; but other visual perceptions—e.g.
> those of the movements of his hands—will coincide in the sub-
> ject with memories of quite similar visual perceptions of his
> own, of his own body, [memories] which are associated with
> memories of movements experienced by himself. Other percep-

tions of the object too—if, for instance, he screams—will awaken the memory of his [the subject's] own screaming and at the same time of his own experiences of pain. Thus the complex of the fellow human-being falls apart into two components, of which one makes an impression by its constant structure and stays together as a *thing*, while the other can be *understood* by the activity of memory—that is, traced back to information from [the subject's] own body. (SE, 1:331)

As Freud presents it here, reference to the sense of one's own body, its movements and position in space, plays a foundational role in all judgment. "As regards judging . . . ," Freud says, "its basis is obviously the presence of bodily experiences, sensations and motor images of one's own" (SE, 1:333). Such body reference lends to perception a kind of baseline of comparison that Freud calls "imitation-value." The question of identity is posed against this baseline reference to one's own corporeality. It is essentially a question of "like me or unlike me" that leads to the positing of the Thing in the case of a failure to establish identity. Of course, the process involved is most readily apparent in the case of the relation to the fellow human being but it is operative in all perceiving to the extent that all objects of perception occupy definite positions in space, at rest or in movement. It is with respect to this bodily basis of judgment that Freud claims to have demonstrated "the eminently practical sense of all thought-activity" (SE, 1:332). Freud's theory thus insists on the fundamental part played by the awareness of embodiment for setting in motion the whole process of cognition. Every cognition takes its point of departure and implicitly defines itself in relation to the body schema. Yet the ultimate point of Freud's construction is to suggest how cognition comes to concern itself with objects over and beyond the body and unlike it—the unassimilable dimension of the Thing. On the basis of the preceding discussion, the phoneme emerges as the privileged element that inaugurates this action of judgment in the function of speech. As the hinge between the body-relative register of differential features and the open horizon of semantic content, the phoneme is the gateway to the Thing.

The likeness of the view we are proposing to Freud's theories can be made on a more general level. In some of his earliest letters and papers, Freud sought to explain the mechanism of repression—and by extension the very existence of the unconscious—by way of a theory of "double inscription."[5] The dynamics of consciousness and unconsciousness become possible because psychical material is laid down in multiple inscriptions. The most basic division of these different inscriptions is that between images and words. It is this distinction that returns in Freud's later formulation of the relation between thing-presentations and word-presentations. What we have proposed concerning the underlying structure of language is in its own way a system of double inscription. The functioning of language depends upon two layers of opposition that partly reflect or redouble one another while also remaining distinct.

2. The dynamics of opposition that operate variously on the vocal-physiological level of differential features and on the semantic level of morphemes are stabilized in relation to one another by the fact that the phonemes constitute an ordered *system*.

We have said that the phoneme functions to hinge two orders of opposition. By this we mean that the phoneme serves to carry over into the more complex structures of language something of the felt necessity of alternation that inhabits the binary opposition of differential features. At the same time, however, the bundling of differential features in the phoneme frees that force of necessity from its anchorage in any specific form. With the presentation of any differential element (say, the enunciation of a rounded vocalization), the opposing character (of unroundedness) is necessarily called up by virtue of a kind of reflex response. The binarisms of the differential features entrain physiological structures of action and reaction. Such action-reaction structures are likely akin to the innervative patterns of contraction and relaxation described by C. S. Sherrington as essential to the functioning of all motor responses. Packed into the complex of the phoneme, however, the binarism of the differential feature no longer calls for a particular alternation but grounds a general force of expectancy that is available for deployment on a new level of linguistic structure, the system of phonemes constitutive of a given language. In this way, the phoneme succeeds in establishing the essential condition of all linguistic signification, that is, the generation of an open and indeterminate readiness-for-meaning.

Consider the way in which these points bear on the very essence of the linguistic sign. Put in the most elementary terms, the linkage between the signifier and signified involves a process by which the perception of one thing leads to the thought of another. This shift, at bottom a kind of exchange of one object of thought for another, is characteristic of all signs but is especially striking in the case of linguistic signification. For the practiced speaker of a given language, the linkage of signifier and signified becomes a virtual identity, the apparent naturalness and irresistibility of which obscures the fact that an otherwise arbitrary connection has been established. Ultimately, however, what is most distinctive about language requires an additional determination, as the substitutive function just pointed to applies equally well to many forms of animal communication that cannot properly be called languages. When a beaver slaps its tail on the water to indicate an approaching danger, for example, perception of one thing immediately calls up awareness of something else.[6] What really separates human language from other sign systems is most clearly evidenced not in the instance of a signifier that we know but in one that we don't know. That is to say, the real power of linguistic signification lies not merely in establishing an otherwise arbitrary linkage between signifier and signified but in generating a pure and virtual sense of meaningfulness around an unfamiliar word. For such a word, we can supply no definite meaning, yet tend ineluctably to attempt one. In the unknown word, we experience something like a pure potentiality-for-meaning. In the course of his *Six Lectures,* Jakobson takes special note of this tendency. Thus "even when we hear, in a discourse composed of words which we know, one word with which we are completely unfamiliar, we do not *a priori* consider this word to be lacking in meaning. A word is always for us a particular semantic element and, in the present case, the signified of this particular semantic element is zero" (SM, 58). The unknown word sets in motion an unfulfillable vector of significance. It initiates a particular force of felt necessity, a pure preparedness for meaning.

> In the novel *Hunger* by Knut Hamsun the hero invents the
> word "*Kuboa.*" "I have the right," he says, "to endow it with
> whatever meaning I judge appropriate: I do not know yet
> myself what this word means." To put it another way, as soon as
> a certain group of phonemes is conceived to be a word, it looks
> for a meaning for itself. In other words it is a potential seman-
> tic content. (SM, 58)

The point here is not, of course, that we can make up words at will and endow them with any meaning we wish, as if we could deliberately re-create the miracle of meaning that is achieved by words in the already existing lexicon of the language that we speak. The purpose of the Hamsun example is rather to highlight our tendency to endow unknown words with a kind of open space of semantic potential in which a meaning *could* be specified. The recognition of something wordlike calls our attention to a pure readiness-for-meaning. The key point concerns this pure readiness-for-meaning, this as-yet-indeterminate semantic pressure. Such readiness-for-meaning is precisely the relation to the Freudian Thing that we have been looking for. The question is where it comes from. What produces it? An indispensable part of the answer lies along the line we have been pursuing: the felt pressure-toward-meaning at stake here, a pressure that constantly animates the speech stream and that is high-lighted by the example of the unknown word, is rooted in the necessity that binds together the binarism of differential features. Passed onto the level of the system of phonemes but freed from its bondage to a particular couplet of differential features, the sound texture of language creates an obscurely felt force of necessity that animates the spark of meaning that will cross the gap between signifier and signified.

What enables passage of this spark is the organization of phonemes in a system. The phonological system enables the speaker of a given language to identify an unknown word as belonging to the language and to reserve in advance a space in which its meaning will come to be specified. "So we see that even when a word is unfamiliar its phonemes enable us to assign to it a virtual place in our language and to recognize different words, i.e., to recognize that they differ in meaning" (SM, 56-57).

In effect, every utterance of a phoneme both depends upon and rein-forces the sense of language as system. This consideration recalls the observation of William James about the distinctive character of a given language. Having once begun to speak a given language, the speaker is predisposed to continue in that language.

> If we know English and French and begin a sentence in French,
> all the later words that come are French; we hardly ever drop
> into English. And this affinity of the French words for one
> another is not something merely operating mechanically as a

brain-law, it is something we feel at the time. Our understanding of a French sentence heard never falls to so low an ebb that we are not aware that the words linguistically belong together. . . . Such a vague sense as this of the words belonging together is the very minimum of fringe that can accompany them, if 'thought' at all. (P, 1:262)

The phenomenon remarked here by William James could be called "linguistic disposition." It is quite obviously an example of dispositionality in the sense we have sought to define. When viewed from the perspective opened up by Jakobson, such linguistic disposition is seen to be based upon the phonemic system of a given language, that is, the way the phonemic pattern of a language represents a selection from the table of differential features.

3. The phoneme constitutes a unique intersection of positionality and dispositionality.

The function of the phoneme as a hinge between sound and meaning is demonstrable in a particularly striking way. The entire validity of structuralist linguistics rests upon the assumption that understanding the meaning of speech requires some minimal yet accurate perception of the phonemes from which speech is constructed. The challenging aspect of this assumption, however, is the difficulty of seeing how the requisite perception of phonemic structure is achieved given the immense complexity of the sounds involved, the very slight differences that distinguish one phoneme from another, and the variations to which speech is constantly subject under the influence of dialect, accent, voice pitch and timbre, and other idiosyncratic factors. As Jakobson points out, perceptual registration of phonemic content would be all but impossible if speakers were forced to rely solely on the clue provided by sound. There must be a guiding contribution from the side of meaning. The capacity of a native speaker reliably to perceive minute differences of phonemic structure becomes explainable only when we allow for the preparatory role played by the anticipation of meaning. In effect, speech becomes understandable only because the perception of the sound chain is pre-informed by a grasp of the meaning of what is being said.

The auditory differences between the various phonemes of any given language are often so minute and so subtle that it is sometimes difficult to detect them even with sensitive instruments. Modern specialists in the field of acoustics wonder with bewilderment how it is possible that the human ear has no difficulty in recognizing the great variety of sounds in a language given that they are so numerous and their variations so imperceptible. Can it really be that it is a purely auditory faculty that is involved here? No, not at all! What we recognize in spoken language is not sound differences in themselves but the different uses to which they are put by the language, i.e., differences which, though without meaning in themselves, are used in discriminating one from another entities of a higher level (morphemes, words). The minutest phonic differences, to the extent that they perform a discriminative role in a given language, are accurately perceived by all the native speakers of that language without exception, whereas a foreigner, even a trained observer, or even a professional linguist, often has great difficulty in perceiving these differences if they do not perform this discriminative function in his native language. (SM, 74-75)

Jakobson underlines the point at stake here by asking us to imagine the extreme difficulty of memorizing a passage written in an exotic script. In such a case, the fact that we are able plainly to perceive the shape of the written characters, and indeed, might even be free to examine them over a considerable length of time, in no way lessens the virtual impossibility of the task.

Suppose that we want to learn an unfamiliar script, for example the Coptic script. This would be an extremely arduous task if it involved a mere conglomeration of meaningless arabesques. It would, for example, be horribly difficult to reproduce a Coptic text from memory if we had no idea of the value of its components, but the task would be an easy one if each of the letter had for us a positive, fixed, and specific value. (SM, 77-78)

In the immensely complex and shifting stream of speech, perception of the phoneme is possible only because the register of sound is preoriented by awareness of meaning. The result is a paradox: the transmission of meaning in speech depends upon accurate reception of sound, but reception of sound depends upon some preliminary grasp of meaning. This paradoxical situation has especially significant consequences for our conception of positionality and dispositionality. Suspended between the registers of sound and meaning, the phoneme also marks a unique junction between the functions of positionality and dispositionality. On the one hand, the identity of phonemes must be correctly registered by the auditor of speech. The phoneme is thus a genuine element of language, a discriminable particle in the sound stream. To this extent, it appears that the phoneme must achieve some minimum of positional definition. Presumably, it must in some minimal degree become an object of perception. On the other hand, the function of this positional discrimination is completely exhausted by its purely differential value. What we said in an earlier chapter of the necessarily evanescent character of every signifier (that the sound image must evacuate itself in favor of the vector of its signified) is true of the phoneme in the greatest degree. As Jakobson's analysis demonstrates, the phoneme functions solely as a marker of difference, its signifying role is limited to indicating its contrast from other phonemes from which it is distinct. The positionality of the phoneme is immediately swallowed up by its role in establishing a field of dispositionality.

The phoneme thus appears as a paradoxical entity whose positional registration as an object of perception is entirely in the service of a reinvigoration of a dispositional field. The paradox becomes complete when we recognize that the speaker's grasp of the meaning of what is said enables the activity of perception by which it is actually heard. In the terms we are now using, this means that the positionality of the phoneme, its availability to perception in the first place, is conditioned by the speakers' acquaintance with the very system of differences constituted by the phonemes of a given language. In this way, the phoneme shows itself to be the most extreme example of the conditioning influence of a dispositional field in the production of positionality.

Taken together, these considerations reveal the phoneme as a unique intersection of positionality and dispositionality. The phoneme is a perfect metastasis of the two functions.[7] Indeed, can we not now see that the capacity of the phoneme to found a signifying system of unprecedented power and flexibility resides in precisely this metastatic character? In the second chapter, we pointed to the unfolding dialectical relation of positionality and dispositionality, suggested its relevance as the very structure of experiencing, and remarked that language functions to continually reinvigorate that dialectic. It is now possible to see how the phoneme is the most elemental cell of that dialectic.

It might now be objected that the preceding account assumes that phonemes must become objects of perception, however fleetingly, yet successful communication quite ordinarily occurs between speakers who fail to isolate and identify large numbers of phonemes in one another's speech. An obvious example is provided by the slurred speech of inebriation. We are often able to understand drunken speech in spite of the fact that whole segments of phonemic structure may be missing or mutilated. This success in understanding despite the absence of the proper phonemic clues is explained by our capacity to "fill in" the missing or distorted phonemic material. In view of this admittedly routine phenomenon, it might be objected that phonemes are not necessarily objects of perception and that the dialectic of positionality and dispositionality that we have supposed is therefore undermined. But such an objection would be a misguided and superficial one. Far from supporting an objection to the account we have given, our capacity to understand drunken speech is explainable precisely on the basis of that account. What enables the auditor to successfully "fill in" what is missing in the sound stream is a fore-grasp of what is being said, which fore-grasp is itself predicated upon practiced acquaintance with the phonemic system of the language being spoken. The deficit in positional registration can be made up for only by adequate familiarity with the dispositional field.

It is possible to reread a key debate in the history of linguistics in accordance with the view of the phoneme at which we have arrived, according to which the phoneme is a positional-dispositional metastasis. At the center of that debate was the status of the being of the phoneme. Linguists were continually puzzled about the phoneme's mode of existence. They asked, as Jakobson notes, "where is the phoneme located? in which domain of reality does it have it roots?" (SM, 36) Some linguists, following the lead of Baudouin de Courtenay, grounded the identity of the phoneme in the register of mental images, hoping thereby to explain how perception of discrete phonemes takes place. Such a view stresses status of the phoneme as a bona fide psychological object. Others, like Alfred Schmitt, tried to deny the existence of the phoneme altogether for the reason that phonemes ordinarily do not function as discrete and isolated particles but are thoroughly interwoven with one another. The word, not the phoneme, must therefore be considered the smallest linguistic unit relevant to the actual perceptual experience of speakers. At issue in this debate are precisely the problems of positionality and dispositionality we have struggled to articulate. On the one hand, corresponding to the view of Baudouin de Courtenay, is the insistence that the phoneme must register upon perception. On the other hand, with Schmitt, is the recognition that the function of the phoneme is entirely differential and context dependent. We have sought to show that what is correct and valuable in both sides of the debate emerges only when they are taken together in a dialectical interrelation. The result is to assert for the phoneme something like what the theory of complementarity claims about the nature of light. Just as light can be adequately described neither as a particle nor as a wave but only as both simultaneously, the phoneme is an essentially paradoxical entity. Its positionality serves only to reinforce its dispositionality, yet its participation in a dispositional system contributes significantly to its positional recognition.

CHAPTER 5

Figurations of
the *Objet a*

The previous chapter traced the contours of the Freudian Thing as the uncognizable dimension of every object, the empty site in which judgment seeks to close the gap between memory and perception. Seizing upon this point of Freud's text and radicalizing its reference to the fellow human being, the *Nebenmensch*, Lacan locates in the negative space of *das Ding* the impenetrable nucleus of what is most unknowable in the Other, the enigma of the Other's desire. Lacan then passes beyond anything Freud says of *das Ding* by associating it with the power of language to articulate a pure potentiality-for-meaning. The cardinal function of language resides in the projection of an essential indeterminacy, the establishment of an open horizon of meaning as-yet-to-be-determined. We went on to locate in the structure of the phoneme the most elemental point at which linguistic signification evokes the dimension of *das Ding*. As a hinge between sound and meaning, the pivot point between a level of nonsignifying structure (of differential features) and higher levels of semantic content (of morphemes, words, and sentences), it is the phoneme that makes possible the miracle of linguistic symbolization. Just as the Freudian Thing serves to hold open the site of judgment when comparison to the subject's own body fails to provide adequate orientation, the phoneme functions to link a system of oppositions modeled on a logic of embodiment with a domain of meaning that transcends all reference to the body.

Lacan's reconception of the Freudian Thing radically extends and generalizes Freud's theory of *Nachträglichkeit*. Where Freud was concerned specifically with the delayed effect of childhood trauma, for Lacan a general function of retroaction is constitutive of the very being of the human subject. This Lacanian *Nachträglichkeit* is relevant to the relation between language and perception. The essential action of *Nachträglichkeit* concerns the priority of the word over the image, the way in which the linguistic signifier, though not fully acquired by the human infant until long after functions of perception have brought about crucial formative effects, can be said to have always already played a decisive role. The retroaction of the signifier implies that there is no pure and innocent empiricism, no product of human perception that is uncontaminated by the structuring influence of language. The power of the word has always already prepared every registration of the image in such a way as to disqualify any claim of sensation to absolute originality.

We now turn to a final and decisive topic. In the spaces opened up by this linguistic retroaction, there emerges a distinctive form, a product of the intersection between the image and the word: Lacan calls it "*objet a.*" The *objet a* is a kind of echo of *das Ding*, circuited by the system of signifiers. As Slavoj Žižek has said of it, "*objet petit* a designates that which remains of the Thing after it has undergone the process of symbolization."[1] Like the Thing, the *objet a* marks a locus of indeterminacy, it is linked to bodily structures, but is also crucially distinct from all embodiment. It is ingredient to every act of signification precisely to the extent that it marks a beyond of all signifying.

The Object-Cause of Desire

The concept of the *objet petit a*, a phrase that Lacan prefers to leave untranslated, is perhaps his most original contribution to psychoanalytic theory. The lower case "a," the initial letter of "autre," indicates an essential relation to the Other but is also intended to designate an algebraic variable or "function" in the mathematical sense. Within the compass of

the *objet a* Lacan gathers the familiar psychoanalytic partial objects relevant to the Freudian stages of development—oral, anal, and phallic—but
also adds some of his own. He thus cites as figurations of the *objet a*: "the
mamilla, faeces, the phallus (imaginary object), the urinary flow. (An
unthinkable list, if one adds, as I do, the phoneme, the gaze, the voice—
the nothing.)" (E:S, 315).

Perhaps the most challenging aspect of the *objet a* is its liminal character, and that in two senses. First, the *objet a* is strangely suspended
between the subject and the other, belonging to both and neither. It simultaneously designates what is most other in the Other, yet is intimately
bound up with subject itself. Lacan likens it to the bobbin with which
Freud's grandson replays the departure and reappearance of his mother
(*Fort!* and *Da!*). Paradoxically inner and outer, one's own and foreign, the
objet a is "a small part of the subject that detaches itself from him while
still remaining his, still retained" (FFC, 62). It is perhaps most with the
objet a in mind that Lacan coined the phrase "extimate." It is something of
the subject's own, indeed, the most intimate part, yet it always appears
elsewhere, outside the subject and eluding its grasp.

But the *objet a* is also liminal in a second sense: it participates in all
three of Lacan's fundamental categories of imaginary, symbolic, and real,
yet belongs exclusively to none of them. It is an object that finds its most
primitive representatives in the imaginary, as clearly imaged parts of the
body (the breast, the feces . . .), and yet is intended by Lacan to mark the
limit of what is imaginable. The *objet a*, as "what is lacking, is non-specu-
lar, it is not graspable in the image."[2]

Then again, the *objet a* is intimately related to the linguistic signifier
and is a kind of constitutive effect of signification. Thus Lacan claims to
have "defined a as the remainder of the constitution of the subject at the
locus of the Other in so far as it has to constitute itself as a speaking subject, a barred subject, \$" (S.X, 6-12-63). Yet if it could not exist without
the signifier, the *objet a* is also essentially resistant to symbolization. As
Lacan says, it "symbolizes what in the sphere of the signifier is always what
presents itself as lost, as what is lost to signification" (S.X, 3-13-63). *Objet
a* is a kind of remainder, a scrap or residue unassimilable by either the
imaginary or the symbolic. As such, it is attributable to the real. It is, as
Lacan sometimes says of it, an impossible object, an object that paradoxically can never appear as such.

Lacan emphasizes the retroactive character of the *objet a*, describing it as the "object-cause" of desire. What is at stake in this effect of retroaction is nothing less than the constitution of the subject itself. The tendency of common sense, rooted in grammatical habit, is to suppose that there must first be a subject who desires before there can be any question of the object upon which desire fixes. By contrast, Lacan insists that there is always already an object of desire in relation to which the desiring subject is constituted in the first place. But not just any object. The object that functions as the cause of desire is a primordially lost or essentially lacking object, a profoundly negative object which is absent before it can be present, whose non-being precedes its being. By virtue of its paradoxical constitution the *objet a* can only be described topologically as the perpetually absent locus around which the drives revolve. The *objet a* is thus the psychoanalytic object *par excellence*. It is "that object around which the drive moves. . . that object that rises in a bump, like the wooden darning egg in the material which, in analysis, you are darning—the *objet a*" (FFC, 257).

> The *objet a* is something from which the subject, in order to
> constitute itself, has separated itself off as organ. This serves as a
> symbol of lack, that is to say of the phallus, not as such, but in
> so far as it is lacking. It must, therefore, be an object that is,
> firstly, separable and, secondly, that has some relation to the
> lack. (FFC, 103)

To summarize these preliminary indications: the *objet a* emerges with a special necessity in the relation of the subject to the other. Like the Freudian Thing of which it is a kind of descendent or successor, the *objet a* is spun off from the process of representation as an unassimilable "something-or-other," a locus of unthinkability, that is continually generated at the limits of the imaginary and the symbolic. In one sense, it is a kind of useless excess, like the intractable piece of gristle that falls to the floor under the butcher's table. And like a piece of gristle, it remains for the subject an indigestible bolus, an unswallowable mass. In another sense, however, nothing could be more crucial for the incitement of desire, for the *objet a* functions as a stimulus, an intensive vortex around which the drives rotate. It is able to do so by virtue of its essential negativity, the way in which it represents an incarnation of lack. The *objet a* is at once impossible to possess and impossible to live without. In these ways, the *objet a* is an embodiment of perfect contradiction. Both inner and outer, subjective and objective, it is at every point both/and and neither/nor. This angle of view sheds light on Lacan's formula for phantasy in which the subject stands in relation to the *objet a*: $ \mathcal{S} \lozenge a $. The central term of the formula, the *poinçon*, fuses the logical symbols of conjunction and disjunction, indicating both inclusion and exclusion, both necessity and contingency, both implication and impossibility. The *objet a* is the point at which the subject assumes a certain paradoxical consistency precisely by virtue of marking the impossibility of coincidence of the subject with itself.

We can further elaborate the concept of this specifically negative object, this paradoxical object that functions as cause of desire by virtue of its very negativity, by reference to Lacan's tenth seminar on Anxiety, in which he retraces the trajectory of the familiar oral and anal stages of development. A key point in this rereading is the concept of a "cedable object" (*objet cessible*). In each of the stages, the child "cedes" or gives up an object—the breast or the feces. The crucial point centers on the action of the "ceding" itself. At stake is the very constitution of the subject and its desire.

To see more clearly what Lacan has in mind, let us take his discussion of weaning, which is particularly challenging, at least for the conventional interpretation of the Freudian teaching. According to the received view, one of those commonplaces of psychoanalytic theory that have passed into general circulation, the infant clings to the breast as long as possible and must be torn away by weaning. Indeed, isn't this the ordinary meaning of the Oedipal drama: the child is split off from the maternal body under the father's threat of castration? By contrast, in recasting the breast as a "cedable object," Lacan invites us to think of it as something the child yields or gives up. Thus he remarks that "it is not essentially true that the child is weaned: he weans himself, he detaches himeslf from the breast, he plays . . . at detaching himself from this breast and taking it up again" (S.X, 7-3-63).

A number of fascinating and far-reaching reflections follow from this supposition. We are reminded, for example, of Freud's discussion in the first part of *Civilization and its Discontents*, in which he describes the process by which the ego progressively splits itself off from the external world. Freud remarks that "originally the ego includes everything, later it separates off an external world from itself. Our present ego-feeling is, therefore, only a shrunken residue of a much more inclusive—indeed, an all-embracing—feeling which corresponded to a more intimate bond between the ego and world about it" (SE, 21:68). We are reminded, too, of our earlier discussion of sacrifice. Weaning, in Lacan's view, is tantamount to a primordial act of sacrifice in which the child in some sense offers the breast to the mother. Indeed, in the light of Lacan's notion of the cedable object, we are led to suppose that the entirety of the world has its origin in an activity of subjective ceding or yielding. Ultimately, the world itself is an object of sacrifice.

Sacrifice to whom and for what? The object is ceded as a way to avoid anxiety. Again Lacan's approach runs contrary to a commonplace of psychoanalytic theory according to which anxiety is triggered by loss. On the Lacanian view, anxiety predates the loss of the object—"the function of anxiety is prior to this ceding of the object" (S.X, 7-3-63). Moreover, the object is given up precisely in order to quell anxiety. Why? The reason is to be found in Lacan's distinctive interpretation of anxiety, namely that "anxiety . . . is linked to the fact that I do not know what object a I am for the desire of the Other" (S.X, 7-3-63). The infant at the breast is confronted above all by the unanswerable question of the mother's desire. It is in the face of this question that the mother assumes the proportions of *das Ding*, not the little other of the imaginary object, the mirror image of the other human being, but the unknowable, unmasterable, and monstrous big Other. Crudely considered, the strategy of the infant at this point seems comparable to that of certain species of lizards, whose mode of escape from the clutches of a predator is to give up that portion of their tail that is capable of regeneration. In like fashion, the breast, heretofore part of the infantile ego itself, is given up, or ceded, to the other. But the Lacanian point is more subtle. The action of ceding is more precarious, more ambiguous. The infant does not detach the breast from its own body, as if amputating one part in order to preserve the whole, but rather comes to experience itself as a body for the first time with the separation or ceding of the breast. Thus Lacan speaks of "this function of the cedable object as a separable fragment carrying in a way primitively something of the identity of the body which antecedes the body itself as regards the constitution of the subject" (S.X. 6-23-63).

The trickiest point concerns the granting of agency to the infant, as if the action of ceding could be conceived as an intentional tactic of survival, as if it could be thought of as an act at all. Lacan's point is much more radical and paradoxical: far from it being the case that there exists an infantile subject who voluntarily or deliberately yields the breast, it is only in the moment of ceding the object that the subject can be said to come into being at all. "This primitive mythical subject who is posed at the beginning as having to constitute himself in the confrontation, [is what] that we never grasp—and for good reason—because the [little] *a* has preceded him, and because it is in a way itself marked by this primitive substitution, that it has to re-emerge beyond" (S.X, 6-26-63). In ceding the object, the locus of the subject emerges for the first time, the loss of the part establishes the whole virtually, negatively, retroactively. What is at stake, Lacan insists, is "what one could call the most radical essentiality of the subject" (S.X, 6-26-63). Put back into the language of sacrifice, the being of the sacrificer emerges for the first time only with the loss effected by the act of sacrifice.

The paradox at issue here can be seen from another angle of view when we consider the relation between the ceding of the object and the genesis of desire. The object is ceded not in order to preserve an already formed desire but, in the most radical sense, desire originates precisely in such ceding. The object is thrust away so that it can be desired, it is lost so that it can be found for the first time. Desire paradoxically comes into being in and through its limitation, the upsurge of desire is thus coincident with its inhibition. As Lacan continues, "the first developmental form of desire is thus and as such akin to the order of inhibition. When desire appears for the first time, it opposes itself to the very act through which its originality as desire is introduced" (S.X, 7-3-63).

Lacan explicitly links the cedable object to the object of sacrifice and reilluminates our earlier discussions of sacrifice. The real function of sacrifice, he insists, is less to enact a specific transaction, any particular *quid pro quo* with the other, than to determine the Other as a desiring being; less to effect a specific exchange than to establish the very possibility of exchange. Sacrifice serves to bring the desire of the other out of the real, out of the monstrous domain of *das Ding*, and to anchor it in a symbolic order. Thus Lacan claims that "sacrifice is destined, not at all to be an offering or a gift which spreads itself into a quite different dimension, but to be the capture of the Other as such in the network of desire" (S.X, 6-5-63). Ceding the breast in order to avoid the anxious confrontation with the real of the maternal Thing, the child repeats with the mother the essential gesture of sacrifice to the ancient gods. Subjective ceding founds the desire of the subject precisely to the extent that it gives form, through the mediation of the object, to the desire of the Other. "The whole question was to know whether these gods desired something. Sacrifice consisted in behaving as if they desired like us. . . . That does not mean that they are going to eat what is sacrificed to them, nor even that it can be of any use to them; but the important thing is that they desire it and, I would say further, that this does not provoke anxiety in them. . . . To tame the god in the snare of desire is essential, and not to awaken anxiety" (S.X, 6-5-63).

In Lacan's view, the subject emerges as a kind of remainder, an effect of the negative space hollowed out in the ceding of the object. As *objet a*, this object is not identical with the subject, but is a kind of negative stand-in for it. The *objet a*, says Lacan, "is the substitute (*suppléant*) for the subject" (S.X, 6-26-63). But to say that the *objet a* is a substitute for the subject is also to insist on some separation between them. The sustainability of desire depends upon the moment of difference, or negation, signified by the *poinçon* in the formula $\mathcal{S} \lozenge a$. In this way, we can make sense of the relation—which must strike any reader familiar with Lacan's work—between Lacan's discussion of the cedable object and his other reliance on the word "cedable" to characterize the ethical import of psychoanalysis as a question of "not ceding on one's desire." "From an analytic point of view the only thing of which one can be guilty is of having ceded (of having given ground or compromised) relative to one's desire" (S.VII, 319). Are we not to read these two usages of *céder* in correlation with one another? Is the point not that the Lacanian subject is enjoined to give up the object, but to not give up the negative space left by its lack? The two moments of ceding are exactly complementary: the subject must cede the object in order not to cede on its desire.

"You don't love me . . . you just don't give a shit."

Along with the breast, the other great "cedable object" of infancy is, of course, the feces, and with respect to the excremental object, this second great figure of the *objet a*, the relation between the *objet a* and the desire of the other emerges with special clarity.

Lacan begins by acknowledging the "natural attitude" toward excrement. For the animal "excrement is characterized . . . as something rejected and as a consequence it is rather in the sense, in the current, in the flow of that which the living being as such tends to disinterest himself in. What interests him is what enters; what goes out seems to imply in the structure that he has no tendency to retain it" (S.X, 6-19-63). By contrast with the animal, however, the developing human being becomes aware from a very early age that everything surrounding the substance of feces appears to be of the very greatest import. The appearance of excrement typically elicits meticulous attention on the part of the mother or caretaker—attention that is clearly marked by anxious concern. How could the infant fail to conclude that this otherwise worthless substance is in fact the most valuable stuff in the world? And how could the infant fail to realize that the zone of the body which produces it links the infant to the mother in a particularly constant and intimate way? In Lacanian terms, the infant's feces is the privileged object of the mother's demand.

> Along what path does excrement enter into subjectification? . . .
> it involves education in what is called cleanliness, which com-
> mands the child to retain . . . the excrement and because of this
> already to outline its introduction into the domain of belonging,
> of a part of the body, which for at least a certain time must be
> considered as not to be alienated, then after that to release it,
> always on demand . . . thanks to the fact that the demand also
> becomes here a determining part in the releasing in question . . .
> the subject has some apprehension he is taking on, this part
> becoming at least valorised by the fact that it gives its satisfac-
> tion to the demand of the Other. (S.X, 6-19-63)

The consequences of this insertion of the feces into the circuit of demand of the other are far from trivial. Consider, first, their influence on the subject's own body. Toilet training attests to the fact that the Other is intensely interested in the most primitive and quasi-automatic functions of the infant's physiology. By this means, the anus is charged with the demand of the other. For this reason, the anal sphincter, despite the socially rehearsed repugnance that attaches to everything excremental—or rather precisely because of that repugnance—must be considered the most profoundly social organ of the body. It is the site at which the most elemental physiological functions, the rhythmic movements of peristalsis, are entwined with the most subtle psychological and interpersonal dynamics, laid down by the subject's experience of the other's love or rejection. In toilet training, the anus is "colonized," to invoke a happily apt pun, by the other's desire. Throughout the future life of the individual, the contractions and relaxations of the anal muscle will inevitably call up immensely more global connotations of mastery or submission, independence or dependence.

Taken up into this physiologico-emotional complex, the fecal material becomes freighted with significance that utterly outstrips all natural or animal attitudes toward excrement. In accord with a symbolic equivalence already familiar to Freud, the feces become privileged tokens in an exchange of love—excrement as primordial gift. In this way is accomplished a radical "revaluation of all values." By fixing upon what is most naturally worthless, the range of possible objects of human desire is henceforth established as formally infinite, potentially inclusive of even the most abject and revolting content. At the same time, this elevation of excrement to the level of the very index of love will color all subsequent experience of the libidinal bond with a profound ambivalence. In the heart of the love relation is something that may at any moment reveal itself to be repulsive and worthless. Jokes about the sexual function thus become "dirty jokes." Love is perpetually haunted by the deeply rooted suspicion—a reality on the level of the unconscious—that it is "much ado about nothing." Something similar can be said about the way in which the drama of toilet training establishes an ambivalence concerning the entirety of human social life and the institutions that structure and support it. In a very real sense, the human being enters civilized life by way of an unnatural investment of libidinal interest in functioning of its bowels. The edifice of civilization is founded upon the unconscious libidinalization of excrement.

The identification of the *objet a* with the anal object is especially illuminating for Lacan's definition of the *objet a* as produced at the site of the body's orifices, as a function of the organs that possess a "rim," the line at which what is inner is separated from what is outer and other. In this invocation of the rim, we see especially clearly the imaginary staging of the *objet a*, not only its positioning at the unstable in-between of the subject and the other, but also its role as an interrruption or discontinuity of the bodily gestalt. As a breaching of the body's inetgrity, the fecal object sites the question of what other monstrosities of the real are hidden and contained by the skin.

It is at this point that we can append a remark about the relation of the *objet a* to the psychological function of the stain so often pointed to by Lacan. The irregular blotch of the stain violates the field of an homogeneous surface and thus serves to evoke the question of what lies behind the surface, what more there is than the image. The capacity of the *objet a* to instantiate lack, to body forth a registration of the negative, is here based on a marking of the body surface by a blemish. Lacan illustrates this point by reference to the beauty mark, the charming effect of the discrete mole off to one side of the otherwise flawless face. The source of this charming effect resides in its serving to evoke the *objet a*. The beauty mark "shows the place of *a*, here reduced to the zero point whose function I evoked the last time. The beauty spot, more than the shape that it stains, is what looks at me" (S.X, 5-22-63) "With the stain there appears, there is prepared the possibility of the resurgence, in the field of desire, of what is hidden behind" (S.X, 6-5-63).

Lacan's reinterpretation of the oral and anal stages shows clearly how the drive in the human being emerges in the context of natural functions of suckling and defecating but only by deflecting those functions into new and denaturalized strivings. Eating and eliminating become truly human only when they are drawn into the orbit of a demand for something wholly superfluous to the satisfaction of any natural need. This extranatural element, split off from the exigencies of biological need and established as an independent power, the eccentric locus around which the drive will perpetually revolve without ever achieving fulfillment, is the *objet a*. Thus Lacan concludes that "the *objet petit a* is not the origin of the oral drive. It is not introduced as the original food, it is introduced from the fact that no food will ever satisfy the oral drive, except by circumventing the eternally lacking object" (FFC, 180). For the same reason, the "development" of the human child through successive "stages," far from being attributable to any natural evolution of maturation, must rather be understood as a migration of the function of the *objet a*, passing like a restless and irremediable exile from one organ system to another.

> The passage from the oral drive to the anal drive can be produced not by a process of maturation, but by the intervention of something that does not belong to the field of the drive—by the intervention, the overthrow, of the demand of the Other. . . .

There is no natural metamorphosis of the oral drive into the anal drive (FFC, 180).

Between the Look and the Gaze

We have yet to describe a key aspect of the Lacanian *objet a*, one that is especially significant for the trajectory of argument we have been following in this book. It is an aspect that is particularly well illustrated by Lacan's identification of the *objet a* with the gaze.

Introduction to Lacan's concept of the gaze can usefully be made by way of the theory developed by Sartre in *Being and Nothingness*. Lacan more than once refers to Sartre's view, though ultimately in order to rigorously distinguish his own position from it. It is convenient, therefore, that the French word used in both instances, *le regard*, is generally translated differently in Sartre's case, not as "gaze" but as "look."

Lacan is not unappreciative of Sartre's contribution, which he calls "magisterial" and "essential reading for an analyst" (S.I, 215). To his credit, Sartre recognizes both the primordiality of the phenomenon and its centrality for the experience of the other human being. Sartre is right to insist, as Lacan puts it, that "the human object is originally distinguished, *ab initio*, in the field of my experience, and cannot be assimilated to any other perceptible object, by virtue of being an object which is looking at me" (S.I, 215). Sartre also rightly maintains that what is at stake in the gaze far transcends the literal presence of the other's eyes. Lacan underlines this point by suggesting that the most intense experience of the gaze may be produced by "the blankness of the eye of the blind man" or by the lowered eyelids so characteristic of statues of Buddha (S.X 5-22-63). Thus the experience of the gaze may be less intensely aroused by the eyes of the other *per se* than by an oblique evidencing of their presence. "If you turn to Sartre's own text," Lacan reminds us, "you will see that, far from speaking of the emergence of this gaze as of something that concerns the organ of sight, he refers to the sound of rustling leaves, suddenly heard while out hunting, to a footstep heard in a corridor" (FFC 84).

> The gaze in question must on no account be confused with the fact, for example, of seeing his eyes. I can feel myself under the gaze of someone whose eyes I do not even see, not even discern.

All that is necessary is for something to signify to me that there may be others there. This window, if it gets a bit dark, and if I have reasons for thinking that there is someone behind it, is straightaway a gaze (S.I, 215).

Few people are wholly unfamiliar with Sartre's view, if only because it implicitly informs so many recent feminist discussions of the objectifying male attitude toward women's bodies. Sartre's basic idea—itself modeled on another account, that of the Hegelian dialectic of master and slave—supposes a kind of duel between one consciousness and another. Only one of them will emerge as a true subject; the other will be objectified under the force of the look. Sartre's paradigmatic example is the experience of shame that overcomes the voyeur when, poised at the keyhole in the act of enjoying another's objectification, he is himself objectified under the look of a third person who happens along and discovers him. The relevance of Sartre's account for a feminist critique is well displayed by considering what is probably the quintessential fashion pose, countless examples of which crowd the pages of magazines like *Vogue, Glamour, Elle*. In this gesture, far more commonly adopted by female models than by their male counterparts, the model languorously casts her look away from the viewer. Whether the eyes are demurely turned down, thrown distractedly off to one side, or allowed to float vaguely upward, the defining characteristic of this pose is that the eyes appear not to focus on anything. They seem willingly to evacuate any intention of their own, to abdicate their own power of seeing. The purpose of this aimless look is not difficult to determine: it signals a suspension of the model's own claim to subjectivity and thereby grants the prerogative of looking to the other who enjoys unchallenged visual access to her body. To the gaze of the other these eyes say "Take me!" Given this sort of example, one might well ask, with Laura Mulvey, Ann Kaplan, and others, "Is the Gaze Male?"

Sartre's account interests Lacan in part because it identifies "a register in which you have to recognize the plane of the imaginary" (S.I, 215). Yet therein consists its limitation as well. For Sartre's conception of the look remains essentially dyadic. It is a binarism that shows itself in Sartre's reduction of love to a dialectic of sadism and masochism, but also and more generally informs his most fundamental categories of the for-itself and the in-itself. This binary model raises a number of problems, among which is Sartre's tendency to assume an either/or relation between the two poles it identifies: either the other retains his rights as a subject by objectifying me with his look, or he is himself rendered an object under my look. From a Lacanian point of view, however, there is nothing to prevent both positions from being occupied simultaneously. To cite an example, let us return to the glossy fashion magazine. Especially during the 1980s, the covers of these magazines typically displayed the dazzling image of the "cover-girl," indeed the presence of this intensely focused face, this modern-day icon, virtually defined the genre of women's fashion magazines.

In order to grasp the function of the cover-girl face, it is essential to notice how it simultaneously produces two distinct but interrelated effects. On the one hand, and most immediately, the cover girl presents an image-object of uncommon fascination. Extraordinary care is taken, formerly by airbrush and now by computer retouching, to produce an epiphany of uncannily flawless beauty. The result is a magical image of mesmerizing power. On the other hand, the cover-girl face typically looks directly back at the viewer with an almost unbelievably intense gaze. Here, too, very deliberate care is taken to achieve the effect. Reflective highlights in the eyes are strategically placed in order to produce an electrifying stare. Whatever the captivating attractiveness of the rest of the face, these glittering, jewel-like eyes stand out with such unmistakable brilliance that they exert an arresting effect all their own.

The cover girl thus seems to embody the two poles of the Sartrian look: the captivating object *and* the gazing subject. And proceeding on Sartrian premises, we might suppose that the viewer is doomed to fall one way or the other. Either the fascinating object-character of the face is privileged, thus undergirding the self-possession of the viewer-subject in confrontation with the inert object, or else the viewer wilts under the extraordinary force of the gaze, the effect of which is to produce in the viewer a disabling, shaming self-consciousness, a painful awareness of the viewer's own objectification. But it is not difficult to conclude that the real power of the cover-girl image lies precisely in its capacity to induce both effects at once. Indeed, the two moments dialectically reinforce each other: the more the viewer feels undone by this penetrating gaze, the more the face is reinvested as a fascinating object of beauty. Conversely, the more the face is inflated with the value of the beautiful, the more commanding and dangerous its gaze becomes. And this double function shouldn't surprise us. Its resulting dialectic of shame and fascination provides the perfect mechanism for selling magazines to women anxious about their own appearance. At the same time that the cover-girl gaze excites a feeling of self-doubt it also promises an escape from doubt and shame by providing a marvelous and remobilizing image upon which the threatened ego can feed, the wherewithal to mimic which is available for sale within the pages of the magazine.

The example of the cover girl helps point us toward the essentials of the Lacanian notion of the gaze. The key point is the distinction Lacan draws between the eye and the gaze. The eye fixes upon visible objects precisely in order to escape from the gaze. It is this distinction between the eye and the gaze that most separates Lacan's account from Sartre's. For Lacan, the structure of the gaze is not dual but triadic. It includes the subject (the one who sees), the visual object (the other who is seen), and the gaze (a third locus that fails to coincide with the visual other).[3] Thus Lacan remarks that "Sartre does not perceive that the intersubjective field cannot but open on to a numerical structuration, on to the three, the four, which are our bench-marks in the analytic experience" (S.I, 224).[4]

How does this Lacanian distinction of eye and gaze work in the example of the cover girl? Notice, first, the way in which it parallels our discussion of the Thing. The cover-girl face is a perceptual complex in the sense Freud defines it: it presents a familiar object to the extent that it mirrors the viewer's own body image. But it also calls up an unencompassable dimension, the otherness of this Other, alive in the question that is thrown back on the viewer about what this intense gaze sees. Behind this threatening gaze lurks the question of *das Ding*. As we have just seen, both these levels are operative in the encounter with the cover-girl face. Consciously, the cover girl appears as a supremely attractive object. But this attractiveness (along with the promise of an identification with the beautiful model who embodies it) is coupled with a simultaneous excitement of anxiety (which arises with the viewer's painful recognition of how little she resembles the beauty queen displayed on the magazine cover). In order for the cover-girl image to succeed in its basic purpose—that of selling the magazine—the anxiety it arouses must be controlled in some way. How? The anxiety remains unconscious by means of a reinvestment in the radiant image of beauty. The attractiveness of the cover-girl object is substituted for the monstrous presence of the Thing. The beauty of the face gets repainted over the hole opened up by the Thing. In Lacanian terms, the eye triumphs over the gaze. A precisely similar process operates in the adoration felt by the lowly peasant for the radiant King or Queen. What might otherwise emerge as uncontrollable panic in the presence of the sovereign power is transformed into an enormously magnified sense of aesthetic awe.

Lacan extends this distinction between eye and gaze to propose a general theory of vision in which the act of seeing functions precisely to avoid the gaze. He thus suggests that painting produces a "pacifying, Apollinian effect" that feeds the eye with reassuringly stable objects in order to allow the viewer to put the gaze out of play. In painting, "something is given not so much to the gaze as to the eye, something that involves the abandonment, the *laying down*, of the gaze" (FFC, 101). How are we to understand this laying down of the gaze? The painter offers the picture to molify the gaze of the spectator, as if the gesture of painting were a matter of escaping from a predator by distracting it with a piece of meat.

> The painter gives something to the person who must stand in front of his painting which, in part, at least, of the painting, might be summed up thus—*You want to see? Well, take a look at this!* he gives something for the eye to feed on, but he invites the person to whom this picture is presented to lay down his gaze there as one lays down one's weapons. (FFC, 101)

By referring the act of seeing to some third point off the axis of seer and seen, Lacan succeeds in revealing the internal complexity of the scopic drive. The third position, itself invisible yet functioning continually to reenergize the subject's investment in the object of sight, is none other that the *objet a*. Its presence-by-absence serves to produce "the ambiguity that affects anything that is inscribed in the register of the scopic drive" (FFC, 83). To illustrate this point, we can return to the example of the voyeur who, relentlessly goaded on by the scopic drive, is most completely reclaimed by the force of the drive precisely when he fails to see what he is looking for. That is to say, as a search for the *objet a*, an object that by definition cannot be given, the scopic drive is most surely reinforced and recreated at the moment when it appears to draw closest to its objective, yet fails to grasp it. It is as if this very failure is the evidence that the *objet a* is there. The point is perfectly demonstrated by the essential pose, the veritable *sine qua non*, of soft-core pornographic magazines: the so-called spread shot. The centerpiece of this shot is the vulva spread wide for the camera to inspect. Seeking to explain the appeal of this defining image we might naively suppose that the spread shot satisfies insofar as it "shows all." It leaves nothing to the imagination. The viewer has finally won unimpeded visual access to the inner secret of the feminine. From a Lacanian point of view, however, the conclusion is exactly the opposite. What attracts the scopic drive to the vaginal spread shot is precisely what it doesn't show, to what in fact cannot be shown. The result of the "show all" strategy is to create even more intense hunger for the thing that cannot be imaged: the *objet a*. The more you see, the less you find what you are really looking for. The "proof" of the Lacanian view lies in the compulsiveness with which the consumer of pornography moves from one girlie image to another, to another, and so on. If the spread shot really succeeded in "showing all," then one image would be enough. But the pornographic drive shows its real essence less in the excitement created by one image than by the insatiable hunger it generates for *yet another image*. The enormous commercial potency of pornography derives in part from the fact that it succeeds in continually restimulating the very hunger it promises to satisfy.

The investment of interest in pornography depends upon the subject's relation to something that ceaselessly escapes the roving, lustful eye, some moment of ultimate satisfaction that is continually promised but never fully given. In this way, the example of the pornographic image shows very well what Lacan means by saying that the *objet a* is not the aim of the drive but rather the perpetually eccentric point around which the drive revolves. The point of crucial theoretical importance in all of this concerns the way in which the *objet a* irrecoverably triangulates the subject's relation to the aim of the drive. Despite the fact that his conclusions are repeatedly pressed back into the mold of one or another dualism, Sartre's account of the gaze comes close to acknowledging this essential triangularity of the gaze. In the paradigmatic example of the voyeur discovered at the keyhole, for example, the relation of the subject and his object is disturbed by the upsurge of another look, a third position. To be caught in this way by the appearance of a third party, says Lacan, "changes all perspectives, the lines of force, of my world" (FFC. 84). It is a similar rupture of the dual axis of sight that Lacan analyzes in Holbein's painting *The Ambassadors*. In order to see that the strange, oblong object floating in the foreground is in fact a skull, the viewer must shift position altogether, looking back at the painting from a new stance lower down and far to one side—shifting, that is, to a third position that lies off the dual axis described by the previously established line of sight. But the central Lacanian point is that this third position is always there, always exerting a constitutive influence on what emerges on the stage of awareness. In effect, the voyeur is always already seen by the gaze. Indeed, the deliciously anxious excitement of his act of peeping is constituted by this very exposure to the gaze. At the deepest level, the voyeur's thrill derives less from his enjoyment of a stolen view of another's private moments than from the way in which this theft is itself seen by the gaze. What is most profoundly seen in voyeurism is the voyeur himself.

By identifying the gaze with *objet a*, Lacan describes a structure that in principle cannot be mapped in a linear fashion but can be described only by recourse to topology. What, then, is the gaze as *objet petit a*? In the terms we have evolved over the course of this essay, the *objet a* must be located in the dispositional field. What distinguishes this object from all others is the fact that it cannot occupy the positional focus of attention. Yet it remains active in the invisible framing that produces all positional awareness. This, then, is what it means that the *objet a* is not the aim or object of desire but its object-cause. The *objet a* is a dispositional object. It is the dispositional character of the gaze that accounts for what Lacan calls its "inside-out structure." The gaze forms what he calls the "underside of consciousness" (FFC, 82- 83). Where for Sartre the revelation of the other's look threatens an extinction of my consciousness, for Lacan the gaze is the very condition of consciousness. The gaze is the horizon within which the realm of the visible is established. With respect to the structuring of the scopic domain, the distinction between the eye and the gaze is a way of specifying the dependence of consciousness upon the structure of the unconscious: behind the coming to presence of all the objects of my world there lurks a constitutive absence that is animated by the desire of the other.

There is something intrinsically ungraspable, unmasterable, about this horizon of the visible. Even as it makes possible the emergence of things into visibility, the gaze remains "unapprehensible," subject to a primordial "scotoma" (FFC, 83). Ultimately, what Lacan means by the gaze thus has less in common with the quasi-Hegelian duel of objectifying looks described by Sartre than it does with Merleau-Ponty's effort to radicalize metaphysics through a meditation on the visible and the invisible. The point, as Lacan remarks in the last session of his eleventh seminar, is that "there is something that looks before there is a view for it to see" (FFC, 273). This gaze does not emanate from any particular pair of eyes, but precedes and possibilizes the field of the visible altogether. It is an all-encompassing survey that simultaneously takes in the position occupied by the other human being who looks at me *and also my own position.* "What we have to circumscribe," says Lacan, ". . . is the pre-existence of a gaze—I see only from one point, but in my existence I am looked at from all sides" (FFC, 72). In the light of this all-seeing gaze that is always already there and belongs to no one in particular, the particular example of painting becomes a subset of a more general phenomenon of the picture, the very body of the visible, as screen for the gaze.

> That which is light looks at me, and by means of that light in the depths of my eye, something is painted—something that is not simply a constructed relation, the object on which the philosopher lingers—but something that is an impression, the shimmering of a surface that is not, in advance, situated for me in its distance. This is something that introduces what was elided in the geometral relation—the depth of field, with all its ambiguity and variability, which is in no way mastered by me. It is rather it that grasps me, solicits me at every moment, and makes of the landscape something other than a landscape, something other than what I have called the picture.

> The correlative of the picture, to be situated in the same place as it, that is to say, outside, is the point of gaze, while that which forms the mediation from the one to the other, that which is between the two, is something of another nature than geometral, optical space, something that plays an exactly reverse role, which operates, not because it can be traversed, but on the contrary because it is opaque—I mean the screen. (FFC, 96)

Lacan's concept of the gaze thus enables us to rejoin our point of departure in the concept of the dispositional field. To the extent that the

Lacanian gaze becomes constitutive of vision, it establishes the very possibility of the visible in a way precisely parallel to the effects of lighting that Monet called the *enveloppe*. For Lacan, it is in the unlimited medium established by the *enveloppe* of the gaze that the desire of the Other addresses itself to us. The gaze is that moment of the Other that escapes from the merely imaginary aspect, it is the Other in the other. The gaze is the moment of dispositionality in the other.

The Lacanian gaze is thus understandable only in the triadic structure of desire, the Oedipal structure in which the subject is faced with the question of the Other's desire. In the actual experience of the Oedipal stage, the experience of the gaze begins to unfold when the mother no longer simply presents an image to the child but is seen to be looking for something herself, the moment when the suspicion dawns that the mother's desire is directed beyond the child itself to some third position. Said otherwise, the gaze is one of the prime figures in which the imaginary relation opens out upon a symbolic horizon. It is by virtue of its capacity to excite an experience of this dimension of the gaze, precisely through preventing the analysand from seeing the eyes of the analyst, that psychoanalysis sets up the special force field of the transference. Its place will come to be occupied by the entirety of the symbolic order. In the place of the gaze, the subject will come to experience the call of the signifier. Correlatively, it is a certain suspension or avoidance of the gaze that founds the entirety of the imaginary register, both the ego and its objects. This elision of the gaze is the very essence of imaginary *méconnaissance*. Lacan therefore asks of narcissism and of the "satisfaction, not to say self-satisfaction, that diffuses from it, which gives the subject a pretext for such a profound *méconnaissance* . . . —can we not also grasp that which has been eluded, namely, the function of the gaze?" (FFC, 74).

To give a final suggestion of what is at stake in this aspect of the gaze, let us take another example: that of the monumental architecture designed for Adolf Hitler by Albert Speer. Speer's architecture is precisely calculated to stage a certain experience of the gaze. In the enormity of this architecture, it is the negative space, the yawning, open expanses, that are most important. This architecture is meant less to be seen by a viewer, than to produce in the viewer an experience of being seen in and by it. Individuals find themselves taken up into an overwhelming embrace precisely because the spectacle of which they are a part is too enormous to be the object of any single human eye. This experience of a gaze that is unencompassable, that surpasses every particular viewpoint, uplifts and transforms the viewers' sense of themselves, of their aspirations, their motivations, their possibilities. The experience of being projected ecstatically outside oneself is coextensive, as the title of Speer's memoir suggests, with being "inside the Third Reich." A parallel solicitation of the gaze is powerfully present in Leni Riefenstahl's *Triumph of the Will*, the opening sequence of which features footage taken from an airplane. This opening shot lingers for a long time among the clouds before finally descending upon the columns of marching soldiers and cheering throngs that line the village streets. Only when the plane lands and Adolf Hitler steps out does this evocation of the gaze become particularized: it is the gaze of the Fürher himself.

What is absolutely crucial in this fascistic incitement of the gaze is its collective character, the way in which it is not the individual but the solidarity of the group that is its object. It is at this point that a Lacanian analysis contributes significantly to Freud's theory of the ego ideal in mass psychology. In and through its collectivizing effect, the overwheming sense of the gaze in mass psychology brings the subject into a position of being completely dominated by the desire of the Other. It is the precise opposite of the function of the gaze in the analytic transference. Both situations result in the incitement of aggressivity. What distinguishes them is that in the case of mass psychology the violence will be directed outside the group in the name of the leader who instantiates the gaze. In the analytic situation, by contrast, an aggressive impulse will finally erupt toward the very locus of the gaze, the unseen analyst whose desire remains an enigma, and will initiate the process by which the subject reclaims some greater portion of his or her own desire.

Why One and One Make Four

The foregoing discussions have placed the Lacanian *objet a* into the architecture of concepts we have developed over the course of this study. In the terms we have evolved, the *objet a* must be conceived as a dispositional object. It cannot be given as a positional locus. It is a kind of paradoxical, negative object, the unconscious object *par excellence*. Indeed, even to refer to it as an "object" involves a measured abuse of language, for the *objet a* is less an object than the function by which objects will be established. It is,

Lacan says, "the object of objects," less an instance of objectivity than a function of "objectality" (S.X, 5-8-63)

> To designate the *petit a* by the term object is, as you see, a metaphorical usage, since it is borrowed precisely from this subject-object relationship from which the term object is constituted, which no doubt is suitable for designating the general function of objectivity; and this object, of which we have to speak under the term *a*, is precisely an object which is outside any possible definition of objectivity. (S.X, 1-9-63)

Yet there no doubt remains good deal about this crucial Lacanian concept that is stubbornly mysterious. How to further specify its meaning? It might fairly be said that Lacan himself had the same problem, and no wonder, given the novelty and radicality of his intention. In the last years of his teaching, Lacan sought to theorize the nature and function of the *objet a* by relying on analogies to mathematical topology and by developing a series of terse symbolic expressions, his so-called mathemes, such as the formula for the phantasy, $\cancel{S} \lozenge a$. In this formula, the subject S is "barred" by virtue of its submission to the law of the signifier and placed in a complex relation to the *objet a*. Toward the same end, Lacan also employed a number of graphs and schemata, such as the Schema L, to which we have already referred more than once, and his later Schema R. Let us now make the experiment of trying to clarify the *objet a* by redrawing those schemata.

We begin by placing the Thing opposite the subject, on the side of the other, but distinguished from it, to signify that the Thing concerns that aspect of the other that remains unrepresentable, uncognizable (Fig. 16). The Thing is that ungraspable dimension of the *Nebenmensch*, called up especially by the sounding of the voice, that overflows the body image of the other.

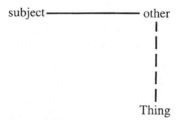

Figure 16

This arrangement immediately begins to resemble the three corners Lacan's Schema L (cf. Fig. 4, page 83 above), and for good reason: the Thing locates precisely what is most Other about the other. It provides a first orientation to what Lacan calls "the big Other," the Other with a capital "O." Moreover, we have already seen how this relation to the Thing has the effect of rebounding on the subject itself. There is a profound resonance between the Thing, as the unencompassable kernel at the heart of the object, and the as-yet-unknown dimension of the subject's desire, the unrepresented pulsional interior. There is a correspondence between *das Ding* and *das Es*. We can add this correspondence to our developing graph by connecting the positions of Thing and subject with a dotted line to indicate its character as a relation to-be-realized (Fig. 17).

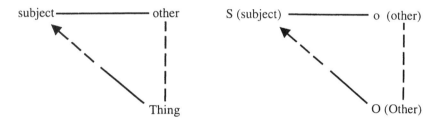

Figure 17

The real of the Thing, we have said, is approachable only by means of the signifier and the diacritical system in which it is situated. This action of the signifier is a genuinely mediating function, as it serves simultaneously to link the subject to the Thing and also to keep them separate. The necessity of this mediating function, stablizing a relation to the Thing without collapsing the distance that separates the subject from it, cannot be overestimated. For Lacan, it is nothing less than the fundamental meaning of the prohibition of incest (S.VII, 67-69). Its failure, as we see it in the Schreber case, triggers descent into psychosis. For Schreber, *das Ding* appears in the place of the imaginary other, but with all the power and uncanny monstrousness of the primordial object. Thus Schreber becomes the victim of the desire of the Other in a completely unmediated way—he becomes the beloved of God.

With these points in mind, we can complete the parallel between the diagram we have constructed and Lacan's Schema L (Fig. 18). The Lacanian Big Other (O), which represents what in the Other escapes from the relation to the imaginary other (o), is located in the lower right of the schema. It is this Big Other that Lacan associates with the locus of the signifying code, the Other at stake in the Lacanian claim that the unconscious is the discourse of the Other. But immediately we notice that in the alignment we have proposed, the locus of the Big Other, associated by Lacan with the father, coincides with that of the Thing, linked most closely with the mother.

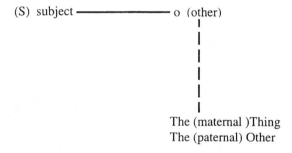

Figure 18

In collapsing the maternal and paternal positions, has our attempt at a schema already gone awry? Not at all. The coincidence of these two positions is precisely what the Lacanian theory of the paternal metaphor suggests. The function of the paternal metaphor is to submit the desire of the Mother (which is of the order of the Thing) to the law of the Father (which comprises the totality of the signifying system, the structure of the symbolic order). The primary achievement of the Oedipus complex is to effect this shift in the lower right corner of the schema from the maternal Thing to the paternal Law. Clarifying this point avoids what might initially appear to be a contradiction, but also indicates that the schema represents positions that are tensed with a temporal unfolding. The schema represents a relation of the subject to the Thing that develops over time. As we will see, the *objet a* emerges as an effect of that development.

Let us now take account of the other thread of our inquiry, in accordance with which we have tried to bring certain key points of the psychoanalytic theory into relation with the lessons of Gestalt psychology. It is not difficult to suggest a translation of our first diagram into the Gestaltist terms of figure and ground (Fig. 19).

Figure 19

In this scheme, the function of the ground is attributed to the primitive subject and the heterogeneity of impulses that animate it. The image of the other in relation to which the subject first mobilizes itself is fittingly compared with the gestalt figure. This is the moment of identification with the other in the mirror phase. It represents the other as mere image, as perceptual registration of an object. Given this initial couplet of ground and figure, the Thing occurs initially in purely negative terms as "Not Figure." It is plainly opposite to the subject (thus differentiated from the inchoate ground) and is implied by the other/object but is not identical with it (thus "not figure").

At this point, the schema we are developing in Lacanian terms can be recognized as homologous with the basic schema of structuralism, based on the logic of the Klein Group and most evocatively worked out in the semiotic square of A. J. Greimas. Rosalind Krauss makes exactly this point in her study of *The Optical Unconscious*.[5] Greimas's semiotic square presents a logic of "contraries," represented by the two top terms, S_1 and S_2, and relations of "implication," corresponding to the diagonals linking the upper and lower corner terms, S_1 and $\sim S_2$, S_2 and $\sim S_1$. The vertical segments (S_1 and $\sim S_1$, S_2 and $\sim S_2$,) represent relations of "contradiction." The resulting square is presented in Fig. 20.

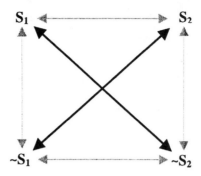

Figure 20

The overarching aim of Greimas's semiotic square is to define the most elementary structure of meaning. It does so by presenting a logic of semantic implication by means of which a given term is opened up to the dimensions of difference that define its particular semantic field. The procedure begins by setting the initial term in binary opposition to its contrary—we cannot define "white," for example, apart from its opposition to "black." However, for each of the contraries, it is possible to posit contradictories (non-white, non-black) which open a larger and more complex field of meaning. The resulting relations can be mapped as shown in Fig. 21.

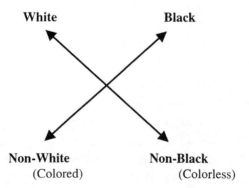

Figure 21

Greimas's construction is broadly applicable for analyzing systems of meaning. The contraries of "having-to-do" and "having-not-to-do" (being obligated vs. being prohibited), for example, generate a square that describes the dynamics that govern many sets of cultural rules (Fig. 22).

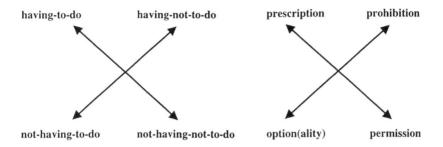

Figure 22

When this scheme is applied to a specific set of rules (as, for example, those governing sexual relations) we notice how groupings of terms can be made (e.g., S_1 and $\sim S_2$, S_2 and $\sim S_1$) that describe new conceptual distinctions—in this case, the opposition between "culture" and "nature" (Fig. 23).

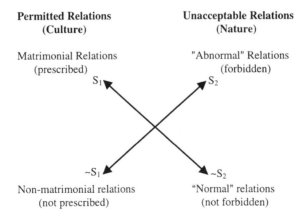

Figure 23

Completing our diagram of gestalt concepts along the lines of Greimas's square, we arrive at Fig. 24:

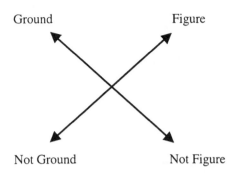

Ground   Figure

Not Ground   Not Figure

Figure 24

When we now try to align this graph of gestalt concepts with the Schema L, however, we notice a wrinkle. The problem is that the position of the imaginary ego (in the lower left corner of the Schema L) must be identified with the locus of the "not-ground." Aside from the fact that it is not yet clear what "not-ground" might mean here, the whole point of Lacan's theory of the imaginary ego is to assert an equivalence between the imago of the other—a kind of gestalt figure—and the primitive identity of the ego. In gestaltist terms, the ego is a figure. How are we to clarify all of this?

The way beyond this impass—and the way toward a more satisfying elaboration of our entire discussion—lies in recognizing that the gestaltist square we have proposed cannot be aligned with the Schema L without qualification. It can, however, be aligned with another of Lacan's basic schemata: the so-called Schema R. Lacan first develops this schema in his discussion of the Schreber case. It is presented there as shown in Fig. 25.

This schema is roughly homologous with the Schema L, whose two cardinal terms—S and O (the subject and the Other)—are inscribed just inside the two corners of the square. To briefly translate the other terms: at the outside of the upper left and lower right corners we have Φ (the phallus), M (the "signifier of the primoridal object," the maternal Thing), F (the father and the symbolic law he represents or "Name-of-the-

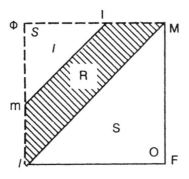

Figure 25

Father"), and I (the ego ideal). Completing the central trapezoid are two additional points: m (for the ego, or *moi*) and i (for the imaginary other).[6] I, R, and S, describe the domains of the imaginary, real, and symbolic.

It is now possible to plot the square of gestalt concepts in relation to the Lacanian schema in a way that is illuminating for both. What is new in this alignment is that the positions of figure and not-ground are no longer merely single points or corners of the graph but are distributed along two internal axes. The first axis, that of the figure, connects the imaginary other and the ego. The second axis, associated with "not-ground," extends between the ego ideal (I) and the primordial signifier of the Other (M). Even without yet working out all the implications, we can immediately recognize the sense this association makes: the ego ideal is precisely a function of identification that moves beyond the imaginary, it is a shaping of identification that is at once unimagable (it is not an imaginary figure), though it is also something differentiated from the archaic and formless ground of the subject (therefore not-ground). The symbolic identification of the ego ideal (I) thus becomes a locus of a purely virtual positionality, an unimaged figure or "not-ground."

This alignment of the terms allows us to adjust and correct our previous schematization while also revealing the underlying dynamics of the Lacanian diagram with special clarity. The key point concerns the inner trapezoid described by points m, i, I, and M. Lacan associates this trapezoid with the real. Its space is opened up by the action of the symbolic and enables the subject to make two complementary differentiations: on the one

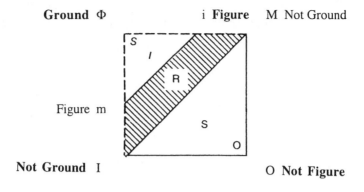

Ground Φ   i **Figure**   M Not Ground

Figure m

Not Ground I   O **Not Figure**

Figure 26

hand, between the imaginary other and an unimaged beyond of the other (the Thing), and, on the other hand, between the imaginary ego and an unimaged identification that transcends the ego (the ego ideal). Plotted onto the basic frame of the Schema R, this movement of differentiation separates two planes or axes, the properly imaginary plane of the figure that links the imaginary ego and its specular other (m and i) and a symbolically mediated plane stretching between the ego ideal and the locus of the primitive object, the Thing (I and M). We can represent it as shown in Fig. 26.

The four terms of our original square of gestalt concepts are printed in bold type. In the resulting schema, the ego (m) is associated, as it should be, with the gestalt figure, and is coupled with its specular double, the imago of the other (i). Together, they form an imaginary axis, the base of the triangle of the imaginary marked with a bold capital I. Correlative with this axis (but separated from from it by the space of the real) is another, non-imaginary axis, that between the ego ideal (I) and the signifier of the primordial object (M). As the two pairings of lower and upper case letters indicate, the mid-section of the Schema R, the trapezoid associated by Lacan with the zone of the real, is susceptible to an opening or closing as the non-imaginary axis I–M is differentiated from its imaginary counterpart m–i. The process that opens the space between the two diagonal axes of the Schema L is the movement by which the sign is differentiated from the image, the move-ment semioticians call "demotivation." (Indeed, we could even associate the two axes, the first tied to the image-registration of the object and second differentiated from the first by the mediation of a symbolic function, with the signifier and signified respectively.) It is a movement of differentiation made possible by the existence of a symbolic code (O).

Plotting these associations onto the schema is especially satisfying because it so clearly shows the opening up of the signifying function between a subject and the locus of the symbolic code. The differentiating action of demotivation is what Lacan refers to as symbolic castration. The task of castration, as we have seen in earlier chapters, is to introduce a fundamental shift in the subject's relation to the image, that is, to relate the positional moment of the image to the dispositional horizon of a symbolic system. The Schema R thus serves to map an essentially temporal process. The central trapezoid of the real forms a kind of ventricle that pulses open under the influence of the signifier and then restablizes in relation to new imaginary formations.

Explicating the Schema R in this way allows us to clarify its relation to the Schema L. If the movement of demotivation fails, the symbolic axis of the ego ideal fails to be differentiated from the imaginary. The result, in which a defensive and narcissistic over-investment in the imaginary ego resists symbolic mediation, is precisely the situation mapped by the Schema L. It is from this point of view that the Schema L is rightly interpreted as the schema of the analytic situation. What the Schema L really shows is the neurotic inflection of the personality in which the ego assumes the status, as Lacan says, of the symptom *par excellence*. The trick for the analyst is to engage the imaginary transference along the axis o'–o, and then, by occupying the position of the big Other (O) of the symbolic code, to open it to the influence of the signifier. The aim is to open the real under the influence of the signifying function with the result of bringing the subject into a new relation both to the Thing and to the ego ideal. By contrast to the Schema L, which is more specific to the analytic situation, the Schema R charts the inner workings of the Oedipus complex in symbolic castration and thus represents a fuller and more "normal" picture of psychical structure.

How the Real World Became a Phantasy

Where, then, in all of this is the *objet a*? In fact, Lacan offers the entire Schema R as "a mapping of the *objet a*":

What the Schema R shows is a projective plan. In particular the points, and it is not by chance (or by a sense of play) that I chose the letters that correspond to them—m, M, i, I—and which are those that frame the only valid cut in this schema (the cut m M, i I), are sufficient indication that this cut isolates a Moebius strip in the field. . . . I mean that only the cut reveals the structure of the entire surface from being able to detach from it those two hetero-geneous elements (represented in my algorithm ($ ◊ a) of the phantasy: the $, S barred by the strip to be expected here in fact, that is to say, covering the field R of reality, and the a, which cor-responds to the fields I and S. It is as representative of the respre-sentation in phantasy, therefore, that is to say as the originally repressed subject that $, the barred S of desire, here supports the field of reality, and this field is sustained only by the extraction of the *objet a*, which, however, gives it its frame. (E:S, 223).

Let us conclude this chapter with an explication of this passage. Of key importance is the moment of the cut, originally a cut in the body of the imaginary object by which a series of partial objects (the breast, the feces, the phallus, voice, gaze, etc.) are separated from the body of the other. By means of this separation, a succession of objects are established that will mediate symbolically between the subject and the other. It is in this sense that Lacan claims that the *objet a* is a "remainder in the dialectic of the subject and the other" (S.X 5-15-63). Said otherwise, the successive figurations of the *objet a* offer to the subject a means, like a series of stepping stones that both dif-ferentiate and connect, by which the desire of the Other as Thing is sepa-rated from the imaginary order and passed into the symbolic circuit. Each step in this succession provides the symbolic wherewithal by which the sub-ject is able to represent the moment of lack that is constitutive of desire. That is to say, each incarnation of the *objet a* allows the subject, not to pro-vide any final answer to the question of the Other's desire, the unthinkable dimension of the imaginary other that emerges primitively as *das Ding*, but to pass that question into the unfolding of a symbolic processs. The stakes of desire become oral, anal, phallic, scopic and, finally, with the emergence of the phoneme and the voice, verbal. This process of representation of lack is what opens the space between the imaginary and symbolic axes that cross the Schema R on the diagonal, the space of the real.

The final terms of this process are indicated in the opposing corners of the schema, the outer points of the imaginary and symbolic triangles, the phallus and the locus of the Code or Name-of-the-Father. Why does the subjective side of this differentiation come to be associated with the phallus? What outfits the phallus in particular to assume the status of a master signfier? Why, said otherwise, does the ultimate form of the cut take the form of the phantasy of castration? We already sketched part of the answer in a previous chapter: the phallus offers an especially fortuitous junction of the imaginary and symbolic. The male member is at once a privileged representation of the cut (it is actually missing in the body image of the female) and readily models the binary opposition of the signifier (as it marks sexual difference between male and female). To which we can now add: the phallus is the last in a series of figurations of the *objet a* that display a conspicuously imaginary character (the imaginary dimension, the reference to a part of the body, is obviously diminished in the case of the gaze and the voice). It is for this reason that the range of perversions—those efforts to side-step or short-circuit the effects of castration: in fetishes, scopophilic compulsions, pederasty, etc.—will take the imaginary phallus as a privileged point of reference. Moreover, unlike the breast or feces, the phallus inevitably points away from the mother toward the third position of the father, off the axis of relation that binds the imaginary ego to the mother. For all of these reasons, the phallus is not merely one figure of the *objet a* among others but assumes a special status.

Reference to castration serves to remind us that the cut that issues in the *objet a*, if it is primitively figured in the body of the other, is also a cut internal to the subject itself. As we have already seen, the unimagable dimension of *das Ding* in the other is correlative with a similarly unthinkable dimension in the subject, *das Es*. Among the effects of the process by which the Thing is established in a symbolic dimension, increasingly independent from the imaginary form in which it was originally anchored, is thus not only a differentiation of the image of the other (i) from the question of its desire (M), but also the imaginary form of the ego (m) from the ego ideal (I). That these two moments of differentiation—i and M, m and I—occur together is part of what Lacan means by comparing the quadrilateral described by the four points to a Moebius strip. Prior to the submission of the subject to symbolic castration, the imaginary and symbolic functions are collapsed upon one another, just as the two sides of a

Moebius strip are in fact only a single side. By cutting the strip, that is, by opening up the moment of separation between imaginary and symbolic under the influence of an established code (the function Lacan calls the Name-of-the-Father), a novel modality of symbolically mediated identification becomes possible in the form of the ego ideal. The emergence of the ego ideal mobilizes the desire of the subject in the pursuit of aims and objects that transcend the register of the image. The properly symbolic function of desire is set in motion, one in which the subject, as Lacan says, is represented by a signifier for another signifier.

The Schema R is thus, quite literally, a homologue of the formula $S \lozenge a$. In the rectangular *poinçon* at the center of the formula we recognize the trapezoidal band of the real that slices across the Schema R. The bar that crosses the S of the subject indicates that this function of the real has been taken into the subject by means of a symbolic mediation. The effect of this submission to the signifier is a passage beyond the captures of the imaginary. It is a transformation that is made possible by the way in which the lack, the deficit in the subject's capacity to know the desire of the other, a lack marked provisionally in the successive figures of the *objet a*, is increasingly passed into the defile of the signifier. The result is not that the unthinkable Thing is now thinkable, but rather that the question of the Thing becomes circuited by the chain of signifiers. Desire, as the ceaseless posing of that question, assumes its symbolic destiny as an unending metonymy.

We can now better appreciate the significance of the fact that the internal trapezoid of the real borders the imaginary on one side and the symbolic on the other. This circumstance graphically represents the distinction, so central to Lacan's entire outlook, between everyday "reality" (the predictable, even banal, domain of stable objects and routinized actions in which we ordinarily live) and the "real" in the properly Lacanian sense (as an uncanny and ultimately unknowable dimension of Otherness). The world of everyday reality, comparable to Heidegger's notion of the inauthentic domain of *Dasein's* everydayness overseen by the authority of an anonymous "they," is the domain of the ego in relation to its imaginary objects. It is represented in the Schema R by the axis between m and i. Under the influence of the signifier, the subject is opened to the movement of desire beyond the image, to a world beyond the familiar confines of the ego and its banality. In all fairness, then, the line in the Schema that indicates the border of this symbolic dimension (joining I and M) ought not be represented by a line at all, but rather by a kind of semi-permeable zone through which the subject is drawn beyond its capacity to know itself as image. It is in passing into this zone that the subject is "barred," as it can no longer identify itself simply as this or that (a particular social role, etc.) but becomes ecstatically unknowable to itself.

How and why does Lacan link the frame of the real to phantasy? The answer is related to the profound ambiguity of all phantasy, for phantasy is always a picturing, a imaginal figuration, yet also aims toward something unimagable. What is most deeply sought by desire in the phantasy cannot be given in the register of the image. This ambiguous, Janus-faced character of phantasy is an effect of its middle position between imaginary and symbolic. And it is that middle zone that is mapped in the trapezoid of the real. On the side of the ego's stabilization in everyday reality, what we have is an elaboration of the imaginary register, a kind of taming of the real in a matrix of objects. But this everyday reality is precisely a phantasy, now in the quasi-derogatory sense, to the extent that it excludes the unknowable kernel at which desire aims. As such it is intrinsically unstable and liable to eruptions of something "untoward" and ill-fitting (as, for example, when the man who has settled comfortably into the "good life" of the modest career, the wholesome family, etc. symptomatically pursues some "crazy" or even ruinous act—his visits to a prostitute, his compulsion to gamble—the sort of thing about which he is forced to say afterwards "I don't know what caused me to do it, I must have been out of my mind").

We now recognize the fuller meaning of the formula for the phantasy, $\mathcal{8} \lozenge a$. The *objet a* is there, in the space beyond the imaginable, and functions to keep the phantasy open to its ultimate destination in the real of desire. Moreover, we see how and why Lacan associates the end of analysis with a "traversing of the phantasy." In the analytic situation, the analyst occupies the position of the *objet a* with the result that the analysand is progressively drawn beyond the imaginary sedimentations of phantasy toward a symbolic horizon in which the lack that stimulates desire remains open to the play of signifiers. "Traversing the phantasy" thus does not mean that the subject somehow abandons its involvement with fanciful caprices and accomodates itself to a pragmatic "reality," but precisely the opposite: the subject is submitted to that effect of the symbolic lack that reveals the limit of everyday reality. To traverse the phantasy in the Lacanian sense is to be more profoundly claimed by the phantasy than ever, in the sense of being brought into an ever more intimate relation with that real core of the phantasy that transcends imaging.

This discussion also illuminates our earlier characterization of the *objet a* as a dispositional object. The *objet a* functions to "dispose" the subject in the direction of the ungraspable horizon of the Thing. As such, it founds a "disposition" in the more ordinary connotation of the word as an internal orientation of the subject toward an end, aim, or action. But the *objet a* is also appropriately called "dispositional" in the sense, as we have seen, that it cannot be presented as such. It is a paradoxically non-objective object.

We can now take a further step toward clarifying this paradoxical status by returning to our effort to show the Lacanian schemas in overlay with a structural square of Gestalt concepts—figure and ground, not-figure and not-ground. The *objet a* is appropriately identified with the "not-ground." Of the primitive Thing, it was possible initially only to say that it is "not-figure." The Thing marks the limit of the image of the other, but as such is strictly negative and utterly unknowable. But as the space of the Thing comes to be imbricated in the system of signifiers, it is as if a wholly virtual object is thrown into relief. By means of its systemization, the not-figure thus gives rise by a special effect of retroaction to a not-ground. This new locus of a not-ground, as an indeterminate figure, then displays the ambiguity of the phantasy, indeed the not-ground of the *objet a* describes the very structure of phantasy. On the one hand, it inevitably tends to be filled out with imaginary contents, the familiar clothing of phantasies. It is on this side of its function that the *objet a* is launched in the parade of part-objects (the breast, feces, phallus, etc.). On the other hand, as it continues to be evacuated of content by the open-endedness of signfication. The not-ground of the *objet a* remains unspecified, a figure of pure lack. It is that around which the traverse of the phantasy revolves.

In identifying the *objet a* as "not-ground," we are able to make new sense of Lacan's claim that the *objet a* serves to "frame" the experience of the real. As "not-ground," the *objet a* functions as a particular enhancement, we might even say a "focusing," of the dispositional field. It is in this sense that the *petit a* constitutes the "cause" of desire. It entrains the movement of desire precisely because it is not and cannot be the aim or object of desire, but "disposes" desire from a perpetually eccentric locus.

The *objet a* is intrinsically paradoxical, even contradictory—a circumstance expressed by the oxymoronic term we have chosen to describe it, that of a "dispositional object." As dispositional, it is something that in principle cannot be made present to awareness. At the same time, however, it has the character of a discrete entity. The psychoanalyst must therefore postulate its existence somewhat in the way that astronomers theorize about black holes, the super-dense remnants of dead stars whose gravitational field is so great that all radiation emanating from them is immediately sucked back in. We know of their existence only by observing their influence on other visible objects that surround them.

If we cannot simply point to the paradoxical *objet a*, we can nevertheless locate its effects in perfectly classical Freudian terms (and thereby recognize that we aren't dealing with some "foreign import" of Lacanianism) by reminding ourselves of the most basic assumption of the psychoanalytic theory of love. If a man is to find satisfaction in love, the object of his erotic attentions must succeed in revivifying the archaic memory of the mother (because love is a refinding of the lost object). But at the same time, it is equally indispensable that the object *not* be the mother (because the prohibition against incest must be preserved). Happiness in love thus requires that the love object *both be and not be* the mother. This means that love is never related simply to the given object before us but to another object that remains paradoxically suspended between presence and absence.

Every experience of love has this structure. Passion reaches beyond the sum of the object's actual qualities toward another dimension projected beyond it. This ungraspable dimension is the real core-generator of the power of love. The virility of a man or the allure of a woman, for example, continually evoked by a variety of clues, is never wholly present but resides in a kind of "fourth dimension" of the love object. It is with respect to this dimension of a beyond-of-the-object, the dimension of the *objet a*, that we can make sense of Lacan's definition of love as "giving what one doesn't have." What the lover finds in the beloved is something the beloved doesn't actually possess, something that is never concretely present in the beloved but—we can now use the word with the full weight of its meaning in Lacanian theory—is *signified* by them.

This view of the matter explains the familiar "blindness" of love, the way in which the lover overlooks the flaws in the beloved. The tableau presented by the actually perceived qualities of the beloved is continually repainted under the magical influence of a hidden, inward quality. Love routinely transforms a sow's ear into a silk purse. By a kind of refraction, the captivating force of the *objet a* illuminates the mundane object from beyond it. The mechanism at work is related to the effect we noted earlier in the cover-girl face, in which the anxiety elicited by her over-intense gaze is circuited back into a revivified sense of her transcendent beauty. It is in this sense that love is truly blind: the lover remains unaware of the way in which the two levels that we here distinguish theoretically—the level of the image and of something in the ungraspable beyond of the image—are always collapsed in the actual experience of love. To fall in love is to become subject to the spell of this illusion. It is also this illusion that operates in the most successful instance of sublimation. The art object, says Lacan in his definition of sublimation, "raises the object to the dignity of the Thing."

We have returned repeatedly to the importance of the central trapezoid of Schema R, the zone Lacan associates with the real. But what relation obtains between the Lacanian sense of the real and the Freudian "reality principle"? The answer offers a last opportunity to clarify the function of the *objet a*. Lacan must be credited with rescuing Freud's idea from the oversimplifications of many of Freud's followers and restoring its true radicality. The great temptation is to conceive the reality principle from a naively empiricist standpoint. From this point of view, the wishful psyche is free to hallucinate its satisfactions until the brute fact of reality is pressed upon it by perception. This notion, or something very like it, underlies the stress on adaptation to reality championed by the school of ego psychology toward which Lacan remained so polemically opposed. It is a notion based on doubly mistaken assumptions.

The first error is to suppose that the essential conflict uncovered by the Freud is that between wishes and their fulfillment, between acting on one's desires versus bumping up against the constraints of external reality. This way of thinking reduces Freud's theory to the most commonsensical view of things. It assumes that we all know what we want (as a function of the pleasure principle) but we are hemmed in by a harsh and unforgiving world (the reality principle). The genuine Freudian insight places the most important site of conflict not between our wishes and the world that limits their fulfillment, but between our wishes and ourselves. The problem is not that we are prevented by reality from fulfilling our desire but that we are prevented from knowing that desire in the first place. The Lacanian innovation is to insist on the rootedness of desire in the real, that is, on the way in which the sources of our own desire are always beyond us, the way in which desire harbors an irreducible opacity, an impossibility not just to satisfy desire but also to represent it to ourselves. We see how this Lacanian "innovation" is hardly new but rather truly a return to Freud's own conception when we recognize the congruence of the Lacanian notion of the real and the Freudian id, the unthinkable "it" at the heart of the subject.

The second error of the naive conception of the reality principle is related to the first. It again has to do with the Lacanian sense of the real but this time in relation to the world outside the subject. The mistake here is to think that the reality principle concerns an accommodation to something simply given in the world, the only problematic aspect of which is the challenge it poses to the subject's powers of adaptation. Lacan reorients us in this respect, forcing us to consider the way in which the reality principle ultimately concerns the real in his sense of the term as the unknowable, even impossible, kernel of the Thing. The key point is that relation to reality, far from being founded upon the certainties of perception, becomes a possibility for the human subject only when perception is destabilized by the influence of the signifier. The sense of reality is predicated upon a discontinuity, the eruption of an uncertainty with respect to the object. Lacan makes this point with special clarity in his discussion of the Schreber case. In the depth of his psychosis, Schreber loses his sense of reality, but he has an unshakable sense of certainty (which forms the basis of his delusions). In fact, this combination of *absolute certainty without reality* could function as a shorthand definition of paranoia. The nonpsychotic orientation to the world, on the contrary, has a firm sense of reality *precisely because it doesn't have absolute certainty*. "Reality testing" is thus almost the exact opposite of what the naive empiricist would have us believe. Far from a way of being grounded in the givenness of objects to perception, the capacity of relating oneself to "reality" is a matter of relating oneself to what is *not there*, to what is missing or incomplete in perception. I relate myself to the reality of the coffee cup in front me by virtue of my capacity to leave open the question of its "true being"—and this in various senses, some as elementary as my awareness that the cup has a backside that is presently hidden from my sight but allowed for in my perception of the cup as an aspect of its "reality." "Reality testing" occurs when the subject experiences what is there in relation to what is not there. Said otherwise, the sense of reality is grounded on the experience of the object in its relation to the Thing.

From this vantage point, we can grasp the core meaning of Lacan's theory of psychosis. The Lacanian formula for psychosis as a foreclosure of the Name-of-the-Father implies that the psychotic suffers an impairment of the relation to the *objet a* due to a deficiency of the symbolic function. What the psychotic lacks is the lack itself. With this point in mind, we can interpret the last enigmatic portion of Lacan's text in which he asserts that the field of reality "is sustained only by the extraction of the *objet a*, which, however, gives it its frame." In order to function as the cause of desire and—what comes to the same thing—in order to ground the genuine experience of reality, there must be something essentially missing. There must be a constitutive blind spot, an empty space in the field, in which the sense of uncertainty can be continuously regenerated. The experience of the "realness" of reality depends on such a continual suspension in uncertainty. By means of a relation to the irrecoverably lost object of the *objet a*, the subject is brought up before the dimension of what is "in me more than me," and simultaneously what is "in the world more than the world."

CONCLUSION

Looking back over the trajectory of this study, it might understandably be asked whether it deserves its title—"Freud as Philosopher." In what sense, first of all, can I claim to have written a book about Freud? Is it not rather a treatise on Jacques Lacan, in which Freud plays the role of a mere accompanist? To see that it is not so, that the Lacanian theory is truly a "return to Freud," is to recognize the singular character of Lacan's relation to Freud, a relation that is perhaps unique in the history of thought. Where else do we find the creative genius of one thinker, in itself highly original and distinctive, so profoundly dedicated to the task of excavating the inner meaning of a predecessor's work? The rule of succession throughout the intellectual history of the West has been one of appropriation by critique and correction. The relation of Aristotle to Plato, or that of Aquinas to Aristotle, Schopenhauer to Kant, Marx to Hegel, Heidegger to Husserl—in all of these instances, respectful apprenticeship to the thought of an influential predecessor serves mainly to stage an assertion of significant difference, of targeted rejection and reformulation. In Lacan's relation to Freud, by contrast, we find innovation constantly harnessed to the labor of recovery. Lacan appears to race far ahead of Freud, yet claims to be merely trying to catch up with him. Ironically, to the extent that intellectual inheritance is typically marked by anxiety of influence and pointed force of critique, Lacan's relation to Freud represents the least Oedipal of intellectual filiations. One of the main objectives of the foregoing study has been to demonstrate the degree to which Lacan's innovations, even when they seem most strikingly foreign to anything we find in Freud's text, succeed in illuminating Freud's inner intention. I have tried to show how the Lacanian theory can be positioned in relation to Freud as a kind of structural overlay which retraces the underlying architecture of Freud's thought and reveals its coherence as if for the first time.

Both for the audacity of its ambition and for the breadth of references on which it relies, Lacanian theory stands virtually alone amidst the body of thought, rehearsed in the officially sanctioned journals of psychoanalysis and familiar to the point of being almost common knowledge, that has been left to us by other followers of Freud. But what makes possible the Lacanian "return to Freud" is a lacuna internal to Freud's own work, the gap between the difficulty of the theoretical problems he faced and the inadequacy of the conceptual tools available to him. Nowhere is this gap more extreme than in the unfinished torso of the metapsychology and the notion of energetics that forms its spine. Freud was forced to conceptualize his experience by relying on physicalistic metaphors—a cobbling of nineteenth century mechanics, hydraulics, and vitalism. That Freud himself was acutely aware of the failure of this effort is signalled by his repudiation of his first great attempt at a systematic integration, the *Project for a Scientific Psychology*. He never returned to the neuro-physiological fantasy that it presents. Nor did he ever succeed in replacing it with a fully elaborated alternative. The projected collection of papers on metapsychology never appeared, seven of the twelve having been not only withheld from publication but destroyed altogether. In his 1915 paper, "Instincts and their Vicissitudes," Freud acknowledged the approximate and provisional character of the basic concepts of psychoanlaysis, prime among them the pivotal theory of the drives. Nearly twenty years later, he was, if anything, even more circumspect, admitting that "the theory of instincts is so to say our mythology. Instincts are mythical entities, magnificent in their indefiniteness" (SE, 22:95). What the Lacanian transformation of Freud provides is the theoretical wherewithal to restore the project of metapsychology.

Or is it the other half of the title that is most problematic—Freud *as philosopher*? Freud remained deeply suspicious of philosophers and their speculations. Fond of repeating his conviction that psychoanalysis has little to learn from philosophy, he more than once compared philosophical systems to the delusions of paranoiacs and suggested that the primary impact of psychoanalysis on philosophy might consist in affording new insight into the personal quirks that motivate philosophical theory-building. The most common error of philosophers, he thought, is their restriction of the sphere of the mental life to conscious activity. But equally objectionable is their tendency to project for themselves a seamless account of reality, their penchant for "clinging to the illusion of being able to present a picture of the universe that is without gaps and is coherent" (SE, 22:160). Among Freud's favorite quotations was Heine's derisive caricature of the philosopher: "With his nightcaps and the tatters of his dressing gown he patches up the gaps in the structure of the universe" (SE, 22:161).

Of course, it is not difficult to be suspicious of Freud's own suspiciousness, and to sense that he doth protest too much. In the eyes of his contemporaries in psychiatry, it was likely Freud himself who appeared in the role of an over-zealous system builder. In any event, the aspersions cast by Freud on academic philosophy cannot obscure the enormity of his own speculative ambition. As Freud himself remarked, "the psycho-analytic consideration of philosophical problems . . . promises to become more and more fruitful" (SE, 17:274-75). The real question is what sort of philosophical implications are to be drawn from psychoanalytic theory. To define them in a provisional way, we can usefully reverse Heine's quip: what is most philosophical about Freud is not the way he spackles over the holes and incoherencies in things, but precisely the opposite. The centerpiece of Freud's discovery is the demonstration of an irremediable gap in the structure of the universe—or at least in the universe of the human subject. Lacan is particularly sensitive to this negative moment in Freud's thought, an aspect of Freud's famous pessimism.

> If I am a psychoanalyst I am also a man, and as a man my experience has shown me that the principle characteristic of my own human life and, I am sure, that of the people who are here—and if anybody is not of this opinion I hope that he will raise his

hand—is that life is something that goes, as we say in French, *à la dérive*. Life goes down the river, from time to time touching a bank, staying for a while here and there, without understanding anything—and it is the principle of analysis that nobody understands anything of what happens. The idea of the unifying unity of the human condition has always had on me the effect of a scandalous lie.[1]

Lacan is adamant that there is no final coherence, no overarching unity, of human life. But the rejection of unity is not incompatible with the assertion of structure. On the contrary, Freud's theory of the human subject establishes that there can be no universal coherence precisely because there is in human desire a structure. As Lacan has said of it, "it is precisely because desire is articulated that it is not articulable" (E:S, 302). In the broadest perspective, this denial of unity *by virtue of* structure is by no means novel. It ought to remind us of the relation between Kant's critical philosophy and his architectonic method. Nor is the comparison to Kant merely incidental. Freud's thought is appropriately placed in the tradition of critical philosophy inaugurated by Kant and radicalized by a long line of thinkers after Hegel. In a manner reminiscent of Nietzsche's perspectivism, of Heidegger's meditations on ontological difference, or of Merleau-Ponty's notion of the *écart*, Freud insists on an essential and constitutive misfit or disjunction, an insurmountable dehiscence, at the heart of the human condition. What Freud contributes is a particularly radical and uniquely challenging way of defining it.

The objective of this study has been to sketch some of the main outlines of that Freudian philosophy. In doing so, we have hardly exhausted what might be said in reprising Freud's metapsychology. At best, we can claim to have cut through a large body of theory along the bias of a highly selective series of concerns. The argument took its point of departure from a two-fold proposition: 1. The key to Freud's novel contribution to a theory of the human subject is to be found exactly where he himself placed it: in his metapsychology and its cardinal concept of energetics, and 2. The real significance of the Freudian metapsychology can very usefully be illuminated in terms of the Lacanian triad of categories, imaginary, symbolic, and real.

The first crucial point was to recognize that the notion of psychical energy is above all a structural concept. It functions to coordinate elements in a system. Freud relied upon it to theorize the derivation of one set of psychical contents, available to consciousness or even hyper-conscious, from another set of contents that remains unconscious. It was to the end of underlining this aspect of energetics and of suggesting its relations with other currents of nineteenth and twentieth century thought that I proposed the concepts of positionality and the dispositional field. From this point of view, Freud's hypothesis of psychical energy is a means by which to conceptualize the dependence of consciousness on an unconscious ground. Correlative with this conception of energetic investment across the line separating conscious and unconscious is the distinction, implicit throughout Freud's work, of two forms of energetic cathexis, a focused and determinate investment characteristic of the perception of objects versus a more subtle and diffuse distribution of investment across a network of relations. Compared by Freud to the perception of images versus words, it is a distinction that parallels the Lacanian categories of imaginary and symbolic.

Transposing Freudian energetics into Lacanian terms affords new insight into the connection between the theoretical framework of metapsychology and the specificity of clinical experience. The dynamics of fixation and symptom formation, of condensation and displacement, of repression, regression, and substitution, all become legible in terms of the categories of imaginary and symbolic as two modalities of representation, two modes of psychical inscription. At the same time, the translation of Freudian into Lacanian categories helps clarify the underlying structure of the topographical theory and the theory of the dual drives that animates it. The ego emerges as a defensive, inhibitory structure that functions, like the discrete images on which it is modeled, to establish a restricted economy of impulses and their discharge. Opposing the attempt of the ego to control the contour of a closed domain is the counter-force of a splintering and pulverizing death drive, through which the most profoundly heterogeneous impulses of the unconscious struggle toward expression. The most abstract Freudian formulations are thus brought closer to the plane of clinical description. The two great drives of Eros and Death, associated by Freud with the opposing forces of unity and disintegration, become understandable in terms of the conflicting claims of the imaginary and the symbolic, the mobilizing effects of imaginary *Prägnanz* versus the agency of the signifier that continually overflows the limit of every imaginary presentation.

Lacan's rereading of Freudian concepts clarifies psychoanalysis as a theory and practice of representation and thus locates it recognizably in the trajectory of post-Kantian thought. But Lacan also allows us to see more clearly what is distinctive in the Freudian discovery by emphasizing the conflictual dynamic at the heart of representation. The Freudian subject is divided by the competing exigencies of the image and the word. The human being, that "forked animal," is situated at the unstable fault line between two interrelated but essentially distinct modalities of representation. The entire problematic of representation is split at its very core. Not only is all representation rooted in a ground of the unrepresented, the processes of representation are divided between two grounds, each governed by different laws. Psychoanalysis reveals representation to be submitted to a double ground, defined by Freud in terms of thing-presentations and word-presentations and rearticulated by Lacan as the split between imaginary and symbolic. From a Lacanian point of view, therefore, psychoanalysis can be seen to form an intersection between two great currents of contemporary theory, phenomenology and structuralism, each devoted to a different facet of the problem of representation. The subject of the unconscious, describable by neither tradition alone, is conceivable only at the junction between phenomenal presentation and structural articulation.

Had Lacan achieved nothing else but identifying the categories of imaginary and symbolic and elaborating their relevance for a new understanding of the formations of the unconscious, the value of his contribution for enriching and clarifying the Freudian legacy would be amply assured. But whatever the explanatory power of the imaginary and the symbolic, it is with respect to the category of the real that Lacanian theory most succeeds in retrieving the essential insights of Freud's metapsychology. And here again, it is the Freudian concept of energetics that is at the heart of the matter. For the ultimate import of the energy assumption lies in marking the unsurpassable limit of representation. From the *Project* onwards, Freud conceives the drives at the limen between the psychical and the somatic, the threshold between that portion of the body's pulsional energies that is prepared for discharge by virtue of being attached to determinate representations and an unrepresented excess of psychically untamed energies. The most crucial idea, rarely stated explicitly precisely because it is so fundamental to Freud's entire outlook, is the assumption of an inevitable and irremediable disjunction between the level of somatic excitations and their psychical representation. There is always a remainder, an irrecoverable left-over, a portion of the body's energies that fail to receive adequate registration in the battery of *Triebrepräsentanzen*. The processes of psychical binding never succeed in exhausting the somatic reservoir of unbound energies. It is at this point that the Lacanian concept of the real is to be grafted on to the armature of Freud's metapsychological theory. Impossible of being imaged or symbolized, the real is the Lacanian analog of the raw force or *Drang* of the Freudian drive.

The pure, unthinkable force of energy was conceived by Freud by appeal to a mythic substance called *libido*. It is this unknown and ultimately unknowable source of energy, a perpetual excess that animates the human subject even as it threatens to blast it apart, that Lacan calls "real." And here Lacan adds something crucial by linking the unrepresentable excess of libido to the Other. The real is the dimension of *das Ding*, of what is in the other more than the other. It is this dimension that is unassimilable in the image and is implicitly animated in every registration of the signifier, in the overflow of meaning by virtue of which every utterance says more than it means to say. Such a reference to the unencompassable dimension of the Other is the key point of Lacan's outlook and a crucial aspect of what he finds in "returning to Freud." Lacan thus reminds us of the essential point of Freud's theory of the Oedipus complex: the notion of an individual psyche is ultimately unintelligible. The structures that establish the lines of desire in every individual are derived from an ineluctably intersubjective field. The Other is always already there in the constitution of the subject. It is, at the same time, the point on which a Lacanian retrieval of metapsychology is centered. At the core of the problem of psychical energy, retraced by Lacan through the progression of need, demand, and desire, is the question of the Other—the Other without whom the infant cannot physically survive, the Other whose vocalizations open up the infinite expanse of signification, the Other whose own desire remains an unanswerable question.

If Lacan distributes Freudian energetics across the triad of imaginary, symbolic, and real, each of the three bearing an essential relation to the unencompassable Other, he then takes the further step of knotting the whole battery of his innovations in the concept of the *objet a*. Never before explicitly named, Lacan claims that it is nevertheless something "well known by all psychoanalysts as all psychoanalysis is founded on the existence of this peculiar object."[2] It is now possible to see how the *objet a* marks a unique contribution of psychoanalysis. We began by pointing to the way in which psychoanalysis shares with a series of other contemporary thinkers a common concern for the unthought ground of thought. We traced it across a range of figures, from William James and Nietzsche, through the Gestalt psychologists to Husserl, Heidegger, and Merleau-Ponty. In one way or another, they are all theorists of the dispositional field, alert to the ways in which the contents of consciousness are conditioned by a field of influences that remains irretrievably outside awareness. Much of the Freudian theory, too, can be interpreted in this way as a particular mapping of the relations of positionality and a dispositional field. But with the Lacanian *objet a* we come upon a concept that has no analog among this cadre of other thinkers. For what Lacan offers in the *objet a* is the notion of a dispositional *object*. There is nothing comparable in the fringe of awareness discussed by James, the unthematized margin of consciousness identified by Husserl, or the transcendence of Being meditated upon by Heidegger. By contrast to all of these attempts to evoke a ground of thought beyond thought, Lacan is alone in his insistence that the unthought condition of thought be related to an object. It is in this sense that he asserts "in imitation of Aristotle, that man thinks with his object" (FFC, 62). The broadest implications of Lacan's rewriting of Freud can be summarized with respect to this distinctively Lacanian concept. Let us mark the highlights in a series of brief points.

1. THE SUBJECT OF LACK

The subject of the unconscious is constituted by lack in the form of the "insistence" of the *objet a*. That is to say, the subject is determined by a relation, not just to a field beyond consciousness that conditions everything that enters awareness, but to a special kind of negative locus, the empty form of the *objet a*. To be sure, consciousness is situated in a determinative field, identifiable not only with the tacitly registered background of perception but also with the nexus of the signifier, the symbolic code. Yet signification is continually organized, continually drawn into the orbit of the *objet a*. Lacan thus defines the symbolic function in the human being in a fashion that transcends the aims of mere communication of information and that goes beyond what linguistics teaches about the operation of language. It is in this way that he claims to have "defined the signifier as no one else has dared."[3] If language is typically engaged with objects in the world, it is even more primordially concerned with an object that is not and cannot be located in the world. It is this influence of the *objet a*, the peculiar gravitation it exerts on the stream of signification, that accounts for the imbrication of desire in language. From a Lacanian point of view, speech and language are freighted, not just with information, but with longing for something beyond every matter of fact. Every letter, we can then say, is a love letter.

2. THE INNER INCOMMENSURABILITY OF REPRESENTATION

The philosophy attributable to Freud is one that insists on an irremediable gap at the heart of the human subject, a gap located in the subject's relation to the *objet a*. The life of desire depends upon this gap remaining open. And we know the Lacanian name for the opening of the gap. It is castration. Castration implies the impossibility of any perfect alignment between the image and the word, a constitutive incommensurability between the imaginary and the symbolic. The movement of desire is initiated by an impossibility of coincidence, not just between the means of representation and the ineffable real, but also between the two great modalities of representation, imaginary and symbolic. By virtue of the perpetually unstable fault line between images and words, the subject is plunged irretrievably into history. It becomes what Lacan calls a "barred subject"—a subject, as the slash across the letter implies, that can never be fully present to itself, a subject that is represented by a signifier for another signifier. For the subject submitted to castration, therefore, the three categories of imaginary, symbolic, and real become dialectically intertwined precisely because they are incommensurable with one another.

3. THE BODY OF PHANTASY

Instantiation of pure lack, the *objet a* nevertheless retains an essential relation to figures of embodiment. We thus arrive at the deeply equivocal character of the *objet a*. On the one hand, it designates a locus of radical negativity, an empty set or zero point. It is by virtue of this perfect emptiness that the *objet a* is able to assume its role as a final cause of signification. At the same time, however, the *objet a* carries with it an echo of the imaginary body from which it was detached. We have seen how the function of the *objet a* emerges in relation to parts of the body, separated from the whole and set up as tokens of mediation between the subject and the other. The *objet a* is thus both the alpha and omega of desire. It retains a kind of virtual impress of the body's imaginary anatomy. On the level of the unconscious, this virtualized embodiment implies a privileged role of the body in all symbolization. Human discourse tends ineluctably to call up the ghost of an organic form, a tendency discernible in the classical comparison of texts to bodies and their appendices. Yet the *objet a* also marks the limit of what is imageable and thus points toward a domain of pure transcendence.

But can Lacan have it both ways? How are we to resolve the contradiction involved in the claim that the *objet a* is simultaneously a locus of lack, "a void that cannot be filled by any object" (FFC, 180) *and* a figure of embodiment in which the forms of the imaginary are retained? We have already encountered this "contradiction" in the constitutive ambiguity of phantasy, at once filled out with imaginal content while harboring an essential emptiness, the space in which desire relates itself to an open horizon. The point to be made here is that *this apparent contradiction is itself the very heart of the matter*. The *objet a* is precisely that "impossible" object that continually functions both to stage the phantasy (by drawing the action of the signifier back into the orbit of the imaginary) *and* to evacuate the phantasy of all positive content (by standing for the "purity" of the signifier, the way it transcends every particularization). The *objet a* functions, as Slavoj Žižek has expressed it, as a "vanishing mediator." It is located between the imginary and the symbolic and belongs, in a sense, to neither.

This mediating action of the *objet a* again displays the degree to which the Freudian theory bears a limited homology with that of Kant. The function of the *objet a* parallels that of the Kantian schematism, whose task it is to provide the point of intersection between intuition and understanding. Or rather, there *would be* a parallel had Kant recognized the necessity of an additional step, namely that the schematism can perform its work of mediation only by straddling the line separating consciousness from the unconscious. What separates the imaginary and symbolic dimensions of the *objet a*, what thus constitutes it as an embodiment of contradiction yet also resolves it, is the action of primal repression. The *objet a* is simultaneously imaginary and symbolic, at once "filled" with content and formally empty, because the subject's relation to its originary figures—the part objects of the breast, the feces, the phallus—has been repressed.

The equivocal, virtually contradictory, character of the *objet a*, functioning on the shifting interface between imaginary forms of the bodily gestalt on the one hand and symbolic exigencies of an indefinite horizon of signification on the other, can now be illuminated from another angle of view. The paradoxical structure we have identified in the *objet a* is far from being something rare and exotic that operates only in exceptional instances. On the contrary, it is precisely the structure that we earlier discovered in the phoneme. Defined by Jakobson as a hinge between sound and meaning, the phoneme conjoins two levels of structure—the battery of differential features defined by various binarisms attributable to the spatiality of the speech apparatus (front versus back, closed versus open, compact versus diffuse, voiced versus unvoiced, etc.) and the level of purely conventional oppositions that comprise a language. Tracing its two-fold nature in this way, the phoneme emerged as a unique point of intersection between positionality and dispositionality. The phoneme is both a sound image (it must register upon the perception of the auditor) and a pure function of difference (which supports and is supported by the sound system of language). This point enables us to recognize how and why Lacan associates the *objet a*, not just with the familiar litany of part objects (the breast, feces, phallus, etc.) but also with the phoneme. In fact, the phoneme deserves to be called the prime figure of the *objet a* inasmuch as it is in and through the phoneme that the *objet a* can be seen to operate in every micro-increment of speech and language.

4. THE MASTER SIGNIFIER

It is only with respect to the equivocal character of the *objet a* (paradoxically imaginary *and* symbolic) that we can make sense of the Lacanian doctrine of a master signifier and his association of that master signifier with the phallus. Without the perpetually unsettled intersection of imaginary and symbolic constituted by the *objet a*, there could be no privileging of any one signifier over another. But the Lacanian subject is no purely cybernetic machine. The claim that the unconscious is strucured like a language must be completed with the additional proviso that the system of signifiers is inflected by an imaginary center of gravity, even as the essential tendency of signification is to enable desire to escape from the captures of the imaginary. Why, then, does this special point of intersection between the symbolic and the imaginary come to be associated with the phallus? The answer is that the phallus marks the last point at which the question of the desire of the other can be posed on the imaginary plane. It for this reason that the process by which the symbolic function gains ascendency over every imaginary formation is associated with the phantasy of castration.

Lacan's "phallocentrism" implies that there is no complete freedom of the symbolic from the imaginary. In every discourse, there will always be at least one point at which the slippage of the signifier is quilted to the imaginary order. And the name Lacan gives to that point of attachment, that rootedness of the symbolic in the ground of the imaginary, is "phallus." At the same time, however, it is the figure of the phallus, in as much as it represents the ultimate object of desire, that marks the outer reaches of longing, the pure transcendence of desire over every imaginary formation. The result is an absolute paradox: as a term of Lacanian theory, the phallus stands simultaneously for the inevitability of imaginary capture *and* the indefinite *telos* of signification.

Tempting though it may seem, it would be a complete misunderstanding to conclude that the Lacanian assertion of the phallus as a master signifier underwrites a superiority of the masculine over the feminine. Far from proving the underlying misogyny of psychoanalytic theory, Lacan's "phallocentrism" shows ever more decisively why masculinity is fraught with a special anxiety of potency and is especially disposed toward the reassurance of fetishistic supplements. On the side of its symoblic function, the phallus is precisely what the subject of desire lacks, it is precisely what cannot be possessed. By the standard of the phallus as a signifier, every mere penis falls infinitely short. The very essence of masculinity is thus bound up with the awful sense that, if anyone truly has the phallus, it is some *other* man. Every man is tormented by the specter of the primal father who "really has what it takes." It is in this sense that an anxious homosexuality lies at the heart of every assertion of masculine prerogative. Lacan enables us finally to understand that penis envy is most profoundly felt precisely by those who have a penis.

5. FREUDIAN "MATERIALISM" AND THE TRANSCENDENCE OF DESIRE

The doctrine of the phallus as master signifier leads us to a conclusion of more general import for the psychoanalytic theory of the unconscious. The essentially contradictory character of the *objet a*, the way in which it is "impossibly" distributed between both an imaginary and a symbolic register, is what accounts for the fact that the unconscious, even as it aims desire toward something beyond all imaging, is also everywhere related to the imaginary body. The infinitude of abstraction is opened up in the very heart of the particularity of embodiment. We see this paradox in the concept of the erotogenic zones identified by Freud. Each of the primitive infantile drives—the oral, anal, and phallic—is set in motion in relation to a specific organ system and its function. Yet each serves to launch a movement of desire beyond the natural. There is in each case an opening up of desire that transcends any merely biologically determined object. Each stage of libidinal development generates a margin of denatured surplus. This margin of surplus is the dimension of *jouissance*—the way in which what is sucked is always more than any breast, what is excreted is always more than mere waste, what becomes erect always stands for something more than the need to copulate. Freud's "materialism" is therefore anything but the notion that the human being is determined by biological "instincts." It is rather a way of insisting that the pulsional forces of the body are subject to an elemental dislocation as they are drawn into the conflictual nexus of representation in the imaginary and the symbolic. The flow of "energy" becomes "drive" when impulses originating in the pressure of natural needs are drawn into the orbit of the *objet a*. That the drive circles around the *objet a*, not as the aim, but as the cause of desire, thus means that desire in the human being is opened to an indefinite range of objects and aims that may have nothing to do with any service of naturally determined ends. Formally speaking, desire is always a useless passion.

6. THE PARADOXES OF *NACHTRÄGLICHKEIT* AND THE TIME OF THE REAL

In speaking of a natural need diverted by the signifier, there is a danger of missing the radicality of the Freudian theory. Indeed, there are two dangers. The first concerns failing to appreciate the full implications of *Nachträglichkeit*. It is impossible to refer back to a primitive state, either in some lost Eden of infancy or in some immediacy of unconscious animality, in which the force of the drive has not been always already stamped by the influence of symbolization. There is no raw purity of impulse that has not already been trellised by the web of representation. Nothing can be said to exist outside the two-cycle machinery of the imaginary and the symbolic. This means that there can be no direct appeal to the primordial object. Said otherwise, the *objet a* is precisely the locus of the primordial object *in its very impossibilty*.

> Such is for Freud the fundmental definition of the object in its guiding function, the paradox of which I have already demonstrated, for it is not affirmed that this object was really lost. The object is by nature a refound object. That it was lost is a consequence of that—but after the fact. It is thus refound without our knowing, except through the refinding, that it was ever lost. (S. VII, 118)

In radicalizing the psychoanalytic concept of *Nachträglichkeit*, a Lacanian point of view reveals the profound appropriateness of Freud's choosing to represent the truth of the unconscious with the drama of Oedipus, a man whose fateful life seems to have embodied Nietzsche's self-description about being "born posthumously." Caught up in a web of circumstances that was knotted long before his birth yet unwaveringly guided the course of his acts, Oedipus is an apt emblem of unconscious determination. That the screw of fate bore in upon Oedipus precisely at the point of a confusion about his own identity makes the appropriateness complete. Oedipus is the perfect instantiation of the Lacanian subject, for whom the assumption of his own being must be described in the future anterior: the subject who will have been.

Related to this first danger is a second: that of substantializing the Lacanian real. Just as it is impossible to point to any original state of desire that antedates the influence of the signifier, there is also no *Ur-stoff* of the real. Here we encounter the deepest mystery of the subject of the unconscious: namely that the ineffability of the real is not prior to the upsurge of the signifier but is, in a certain sense, constituted by it. The Lacanian real is in this respect crucially unlike the blind striving of Schopenhauer's world Will which continually spews forth an infinite range of self-expressions in the myriad forms of the natural world. By contrast to the Schopenhauerian Will, the Lacanian real cannot be said to have any incipent directionality or evolutionary tendency of its own. Rather the real erupts in human life only in and through fractures of the imaginary and failures of the symbolic.[4] Perhaps it is impossible for us to avoid supposing that the real intrudes traumatically upon the subject from beyond the battery of representations like a force from outside the psychical system. It was in exactly this way that Freud himself pictured it in the *Project* as the impingment of energy Q upon the psychical apparatus. Yet any such appeal to an externally impinging force remains a reifying abstraction. As essentially unthinkable and unrepresentable, the real can only be conceived negatively, in terms of disturbances of the imaginary and the symbolic. Even in Freud's case, as we have seen, the real of energy does not remain a mute substance, but is everywhere related to movement within a structure. The real is evidenced only in the misalignments, dislocations, and catastrophes (in the mathematical sense of the term) of the structures of representation. It is in this sense that the *objet a* can be said to function like a "piece of the real." Located at the shifting intersection of imaginary and symbolic, this virtual object is the tell-tale of the tensions and slippages between the two registers.

8. THE TRUTH IN FICTION

We can add a last point, touching upon the paradoxes of truth and untruth in psychoanalysis. From its very inception, Freud was everywhere confronted with the paradox of the truth emerging in the place of error. Slips, parapraxes, and symptoms proved over and again, as Lacan says, that "error is the usual manifestation of the truth itself" (S.I, 263). What is distinctive about the Freudian philosophy is precisely this paradoxical intertwining of truth and fiction.

> The Freudian discovery, while being empirical, does not on account of that make any less of a striking contribution, so striking in fact that one gets blinded to its existence, to this question, a question which seems, taken literally, to be a *metaphysical* one.
>
> What is peculiar to the field of psychoanalysis is indeed the presupposition that the subject's discourse normally unfolds—this is a genuine bit of Freud—within the order of error, of misrecognition, even of negation—it is not quite a lie, it is somewhere between an error and a lie. These are truths of crude common sense. But—this is the novelty—during analysis, within this discourse which unfolds in the register of error, something happens whereby the truth irrupts, and it is not contradiction. . . . In analysis, truth emerges in the most clearcut representative of the mistake—the slip, the action which one, improperly, calls *manquée* [missed, failed, abortive]. (S.I, 265)

From the point of view we have opened up, the *objet a* becomes recognizable as the very nodal point at which these intertwinings of truth and fiction are knotted. As the perpetually unstable intersection of the imaginary and symbolic, this special object—the object of all objects, the function of objectality itself—becomes the privleged site at which the symbolically mediated truth of the human subject is inevitably caught in the net of the imaginary. Here too, Freud's choice of Sophocles' Oedipus as the exemplar of psychoanalytic truth is perfectly apt, not so much for the particulars of his story, but simply for its status *as a myth*. The Lacanian concept of the *objet a* reminds us that the human being is always and forever entangled in a mythic dimension. The Freudian teaching asserts the inevitablility of fiction, the inescapability of myth. The human subject is perpetually and unavoidably immersed in fiction, such that even the pathways to the emergence of the subject's truth typically appear at those moments when it is precisely the wrong choice that is the right one. We can no more escape the influence of the mythic than Oedipus, rushing away from Corinth in a frantic effort to elude the horrible prophecy of his fate, could avoid fulfilling it.

NOTES

Introduction

1. Sigmund Freud, *The Complete Letters of Sigmund Freud to Wilhelm Fliess,* ed. and trans. Jeffrey Masson (Cambridge: Havard University Press, Belknap Press, 1985), Letter #44 of April 2, 1896. This source is hereafter noted parenthetically in the text as "CL" followed by page number.

2. Freud first uses the word "metapsychology" in a letter to Fliess dated February 13, 1896. The first published appearance of the term "psycho-analysis" occurs in a text written in French and sent off to the publisher on February 5, 1896. See Sigmund Freud, "Heredity and the Aetiology of the Neuroses," *Standard Edition of the Complete Psychological Works of Sigmund Freud,* trans. and ed. James Strachey et al. (London: Hogarth Press and the Institute for Psycho-analysis, 1955), vol. 3, pp.143–56. The *Standard Edition* is hereafter noted parenthetically in the text as "SE" followed by volume and page number.

3. I will almost always render Freud's *Trieb* as "drive." Strachey's translation of "instinct" is an especially unfortunate one, as it implies the

operation of a biological necessity of the sort that guides highly fixed and specific animal behaviors (nest building, migration, etc.)—an implication that is not only absent in Freud's concept but that leads to a nearly complete misunderstanding of his meaning. We will return to this point more than once below.

4. It was also a problem for Freud himself. As he remarked in *Beyond the Pleasure Principle:* "The indefiniteness of all our discussions on what we describe as metapsychology is of course due to the fact that we know nothing of the nature of the excitatory process that takes place in the elements of the psychical systems, and that we do not feel justified in framing any hypothesis on the subject. We are consequently operating all the time with a large unknown factor, which we are obliged to carry over into every new formula" (SE, 18:30–31).

5. Roy Grinker, "Conceptual Progress in Psychoanalysis," in Judd Marmor, ed., *Modern Psychoanalysis* (New York: Basic Books, 1968), p. 24.

6. L. Breger, "Motivation, Energy, and Cognitive Structure in Psychoanalytic Theory," in Judd Marmor, ed., *Modern Psychoanalysis* (New York: Basic Books, 1968), p. 44.

7. I have elsewhere offered an extended treatment of the problem of the death drive in Freud and in its Lacanian reinterpretation. See my *Death and Desire: Psychoanalytic Theory in Lacan's Return to Freud* (New York and London: Routledge, Chapman, and Hall, 1991).

8. Ernest Jones, *The Life and Work of Sigmund Freud,* 3 vols. (London: Hogarth Press, 1962), vol. 3, p. 287.

9. David Rapaport, "The Structure of Psychoanalytic Theory," *Psychological Issues,* no. 2, Monograph 6 (1960), p. 50.

10. Henri Ellenberger, *The Discovery of the Unconscious* (New York: Basic Books, 1970), p. 515.

11. Paul Roazen, *Freud and His Followers* (New York: Meridian, 1974), p. xxii.

12. Kenneth Colby, *Energy and Structure in Psychoanalysis* (New York: Ronald Press Co., 1955), pp. 142–43.

13. Jacques Lacan, *Écrits: A Selection,* trans. Alan Sheridan (New York: W. W. Norton & Co., 1977), p. 32. This source is hereafter noted parenthetically in the text as "E:S" followed by page number.

14. Jeffrey Mehlman, translator's introduction to Jean Laplanche, *Life*

and *Death in Psychoanalysis,* trans. Jeffrey Mehlman (Baltimore, Md.: Johns Hopkins University Press, 1976) p. viii.

15. Joseph Conrad, *Heart of Darkness* (New York: Dell, 1960), p. 85.

16. Jacques Lacan, *The Four Fundamental Concepts of Psycho-analysis,* ed. Jacques-Alain Miller, trans. Alan Sheridan (New York: W. W. Norton & Co., 1981), p. 174. This source is hereafter noted parenthetically in the text as "FFC," followed by page number.

17. Jacques Lacan, *The Seminar of Jacques Lacan, Book I: Freud's Writings on Technique,* ed. Jacques-Alain Miller, trans. John Forrester (New York: W. W. Norton & Co., 1988), p. 167. This source is hereafter noted parenthetically in the text as "S.I" followed by page number.

18. Jacques Lacan, *The Seminar of Jacques Lacan, Book II, The Ego in Freud's Theory and in the Technique of Psychoanalysis,* ed. Jacques-Alain Miller, trans. Sylvana Tomaselli (New York: W. W. Norton & Co., 1988), p. 44. This source is hereafter noted parenthetically in the text as "S.II" followed by page number.

19. Jacques Lacan, "The Seminar on the 'Purloined Letter'," trans. Jeffrey Mehlman, *French Freud: Structural Studies in Psychoanalysis, Yale French Studies,* no. 48 (1972): 60.

Chapter One

1. Quoted in *Impressionism,* ed. Jean Clay and the editors of *Réalités* (Secaucus, N.J.: Chartwell Books, 1973), p. 136.

2. Quoted by Joachim Pissaro, *Monet's Cathedral: Rouen 1892–1894* (New York: Knopf, 1990), p. 31.

3. Quoted by Charles Moffet, "Monet's Haystacks," in *Aspects of Monet: A Symposium on the Artist's Life and Times,* ed. John Rewald and Frances Weitzenhoffer (New York: Harry Abrams, 1984), p. 155.

4. Quoted in Rachel Barnes, *Monet: Artists by Themselves* (New York: Knopf, 1990), p. 50.

5. Quoted by Charles Stuckey, "Monet's Art and the Act of Vision," in *Aspects of Monet: A Symposium on the Artist's Life and Times,* ed. John Rewald and Frances Weitzenhoffer (New York: Harry Abrams, 1984), pp. 109–10.

6. Quoted by Virginia Spate, *Claude Monet—Painter of Light,* ed. Ronald Brownson (Auckland: Auckland City Art Gallery, 1985), p. 27.

7. Quoted by John House, "Monet and the Genesis of his Series," in *Claude Monet—Painter of Light*, ed. Ronald Brownson (Auckland: Auckland City Art Gallery, 1985), p. 21.

8. Quoted in Pissaro, *Monet's Cathedral*, p. 7.

9. Pissaro, *Monet's Cathedral*, pp. 21–22.

10. Barnes, *Monet: Artists by Themselves*, p. 36.

11. Quoted in Pissaro, *Monet's Cathedral*, p. 24.

12. Georges Clemenceau, *Claude Monet: The Water Lilies*, trans. George Boas (New York: Doubleday, 1930), p. 119.

13. Quoted by Clemenceau, *Claude Monet*, p. 126.

14. George Heard Hamilton, *Claude Monet's Paintings of Rouen Cathedral* (Williamstown, Mass: Sterling and Francine Clark Art Institute, 1969), p. 17.

15. Quoted by Paul Hayes Tucker, *Monet in the Nineties: The Series Paintings* (New Haven: Yale University Press, 1989), p. 187.

16. William James, *Principles of Psychology*, vol. 1 (New York: Dover Books, 1950), p. 288. This source is hereafter noted parenthetically in the text as "P" followed by page number.

17. Henri Bergson, *Matter and Memory*, trans. Nancy Paul and W. Scott Palmer (New York: Zone Books, 1991), p. 144. This source is hereafter noted parenthetically in the text as "MM" followed by page number.

18. It is a dimension that is central to James's pragmatism, and, indeed, Bergson explicitly cites James in this connection.

19. Friedrich Nietzsche. *Beyond Good and Evil*, trans. Walter Kaufmann (New York: Vintage Books, 1966), #17, p. 24.

20. Friedrich Nietzsche, *The Will to Power*, ed. Walter Kauufman, trans. Walter Kauffman and R. J. Hollingdale (New York: Vintage, 1968), #502, p. 274. This source is hereafter noted parenthetically in the text as "WP" followed by aphorism and page number.

21. Nietzsche, *Beyond Good and Evil*, #36, p. 237.

22. Edmund Husserl, *Ideas Pertaining to a Pure Phenomenology and to a Phenomenological Philosophy: First Book, General Introduction to a Pure Phenomenology*, trans. F. Kersten (Dordrecht: Kluwer, 1982), p. 70. This source is hereafter noted parenthetically in the text as "I" followed by page number.

23. Husserl, Ideas, pp. 71–72. Cf. the Boyce translation: "It is obviously true of all such experiences that the focal is girt about with a 'zone'

of the marginal; *the stream of experience can never consist wholly of focal actualities.*" Edmund Husserl, *Ideas: General Introduction to Pure Phenomenology,* trans. W. R. Boyce (New York: Collier-Macmillan, 1972), p. 107.

24. Martin Heidegger, *Being and Time,* trans. John Macquarrie and Edward Robinson (New York: Harper and Row, 1962), p. 78. This source hereafter is noted parenthetically in the text as "BT" followed by page number.

25. Martin Heidegger, "Origin of the Work of Art," *Poetry, Language, Thought,* trans. Albert Hofstadter (New York: Harper and Row, 1971), pp. 33–34.

26. Martin Heidegger, "The Thing," in *Basic Writings,* ed. David Farrell Krell (New York: Harper and Row, 1977), p. 181.

27. Heidegger, "The Thing," p. 53.

28. Jean-Paul Sartre, *Being and Nothingness: An Essay in Phenomenological Ontology,* trans. Hazel Barnes (New York: Philosophical Library, 1956), p. 22.

29. Sartre, *Being and Nothingness,* p. 24.

30. Sartre, *Being and Nothingness,* pp. 9–10.

31. In his essay "What is Metaphysics?" for example, Heidegger speaks of "nihilative behavior," a term that is strikingly reminiscent of Sartre's concept of "négatités" in *Being and Nothingness.* See Heidegger, "What is Metaphysics?" *Basic Writings,* ed. David Farrell Krell (New York: Harper and Row, 1977), p. 105.

32. The title of Heidegger's essay refers to Sartre's *Existentialism is a Humanism,* and its contents are clearly intended to be a rejection of Sartre's view.

33. Martin Heidegger, "Letter on Humanism," in *Basic Writings,* ed. David Farrell Krell (New York: Harper and Row, 1977), p. 237.

34. Heidegger, "Letter on Humanism," p. 238.

35. Heidegger, "What is Metaphysics?" p. 103.

36. Heidegger, "What is Metaphysics?" p. 105.

37. Maurice Merleau-Ponty, *The Visible and the Invisible,* ed. Claude Lefort, trans. Alphonso Lingis (Evanston: Northwestern University Press, 1968), p. 192. This source hereafter will be noted parenthetically in the text as "VI," followed by page number.

38. Maurice Merleau-Ponty, *Phenomenology of Perception,* trans. Colin

Smith (London: Routledge and Kegan Paul, 1962), pp. 4–6. Hereafter this source is noted parenthetically in the text as "PP" followed by page number.

39. Merleau-Ponty, *Phenomenology of Perception,* p. 143.

40. Michel Foucault, *The Order of Things* (New York: Vintage Books, 1970), p. 16. This source is hereafter noted parenthetically in the text as "OT" followed by page number.

41. Sigmund Freud, *On Aphasia,* trans. E. Stengel (New York: International Universities Press, 1953), p. 73.

42. The phrase is from the inaugural paragraphs of Freud's 1895 manuscript, *Project for a Scientific Psychology,* SE, I:295.

43. Paul Ricoeur provides a useful discussion of phenomenological approaches to the Freudian unconscious and the problems they face. See Paul Ricoeur, *Freud and Philosophy: An Essay on Interpretation,* trans. D. Savage (New Haven: Yale University Press, 1977), pp. 375–418.

Chapter Two

1. Lacan underlines the remarkable character of such moments of presence. There is something not only extraordinary and uncanny but also distinctly uncomfortable about the feeling they produce. "It isn't a feeling that we have all the time. To be sure, we are influenced by all sorts of presences, and our world only possesses its consistency, its density, its lived stability, because, in some way, we take account of these presences, but we do not realise them as such. You really can sense that it is a feeling which I'd say we are always trying to efface from life. It wouldn't be easy to live if, at every moment, we had the feeling of presence, with all the mystery that that implies. It is a mystery from which we distance ourselves, and to which we are, in a word, inured" (S.I, 42).

2. Jacques Lacan, *The Seminar of Jacques Lacan, Book VII, The Ethics of Psychoanalysis,* ed. Jacques-Alain Miller, trans. Dennis Porter (New York: W. W. Norton & Co., 1992), p. 35. This source is hereafter noted parenthetically in the text as "S. VII" followed by page number.

3. Compare, in the light of this discussion, Freud's remark that "repression does not hinder the instinctual representative from continuing to exist in the unconscious, from organizing itself further, putting out derivatives and establishing connections. Repression in fact interferes

only with the relation of the instinctual representative to one psychical system, namely, to that of the conscious" (SE, 14:149).

4. A similar process sometimes occurs when we unexpectedly meet an acquaintance in the street and are unable to adduce their name, as if we are momentarily too occupied with their very presence before us to be able to introduce them correctly to a companion. As the title of a book by Lawrence Wechsler puts it, "seeing means forgetting the name of the thing one sees."

5. Compare, in this connection, Freud's remark that "the word-presentation is not part of the act of repression, but represents the first of the attempts at recovery or cure" (SE, 14:203).

6. "It would be necessary to search for the reason for dividing language into words—for in spite of the difficulty of defining it, the word is a unit that strikes the mind, something central in the mechanism of language—but it is a subject which by itself would fill a volume. Next, we would have to classify the subunits, then the larger units, etc. By determining in this way the elements that it manipulates, synchronic linguistics would completely fulfill its task, for it would relate all synchronic phenomena to their fundamental principle. It cannot be said that this basic problem has ever been faced squarely or that its scope and difficulty have been understood; in the matter of language, people have always been satisfied with ill-defined units." Ferdinand de Saussure, *Course in General Linguistics*, ed. Charles Bally and Albert Sechehaye, with Albert Reidlinger, trans. Wade Baskin (New York: McGraw Hill, 1966), p. 111.

7. "The notion of value envelops the notions of unit, entity, and reality." Saussure, *Course*, p. 110.

8. Roman Jakobson, *Six Lectures on Sound and Meaning*, trans. James Mepham (Cambridge, Mass: MIT Press, 1981), p. 85. Hereafter this source is noted parenthetically in the text as "SM" followed by page number.

9. "Le Séminaire, Livre V, Les Formations de l'inconscient." Transcription based on students' notes. Unpublished translation by Cormac Gallagher. Session of 4–23–58.

10. Compare Lacan's claim that the signifier "connotes presence *or* absence, by introducing essentially the *and* that links them, since in connoting presence or absence, it establishes presence against a

background of absence, just as it constitutes absence in presence" (E:S, 234).

11. For an illuminating discussion of Lacan's concept of the signifier, especially in relation to its roots in Saussure's concept, see Jean-Luc Nancy and Phillipe Lacoue-Labarthe, *The Title of the Letter,* trans. Francois Raffoul and David Pettigrew (Albany: SUNY Press, 1992).

12. The Ratman later styles his relation to Freud along the same axis of high and low social status, but inverts it: where the cruel captain had earlier occupied the position not unlike that of his father as a noncommissioned officer from humble origins, Freud is placed in the superior position. "'How can a gentleman like you, sir,'" the Ratman protests, "let yourself be abused in this way by a low, good-for-nothing fellow like me?'" (SE, 10:209).

13. I owe this insight to Pierre Johannet.

14. Eric Homburger Erikson, "The Dream Specimen of Psychoanalysis," *Journal of the American Psychoanalytic Association,* no. 2 (1954), pp. 5–56.

15. Max Schur, "Some Additional 'Day Residues' of the Specimen Dream of Psychoanalysis," *Freud and his Self-Analysis,* ed. Mark Kanzer and Jules Glenn (New York: Aronson, 1979) pp. 87–116.

16. Schur cites the letter to Fliess of March 8, 1895. Schur, "Some Additional 'Day Residues,'" p. 96.

17. Erikson, "The Dream Specimen," p. 26.

18. Erikson, "The Dream Specimen," p. 27.

19. Schur, "Some Additional 'Day Residues,'" p. 110.

20. Alexander Grinstein, *Sigmund Freud's Dreams* (New York: International Universities Press, 1980), p. 44.

21. Didier Anzieu, *Freud's Self-Analysis,* trans. Peter Graham (London: Hogarth Press and the Institute for Psycho-analysis, 1986), p. 147

22. Barbara Mautner, "Freud's Irma Dream: A Psychoanalytic Interpretation," *International Journal of Psychoanalysis,* 72 (1991), pp. 275–86. I am indebted to Mario Beira for bringing this article to my attention.

23. Mautner, "Freud's Irma Dream," p. 275.

24. Erikson discusses the "analogy between women patients who will not accept solutions, who will not yield to examinations, and who will not submit to advances." Erikson, "The Dream Specimen," p. 12.

25. SE, 4:110 and 111. In a letter to Fliess written six months before the Irma dream, Freud remarks that "there are two kinds of women patients, one kind who are as loyal to their doctor as to their husband, and the other kind who changes their doctors as often as their lovers." Letter of January 24, 1895. (CL, 110).

The passage is significant not only because it puts female patients in the roles of wives and lovers but also because it suggests Freud's sensitivity about women patients who leave him for another doctor. Irma, of course, was such a patient. The proximal stimulus of the dream was a disparaging remark by Oskar Rie (Otto), Irma's *other* doctor.

26. It is perhaps not incidental that Freud puts the word "solution" in quotation marks in his report of the dream. (SE, 4:107).

27. Quoted by Ernst Kris, Introduction, *The Origins of Psychoanalysis*, ed. M. Bonaparte, A. Freud, and E. Kris; trans. by E. Mosbacher and J. Strachey (New York: Basic Books, 1954) p. 6.

28. Freud brings up this issue in his associations to the mention of dysentery in the dream by commenting on the case of a young male patient whose hysterical symptoms were wrongly diagnosed by another physician as dysentery (SE: 4:114–15).

Cf. also Freud's recollection of the response of Jean-Martin Charcot to a colleague's expression of disbelief that a husband's impotence might be the cause of his wife's somatic symptoms: "*Mais, dans des cas pareils c'est toujours la chose génitale, toujours . . . toujours . . . toujours.*" Freud remembered thinking at the time, "Well, but if he knows that, why does he never say so?" (SE, 14:14).

29. In the passage about Charcot cited in the previous footnote, Freud defends the grain of truth in the following joke about the ills of a wife with an impotent husband: "*Rx Penis Normalis dosim repetatur!*" (SE, 14:15).

30. Anzieu explicitly links the "white patch" with "the father's sperm." Anzieu, *Freud's Self-Analysis*, pp. 145–46.

31. Fantasies of fellatio occupy a central place in several of Freud's most famous studies, most notably, as the hidden meaning of the memory of da Vinci's childhood, as a primary element in the fantasy life of Dora, and as it appeared in a dream of the Ratman, in which the dreamer was sexually serviced by Freud's daughter.

32. Jeffrey Masson claims, citing the confirmation of Anna Freud, that

"Irma" was in fact Anna Hammerschlag, the daughter of Freud's old schoolteacher. Jeffrey Moussaieff Masson, *The Assault on Truth: Freud's Suppression of the Seduction Theory* (New York: Farrar, Straus, & Giroux, 1984), p. 205n.

Ernest Jones remarks both on Freud's special affection for Anna Hammerschlag (Anna Freud was named for her) and on the connection between the Hammerschlag family and the family of Josef Breuer: "Freud's eldest daughter was named after Breuer's wife and his youngest after a sister of Breuer's son-in-law—incidently a favorite patient of Freud's. [in a footnote:] Anna Hammerschlag, a daughter of Freud's old teacher. The Hammerschlag and Breuer families, whose flats were in the same building, were intimate friends, and a son of one married a daughter of the other." Jones, *Life and Work of Sigmund Freud,* Vol. I, p. 223.

33. See Freud's comments, SE, 4:115 and again 4:117.

34. Freud comments at some length on sexual exploitation of this sort, precisely in relation to the genesis of hysteria, in his article on "The Aetiology of Hysteria," which appeared a year after the Irma dream.

35. Freud did not confine the possibility of pathogenic sexual contact to childhood. In "The Aetiology of Hysteria," he goes out of his way to "once more stress the fact that every case of hysteria exhibits symptoms which are determined, not by infantile but by later, often by recent, experiences" (SE, 3:214).

36. "Unfortunately, my own father was one of these perverts and is responsible for the hysteria of my brother (all of whose symptoms are identifications) and those of several younger sisters."—letter of February 8, 1897 (CL, 230–31). See also that of September 21, 1897 (CL, 264).

37. The climactic presentations of the two dreams are linked not only by their form but also by their content. The reference to Greece contained in the word "Hella" is also present in the associative train that gives rise to "trimethylamine." From the series "propyl, propyls, . . . proprionic acid" Freud associates to the Propylaea, the gateway to the temple in Athens. (SE, 4:294).

38. Freud seems to have been especially vulnerable to anxiety about Mathilde's health. Ernest Jones attributed Freud's mysterious fainting spell at Bremen in 1912 to anxiety about Mathilde, who had again taken ill. Jones, *Life and Work*, vol. 2, p. 96.

39. I am indebted to Eric Olson for this term.

40. A. J. Greimas, *Structural Semantics: An Attempt at a Method,* trans. Daniele McDowell, Ronald Schleifer, and Alan Velie (Lincoln and London: University of Nebraska Press: 1983), p. 39.

41. See especially Lacan's discussion (E:S, 95–99).

42. "Le Séminaire, Livre V, Les Formations de l'inconscient," Session of 12–11–57.

43. Jacques Lacan, *The Seminar of Jacques Lacan, Book III: The Psychoses,* ed. Jacques-Alain Miller, trans. Russell Grigg (New York: W. W. Norton & Co., 1993), p. 226. This source is hereafter noted parenthetically in the text as "S.III," followed by page number.

44. Lautréamont [Isidore Ducasse], *Maldoror (Les Chants de Maldoror),* trans. Guy Wernham (New York: New Directions, 1965), p. 263.

45. Quoted in Sarane Alexander, *Surrealist Art,* trans. G. Clough (London: Thames and Hudson, 1985), p. 62.

46. For a discussion of field dependence and independence in view of some of its psychoanalytic implications, see Helen Block Lewis, *Shame and Guilt in Neurosis* (New York: International Universities Press, 1971), pp. 47 ff.

47. Roman Jakobson, "Two Aspects of Language and Two Types of Aphasic Disturbances," in Roman Jakobson and Morris Halle, *Fundamentals of Language* (The Hague: Mouton, 1956), p. 79.

48. Jakobson, "Two Aspects of Language," p. 81.

49. Jakobson, "Two Aspects of Language," p. 80.

50. Jakobson, "Two Aspects of Language," p. 86.

Chapter Three

1. Philippe Julien, *Le Retour à Freud de Jacques Lacan: L'application au miroir* (Toulouse: Éditions Erès, 1985), p. 225.

2. It was at Wallon's request that Lacan published an important treatment of the role played by the imaginary in infantile development, the 1938 *Encyclopédie française* article on "La famille."

3. "We would say, then," claims Lacan, " that the behavior can be called imaginary when its direction to an image . . . renders it displaceable out of the cycle within which a natural need is satisfied." Jacques Lacan and Wladimir Granoff, "Fetishism: The Symbolic, the Imaginary, and the

Real," in *Perversions: Psychodynamics and Psychotherapy,* ed. S. Lorand and M. Balint (New York: Gramercy Press, 1956), p. 272.

4. Jacques Lacan, *Ecrits,* (Paris: Editions du Seuil, 1966), p. 181. This source is hereafter noted parenthetically in the text as "E" followed by page number.

5. Jacques Lacan, "The Seminar on the 'Purloined Letter'," p. 39.

6. Jacques Lacan, "Some Reflections on the Ego," *International Journal of Psycho-Analysis,* vol. 34, 1953, p. 12.

7. Anika Lemaire, *Jacques Lacan,* trans. by D. Macey, with introduction by Jacques Lacan (London: Rouledge & Kegan Paul, 1977), p. 176.

8. Lacan, "Some Reflections on the Ego," p. 15.

9. Jacques Lacan, *De la psychose paranoïaque dans ses rapports avec la personnalité* (Paris: Éditions du Seuil, 1980), p. 256.

10. Jacques Lacan, *Le Séminaire Livre IV, La Relation d'objet,* ed. Jacques-Alain Miller (Paris: Editions du Seuil, 1994), p. 33.

11. Jacques Lacan, *Le Séminaire Livre IV,* p. 44.

12. Lacan, "Some Reflections on the Ego," p. 15.

13. Plato, *Collected Dialogues of Plato,* ed. Edith Hamilton and Huntington Cairns (Princeton, N.J.: Bollingen Press, 1961), p. 642.

14. Lacan, "Some Reflections on the Ego," p. 16, emphasis added.

15. Lacan and Granoff, "Fetishism," p. 272.

16. I have elsewhere devoted an extended discussion to this point. See my *Death and Desire: Psychoanalytic Theory in Lacan's Return to Freud* (New York: Routledge, Chapman, and Hall, 1991).

17. Serge Leclaire, *On tue un enfant: Un essai sur le narcissisme primaire et la pulsion de mort* (Paris: Éditions du Seuil, 1975), p. 69.

18. Jacques Lacan, "Of Structure as an Inmixing of an Otherness Prerequisite to Any Subject Whatever," in *The Structuralist Controversy,* ed. Richard Macksey and Eugene Donato (Baltimore: Md.: Johns Hopkins University Press, 1970), p. 194–95.

19. Jacques Lacan, "Le Séminaire V, Les Formations de l'inconscient," Session of 6/18/58.

20. Lacan, "Seminar on the 'Purloined Letter'," p. 53.

21. Thus Lacan remarks in the seminar on "The Formations of the Unconscious," that the phallus is "a detachable object. We can never insist enough on the enigmatic articulation that is involved in the castration complex of penis envy, namely that this something which

is after all well and truly something which belongs to the body, and which after all nothing threatens any more than any other member, or arm, or leg, even the nose or the ear, this element which after all is only a pleasure-point on one's body." Lacan, "Les Formations de l'inconscient," Session of 6–25–58.

22. Jacques Lacan, *Le Séminaire, Livre XX, Encore,* ed. Jacques-Alain Miller (Paris: Editions du Seuil, 1975), p. 10.

23. Cf. Godfrey Lienhardt, *Divinity and Experience: The Religion of the Dinka* (Oxford: Oxford University Press, 1961).

24. Henri Hubert and Marcel Mauss, *Sacrifice: Its Nature and Functions.* trans. by W. D. Halls (Chicago: University of Chicago Press, 1964), p. 26. See also J. C. Heesterman, *The Broken World of Sacrifice: An Essay on Ancient Indian Ritual,* (Chicago: University of Chicago Press, 1993).

25. Cf. Luc de Heusch, *Sacrifice in Africa: A Structuralist Approach,* trans. by Linda O'Brien and Alice Morton (Bloomington: Indiana University Press, 1985), p. 195.

26. Walter Burkert, *Homo Necans: The Anthropology of Ancient Greek Sacrificial Ritual and Myth,* trans. Peter Bing (Berkeley: University of California Press, 1983). p. 11.

27. For a good general presentation of Aztec sacrificial practices, see Inga Clendinnen, *Aztecs: An Interpretation* (Cambridge: Cambridge University Press, 1991).

28. See Joseph Henninger, "Ist der sogennante Nilus-Bericht eine brauchbare religionsgeschichtliche Quelle?" *Anthropos* 50 (1955): 81–148.

29. Sir Edward Burnett Tylor, *Primitive Culture,* 2 vols. (1871; reprint, New York: 1970).

30. Wilhelm Schmidt, "Ethnologische Bermerkungen zu theologische Opfertheorien," in *Jahrbuch des Missionshauses St. Gabriel,* vol. 1 (Mödling, 1922).

    Anton Vorbichler proposes a similar idea, although his understanding is that sacrifice of the firstlings is less a granting to divinities the portion of food that is due them than as a returning of the spark of life to the divine origin from which it sprang. Cf. his *Das Opfer auf den uns heute noch erreichbaren ältesten Stufen der Menschheitsgeschichte: Eine Begriffsstudie* (Mödling, 1956).

31. Gerardus van der Leeuw, "Die *do-ut-des*-Formel in der Opfertheorie," *Archiv für Religionswissenschaft* 20 (1920–21):241–53.

32. Hubert and Mauss, *Sacrifice: Its Nature and Functions,* p. 13.

33. Georges Bataille, *The Accursed Share,* vol. 1., trans. Robert Hurley (New York: Zone Books, 1991), pp. 58–59.

34. René Girard, *Violence and the Sacred,* trans. Patrick Gregory (Baltimore: Johns Hopkins University Press, 1977), p. 259.

35. Girard, *Violence and the Sacred,* p. 235.

36. Girard, *Violence and the Sacred,* p. 198.

37. Girard, *Violence and the Sacred,* p. 188.

38. Girard, *Violence and the Sacred,* p. 185.

39. Rudolf Otto, *The Idea of the Holy,* trans. John Harvey (London: Oxford Press, 1923).

40. Georges Bataille, *Theory of Religion,* trans. Robert Hurley (New York: Zone Books, 1992), p. 19.

41. Bataille, *Theory of Religion,* p. 43.

42. This view is similar to that offered by Roberto Calasso in *The Ruin of Kasch* (Cambridge: Harvard University Press, 1994). Compare, for example: "The very act of naming, the arbitrary decision that enables a thing to be annulled and replaced with a sound, contains the same primordial murder that the sacrifice at once exposes and tries to heal" (p. 137). "Sacrificing something that *stands for* something else sets in motion the very machinery of language" (p. 165). "Pure exchange, which systematizes substitution, gradually expels uniqueness, the vestige of the primordial victim" (p. 166). "There are two modes of effecting substitution: by convention (murder) and by substantive correspondence (sacrifice)" (p. 16).

Chapter Four

1. We might note in passing that in the transition from demand to desire a genuine relation to the particulars of desire can be opened up for the first time—ice cream becomes enjoyable as ice cream and not merely as a counter in a battle for love.

2. Lacan, *Le Séminaire, Livre IV, La Relation d'objet,* p. 293.

3. G. W. F. Hegel, *Logic, Being Part One of the Encyclopedia of the Philosophical Sciences,* trans. William Wallace, (Oxford: Clarendon Press, 1975), p. 181. Hereafter this source will be noted parenthetically in the text as "L" followed by page number.

4. Jakobson provides a good summary statement of this perspective in his essay, with Linda Waugh, on "The Spell of the Speech Sound," in Roman Jakobson, *On Language,* ed. Linda Waugh and Monique Monville-Burston (Cambridge, Mass: Harvard University Press, 1990), pp. 422–47. See also Jakobson's "Quest for the Essence of Language," *op. cit.* pp. 407–21.

5. See especially Freud's letter to Fliess, no. 52 of June 12, 1896.

6. Other examples could readily be offered. Jakobson notes, for instance, how "numerous and varied experiments have demonstrated that dogs are capable of distinguishing and identifying the most subtle auditory signals. Pavlovian biologists have demonstrated that if the arrival of a dog's food is always signalled to it by a sound of a particular pitch then the dog will show that it can recognize the meaning of this pitch, and can distinguish it from all others, even those which are very close to it" (SM, 73).

7. The term "metastasis," taken from Sartre's *Being and Nothingness,* is intended to indicate a perpetual oscillation.

Chapter Five

1. Slavoj Zizek, *The Plague of Fantasies* (London & New York: Verso, 1997), p. 81.

2. Jacques Lacan, "Le Séminaire, Livre X, L'Angoisse," Transcript based on students' notes. Unpublished translation by Cormac Gallagher. Session of 5–22–63. This source is hereafter noted parenthetically in the text as "S.X" followed by session date.

3. "There is never a simple duplicity of terms. It is not only that I see the other, I see him seeing me, which implicates the third term, namely that he knows that I see him. The circle is closed. There are always three terms in the structure, even if these three terms are not explicitly present" (S.I, 218).

4. "All dual relations are more or less of an imaginary style; and in order for a relation to take its symbolic value, it is necessary that there be a meditation by a third person which realizes, by relation to the subject, the transcendent element thanks to which his relation to the object can be sustained at a certain distance." Jacques Lacan,

"Le symbolique, l'imaginaire, et le réel," Unpublished conference paper presented on July 8, 1953.

5. The diagrams offered here that map the Schema L in relation to Gestalt concepts of figure and ground and in relation to the Greimasian semiotic square are exactly those drawn by Rosalind Krauss in her study *The Optical Unconscious* (New York: MIT Press, 1994). See especially pages 13–14.

6. The presentation of the Schema R in the English translation of Lacan's *Écrits* marks the position of the ego with an "e" rather than an "m" (for moi). The unfortunate aspect of this translation is that the reader misses the double pairing of terms in the central trapezoid: i and I, m and M.

Conclusion

1. Jacques Lacan, "Of Structure of an Otherness Prerequisite to Any Subject Whatever," in *The Structuralist Controversy,* ed. Richard Macksey and Eugenio Donato, (Baltimore and London: The Johns Hopkins University Press, 1972), p. 190.

2. Lacan, "Of Structure as an Inmixing . . . " p. 194.

3. Compare, in this connection, Lacan's remark in his seventh seminar about the minimal structure required to launch the function of the signifier. "I have already asked the question here as to what the critical conceivable minimum is for a signifying scale, if the register of the signifier is to begin to organize itself. There cannot be a two without a three, and that, I think, must certainly include a four, the quadripartitie, the *Geviert,* to which Heidegger refers somewhere." (S.VII, 65–66)

4. It is thus an error to think of the Lacanian real as a vitalist *élan,* the pure and unmediated life-flow of *Lebensphilosophie.* In a synopsis of my *Death and Desire:Psychoanalytic Theory in Lacan's Return to Freud,* Slavoj Žižek accused me of making this mistake. (See his *Tarrying with the Negative: Kant, Hegel, and the Critique of Ideology* (Durham: Duke University Press, 1993), pp. 178–180). Such a substantializing of the real was not at all my intention there, and I hope that the present discussion, which I take to be wholly consistent with the earlier book, clarifies this point.

BIBLIOGRAPHY

Alexandrian, Sarane. *Surrealist Art.* Translated by G. Clough. London: Thames and Hudson, 1985.

Anzieu, Didier. *Freud's Self-Analysis.* Translated by Peter Graham. London: Hogarth Press and the Institute for Psycho-analysis, 1986.

Barnes, Rachel. *Monet: Artists by Themselves.* New York: Knopf, 1990.

Bataille, Georges. *The Accursed Share.* Vol. 1. Translated by Robert Hurley. New York: Zone Books, 1991.

Bataille, Georges. *Theory of Religion.* Translated by Robert Hurley. New York: Zone Books, 1992.

Bergson, Henri. *Matter and Memory.* Translated by Nancy Paul and W. Scott Palmer. New York: Zone Books, 1991.

Boothby, Richard. *Death and Desire: Psychoanalytic Theory in Lacan's Return to Freud.* New York: Routledge, Chapman, and Hall, 1991.

———, "Revisiting the 'Specimen' Dream of Psychoanalysis." *Clinical Studies: An International Journal of Psychoanalysis,* Vol. 4, No. 1, 1998. pp 1–25.

———. "Altar-Egos: Psychoanalysis and Blood Sacrifice." *Journal for*

Psychoanalysis of Culture and Society, Vol. 1, No. 2, Fall 1996, pp. 47–61.

———. "Lacanian Castration: Body-Image and Signification in Psychoanalysis." *Crises in Continental Philosophy,* ed. Arleen Dallery & Charles Scott, Albany: SUNY Press, 1990. pp. 215–229.

Breger, L. "Motivation, Energy, and Cognitive Structure in Psychoanalytic Theory." *Modern Psychoanalysis.* Edited by J. Marmor. New York: Basic Books, 1968.

Burkert, Walter. *Homo Necans: The Anthropology of Ancient Greek Sacrificial Ritual and Myth.* Translated by Peter Bing. Berkeley: University of California Press, 1983.

Calasso, Roberto. *The Ruin of Kasch.* Cambridge: Harvard University Press, 1994.

Clay, Jean. et al. (eds.) *Impressionism.* Secaucus, N. J.: Chartwell Books, 1973.

Clemenceau, Georges. *Claude Monet: The Water Lilies.* Translated by George Boas. New York: Doubleday, 1930.

Clendinnen, Inga. *Aztecs: An Interpretation.* Cambridge: Cambridge University Press, 1991.

Colby, Kenneth. *Energy and Structure.* New York: Ronald Press Co., 1955.

Conrad, Joseph. *Heart of Darkness.* New York: Dell, 1960.

de Heusch, Luc. *Sacrifice in Africa: A Structuralist Approach.* Translated by Linda O'Brien and Alice Morton. Bloomington: Indiana University Press, 1985.

Ellenberger, Henri. *The Discovery of the Unconscious.* New York: Basic Books, 1970.

Erikson, Eric Homburger. "The Dream Specimen of Psychoanalysis." *Journal of the American Psychoanalytic Association,* No. 2, 1954, pp. 5–56.

Foucault, Michel. *The Order of Things.* New York: Vintage Books, 1970.

Freud, Sigmund. *On Aphasia.* Translated by E. Stengel. New York: International Universities Press, 1953.

———. "Project for a Scientific Psychology." *The Standard Edition of the Complete Psychological Works of Sigmund Freud.* Edited & translated by James Strachey, *et al.* 24 Vols. London: Hogarth Press, 1958. Vol. 1, pp. 281–397.

———. "Heredity and the Aetiology of the Neuroses." *Standard Edition*, Vol. 3, pp. 143–156.

———. "The Aetiology of Hysteria," *Standard Edition*, Vol. 3, pp. 187–222.

———. "The Psychical Mechanism of Forgetfulness." *Standard Edition*, Vol. 3, pp. 287–298.

———. "Screen Memories." *Standard Edition*, Vol. 3, pp. 299–322.

———. *The Interpretation of Dreams. Standard Edition*, Vols. 4 & 5.

———. *The Psychopathology of Everyday Life. Standard Edition*, Vol. 6.

———. *Three Essays on the Theory of Sexuality. Standard Edition*, Vol. 7, pp. 123–246.

———. "Notes upon a Case of Obsessional Neurosis." *Standard Edition*, Vol 10, pp. 152–318.

———. *Totem and Taboo. Standard Edition*, Vol. 13, pp. 1–161.

———. "On the History of the Psycho-analytic Movement." *Standard Edition*, Vol. 14, pp.1–66.

———. "On Narcissism: An Introduction." *Standard Edition*, Vol. 14, pp. 67–104.

———. "Instincts and Their Vicissitudes." *Standard Edition*, Vol. 14, pp. 109–140.

———. "Repression." *Standard Edition*, Vol. 14, pp. 141–158.

———. "The Unconscious." *Standard Edition*, Vol. 14, pp. 159–216.

———. "A Metapsychological Supplement to the Theory of Dreams." *Standard Edition*, Vol. 14, pp. 217–236.

———. "Victor Tausk." *Standard Edition*, Vol. 17, pp. 273–275.

———. *Beyond the Pleasure Principle. Standard Edition*, Vol. 18, pp. 1–64.

———. *Group Psychology and the Analysis of the Ego. Standard Edition*, Vol. 18, pp. 65–144.

———. *The Ego and the Id. Standard Edition*, Vol. 19, pp. 1–66.

———. "The Infantile Genital Organization: An Interpolation into the Theory of Sexuality." *Standard Edition*, Vol. 19, pp. 141–148.

———. "Negation." *Standard Edition*, Vol. 19, pp. 235–240.

———. *Inhibitions, Symptoms, and Anxiety. Standard Edition*, Vol. 20, pp. 71–176.

———. *Civilization and its Discontents. Standard Edition*, Vol. 21, pp. 57–146.

———. "Fetishism." *Standard Edition*, Vol. 21, pp. 147–158.

———. "Anxiety and Instinctual Life," *Standard Edition,* Vol. 22, pp. 81–111.

———. "The Question of a Weltanschauung." *Standard Edition,* Vol. 22, pp. 158–182.

———. *Moses and Monotheism. Standard Edition,* Vol. 23, pp. 1–138.

———. "Analysis Terminable and Interminable." *Standard Edition*, Vol. 23, pp. 209–254.

———. *The Complete Letters of Sigmund Freud to Wilhelm Fliess.* Edited and translated by Jeffrey M. Masson. Cambridge: Harvard University Press, Belknap Press, 1985.

Girard, René. *Violence and the Sacred.* Translated by Patrick Gregory. Baltimore: Johns Hopkins University Press, 1977.

Greimas, Algirdas Julien. *Structural Semantics: An Attempt at a Method.* Translated by Daniele McDowell, Ronald Schleifer, and Alan Velie. Lincoln & London: University of Nebraska Press: 1983.

Grinker, Roy. "Conceptual Progress in Psychoanalysis." *Modern Psychoanalysis.* Edited by J. Marmor. New York: Basic Books, 1968.

Grinstein, Alexander. *Sigmund Freud's Dreams.* New York: International Universities Press, 1980.

Hamilton, George Heard. *Claude Monet's Paintings of Rouen Cathedral.* Williamstown, MA: Sterling and Francine Clark Art Institute, 1969.

Heesterman, J. C. *The Broken World of Sacrifice: An Essay on Ancient Indian Ritual.* Chicago: University of Chicago Press, 1993.

Hegel, G. W. F. *Logic.* Translated by William Wallace. Oxford: Claarendon Press, 1975.

Heidegger, Martin. *Being and Time.* Translated by John MacQuarrie & Edward Robinson. New York: Harper and Row, 1962.

———. "Letter on Humanism." in *Basic Writings.* Edited by David Farrell Krell. New York: Harper and Row, 1977.

———. "The Origin of the Work of Art." *Poetry Language Thought.* Translated by Albert Hofstadter. New York: Harper and Row, 1971.

———. "The Thing." *Basic Writings.* Edited by David Farrell Krell. New York: Harper and Row, 1977.

———. "What is Metaphysics?" *Basic Writings.* Edited by David Farrell Krell. New York: Harper and Row, 1977.

Henninger, Joseph. "Ist der sogenannte Nilus-Bericht eine brauchbare religionsgeschichtliche Quelle?" *Anthropos* 50 (1955): 81–148.

House, John. "Monet and the Genesis of his Series," *Claude Monet—Painter of Light*. Ronald Brownson ed. Auckland: Auckland City Art Gallery, 1985.

Hubert, Henri and Mauss, Marcel. *Sacrifice: Its Nature and Functions.* Translated by W. D. Halls. Chicago: University of Chicago Press, 1964.

Husserl, Edmund. *Ideas Pertaining to a Pure Phenomenology and to a Phenomenological Philosophy: First Book, General Introduction to a Pure Phenomenology.* Translated by F. Kersten. Dordrecht: Kluwer, 1982.

———. *Ideas: General Introduction to Pure Phenomenology.* Trans. W. R. Boyce. (New York: Collier-Macmillan, 1972

Jakobson, Roman. *On Language.* Edited by Linda Waugh and Monique Monville-Burston. Cambridge, MA: Harvard University Press, 1990.

———. "Quest for the Essence of Language." *Diogenes*, 51, 1965.

———. *Six Lectures on Sound and Meaning.* Translated by James Mepham. Cambridge: MIT Press, 1981.

———. & Morris Halle. *Fundamentals of Language.* The Hague: Mouton, 1956.

James, William. *Principles of Psychology.* 2 Vols. New York: Dover Books, 1950.

Jones, Ernest. *The Life and Work of Sigmund Freud.* 3 Vols. London: Hogarth Press, 1962.

Julien, Philippe. *Le retour à Freud de Jacques Lacan, L'application au miroir.* Toulouse: Editions Erès, 1985.

Katz, David. *Gestalt Psychology: Its Naure and Significance.* Trans. Robert Tyson. New York: Ronald Press, 1950.

Krauss, Rosalind. *The Optical Unconscious.* New York: MIT Press, 1994.

Kris, Ernst. "Introduction." Sigmund Freud. *Origins of Psychoanalysis.* Edited by Marie Bonaparte, Anna Freud, & Ernst Kris, translated by E. Mosbacher & J. Strachey. New York: Basic Books, 1954.

Lacan, Jacques. "Some Reflections on the Ego." *International Journal of Psycho-Analysis,* Vol. 34, 1953.

———. and Granoff, Wladimir. "Fetishism: The Symbolic, the Imaginary, and the Real." *Perversions: Psychodynamics and Psychotherapy,* Edited by S. Lorand and M. Balint. New York: Gramercy Press, 1956.

———. "Le Séminaire V, Les Formations de l'inconscient," 1957–58. Unpublished transcription based on students' notes.

———. "Le Séminaire X, "L'Angoisse," 1962–63. Unpublished transcription based on students' notes.

———. "Le Symbolique, L'Imaginaire, et Le Réel." *Bulletin de Psychologie*, 1962.

———. *Écrits*. Paris: Editions du Seuil, 1966.

———. *Speech and Language in Psychoanalysis*. Translated, with notes and commentary by A. Wilden. Baltimore: Johns Hopkins University Press, 1968.

———. "Of Structure as an Inmixing of Otherness Prerequisite to Any Subject Whatever," Richard Macksey and Eugene Donato, editors. *The Structuralist Controversy*. Baltimore: Johns Hopkins University Press, 1972.

———. "The Seminar on the 'Purloined Letter'." Translated by Jeffrey Mehlman, *French Freud: Structural Studies in Psychoanalysis, Yale French Studies*. 48, 1972.

———. *Le Seminaire, Livre XX, Encore*. Edited by Jacques-Alain Miller. Paris: Éditions du Seuil, 1975.

———. *Écrits, A Selection*. Translated by Alan Sheridan. New York: Norton, 1977.

———. *De la psychose paranoïaque dans ses rapports avec la personnalité*. Paris: Éditions du Seuil, 1980.

———. *The Four Fundamental Concepts of Psycho-analysis*. Edited by J-A. Miller, translated by A. Sheridan. New York: W. W. Norton, 1981.

———. *Le Séminaire, Livre XX, Encore*. Edited by J-A. Miller. Paris: Editions du Seuil, 1981.

———. *Feminine Sexuality*. Edited by Jacqueline Rose and Juliette Mitchell. New York: W. W. Norton, 1982.

———. *Les Complexes Familiaux*. Dijon: Navarin Editeur, 1984.

———. *Television*. Translated by Denis Hollier, Rosalind Krauss, & Annette Michelson, *October*, Vol. 40, Spring 1987.

———. *The Seminar of Jacques Lacan, Book I, Freud's Papers on Technique*. Edited by Jacques-Alain Miller. Translated by John Forrester. New York: W. W. Norton & Co., 1988.

———. *The Seminar of Jacques Lacan, Book II, The Ego in Freud's Theory*

and in the Technique of Psychoanalysis. Edited by Jacques-Alain
Miller. Translated by Sylvana Tomaselli. New York: W. W. Norton
& Co., 1988.

———. *The Seminar of Jacques Lacan, Book VII, The Ethics of
Psychoanalysis.* Edited by Jacques-Alain Miller. Translated by Dennis
Porter. New York: W. W. Norton & Co., 1992.

———. *The Seminar of Jacques Lacan, Book III, The Psychoses.* Edited by
Jacques-Alain Miller. Translated by Russell Grigg. New York: W.
W. Norton & Co., 1993.

———. *Le Séminaire, Livre IV, La Relation d'object.* Edited by Jacques-
Alain Miller. Paris: Editions du Seuil, 1994.

Laplanche, Jean. *Life and Death in Psychoanalysis.* Translated by Jeffrey
Mehlman. Baltimore: Johns Hopkins Univ. Press, 1976.

Lautréamont [Isidore Ducasse]. *Maldoror (Les Chants de Maldoror).*
Translated by Guy Wernham. New York: Directions, 1965.

Leclaire, Serge. *On tue un enfant: Un essai sur le narcissisme primaire et la
pulsion de mort.* Paris: Éditions du Seuil, 1975.

Lemaire, Anika. *Jacques Lacan.* Translated by D. Macey, with intro. by
Jacques Lacan. London: Rouledge & Kegan Paul, 1977.

Lewis, Helen Block. *Shame and Guilt in Neurosis.* New York:
International Universities Press, 1971.

Lienhardt, Godfrey. *Divinity and Experience: The Religion of the Dinka.*
Oxford: Oxford University Press, 1961.

Masson, Jeffrey Moussaieff. *The Assault on Truth: Freud's Suppression of
the Seduction Theory.* New York: Farrar, Straus, & Giroux, 1984.

Mautner, Barbara. "Freud's Irma Dream: A Psychoanalytic Interpretation,"
International Journal of Psychoanalysis, 1991, Vol. 72, pp. 275–86.

Merleau-Ponty, Maurice. *Phenomenology of Perception.* Translated by
Colin Smith. London: Routledge and Kegan Paul, 1962.

———. *The Visible and the Invisible.* Edited by Claude Lefort.
Translated by Alphonso Lingis. Evanston: Northwestern University
Press, 1968.

Moffet, Charles. "Monet's Haystacks," in *Aspects of Monet: A Symposium
on the Artist's Life and Times.* Ed. by John Rewald and Frances
Weitzenhoffer. New York: Harry Abrams Inc., 1984.

Otto, Rudolf. *The Idea of the Holy.* Translated by John Harvey. London:
Oxford Press, 1923.

Nancy, Jean-Luc and Lacoue-Labarthe, Phillipe. *The Title of the Letter.* Translated by Francois Raffoul and David Pettigrew. Albany: SUNY Press, 1992.

Nietzsche, Friedrich. *Beyond Good and Evil.* Translated by Walter Kaufmann. New York: Vintage Books, 1966.

———. *The Will to Power.* Edited by Walter Kaufmann. Translated by Walter Kaufmann & R. J. Hollingdale. New York: Vintage Books, 1967.

Pissaro, Joachim. *Monet's Cathedral: Rouen 1892–1894.* New York: Knopf, 1990.

Plato. *Collected Dialogues of Plato.* Edited by Edith Hamilton & Huntington Cairns. Princeton: Bollingen Press, 1961.

Rapaport, David. "The Structure of Psychoanalytic Theory." *Psychological Issues,* No.2, Monograph 6, 1960.

Ricoeur, Paul. *Freud and Philosophy: An Essay on Interpretation.* Translated by D. Savage. New Haven: Yale Univ. Press, 1977.

Roazen, Paul. *Freud and His Followers.* New York: Meridian, 1974.

Sartre, Jean-Paul. *Being and Nothingness.* Translated by Hazel Barnes. New York: Philosophical Library, 1956.

Saussure, Ferdinand de. *Course in General Linguistics.* Edited by C. Bally & Albert Sechehaye with A. Reidlinger, translated by Wade Baskin. New York: McGraw Hill, 1966.

Schmidt, Wilhelm. "Ethnologische Bermerkungen zu theologische Opfertheorien." in *Jahrbuch des Missionshauses St. Gabriel,* vol. 1, Mödling, 1922.

Schur, Max. "Some Additional 'Day Residues' of the Specimen Dream of Psychoanalysis." *Freud and his Self-Analysis.* Edited by Mark Kanzer & Jules Glenn. New York: Aronson, 1979. pp. 87–116.

Spate, Virginia. *Claude Monet—Painter of Light.* Ronald Brownson, ed. Auckland: Auckland City Art Gallery, 1985.

Stuckey, Charles. "Monet's Art and the Act of Vision," in *Aspects of Monet: A Symposium on the Artist's Life and Times.* Ed. John Rewald and Frances Weitzenhoffer. New York: Harry Abrams, 1984.

Tucker, Paul Hayes. *Monet in the Nineties: The Series Paintings.* New Haven: Yale University Press, 1989.

Tylor, Sir Edward Burnett. *Primitive Culture.* 2 Vols. Reprint, New York: 1970.

van der Leeuw, Gerardus. "Die *do-ut-des*-Formel in der Opfertheorie."
   Archiv für Religionswissenschaft 20 (1920–1921):241–253.

Vorbichler, Anton. *Das Opfer auf den uns heute noch erreichbaren ältesten
   Stufen der Menschheitsgeshichte: Eine Begriffsstudie.* Mödling, 1956.

Žižek, Slavoj. *The Plague of Fantasies.* London & New York: Verso, 1997.

———. *Tarrying with the Negative: Kant, Hegel, and the Critique of
   Ideology.* Durham: Duke University Press, 1993.

INDEX

Incest prohibition, 215, 263, 277
Instinctual representative
    (*Triebrepräsentanz*), 137,
    287
Irma's Injection, Freud's dream of,
    99–114, 119

Jackson, Hughlings, 65
Jakobson, Roman, 88, 92, 130,
    170, 224–30, 234–39, 291,
    303, 307, 311
James, William, 17, 26–31, 34, 37,
    54, 119–20, 125, 235–36,
    288, 300
Jensen, Adolph, 180
Johannet, Pierre, 304
Jones, Ernest, 3, 7, 298, 306
Jouissance, 159–60, 174, 293
Julien, Philippe, 134, 307

Kant, Immanuel, 24, 204, 223,
    281, 284, 286, 290
Kaplan, Ann, 253
Klein group, 265
Koffka, Kurt, 39
Köhler, Wolfgang, 38
Krauss, Rosalind, 265, 312
Kris, Ernst, 12, 305

Lacan, Jacques
    analysis of the Irma dream by,
        101–04
    critique of ego psychology,
        12
    difficulty of style, 10–11
    innovations in psychoanalysis,
        9, 11–14

treatment of energetics, 14,
    146–47, 285–87
Lacoue-Labarthe, Phillipe, 304
Lautréamont [Isadore Ducasse],
    307
lamelle, 149–50
language acquisition, 129, 155,
    162–74, 197
Leclaire, Serge, 308
Lemaire, Anika, 142, 308
Levi-Strauss, Claude, 14
Lewis, Helen Block, 307
Lienhardt, Godfrey, 309
Lorenz, Konrad, 135
Lowenstein, Rudolph, 12

Marx, Karl, 281
Masochism, 150, 152, 156
Mass psychology, 261
Masson, Jeffrey, 305–06
Master signifier, 273, 291–92
Mathemes, 262
Mauss, Marcel, 178–79, 185,
    309–10
Mautner, Barbara, 105, 304
Méconnaissance, 13, 75, 78, 144,
    260
Mehlman, Jeffrey, 10, 298
Merleau-Ponty, Maurice, 17,
    54–61, 68, 116, 229, 259,
    284, 288, 301–02
Metaphor, 124–132
Metapsychology xlii, 2, 3, 4, 6, 8,
    14, 15, 17, 71, 120, 147, 153,
    161, 282, 284, 286–87,
    297–98
Metonomy, 77, 124, 129–132